Handbook of Dehumidification Technology

Handbook of Dehumidification Technology

G.W. Brundrett, BEng, PhD, CEng, MIMechE, MCIBSE, FRSH
Head of Applied Environmental Research,
The Electricity Council Research Centre

Butterworths
London Boston Durban Singapore Sydney Toronto Wellington

First published 1987

British Library Cataloguing in Publication Data

Brundrett, G.W.
Handbook of dehumidification technology.
1. Humidity—Control
I. Title
660.2′8429 TP363

ISBN 0–408–02520–4

Library of Congress Cataloging-in-Publication Data

Brundrett, G. W. (Geoffrey Wilmot)
Handbook of dehumidification technology.

Includes bibliographies and index.
1. Drying apparatus. I. Title.
TP363.B78 1987 664′.0284 86-18042
ISBN 0–408–02520–4

Typeset by Scribe Design, Gillingham, Kent
Printed and bound in Great Britain by
Anchor Brendon Ltd, Tiptree, Essex

Preface

Justig von Liebig, the pioneer food technologist, always sought the limiting factor in any growth process. Dehumidification processes are developing more slowly than I want. My experience over the last fifteen years has shown me that the limiting factor is ignorance of what the process can do and how it can do it. This book is my contribution to assisting more rapid development.

I am conscious of the debt I owe to my technical colleagues. From our Research Centre, Chris Blundell took up the early ideas and recognized immediately the need for computer modelling to deal with the complex interactions of refrigeration components. Frank Sharman developed and widened the model's capabilities and even stepped outside his mathematical discipline to enjoy the delights of planned experimentation. He also read and improved Chapter 3. Tony Flannery ran the environmental tests and built and monitored prototypes. Russell Benstead shared his industrial experience and read and improved Chapter 6. Carlos Lopez-Cacicedo also helped with data from recent heat-pump conferences. Ruth Canavan patiently organized the endless stream of references. Geoff Ratcliff spent a lot of his leisure time professorily improving the manuscript to make it much more readable. Derrick Braham, from our Marketing Department, showed us how professional skills and enthusiasm could sell the concepts to swimming pool operators. He also read and improved Chapter 5. John Fuller, Commercial Director of South Eastern Electricity Board, made history in putting domestic dehumidifiers for sale into his showrooms.

Outside our own industry I must thank John Elliott of Ebac who, despite making his living manufacturing dehumidifiers, still has time to spare to help researchers. Pat Cassey of Thermacon has a commercial flair matched with technical ingenuity which always cheered us. Jim Lawley of Pall Pneumatics spent much of his busy time helping me to understand the world of compressed-gas dryers and kindly read and improved Chapter 8. Chris Sanders of the Building Research Station, Scotland, has helped us understand the moisture problems in housing and has experimented with dehumidifiers. He has also read Chapter 4 and improved it, although my view of the domestic applications is still more optimistic than his. Terry Hynes of Sifan Systems guides us on fan design and has given permission to reproduce performance data in Chapter 3. David Didion of the National Bureau of Standards, Washington, USA, showed us great generosity in giving us parts of his mathematical model, and helped us to establish our own model. Bernard Geeraert of Laborelec, Belgium, was equally generous in revealing his own thoughts on dehumidification, particularly in timber drying, and much of Chapter 6 is based on his work. Marc Delandre of Électricité de France has guided us to French research and you will find many references in the text to translations from the French which we have sponsored. Peter Kalischer of RWE Essen has kindly allowed me to reproduce material from his company's excellent guide to building services. Bent Nielsen of DEFU, Denmark, made sure that I was aware of the practical Danish experience in the related heat-pump field. Niels Josiassen of Danfoss guided me through the intricacies of small-compressor design.

I owe an equal debt to my family. The book had to be written at home. This required near infinite patience, over a sustained period, from Janet, my wife, and our children Timothy and Jane. They had to put up with minor inconveniences of both a positive nature, such as the debris naturally surrounding an author, and of a negative nature, such as the unattended dripping tap or the shelves which never got assembled. It is for them that I will search for a good book review.

Finally, the book would never have got to the publisher if it hadn't been for the care, the skill and the cheerful attention of Joan Hughes, who typed it all. My thanks.

May those who read it learn as much as I did when I wrote it.

G.W. Brundrett

Contents

Chapter 1

Introduction

1.1 Background

Dehumidification is the process of removing water vapour from damp air. A high water vapour content in air can introduce a number of problems.

1.1.1 Create physiological stress and discomfort

Under hot conditions a person controls his body temperature by the evaporative cooling effect of sweating. This cooling effect becomes progressively more difficult to achieve with increasing relative humidity. The physiological system then becomes stressed as the heart rate increases to recirculate blood faster. The general effect is illustrated in *Figure 1.1* for skin temperature, heart rate and sweating[1]. Humidity is the critical factor for heat stress, and in very hot conditions it should be as low as practicable[2]. Mild discomfort can also occur in less extreme conditions. Fabrics feel damp when stored in rooms of high relative humidity[3,4]. Relative humidities below 70% are necessary for fabrics to feel comfortable (*Figure 1.2*).

1.1.2 Encourage ill health

Many of the early nineteenth century urban housing problems were associated with poor ventilation and damp conditions. Compulsory controls through building legislation have removed most of the design problems but damp conditions and condensation problems are recurring due to our changing lifestyles and the house occupier's desire to save energy by reducing ventilation. Recent studies on night-time asthma show it to be closely linked to the house mite population. These mites breed particularly successfully in damp conditions (*Figure 1.3*)[5,6].

1.1.3 Germinate mould spores and grow mould

Outdoor air is well endowed with a wide variety of suspended mould spores and these are small enough (10 μm diameter) to be carried indoors

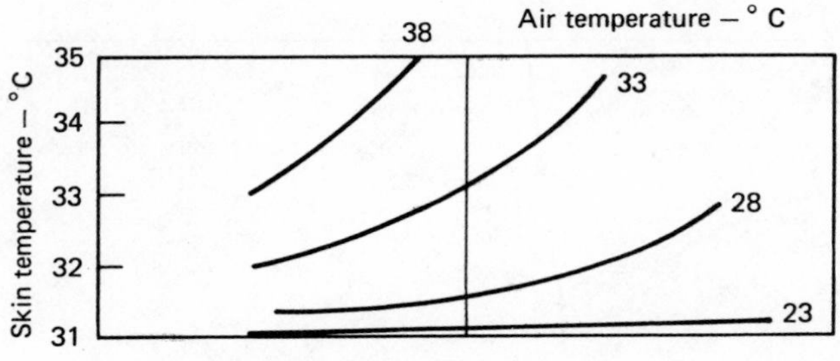

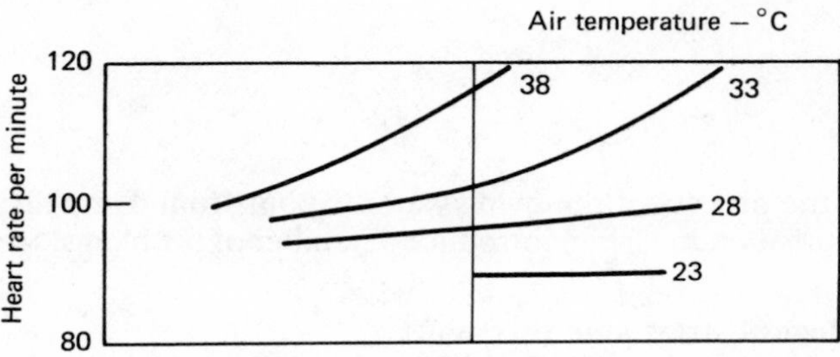

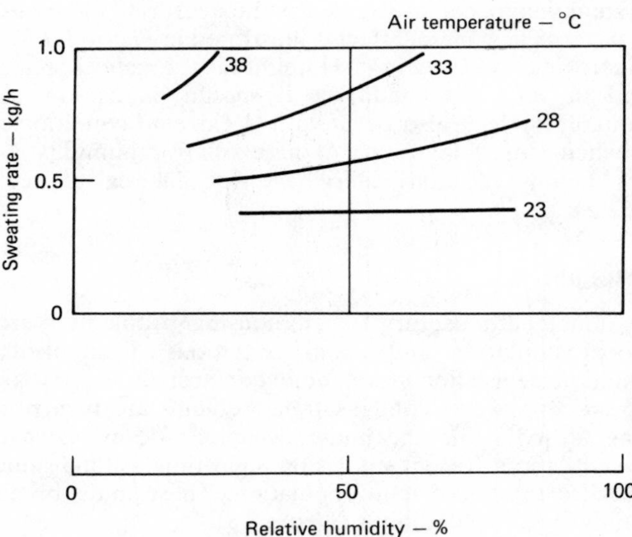

Figure 1.1 Physiological stress is caused by the combination of high temperature and high humidities (Robinson, 1949)[1]

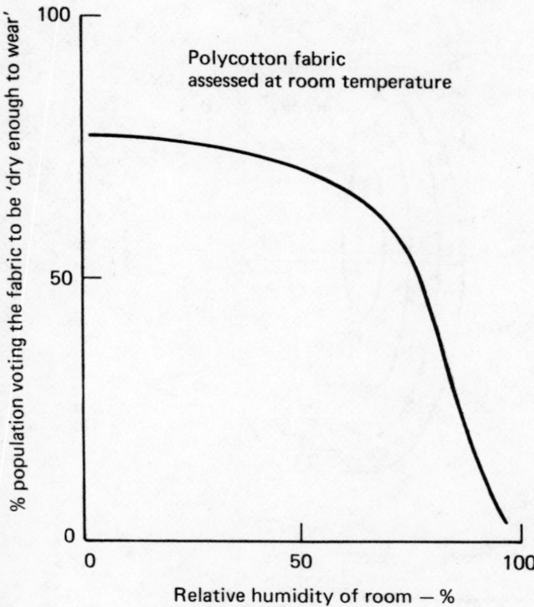

Figure 1.2 Perceptions of 'dryness' for a modern fabric in equilibrium with different room relative humidities (Lake and Lloyd-Hughes, 1979)[4]

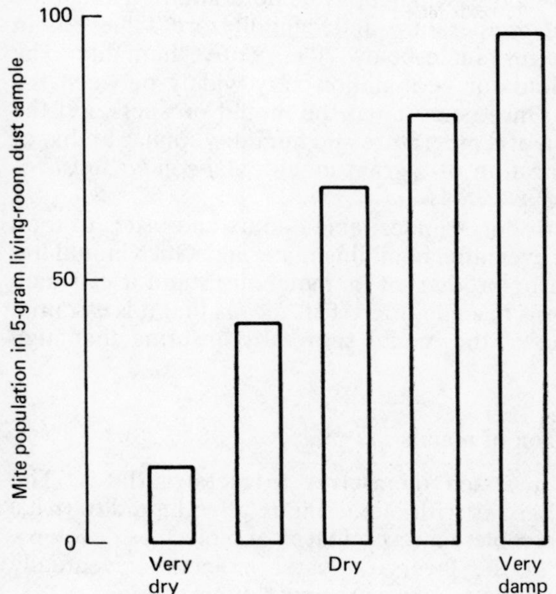

Figure 1.3 The house mite population increases with house dampness (Varenkemp *et al*, 1966)[6]

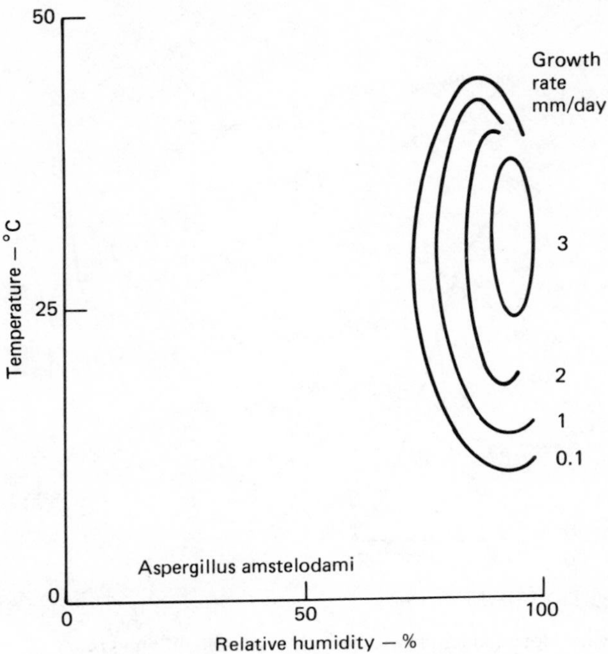

Figure 1.4 Growth rates of a typical grain fungi (Ayerst, 1969)[8]

and eventually to settle. The spores will happily lie dormant for a long time until suitable conditions of temperature and humidity are achieved. In general the spores will not germinate below 70% relative humidity. The actual temperature conditions for germination vary widely between the different types of mould[7]. Once germinated the mould prospers and the speed of growth is a function of temperature and humidity similar to that of germination time. An illustration of a grain mould, *Aspergillus amstelodami*, is given in *Figure 1.4*[8].

Mould growth rapidly introduces undesirable odours and tastes to food products and over time can even affect building materials. Once mould has started to grow, water is a by-product of its metabolism and it can then succeed even when conditions become drier. This means that it is essential to prevent the germination of the mould spores by ensuring that high humidities are avoided.

1.1.4 Accelerate the corrosion of metals

Molecules of water vapour attach themselves to metal surfaces. The concentration of molecules grows with increasing relative humidity (r.h.) and when the first layer is complete a second layer of molecules develops. This molecular thickness of the layers of water molecules eventually permits ionic conduction which accelerates the rate of corrosion.

The actual corrosion rate is a complex function of many factors but the three most important are the passivity of the metal surface, the degree and

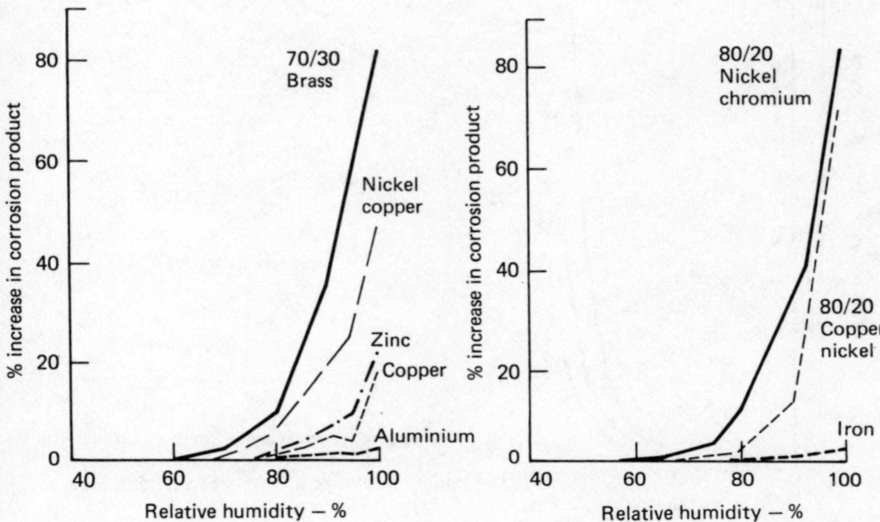

Figure 1.5 Increase in weight after exposure to successive periods of 24h to atmospheres of increasing humidity at 20°C (Hudson, 1929)[9]

type of surface contamination and the physical conditions of temperature and humidity. Experiments to measure the change in corrosion rate at room temperature for different relative humidities are illustrated in *Figure 1.5*[9]. This suggests that relative humidity should be kept below 60% r.h. to avoid accelerated corrosion of metallic surfaces.

In practice, lower values of relative humidity could be required if surface contamination is severe or if corrosion gases are present. Industrial pollutants such as sulphur dioxide will enhance the corrosion rate. Salt deposits, which could easily occur in coastal areas, also benefit by lower relative humidities[10].

1.1.5 Reduce the electrical resistance of insulators

Electrical insulators must not conduct electricity either through the body of the insulator or over the surface. However, the concentration of these ionic water molecules on the surface of a body increases as the relative humidity increases. The actual relationship between water molecule concentration and relative humidity varies with the material and any surface treatment applied to it. Early studies on a very carefully cleaned piece of glass showed that the water molecule concentration built up steadily with increasing relative humidity up to 70% r.h. A single layer of water molecules covered the surface at 50% r.h. Above 70% r.h. the layers of water molecules increase much more rapidly with increasing relative humidity[11].

Electrical surface conductivity tests on a piece of Pyrex showed similar features. The electrical conductivity was almost zero up to 50% r.h. Above 50% r.h. the conductivity increased to 60–70% r.h. and then increased

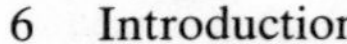

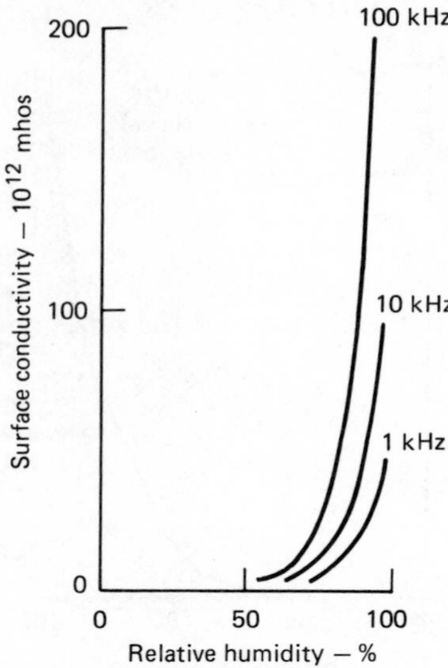

Figure 1.6 The increase in surface conductivity of an insulator (Pyrex glass) with increasing ambient relative humidity (Yaker and Morgan, 1931)[12]

very rapidly at high humidities. These results are illustrated in *Figure 1.6* for a range of measurement frequencies[12].

The more modern problem is low-voltage breakdowns between adjacent circuits on printed circuit boards. The developing microminiaturization of circuits makes the problem a growing one. Preliminary studies on the effect of relative humidity on the intercircuit insulation of a board placed at the coast and one placed in a city, showed that below 60 r.h. there was a pronounced improvement in electrical insulation in both, although the actual magnitude of the breakdown voltage in the city atmosphere was 70% of that in the rural environment[13].

Relative humidities below 60% are recommended for electrical insulators. Prevention of discharge is most important because, when discharges occur, the surface is often damaged irreparably.

1.1.6 Create plant breakdowns in icy conditions

Pneumatic controls and power supplies are widely used in industry, particularly in hazardous areas of potential fire or explosion hazard. The unexpected presence of water or ice can block pipes and valves, sieze linkages and falsify instrument readings whenever very cold weather occurs. The safety implications of this make it imperative to protect against such occurrences, and the simplest solution is to dry the pneumatic air supply[14].

1.1.7 Spoil surface finishes

Moisture droplets either blown or condensing onto surfaces during manufacture can spoil the appearance and lead to more irritating corrosion blemishes later. Dry-air supplies or dry-air curtains are essential in humid climates.

1.1.8 Induce premature chemical breakdown

Many chemicals react with water vapour, particularly at high temperatures. This can lead to unexpected corrosion compounds and early failure in chemical process plant. Moisture can also inhibit catalysts and shorten plant operation time.

Refrigerant cycles are a particularly good example of where the presence of water vapour in the refrigerant gas can be destructive. Reactions between the fluorinated refrigerant and the water vapour can lead to the creation of acids which can take copper into solution from the pipes and deposit it on cast-iron surfaces such as pistons, thus causing seizure. The acid could also attack the thin copper wire insulation and lead to electrical failure. All refrigerant gases are therefore particularly well dried, and special precautions are taken during maintenance work to retain this dryness.

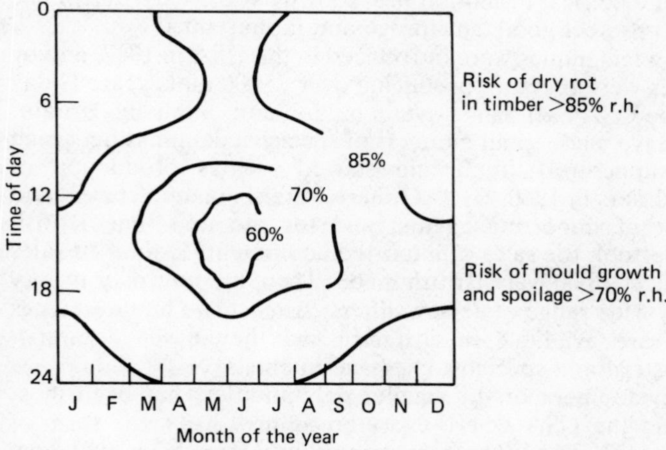

Figure 1.7 Variations in relative humidity over the day and the year. Mean values for London 1957–1966 (Lacy, 1977)[15]

Britain's climate is traditionally mild and damp with long periods above 85% r.h. (*Figure 1.7*)[15]. The presence of moisture is therefore widespread and prolonged, and to meet this problem dehumidifiers are now becoming available at increasingly competitive prices. This book aims to illustrate the types of equipment available, together with an outline of their characteristics, and to guide the reader into the growing number of their applications.

1.2 Historical development of air drying

In the fifteenth century the scientists at the Academio del Cimento in Florence quantified the amount of moisture in the air by collecting the condensate which formed on the outside of a specially-designed ice-filled jar. However, it was not until the eighteenth century that the science of moisture or 'psychrometrics' was placed on a firm base. The two pioneers were de Saussure of Switzerland[16], who quantified humidity in a reproducible way, and Dalton of England[17] who developed the law of partial pressures and hence provided the necessary scientific background.

The engineering work started in the United States of America with Delahaye in 1874 using a cool stream of water through which the air was cooled and dehumidified. However, it was not until 1902 that Willis Carrier used commercial ice-making equipment to create an air-conditioning system with dehumidification[18]. Domestic-sized refrigeration equipment was in use in America in 1895 and Kelvinator offered their first refrigerator in 1918. General Electric introduced a higher reliability with the invention of the hermetically-sealed refrigeration circuit in 1926. These refrigeration developments were applied to small dehumidifiers and by 1931 a range of dehumidifiers from 1.3 to 3 hp was commercially available. Their first use was to remove dampness in pipe-organ lofts to retain the tuning, to prevent electrical insulation breakdowns in the early telephone exchanges, and to protect goods in storage and in museums.

Mass production techniques were introduced in the USA in 1947, and by 1952 28 companies were together producing over 75 000 units/year. Today both Japan and the USA each make over a million units annually. Britain, Italy and France have made small numbers of specialist dehumidifiers each year. Three manufacturers in Britain started serious production of domestic dehumidifiers in 1980. By 1983 there were six manufacturers and an equal number of importing agents, and for the first time British manufacturers overtook the sales of imported equipment. Estimated sales were 15 000 of which 10 000 were British made. There are now over twenty suppliers of a very wide range of dehumidifiers. Almost two hundred types of dehumidifiers are available in Britain[19] and they cover domestic, commercial, industrial and specialist chemical interests.

The market development of the smaller dehumidifiers has been most rapid in Japan and the USA where every house now has some form of refrigerant dehumidification. The new homes in Japan have the most advanced system to match their damp climate. Their air conditioners operate on heating, cooling or dehumidification.

The French have made remarkable progress with the medium-sized dehumidifiers, particularly for timber drying up to 50°C. Nearly 1000 units were installed between 1970 and 1977 and work is in progress to extend the techniques to other industrial processes[20]. British research has concentrated on operating at higher drying temperatures and commercially-available dryers can now work satisfactorily up to 80°C[21].

The larger dehumidifiers are mostly used in swimming pools. They are in widespread use in both the USA and Europe. This application is a new one brought about by increasing energy prices. In the last ten years in Britain one hundred pools have been either built with or converted to dehumidification as a lower energy alternative to high ventilation rates[22].

The refrigerant cycles are normally all evaporation, compression and condensation ones. The very early units used ammonia as the refrigerant but the safer halogen refrigerants took over in the 1940s and modern designs select the most appropriate halogen refrigerant from an ever increasing selection to match the required temperatures and pressures.

Absorption cycles have been well developed and recent advances have been in improved and more reliable control techniques. Air cycles are actively under review for bulk drying[23].

1.3 Psychrometric charts

Psychrometric charts describe the state of damp air (*Figure 1.8*). The terms used are:

(1) *Humidity mixing ratio*. This is the ratio of the mass of moisture present to that of dry air. It is a measure of the quantity of water present.

(2) *Relative humidity*. This is the ratio of the actual water vapour pressure to that at saturation. It is the important parameter in determining the moisture content of solids in equilibrium with the damp air. It is very similar to *Percentage saturation* which is the ratio of the mass of moisture present to that at saturation. At high relative humidities the two are for all practical purposes the same.

(3) *Dewpoint*. This is the saturation temperature for the humidity mixing ratio of the air. It is the temperature at which moisture just starts to condense out of the air stream.

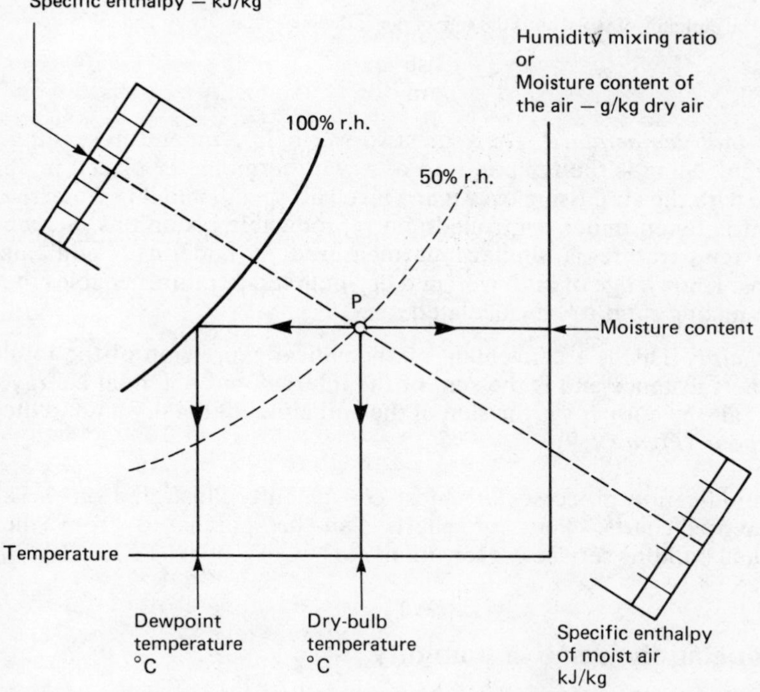

Figure 1.8 Diagrammatic illustration of a psychrometric chart illustrating the characteristics of point P

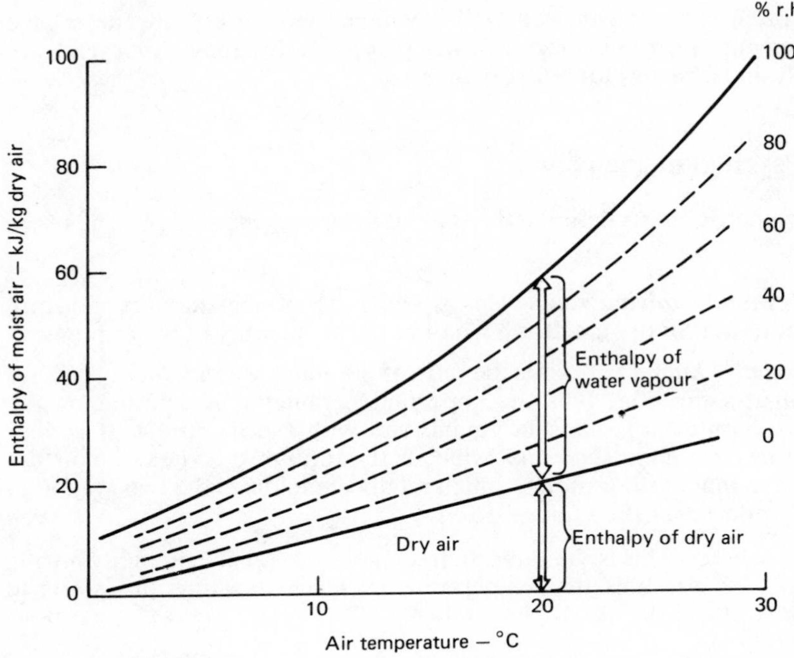

Figure 1.9 The enthalpy of moist air is the sum of the enthalpies of the dry air and the water vapour

(4) *Wet-bulb temperature.* There are two wet-bulb temperatures, 'sling' and 'screen'. Sling is the temperature of a wet thermometer placed in an airstream with the air passing over it at a given air speed, and it is preferred because it is taken under controlled and reproducible conditions. Screen wet-bulb temperature is similar but measured in undefined 'still' air conditions. Knowledge of both wet- and dry-bulb temperatures enables the humidity mixing ratio to be calculated.

(5) *Enthalpy*. This is a convenient mathematical expression of the total heat of the substance and is the sum of the internal and potential energy. For moist air the enthalpy is the sum of the enthalpies of the dry air and the water vapour (*Figure 1.9*).

Dehumidification processes are most conveniently illustrated on these psychrometric charts. Pads of charts can be purchased from the professional building service organizations.

1.4 Reducing the relative humidity

There are four general ways of lowering the relative humidity of moist air, and these can be illustrated on the psychrometric chart (*Figure 1.10*).

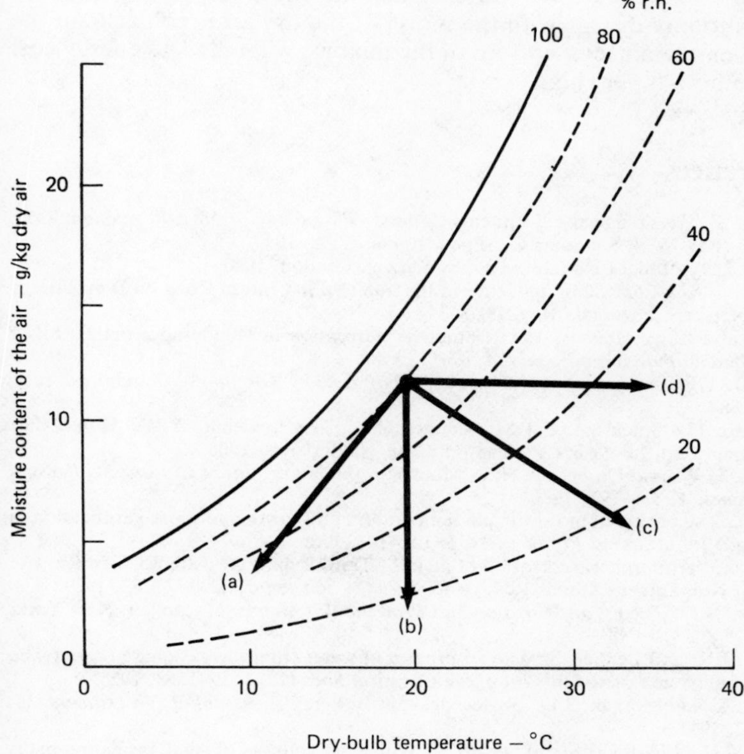

Figure 1.10 Four different ways of lowering the relative humidity of moist air. (a) Dilute with dry air, (b) sorbent drying, (c) refrigerant dehumidifying, and (d) heating

(1) *Increasing the temperature.* Raising the dry-bulb temperature increases the saturation vapour pressure and hence lowers the relative humidity. It does not change the actual amount of water present.

(2) *Heat pump dehumidification.* The heat pump dehumidifier tends to work along lines of constant enthalpy. The latent heat of the condensate is returned to warm up the dry air. Cool moist air is converted to warm dry air of similar enthalpy. Since the high enthalpy of moist air is principally due to the latent heat of the water vapour, the potential recoverable energy is high. In practice, the dehumidifier will add sensible heat to the air passing through it and so the slope of this line on the psychrometric chart will be a little more towards that of 'heating'.

(3) *Moisture removal.* Sorbent systems remove water vapour and this effectively lowers the relative humidity. In practice there will be a small increase in dry-bulb temperatures as the desiccant heats up. The energy penalty of such a system is high because the sorbent has to be regenerated at high temperature.

(4) *Dilution with dry air.* The classical way of lowering the relative humidity is to mix dry air with the moist. If the dry air is colder than the moist air then the air temperature of the mixture will fall. The energy cost for such methods is very high.

1.5 References

1 Robinson, S. 'Physiological adjustments to heat'. *Physiology of Heat Regulation.* L.H. Newburgh (ed), W.B. Saunders Co, Philadelphia, USA, 1949
2 McIntyre, D.A. 'Indoor climate'. *Applied Science*, London, 1980
3 Brundrett, G.W. 'Controlling moisture in the home'. First Intern Cong on Bldg Energy Managet, Oporto, Portugal, May, 1980
4 Lake, B. and Lloyd-Hughes, J.L. 'Dampness perception in laundered articles'. *Jnl of Consmr Studies and Home Econcs*, **4**, 87–95, 1980
5 Galton, D. *Observations on the Construction of Healthy Dwellings.* Clarendon Press, Oxford, 1880
6 Varenkemp, H., Spieksma, F.T.M., Leupen, M.J. and Lyklema, A.W. 'House dust mites'. Paper 2.56, Interasma V Cong, Utrecht, Netherlands, 1966
7 Brundrett, G.W. and Onions, A.H.S. 'Moulds in the home'. *Jnl of Consmr Studies and Home Econcs*, **4**, 311–321, 1980
8 Ayerst, G. 'The effects of moisture and temperature on growth and spore germination in some fungi'. *Jnl of Stored Product Res*, **5**, 127–141, 1969
9 Hudson, J.C. 'Atmospheric corrosion of metals'. Third Rep to the Atmos Corrn Res Cte of the Brit Non-Ferrous Metals Res Assoc. *Faraday Soc Trans*, **25**, 177–252, 1929
10 Tomashov, N.D. *Theory of Corrosion and Protection of Metals.* Macmillan, New York, 1966
11 McHaffie, J.R. and Lenher, S. 'The adsorption of water from the gas phase on to plane surfaces of glass and platinum'. *Jnl of the Chemical Soc*, **127**, 1559–1568, 1925
12 Yager, W.A. and Morgan, S.O. 'Surface leakage of Pyrex glass'. *Jnl of Phys Chemy*, **35**, 2026–2042, 1931
13 Fellman, K.H., Pfeiffer, W. and Schau, P. 'Withstand voltages of small insulating paths and the effect of natural environmental conditions'. *Elektrotechnische Zeitschrift Archiv*, **3**, (4), 117–120, 1981
14 *ASHRAE Handbook: Fundamentals:* Am Soc of Htg, Refrign & Air Condg Engrs, Atlanta, USA, 1982
15 Lacy, R.E. *Climate and Building in Britain.* HMSO, London, 1977
16 Saussure, H.B. de. *Essais sur l'Hygrometrie.* S. Fauche, Neuchâtel, Switzerland, 1793
17 Dalton, J. 'Experimental essays on the constitution of mixed gases'. *Memoirs and Proceedings of the Manchester Literary and Philosophical Society*, **5**, 535–602, 1802
18 Billington, N.S. and Roberts, B.M. *Building Services Engineering: A Review of its Development.* Pergamon Press, Oxford, 1982
19 Brundrett, G.W. 'A guide to packaged dehumidifiers'. Memo by Elecy Ccl Res Cen, Capenhurst, ECRC/M1871, 1984
20 Heap, R.D. *Heat Pumps*, 2nd edn. E. & F.N. Spon, London, 1983
21 Lopez-Cacicedo, C. 'Application possibilities for heat pumps in the higher temperature range'. *Elektrowärme in Technischen Ausban*, Edition A, **38**, A4/5, 281–284, 1980
22 Braham, G.D. and Johnson, A.J. 'A guide to energy cost effectiveness in swimming pools'. Elecy Ccl Mktg Rep, Aug 1977
23 Iles, T. 'The Brayton-cycle heat pump for industrial process application'. *Elektrowarme in Technischen Ausban*, Edition A, **38**, A4/5, 285–294, 1980

Chapter 2

Principles of dehumidification

There are three methods of removing moisture from air. These are sorbent dehumidification, refrigerant dehumidification and air-cycle dehumidification. For completeness vapour recompression is introduced although this is not strictly dehumidification because air is not involved. The required dewpoint determines the technique required. A typical range of applications is given in *Figure 2.1*.

2.1 Sorbent dehumidification

Sorbents are divided into two general categories, *ad*sorbents and *ab*sorbents. Adsorbents are solids which have a large internal surface area on which water molecules condense without changing the nature of the solid. Absorbents are hygroscopic materials which change their nature when taking up moisture. An absorbent is usually a strong concentration of a salt which is exposed to the moist air.

A typical operating cycle for the solid adsorbents is shown in *Figure 2.2*[1]. Moist air is blown through a rotating drum of dessicant. The water vapour condenses on the internal surfaces of the solid, releasing its latent heat of condensation and its heat of adsorbtion. The drier air is therefore raised in temperature by 10 to 20°C and re-enters the conditioned space. The drum of dessicant turns and is reactivated by blowing hot dry air through the matrix. This dries out the dessicant while the hot moist air is blown to waste. The cycle is repeated as the drum rotates. It is an open cycle and about a quarter to one third of the purchased energy goes back into the processed air. Illustrative performance data is shown in *Figure 2.3*.

In recent years this simple cycle has been given variants to meet specific needs. More efficient cycles can be achieved by cooling down the waste hot air from the regenerator and using it to preheat the incoming regenerator supply. Energy savings of about 30 to 40% are claimed by the manufacturers. The principle is illustrated in *Figure 2.4*.

Another version provides a water-cooled condenser on the regenerator loop, thus eliminating the need for a ventilator to the outside. The

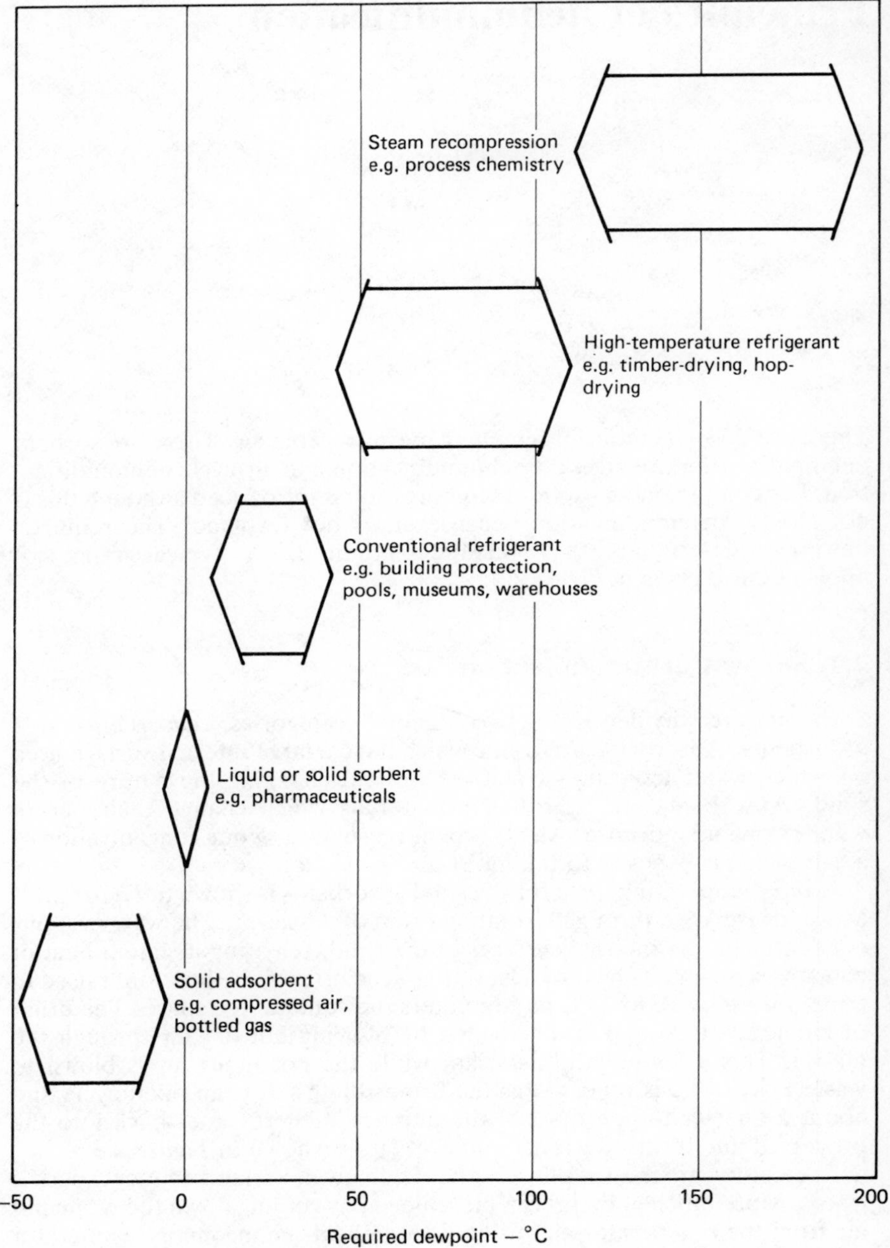

Figure 2.1 The required dewpoint determines the dehumidifying technique

Working zone
Dry air
Process air
Air heater
Wet air
Reactivation air
Driving motor
Reactivation zone

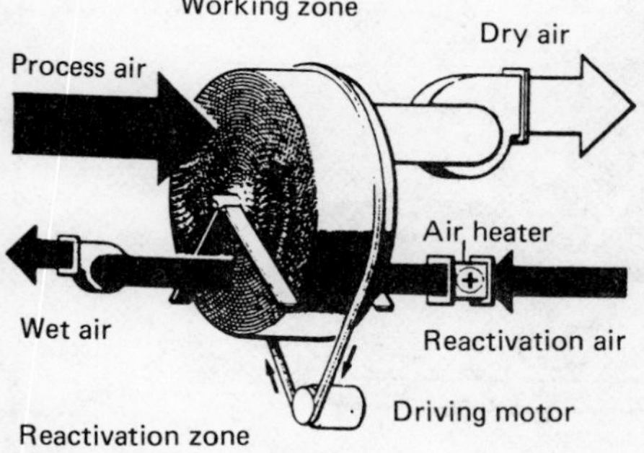

Figure 2.2 Basic design of a solid sorbent rotary dehumidifier (courtesy of Rotaire)[1]

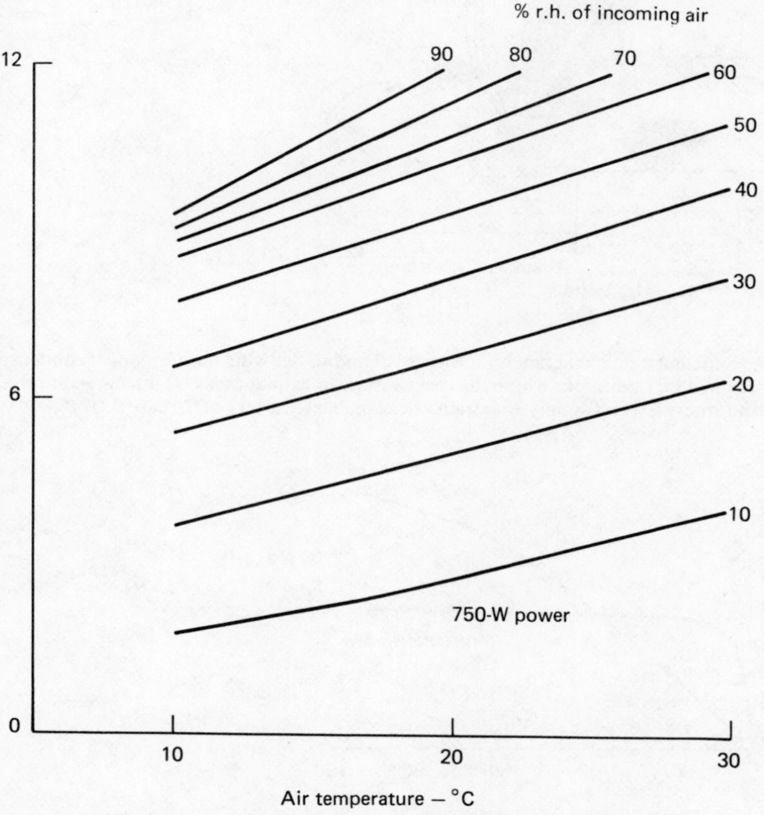

% r.h. of incoming air
90
80
70
60
50
40
30
20
10
750-W power
12
6
0
Water extraction rate – kg/day
10
20
30
Air temperature – °C

Figure 2.3 Illustrative performance of an adsorption dehumidifier (M125, Lithium chloride bed)[1] (courtesy of Rotaire)

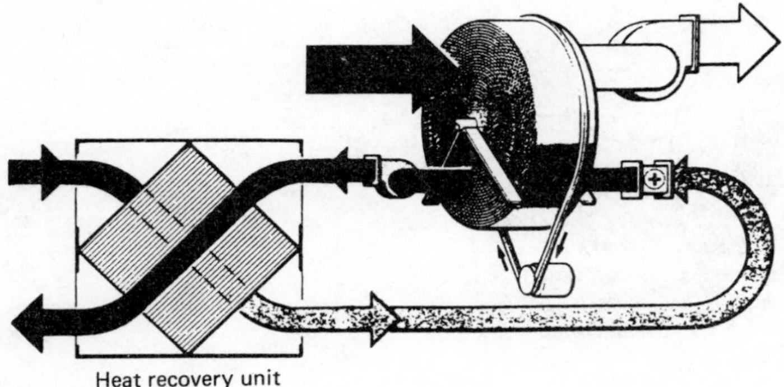

Figure 2.4 Schematic flow diagram for a sorbent dehumidifier with heat recovery; 30–40% energy savings are claimed (courtesy of Rotaire)[1]

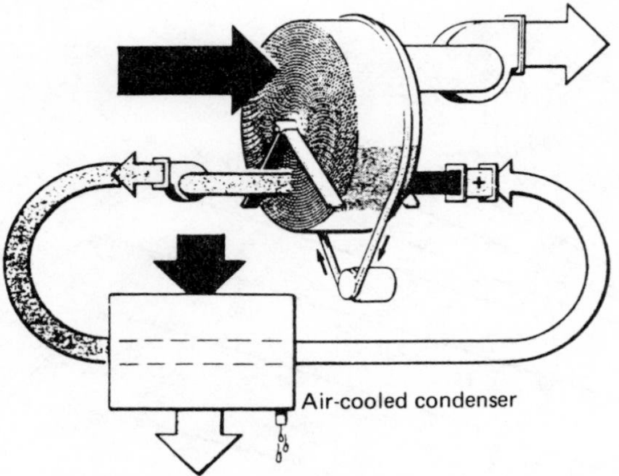

Figure 2.5 Schematic flow diagram for a sorbent dehumidifier with a water-cooled condenser. This is designed for operations where the reactivation air cannot easily be discharged to the outside and where a water supply and drain are available (courtesy of Rotaire)[1]

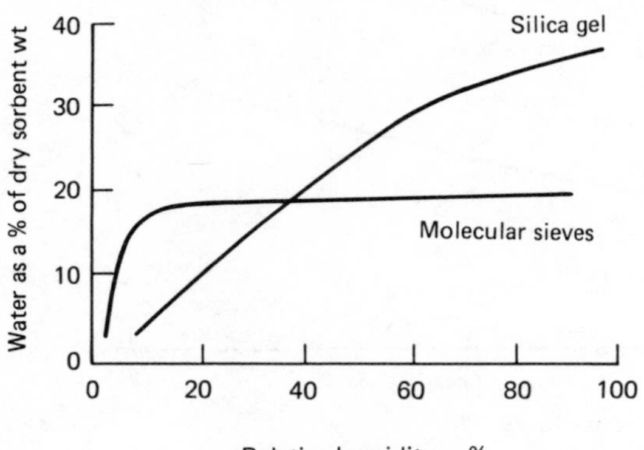

Figure 2.6 Illustrative equilibrium characteristics for two common sorbents

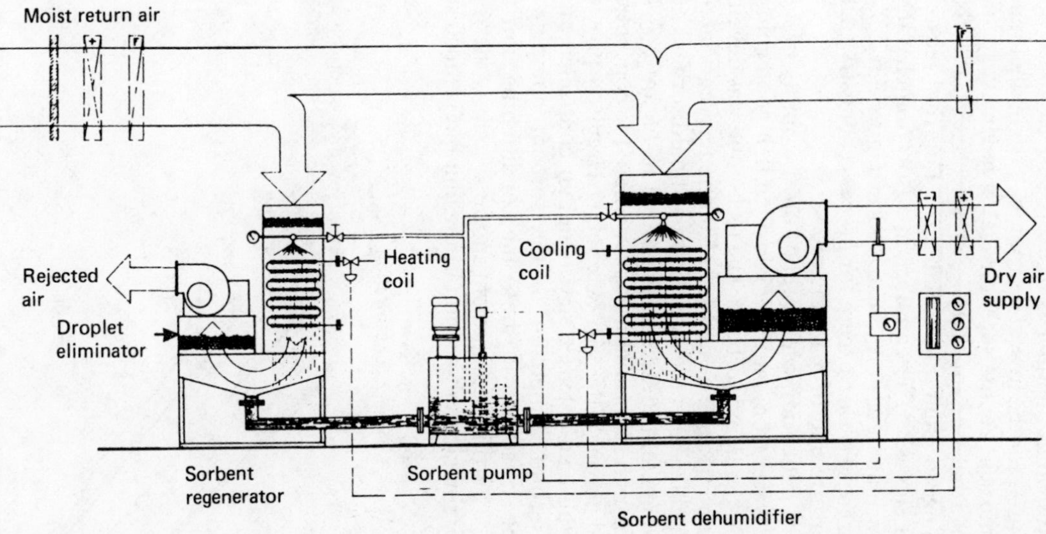

Figure 2.7 Diagrammatic illustration of the three components of the liquid sorbent dehumidifier: the spray dehumidifier, the sorbent pump and the regenerator (Kathabar system)[3]

condensate is collected or run to drain. The principle is illustrated in *Figure 2.5*.

These solid dessicant dehumidifiers are essential for dehumidification to very low dewpoint temperatures. Silica gel is the traditional solid dessicant because of its broad adsorption characteristic over a wide range of relative humidity. Its weakness is its rapid degradation to powder if exposed to water droplets. Activated alumina is more robust to abuse and half the cost. Zeolites are used for the lowest dewpoints. Originally found naturally in modified volcanic ash, zeolites are unusual in having very uniform pore sizes. This means that the material can selectively adsorb or reject molecules according to their molecular size. For this reason they are termed 'molecular sieves'[2]. The equilibrium adsorption characteristics for silica gel and molecular sieves are illustrated in *Figure 2.6*.

Such extreme dryness is rare except for process chemistry such as drying refrigerant gases at the end of manufacture.

Liquid absorbent dehumidification relies on the ability of a strong salt solution to extract water from moist air provided that good contact is made between the air and the liquid sorbent. The technique was developed in the USA in the 1940s and became available in Europe ten years later. A strong solution of lithium chloride is the most popular liquid sorbent. The system has three components and these are illustrated in *Figure 2.7*. Dehumidification takes place in the conditioning spray where the concentrated liquid sorbent is sprayed through the air. A cooling circuit is provided in the tower to remove the heat released and maintain controlled and constant conditions. The second component is the sorbent pumping unit: this provides the supply of sorbent to both the conditioning unit and to the regeneration unit. The third component in the system is the regenerator: this works in a way similar to the conditioning unit but is much smaller and

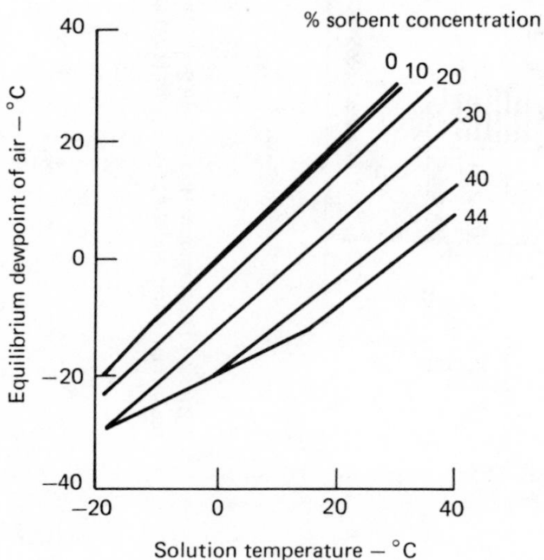

Figure 2.8 Temperature-equilibrium dewpoint characteristics for a typical inorganic absorbent (Engelback, 1969)[4]

is heated. The moisture released is rejected and the more concentrated sorbent returns to the reservoir.

The temperature/equilibrium dewpoint characteristics for a typical absorbent are given in *Figure 2.8*. In practice, concentrations vary from 8 to 44% by weight. The controlled humidity depends upon this salt concentration and the operating temperature, and the concentration is maintained simply by keeping the liquid level in the pumping unit constant. Control is therefore simple and accurate.

The liquid systems cannot achieve the very low dewpoint achieved by the solid dessicants. However, the technique does have two unusual

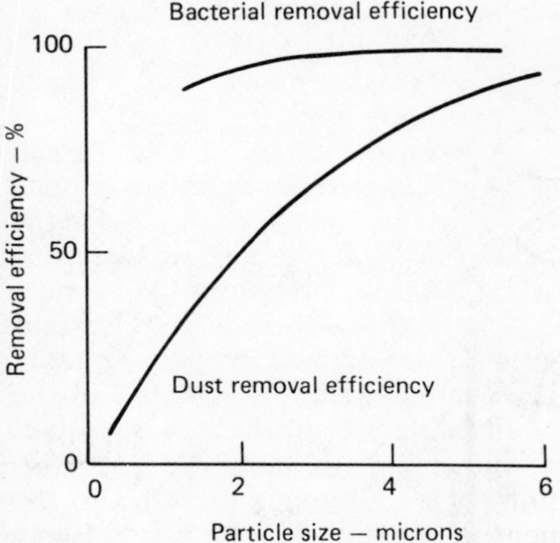

Figure 2.9 Bacteria and dust removal for a Kathabar dehumidifier. The particles were measured with the Anderson Plate sampling technique, and the dust removal was measured according to the National Bureau of Standards Dust Spot Method (manufacturer's own data)

characteristics. The first is that the salt concentration, particularly lithium chloride, has a biocidal effect on the air. The second is that the washing technique is very effective in cleaning the airstream of any suspended solids. Manufacturer's data for normal atmospheric organisms is shown in *Figure 2.9*. The principal applications for the technique are essentially those of the food industry and hospitals. Such industries usually offer the further advantage of a low-cost steam supply for the regenerator operation.

2.2 Refrigerant dehumidification

Refrigerant dehumidification, illustrated in *Figure 2.10*, is unique in converting the enthalpy of the moist air into sensible heat. It achieves this by drawing the moist air over a heat-exchanger surface which is refrigerated to a temperature below the dewpoint of the air. Moisture condenses on this surface, giving up its latent heat of condensation. The cold, drier air is then drawn over the condenser of the refrigerant circuit which is hot. This cycle acts as a heat pump by converting the latent heat of

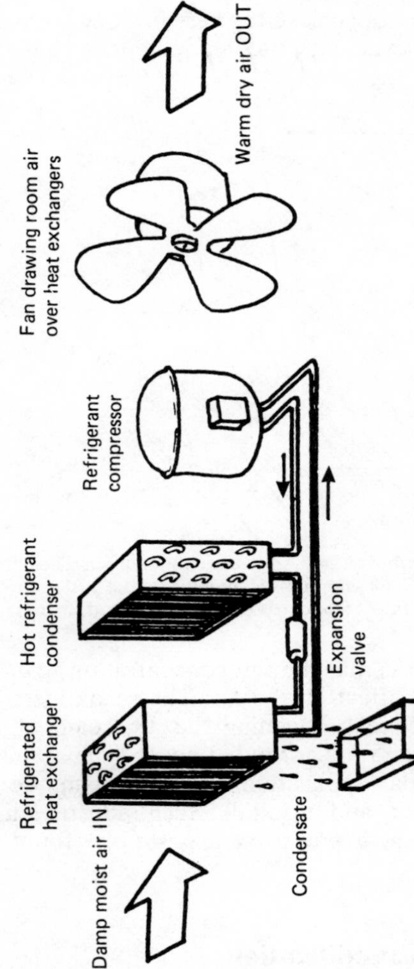

Figure 2.10 The refrigerant dehumidifier

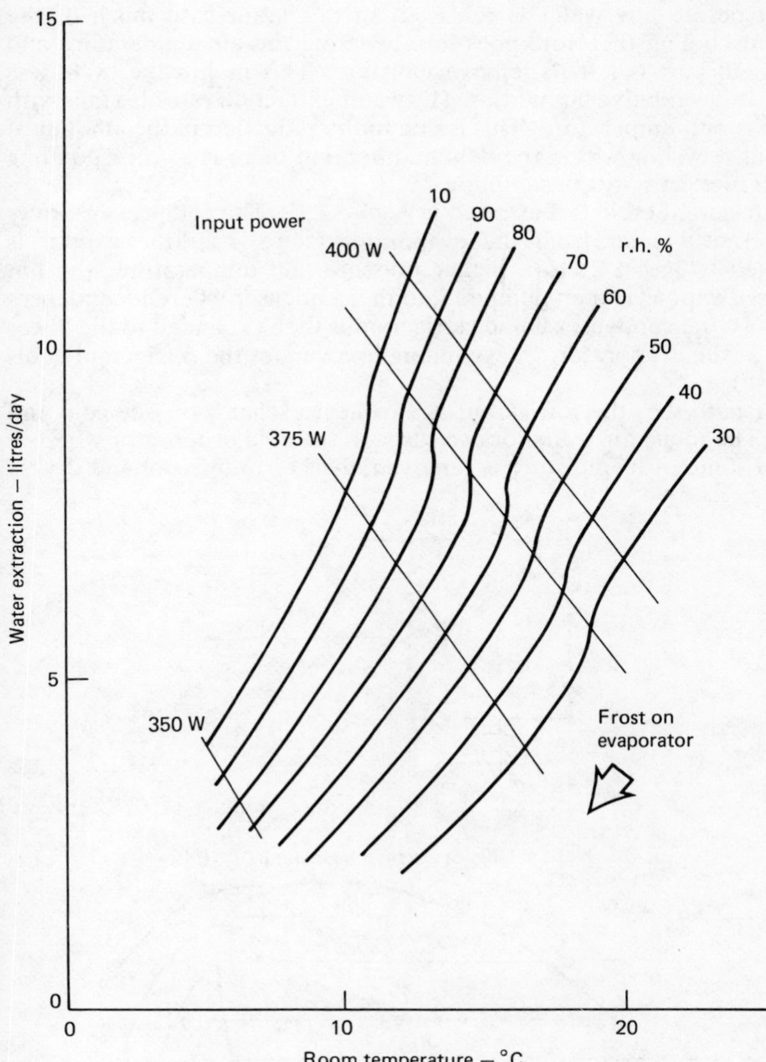

Figure 2.11 Illustrative performance of a large domestic dehumidifier

condensation into sensible heat at the hot condenser. It therefore provides more sensible energy output than the electricity consumed. It can be said to have a 'coefficient of performance' (COP). This is the ratio of sensible heat to the airstream divided by the electricity consumed, and usually this coefficient lies between 1 and 2.

The effectiveness of the dehumidifier depends upon the relative humidity of the incoming air (*Figure 2.11*). The slightest cooling of air which is at 100% relative humidity will result in water being condensed. However, at low relative humidities the air has to be cooled down to its dewpoint before any water is released. In this latter case much of the refrigerant cooling therefore goes into lowering the air temperature and only a small part is left to remove moisture. This makes the cycle less effective at low relative humidities. The water extraction rate also falls with declining room temperature. This is due to the reduction in the amount of refrigerant recycling within the dehumidifier and there is a corresponding reduction in electricity consumption.

The refrigerant cycle is illustrated in *Figure 2.12*. The compressor draws in refrigerant vapour from the evaporator (steps 4-1): the vapour is compressed (stages 1-2) to a higher pressure and temperature: the hot compressed vapour is then pumped into the condenser where it condenses (stages 2-3): the condenser liquid refrigerant is then expanded to the lower pressure of the evaporator. In expanding to a vapour the refrigerant cools (stages 3-4).

The air path sees the refrigerant as two heat exchangers, one cold and one hot. The moist air is first drawn through the cold evaporator where it cools and some of its moisture is removed. This air, now cool and dry, is

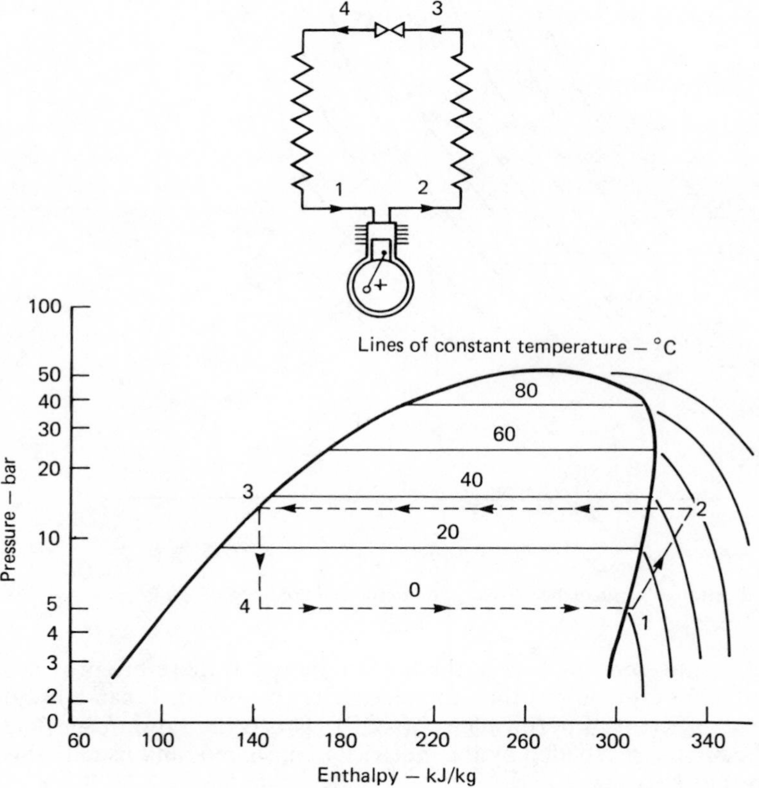

Figure 2.12 The refrigerant cycle for the dehumidifier (R22 refrigerant). 1-2 = the refrigerant gas being compressed from 0°C to 60°C. 2-3 = high-pressure gas condensing and giving up its latent heat. 3-4 = expansion valve or capillary tube which produce a pressure drop. 4-1 = low-pressure refrigerant evaporating at low temperature

then blown through the hot condenser heat exchanger whence it emerges hotter and drier than it was at the start of its path.

Refrigerant dehumidifiers are the ideal solution for winter moisture problems where moisture removal and background heating are needed simultaneously. This meets the need of many applications in Britain's damp and mild winter climate.

2.3 Air-cycle dehumidification

When air is compressed it becomes hot. If this compressed air is cooled at pressure and then expanded, the cooling caused by the expansion will result in the air being chilled and moisture being deposited. This was one of the earliest refrigeration cycles and it was also proposed as a dehumidifier[6]. It has never been used commercially, although research proposals have been made[7,8] for low capital cost vortex-tube dehumidifiers and for large-scale grain drying.

The effectiveness of the cycle depends upon the product of the efficiencies of the compressor and the expander. This, together with its physical bulk, has prevented its development.

2.4 Vapour compression drying

Early pioneering Swiss work in the 1870s recognized that the water vapour itself could be used as the working fluid. Air is excluded from the system. Heat is applied to the wet solids and drives off water vapour. If this water vapour is compressed (*Figure 2.13*) it will rise in temperature. This higher

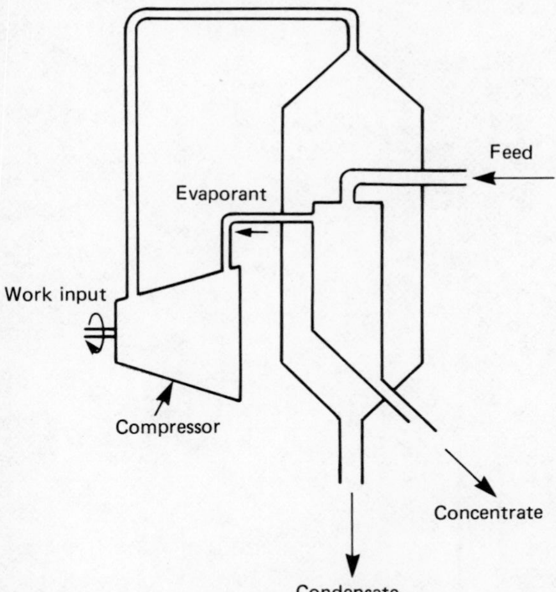

Figure 2.13 Basic operation of a vapour compression cycle (Hardy, Warne and Griffith, 1976)[9]

pressure water vapour will condense at a higher temperature too. The latent heat in the water vapour can therefore be used to heat up the wet solids which are being dried.

This technique is growing in popularity for the higher-temperature drying applications of 100 to 150°C, particularly when large quantities of water vapour are involved. It is now a serious competitor to the conventional air-drying technique[9,10,11].

2.5 References

1 *Rotaire Dehumidifiers*. Company catalogue, 1986

2 Hall, C.W. *Dictionary of Drying*. M. Dekker, New York, 1979

3 *Kathabar Dehumidifiers*. Company catalogue, 1986

4 Engelbach, A.G. 'Air conditioning by means of the chemical absorption process'. *Instn of Htg & Ventn Engrs Jnl*, Aug 1969

5 Heap, R.D. *Heat Pumps*. E. & F.N. Spon, London, 1979

6 Lightfoot, T.B. 'On machines for producing cold air'. *Instn of Mech Engrs Proc*, 105–132, 1881

7 Brundrett, G.W. 'The vortex dehumidifier'. *Design Engg*, 71–72, Dec 1968

8 Iles, T. 'The Brayton-cycle heat pump for industrial process applications'. *Elektrowarme in Technischen Ausban*, Edition A, **38**, A4/5, 285–294, 1980

9 Hardy, W.E., Warne, D.F. and Griffith, M.V. 'A technical and economic appraisal of mechanical vapour recompression'. ERA Rep 76–1023, 1976

10 Hodgett, D.L. and Witt, J.A. 'High-temperature heat pumps for industry'. Elecy Ccl Res Cen, Capenhurst, ECRC/R1803, 1984

11 Taylor, B.J. and Bertinat, M.P. 'The design and evaluation of a 150°C heat pump'. Elecy Ccl Res Cen, Capenhurst, ECRC/M1859, 1984

Chapter 3

Design considerations for refrigerant dehumidifiers

3.1 Introduction

The six basic components of a refrigerant dehumidifier, as illustrated in *Figure 3.1*, are the compressor, the condenser, the expansion valve, the evaporator, the refrigerant fluid, and the fan for recirculating the air.

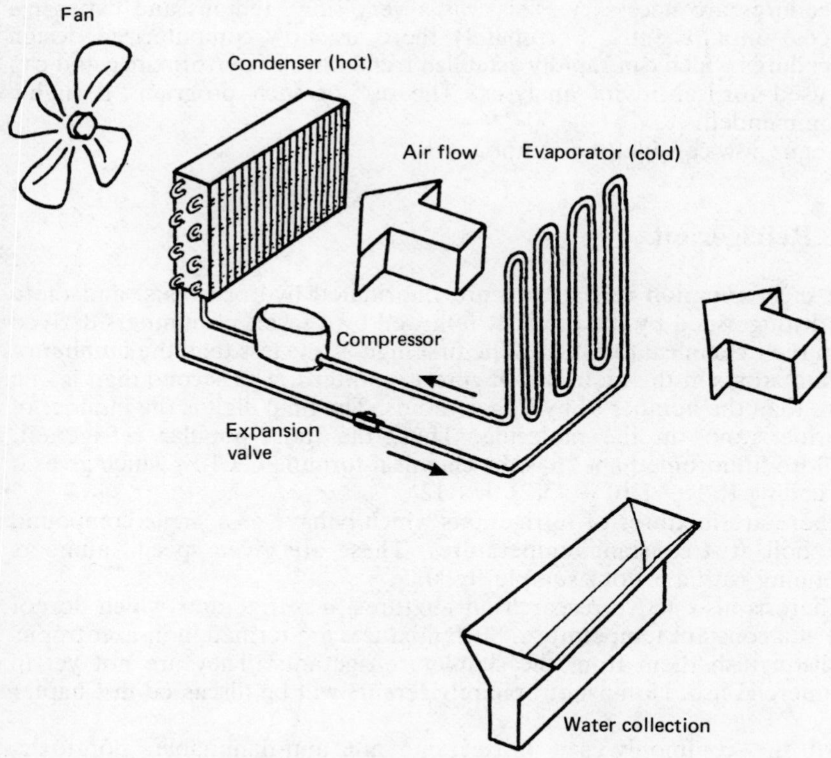

Figure 3.1 Elements of a refrigerant-type dehumidifier

The compressor draws the refrigerant from the lower pressure evaporator and forces it at higher pressure into the condenser. The cycle approximates to two operations, each at constant temperature and pressure. Evaporation of the refrigerant at the low-pressure heat exchanger, the evaporator, requires heat from the air to pass through this heat exchanger. This means that the evaporator operates at a temperature which is very cold and below that of the airstream passing through the heat-exchanger. If the temperature of the evaporator is below the dewpoint of air passing through the heat-exchanger then some dehumidification occurs.

The compressor compresses the refrigerant gas and passes it into the condenser. The refrigerant, now much hotter than the temperature of the air passing through the condenser, therefore condenses, giving up its latent heat to the airstream, thereby heating it up. (A typical compression ratio is 5:1.) The liquid refrigerant is then directed through an expansion valve to enter the evaporator as a wet vapour. The cycle then repeats itself.

In this chapter we will examine these components in more detail and consider general points of integration of a dehumidifier into a drying cycle and methods of assessing the cycle effectiveness.

The simplicity of the design is deceptive because, as in all refrigeration cycles, any change in one component has an effect on the performance of the other components. This strong interaction means that iterative design procedures are necessary. This was a very slow, tedious and expensive process until recently. Fortunately there are now computerized design procedures which can rapidly establish trend lines of performance and can be used for sensitivity analyses. The use of such programs is highly recommended.

Let us now consider the components.

3.2 Refrigerant

The most common refrigerants are fluorinated hydrocarbons, and these are distinguished by the prefix R followed by a series of numbers derived from their chemical formulae. The first digit is one less than the number of carbon atoms in the molecule (if zero is omitted). The second digit is one more than the number of hydrogen atoms. The final digit is the number of fluorine atoms in the molecule. Thus, the most popular refrigerant, dichlorodifluoromethane, has the chemical formula $C\ Cl_2F_2$ which gives it the coding $R(1 - 1)(0 + 1)(2)$ or R12[1].

There are mixtures of refrigerants which behave as a single compound (i.e. boil at a constant temperature). These are given special numbers beginning with a 5, for example R500.

There is also active research on mixtures of refrigerants which do not boil at a constant temperature. Such mixtures are termed 'non-azeotropic' to distinguish them from the simpler refrigerants. They are not yet in commercial use. Non-azeotropic refrigerants will be discussed in Chapter 9.

All the commonly-used refrigerants are non-flammable, non-toxic, non-irritant and normally chemically stable (*Table 3.1*). They possess a

TABLE 3.1 Relative safety of refrigerants

The Underwriters Laboratories' classification system assesses the comparative hazard to life. Their classification is based on acute toxicity tests on guinea pigs. There are six categories:

(1) Gases or vapours which in concentrations of ½ to 1% by volume for durations of exposure of about 5 minutes are lethal or produce serious injury.
(2) As (1) but for ½-hour exposure.
(3) Gases or vapours which in concentrations of 2 to 2½% by volume for durations of exposure of about 1 hour are lethal or produce serious injury.
(4) As (3) but for exposures of 2 hours.
(5) (a) Gases or vapours much less toxic than (4) but more than (6).
    (b) Gases or vapours which available data would classify as either (5)(a) or (6).
(6) Gases or vapours which, in concentrations of up to at least 20% by volume for durations of exposure of about two hours, do not appear to produce injury.

The American Standards Association – B9 Safet Code classify vapours and gases into three groups numbered with the least hazardous in Group 1.

The classifications for common refrigerants are:

Refrigerant	*Name*	*ASA-B9 Safety Code* 1971	*UL Class*	*Flammability*
R11	Trichloromonofluoromethane	1	5	Non flammable
R12	Dichlorodifluoromethane	1	6	Non flammable
R22	Monochlorodifluoromethane	1	5a	Non flammable
R502	Azeotrope of R22 & R115	1	5a	Non flammable
R500	Azeotrope of R12 & R152a	1	5a	Non flammable
R114	Dichlorotetrafluoroethane	1	6	Non flammable

The American Conference of Governmental Industrial Hygienists establishes Threshold Limit Values (TLV) of airborne contaminants. These limits are designed to represent conditions under which it is believed that nearly all workers may be repeatedly exposed day after day without adverse effect. However, a small percentage of workers may experience discomfort because of the wide variation in individual susceptibility at or below the threshold limit.

Two categories apply to the common refrigerants. The first is the Time Weighted Average (TWA) based on an 8-hour day and a 40-hour working week to which nearly all workers may be repeatedly exposed without adverse effect. The second is the Short Term Exposure Limit (STEL) which is the maximum concentration to which workers can be exposed for a period of up to 15 minutes continuously without suffering from irritation or irreversible tissue change or to increase accident proneness.

The two refrigerants classified are:

R11 Threshold Limit Value: TWA 1000 ppm 5000 mg/mg^3
R12 Threshold Limit Values: TWA 1000 ppm (4950 mg/m^3); STEL 1250 ppm (6200 mg/m^3)

high latent enthalpy of vaporization and cover a wide range of temperature/vapour pressure characteristics (*Figure 3.2*). Each application has an appropriate fluid which is usually selected on the basis of evaporating and condensing temperatures. A typical range for a reciprocating compressor is given in *Figure 3.3*[2]. The maximum pressure is determined by mechanical stress considerations. The minimum pressure is determined by mass flow considerations. At low vapour pressures the mass recirculation rate of refrigerant is low.

The refrigerants used in dehumidifiers designed to operate at room temperature are R12, R22 and R500. R12 is readily available and is used

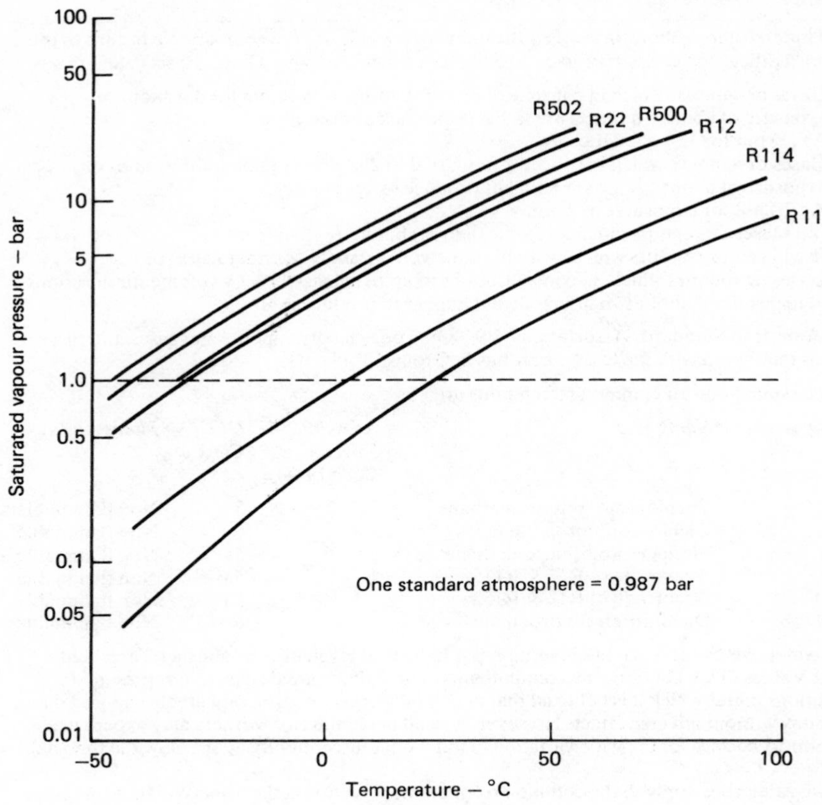

Figure 3.2 Vapour pressure/temperature characteristics of some refrigerants

primarily for conventional refrigeration. It requires a high volumetric flow for a given duty. R22 requires higher operating pressures than R12 and is commonly used in heat pumps and air conditioning. It is less soluble in lubricating oil but less reactive with it, and is a more destructive solvent for wire enamel and some seals. R500 is an azeotrope containing 73.8% of R12 and 26.2% of R152a, and its performance lies between R12 and R22. It is now also readily available and in common use[3,4,5].

Corrosive chemicals can be formed if any of the refrigerants come into contact with moisture. These corrosive compounds can attack the insulation of the motor windings which normally operate at a high temperature. As this leads to premature compressor failure, refrigerants are selected to be above atmospheric pressure during their normal operation. If a minute refrigerant leak occurs then the gas will slowly flow out but moisture will not enter. Repairing the leak, cleaning and recharging with refrigerant should then produce a more satisfactory long-term repair than if the unit had been operating with moisture in the system.

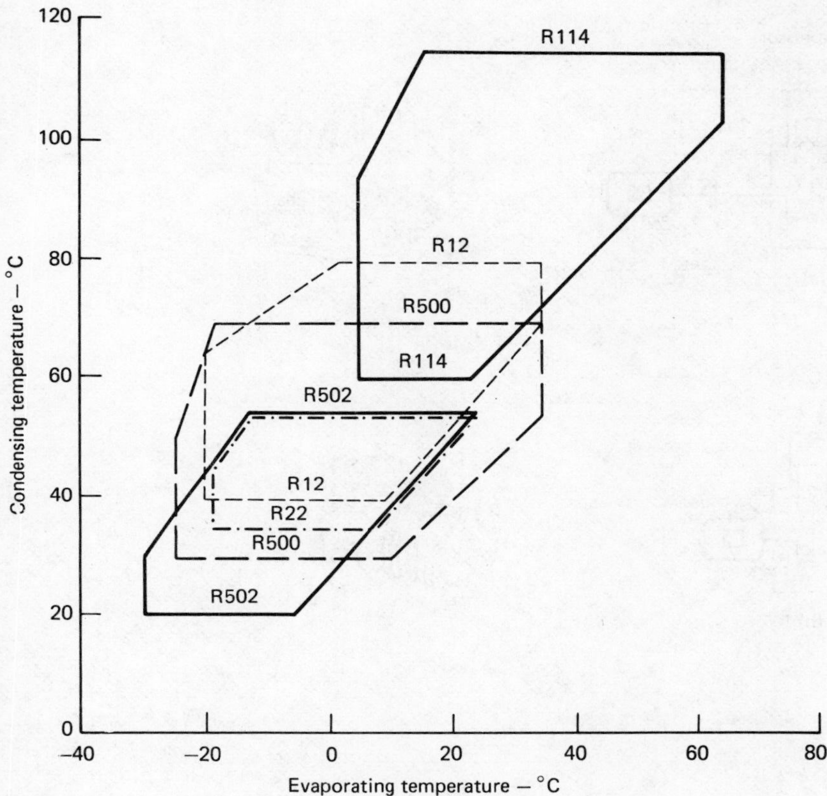

Figure 3.3 Operating temperature range for different working fluids (reciprocating compressor) (Jensen, 1981)[2]

3.3 Compressor

The compressor is described both by its method of manufacture and its mode of operation. The different types of compressor/motor arrangements are illustrated in *Figure 3.4*. 'Open' compressors have a separate motor and compressor linked by a drive shaft. Such compressors are usually driven by fossil-fuelled engines. Low-friction gas-tight seals on the compressor drive-shaft proved difficult to manufacture and therefore most large electrically-driven machines are semi-hermetic. In this type the electric motor is sealed mechanically to the compressor, and the motor operates in the refrigerant and at refrigerant gas pressures. This obviates the need for a compressor drive-shaft seal. The units are serviceable and can be dismantled. Hermetic units have the motor/compressor unit mounted inside a single welded container, and the motor is fully exposed to the refrigerant. Such units are used for domestic refrigerant products and are not repaired but are replaced.

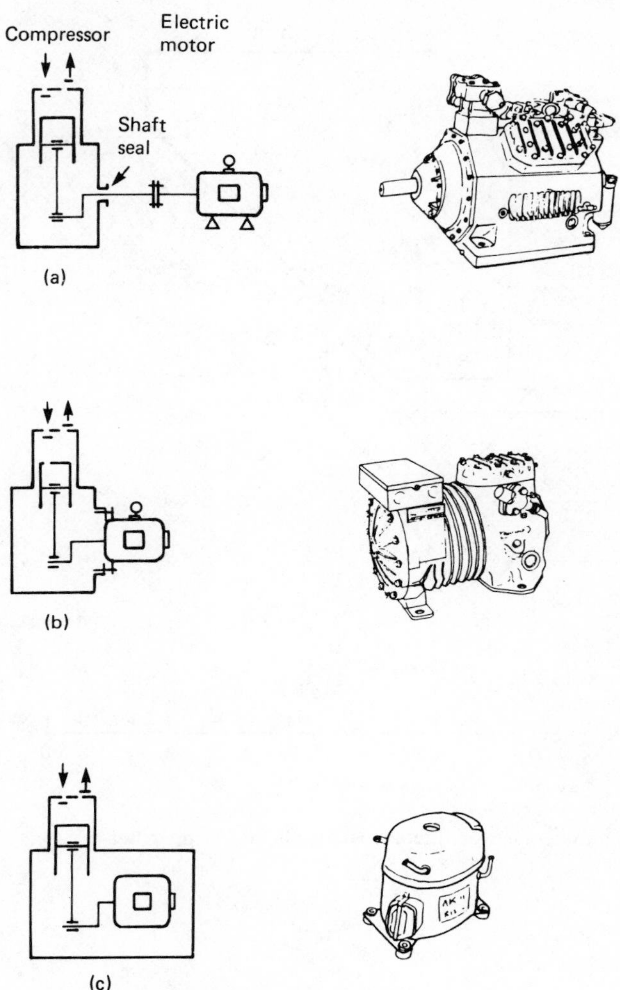

Figure 3.4 A variety of compressor/motor arrangements. (a) Open-type compressor (motor and compressor physically separate). (b) Semi-hermetic compressor (motor and compressor bolted together to avoid shaft seal). (c) Hermetic compressor (motor and compressor permanently sealed together)

The four modes of compression are:

(1) *Reciprocating piston.* This is the conventional means of compression and most dehumidifiers use this technique. It is usually a direct drive and sizes vary from 200 W to 500 kW (*Figure 3.5*).

(2) *Rotary compressors.* The two common types are the rolling-piston and the rotating-vane ones. They are positive displacement direct electric drive units and are characterized by high volumetric efficiency because of the small clearance volumes. The rotating action means less vibration and

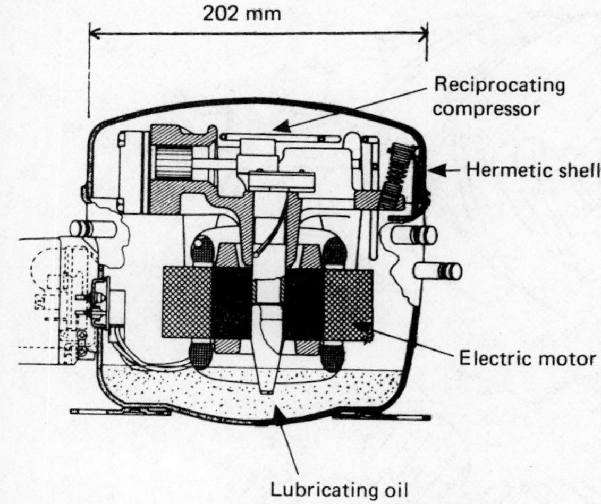

Figure 3.5 A typical small 300 W hermetic compressor (Danfoss FR range, 6.2–10.6 cm^3 displacement; 240 V single-phase 50 Hz. Danfoss, 1984)

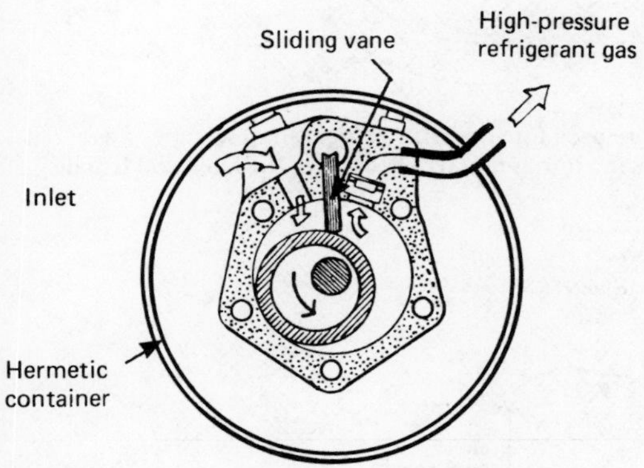

Figure 3.6 Rotary compressor. This form is called a 'rolling piston' type. There is a small spring valve on the exhaust port to prevent backflow

noise. Some small domestic dehumidifiers have such compressors (*Figure 3.6*).

(3) *Screw compressors.* Such units, developed for the process industries, use two mating helically-grooved rotors to provide positive gas displacement. They are available only in large sizes and therefore are not yet used for dehumidification (*Figure 3.7*)[6].

(4) *Centrifugal compressors.* Such units run at high speed and handle very large volumetric flows of refrigerant. They can also operate at high temperature. The pressure rise per compressor stage is low but several stages can be built on one shaft. They also are available only in large sizes and are not yet used for dehumidification (*Figure 3.8*).

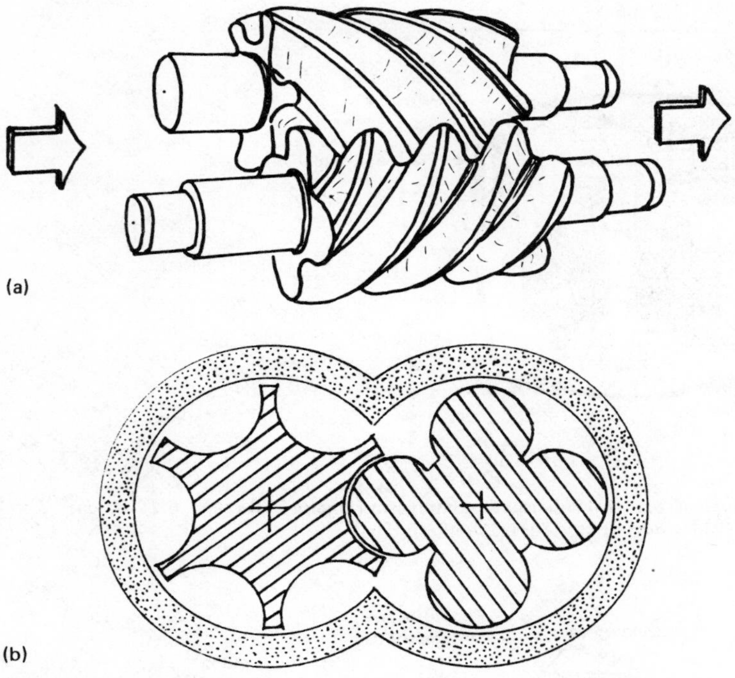

Figure 3.7 Screw compressors. These are used for very large refrigeration schemes. (a) Precision interlocking screws compress the refrigerant. (b) Section of the male and female screws

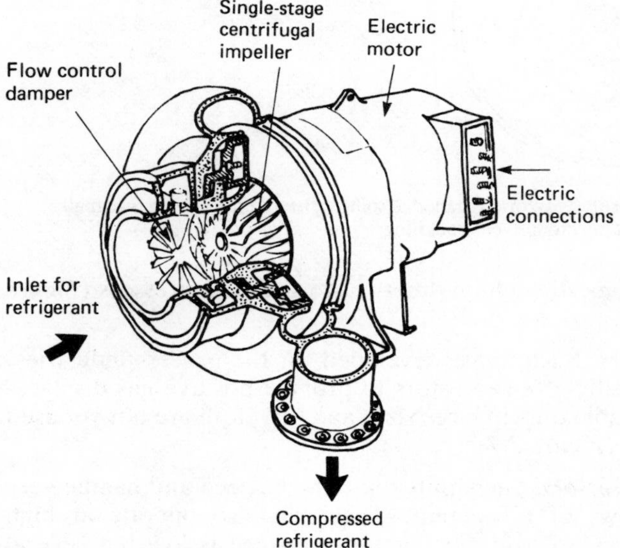

Figure 3.8 Single-stage centrifugal compressor. These are used for very large sizes of refrigerating load, 1–50 MW, and for high temperatures (courtesy of Carrier)

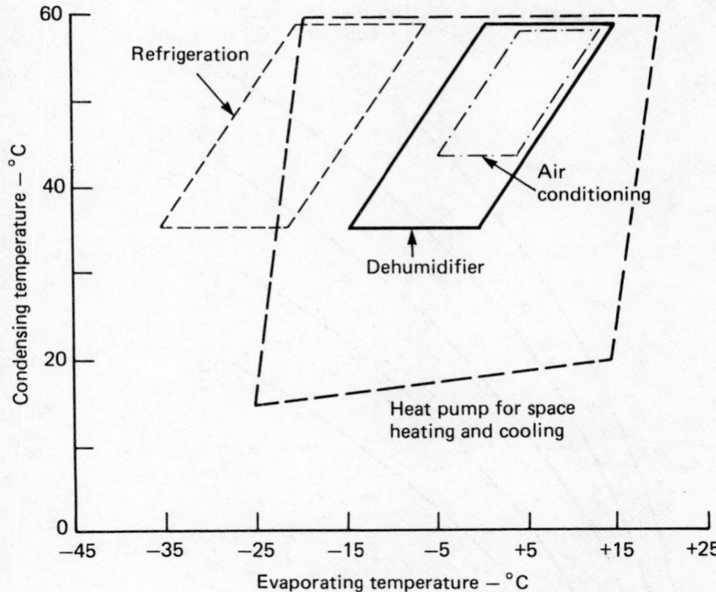

Figure 3.9 Application range for small hermetic compressors (Anon, 1982)[9]

The application duty of compressors for dehumidification is usually wider than that for air conditioning but less severe than for heat pumps. This is illustrated in *Figure 3.9*[7–9].

3.4 Evaporator

Evaporator design is particularly important in dehumidification because a clear distinction has to be made between sensible cooling and water condensation. Sensible cooling is simply related to the difference in dry-bulb temperature between air and refrigerant tube. Water will be extracted only if the evaporator surface temperature is below the dewpoint of the moist air[10].

Dewpoint temperatures are linked to air temperatures and relative humidity, a relationship which is illustrated in *Figure 3.10*. The evaporator surface temperature dictates the lowest dewpoint condition theoretically possible for the air leaving the dehumidifier. An evaporator operating at 0°C could not dehumidify air to below 50% relative humidity (r.h.) at 10°C because such air has a dewpoint of 0°C.

The rate of water extraction is proportional to the difference in water vapour pressure of the moist air and that of the saturated water vapour pressure of the water on the evaporator surface. This relationship is shown in *Figure 3.11*.

Finned heat-transfer surfaces are rarely used in the evaporator unless specifically designed for high relative humidities. Heat flow down the fin means that much of the cooling will be done by the fins at a temperature

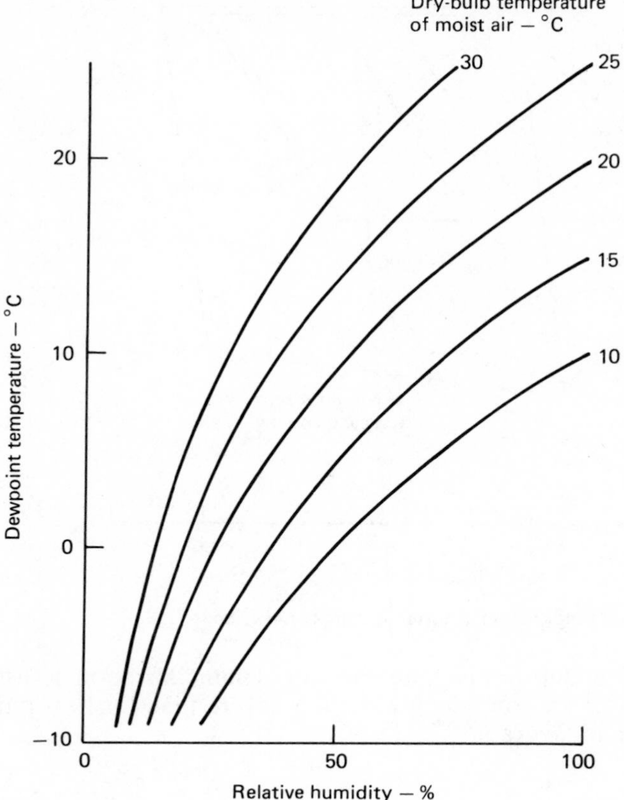

Figure 3.10 Relationship between dewpoint temperature and relative humidity (there is slight ambiguity below 0°C, depending upon whether the water is liquid or ice)

higher than that of the tube surface; therefore, less water will be extracted. The fins also have the tendency to collect and hold water droplets.

The designer's dilemma is that a large heat exchanger working at low air/tube temperature differences will work best at high air-relative humidities, but will have a poor performance at low relative humidities. Low relative humidities require a low evaporator temperature and a high temperature difference between air and tube. Such an evaporator will not work so well at high relative humidities. High temperature differences between air and tube give a high specific heat load on the evaporator. This is measured in watts/m^2 of heat exchanger. The relationship between water extraction rate and specific heat load on the evaporator is illustrated in *Figure 3.12*[11]. Experimental measurements on two Russian dehumidifiers show how the more highly loaded evaporator worked more effectively than the one more lightly loaded in the drier conditions, while the converse was true for the more humid conditions (*Figure 3.13*).

Careful material selection or corrosion protection techniques will be needed for the evaporator when used in many of the industrial drying

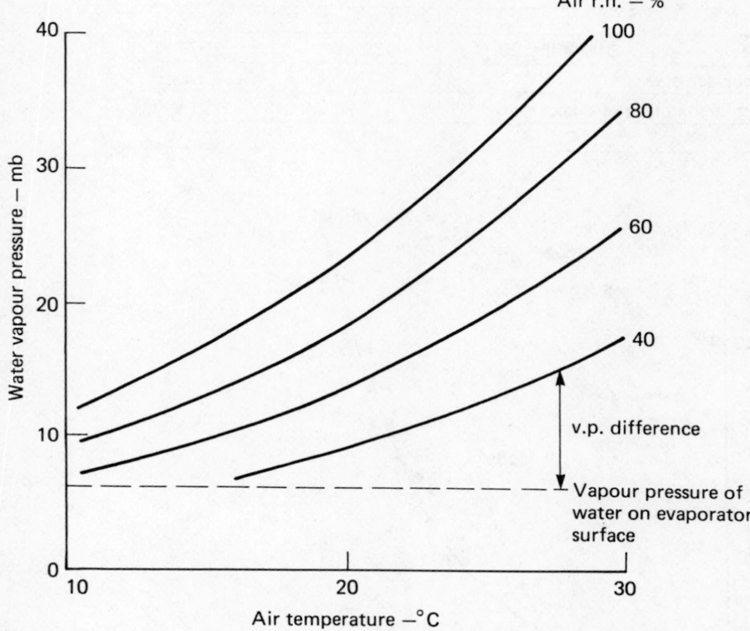

Figure 3.11 The water condensed on the evaporator surface will be related to the difference in vapour pressure between that of the air and that of the refrigerant surface. This illustration is for an evaporator surface at 0°C (6.1 mb)

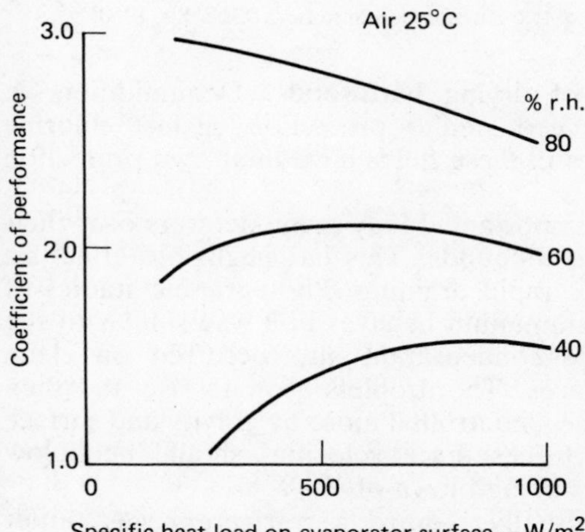

Figure 3.12 Effectiveness, measured in terms of coefficient of performance, as a function of specific heat load on the evaporator surface (Gogolin, 1960)[11]

Model	No 1	No 2
Cooling capacity – evap –5°C; cond 30°C	1326 W	1977 W
Evaporator surface area	3.2 m^2	2.74 m^2
Specific thermal load on the evaporator	414 W/m^2	721 W/m^2
Electric power	500 W	700 W

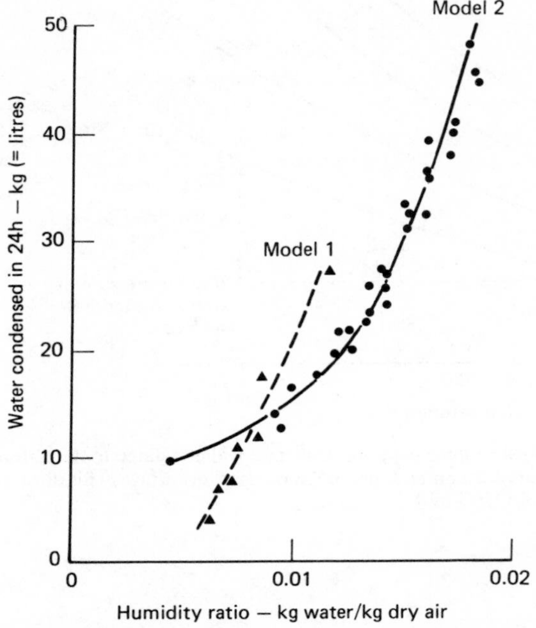

Figure 3.13 Performance characteristics of two Russian dehumidifiers (Gogolin, 1960)[11]

processes, particularly those of drying hardwoods. Dehumidifiers in swimming pool atmospheres need similar protection against chlorine attack. The specialist companies in these fields have their own protection techniques.

Condensate draining is also important. Many manufacturers coat their evaporators with non-wetting compounds. This has negligible effect on heat transfer but does promote rapid draining. Photographic studies of condensation show that clean aluminium behaves in a way similar to the non-wetted surfaces. Dropwise condensation also occurred on clean copper and copper nickel surfaces. The droplets grow in size and then randomly trickle down the surface, controlled more by gravity and surface tension than by aerodynamic forces. Face velocities should be below 2.25 m/s to avoid water droplets being blown off[12,13].

Refrigerant considerations usually require a refrigerant gas outlet velocity of 4 to 5 m/s to ensure an adequate oil return to the compressor and to prevent oil fouling of the inside of the evaporator. Equally the velocity should not exceed 10 to 12 m/s or there will be a large pressure drop between evaporator and compressor with consequent loss of efficiency and reduced refrigerant recirculation rate.

3.5 Condenser

The condenser is usually a finned heat exchanger with about three times the surface area of the evaporator. The thermodynamic cooling efficiency is better with large area, small air/tube temperature differentials. Fin spacing is related to the presence or absence of filtration. Fortunately, the airstream deposits much of its dust on the earlier wet evaporator heat exchanger which then runs to drain. Larger dehumidifiers such as those used in swimming pools filter the incoming air to ensure complete cleanliness of both the evaporator and the condenser.

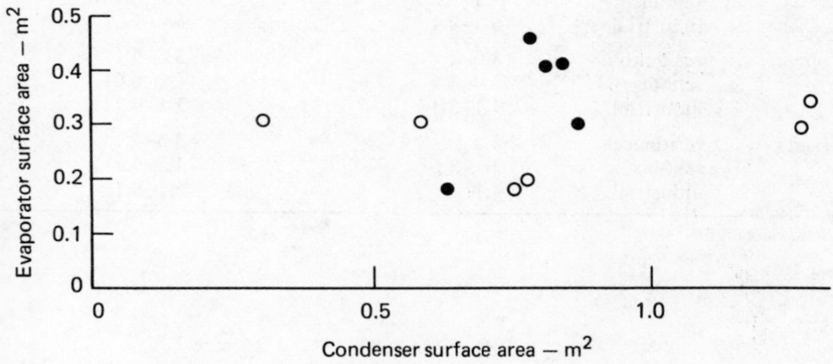

Figure 3.14 Illustration of the range of refrigerant heat transfer surface used by manufacturers in conjunction with a ⅛hp compressor. All condensers are finned. ● = finned evaporators. O = plain evaporators (Peck, 1952)[14]

The relative sizes of condenser and evaporator surfaces for a range of domestic dehumidifiers are shown in *Figure 3.14*[14]. All relate to 1/8-hp compressors built into domestic room dehumidifiers.

Performance data on a wide range of different fin configurations are readily available[15]. These measurements were laboratory ones where flow conditions were as near to perfection as practicable. Field equipment often has less perfect entry conditions, and designers should make some allowance for this.

Recommended air velocities are summarized in *Table 3.2*.

3.6 Expansion valve

The pressure reduction from the high-pressure condenser to the low-pressure evaporator is achieved either by a thermostatically-controlled needle valve or by a length of very fine capillary piping.

TABLE 3.2 Conventional ducting velocities

		Recommended velocity m/s	*Maximum velocity* m/s
Outdoor air intake	residences	2.5	4.1
	schools	2.5	4.6
	industrial	2.5	6.1
Filters	residences	1.3	1.5
	schools	1.5	1.8
	industrial	1.8	1.8
Heating coil	residences	2.3	2.5
	schools	2.5	3.0
	industrial	3.0	3.6
Cooling coil	residences	2.3	2.3
	schools	2.5	2.5
	industrial	3.0	3.0
Main ducts	residences	3.6–4.6	4.1–6.1
	schools	5.1–6.6	5.6–8.1
	industrial	6.1–9.1	6.6–11.2
Branch ducts	residential	3.0	3.6–5.1
	schools	3.0–4.6	4.1–6.6
	industrial	4.1–5.1	5.1–9.1
Branch risers	residences	2.5	3.3–4.1
	schools	3.1–3.6	4.1–6.1
	industrial	4.1	5.1–8.1

ASHRAE Fundamentals, 1981[1]

3.6.1 Thermostatic expansion valve

This valve achieves the required pressure drop and refrigerant flow by forcing the liquid refrigerant through an orifice. The effective size of this orifice can be changed to match changing operating conditions of the dehumidifier. This is achieved by the movement of a spring-loaded and tapered plug inside the orifice. This is illustrated in *Figure 3.15*.

The refrigerant evaporates in the heat exchanger at constant temperature. Once all the liquid has evaporated then the temperature of the vapour rises. This elevation of vapour temperature above temperature at saturation is termed 'superheat'. If this superheat is high then it suggests that the refrigerant flow is too low. The degree of superheat can therefore be used to control the refrigerant flow. This control is achieved in the thermostatic expansion valve by placing a temperature sensor at the outlet of the evaporator. This is a liquid-filled sensor coupled by capillary to the expansion valve. If the refrigerant flow is too low then the superheat rises and the vapour pressure of the fluid in the temperature sensor acts on the diaphragm inside the expansion valve to force it to open a little.

The combination of vapour pressure characteristics of the temperature bulb, refrigerant working pressure, spring characteristics, and plunger/orifice shape, works to provide a constant superheat. For the refrigerant R22 it is normally 5°C superheat.

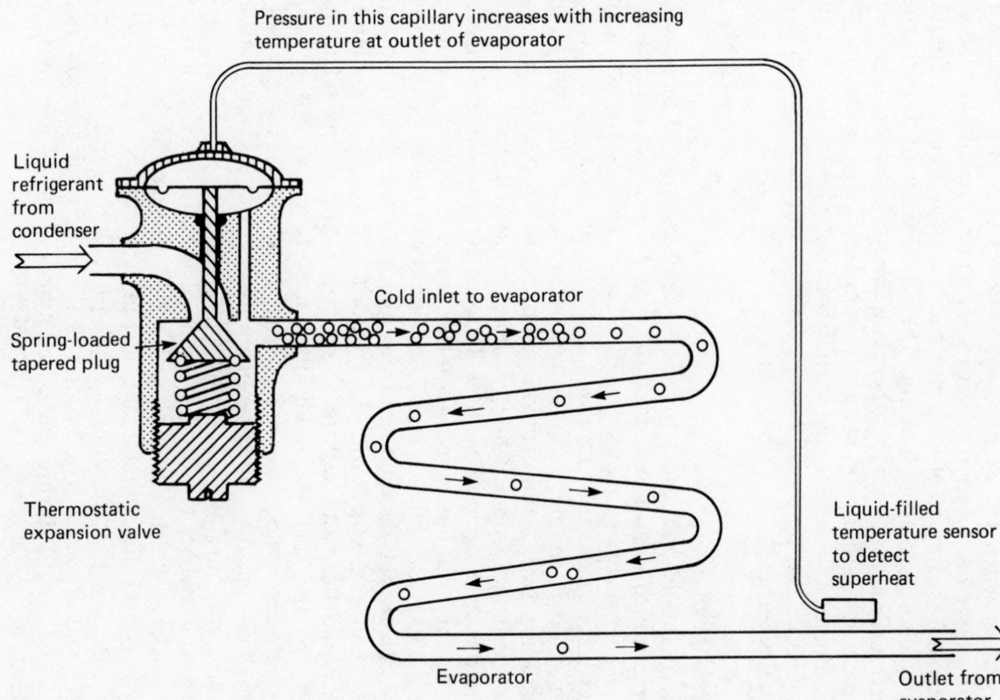

Figure 3.15 Diagrammatic layout of the installation of a thermostatic expansion valve (not to scale)

Adequate sub-cooling is essential to prevent bubbles entering the valve because bubbles significantly reduce the refrigerant flow and cause wild fluctuations. Stable control is typically down to one-third of the rated flow capacity of the valve.

Thermostatic expansion valves are used on the larger dehumidifiers (>5 kW).

A bleed port may be provided to allow pressure equalization of the refrigerant system when the compressor switches off. This reduces the starting torque surge on the compressor motor when it restarts for the next cycle. The dynamic response of the valve and the location of its superheat sensor must be chosen to avoid hunting. The actual value of the superheat will in practice vary a little with the operating conditions of the unit. It will usually increase as conditions move away from the design optimum.

Advanced electrically driven microprocessor controlled valves are now becoming available and these will have the ability to provide much closer control of the superheat.

3.6.2 Capillary tube

All domestic dehumidifiers use a fine-bore capillary tube to provide the necessary pressure drop and to control the liquid flow from condenser to evaporator. The principle involved is that liquid will pass down a fine capillary at a larger mass flow rate than the vapour for a given pressure drop. The method is simple, reliable and of low cost. The liquid flows down the capillary with a uniform rate of pressure drop until, at about two-thirds of the length from the inlet, bubbles occur. The rate of pressure drop associated with this two-phase flow doubles. If insufficient refrigerant is being passed then the liquid refrigerant in the condenser sub-cools and builds up at the capillary inlet. This cooler liquid will travel further down the capillary before bubble point and the high pressure drop associated with the two-phase mixture will be reduced. This will automatically increase the liquid flow and restore correct operation of the refrigerant cycle. The capillary has the additional useful feature of pressure equalisation between evaporator and condenser when the compressor is switched off. This ensures an easier compressor start. Capillaries are usually of 1 to 2 mm bore and a few metres in length.

There are two drawbacks to capillary control. The first is that it is very sensitive to blockage which can occur either by moisture which may have frozen or by minute solid contaminants left in accidentally. The effect of these is minimized by incorporating a small filter dryer in the refrigerant circuit during manufacture. The second is the empirical adjustment of capillary size and length during the development stage. While there are straightforward design techniques available to reach an approximate solution it is usual for several different capillaries to be examined at the prototype stage before deciding on the final choice[16].

3.7 Types of fan

The fan comprises a rotary impeller of various configurations and an electric motor drive.

3.7.1 Impeller

There is a wide variety of fan types, each with its own pressure/flow characteristic, and a number are illustrated in *Figure 3.16*[17]. The maximum efficiencies of the different types are presented in *Figure 3.17*[18]. The three typical factors in selecting the most suitable fan are: the required working pressure rise, the air-flow and the physical size. Efficiency becomes important for the larger sizes of fan and this is independent of the electric-motor efficiency. For pressure rises of up to 2500 Pa

$$\text{Fan total efficiency} = \frac{\text{Volume flow} \times \text{fan total pressure}}{\text{impeller power}}$$

If the duty of the fan is simply to draw air through a heat exchanger, as in a free-standing domestic dehumidifier, then the fan is usually of the propeller type. Such a fan has a low initial cost and a high volumetric capacity. It is normally low in efficiency (20 to 40%) and is restricted to very-low-pressure development. The efficiency and pressure development are strongly influenced by the fan surround. The performance can be enhanced by mounting the fan in a hole in a screen and minimizing the tip clearance between the propeller and the edge of the hold. An illustration of the importance of this tip clearance is shown in *Figure 3.18*[19].

Another popular type of fan for the smaller dehumidifiers is the cross-flow or tangential-flow which is also illustrated in *Figure 3.19*[17]. This is particularly useful for wall-mounted dehumidifiers. In such units the

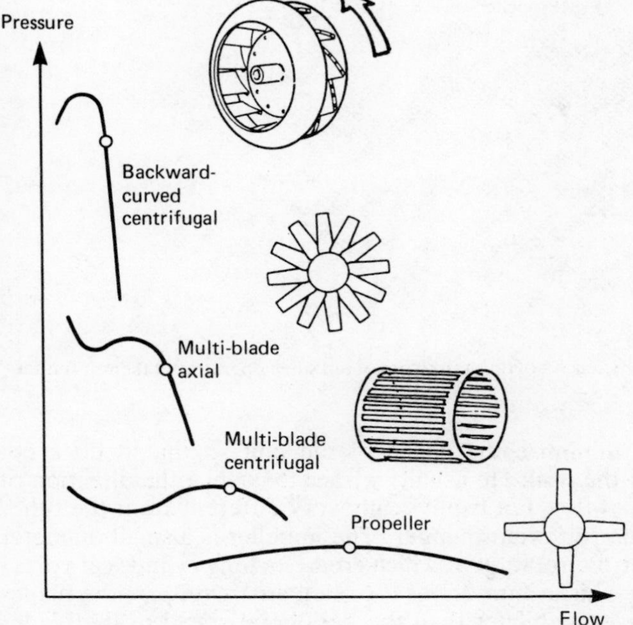

Figure 3.16 Different types of fan have different performance characteristics. Peak efficiency is marked by the circle (Daly, 1979)[17]

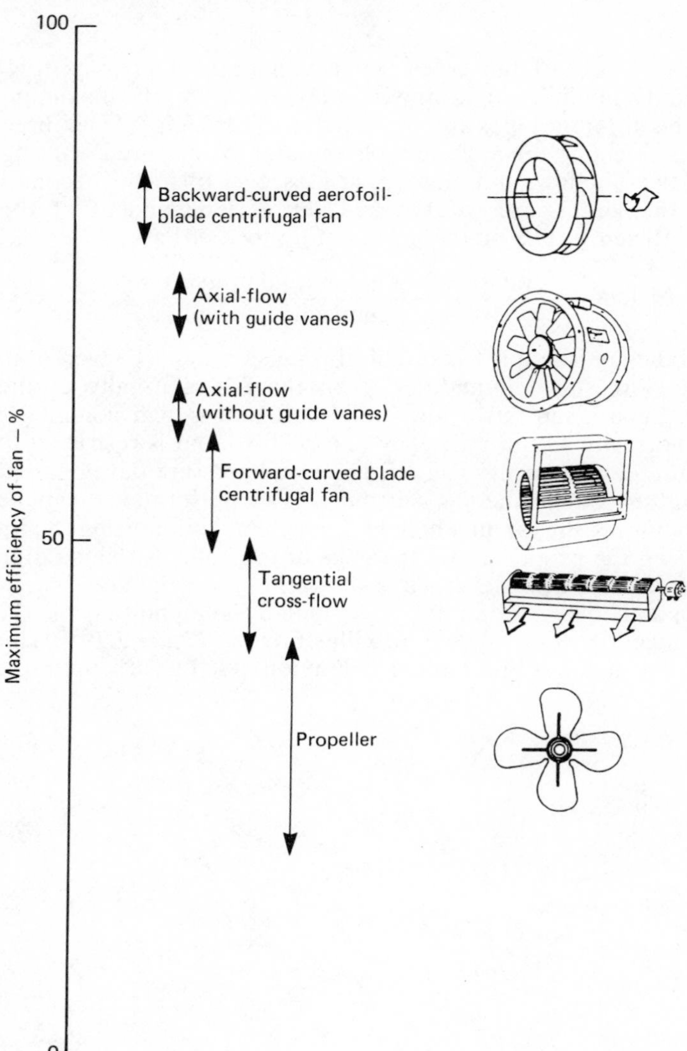

Figure 3.17 Illustrative efficiencies of different types of fan when operating at their optimum (CIBS, 1970)[18]

designer wishes to minimize the depth of the unit so that it does not protrude too far off the wall. He usually wishes to change the direction of the air too. The cross-flow fan is physically very different from the other fans and operates in a different manner. The impeller is a small-diameter long-bladed cylinder the rotation of which creates a long cylindrical vortex within the impeller. This in turn drives the main airstream past the blades of the fan with a velocity higher than the peripheral speed of the blades themselves. The fan efficiency is low (25 to 50%) and its speed range is very narrow. However, its small diameter and its ability to be made in any

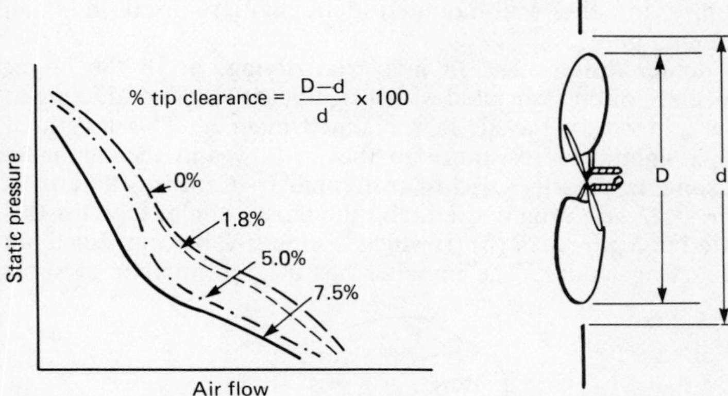

Figure 3.18 The flow characteristics of propeller-type fans are strongly influenced by tip clearance. Designers aim for 2% (Kenny, 1968)[19]

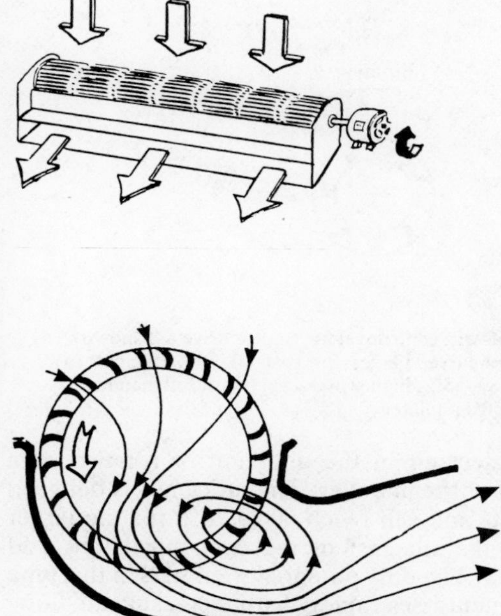

Figure 3.19 Cross-flow fans form a vortex which has its axis parallel to the shaft and near to a point on the impeller circumference. Such fans are slim and can, with suitable intermediate bearings, be made in any length. Fan efficiency is a maximum of 25–50% (Daly, 1979)[17]

length, provided that it is supported with appropriate bearings, give it special suitability for the wall-mounted dehumidifiers used in small domestic swimming pools.

The larger dehumidifiers used in industrial drying, or in the larger swimming pools, are often associated with a significant length of ducting to direct the flow and return the air in a planned manner. This length of ducting offers a significant resistance to the air-flow and the fan must provide a reasonable pressure rise to overcome it. Centrifugal fans as shown in *Figure 3.21*, are usually used, and the most popular type for this duty is illustrated in *Figure 3.20* (b) (i) which is a multi-vane centrifugal fan with forward-curving blades. The impeller has a large number of short

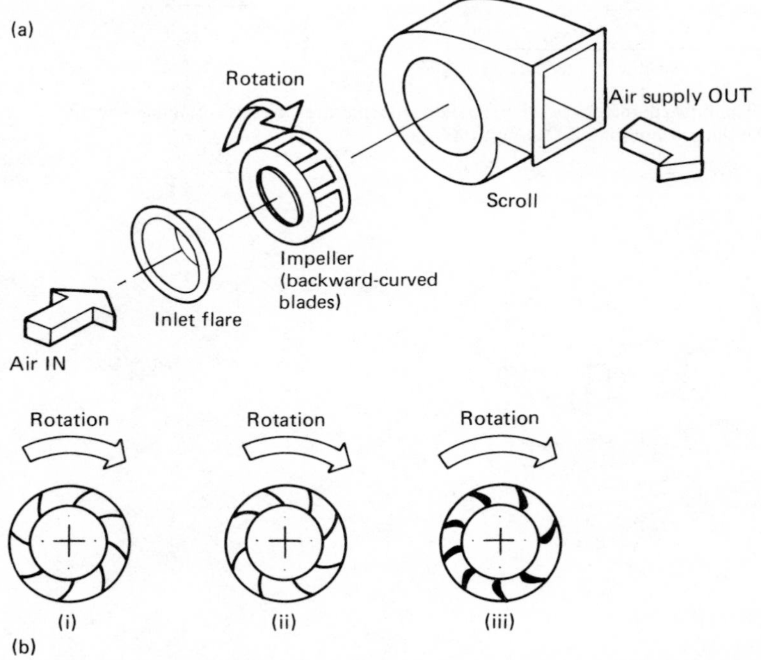

Figure 3.20 Centrifugal fans. (a) Elements of a centrifugal fan (motor drive not shown). (b) Types of centrifugal impeller: (i) Forward-curved blades, low cost, 60–70% efficient; (ii) backward-curved blades, more efficient 80–85%, higher pressure; (iii) aerodynamic backward-curved blades, most efficient 90%, quieter

forward-curving blades which eject air in the direction of rotation at a speed greater than the tip speed of the impeller. The efficiency is between 50 and 60% for the smaller units and can reach 60 to 70% for the larger ones. For a given duty this is the smallest of the centrifugal fans and operates with the lowest tip speed. The only potential weakness in this type of fan is that the power requirement rises rapidly with increasing air-flow. If the designer over-estimates his duct resistance then the actual air-flow will tend to be much higher than intended, with a possible overload on the electric motor. Fan manufacturers usually provide larger margins of motor power with this type of fan to allow for some error.

The very large ducted air supplies associated with large swimming pools may require axial-flow fans (*Figure 3.18*). Such fans are more expensive than other types but are of high efficiency (70 to 75%). The most efficient fans are the backward-curved centrifugal type with aerofoil-section blades (*Figure 3.19*) (b)(iii). These can achieve efficiencies of 80 to 85% and have a correspondingly low noise generation.

The actual selection of a fan is made in two steps. The system designer calculates the flow resistance of the heat-exchanger and the ductwork associated with the air recirculation. This data is available from manufacturers of the heat exchangers for their specific units. The pressure losses associated with the ductwork is well tabled in all the air-conditioning and ventilation guides[1–18]. The summation of these losses can be plotted against a range of air-flows through the ducting, *Figure 3.21*. This flow

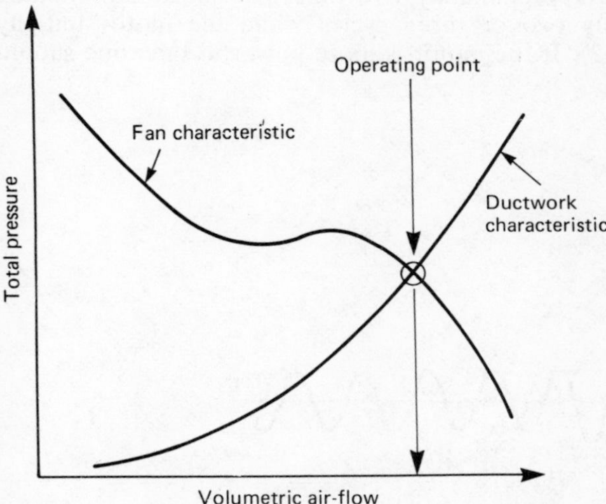

Figure 3.21 Operating point of a fan/motor unit in a ducted dehumidifier air circuit

resistance tends to increase with the square of the air velocity down the duct. The fan performance characteristic can be superimposed on this figure and where the two curves cross will define the operating flow rate. The fan manufacturers data for a range of fans is used to locate a fan which gives the required air-flow.

All these fans have an attractive starting torque characteristic for an electric motor. The torque requirement is very low at low speed but progressively increases as the speed increases. This matches the torque characteristics of electric motors.

3.8 Electrical aspects

3.8.1 Electricity supply

Common single-phase domestic voltages are 240 V in Britain, 220 V in the rest of Europe and 115 V in the USA and Canada. Japan has a range of voltages across its spread of islands. The supply frequency is 50 Hz for Europe and 60 Hz for the USA and Canada. Industrial equipment in all countries is three-phase. Manufacturers often design equipment for more than one country. Transformer tappings can be used to provide the correct voltage but this is rarely done because of the initial cost. The manufacturer usually makes his equipment suitable for voltages 220/240 or 110/120 V. When operated on the 50-Hz supply the motor speed is proportionately down if the unit is designed for 60 Hz supply and the performance characteristics of the dehumidifier have to be modified down accordingly[20–25].

The electricity supply networks are designed for all reasonable loads which usually includes single-phase induction motors up to 1 kW rating. The starting surge for such motors, particularly when driving refrigeration compressors, will take approximately five times the maximum running current, albeit for only two or three cycles while the motor initially accelerates (*Figure 3.22*). If the motor is more powerful then one should

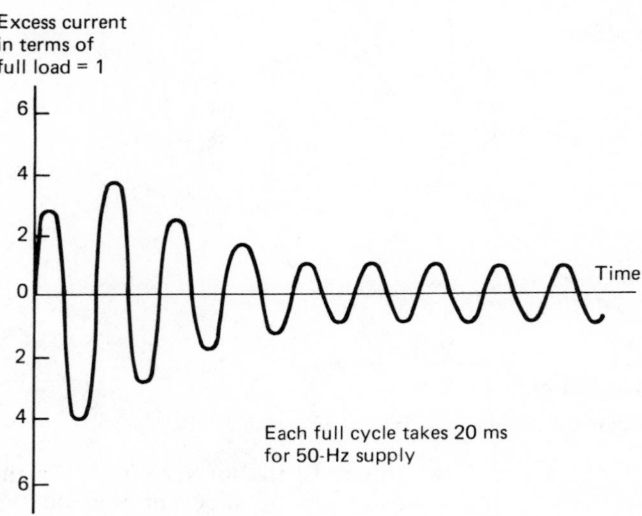

Figure 3.22 Starting current surge associated with an electric induction motor (Elektrizitäts-verwertung, 1981)[26]

consult the local electricity authority who will use their knowledge of the local electrical impedance of the network at that point to calculate the local voltage dip created by the inrush of starting current. The permissible voltage dip is strictly limited. The permitted severity of the dip is a function of how often it occurs. International guidelines are illustrated in *Figure 2.23*. This CENELEC relationship is based on 85% of the population not complaining[27]. Dehumidifiers would normally switch on/off only once an hour, and in bad moisture conditions would run continuously.

If the switching does create a local lighting flicker nuisance then a soft-start circuit should be incorporated. Such circuits are designed to slow down the acceleration of the motor. The voltage dips created by such

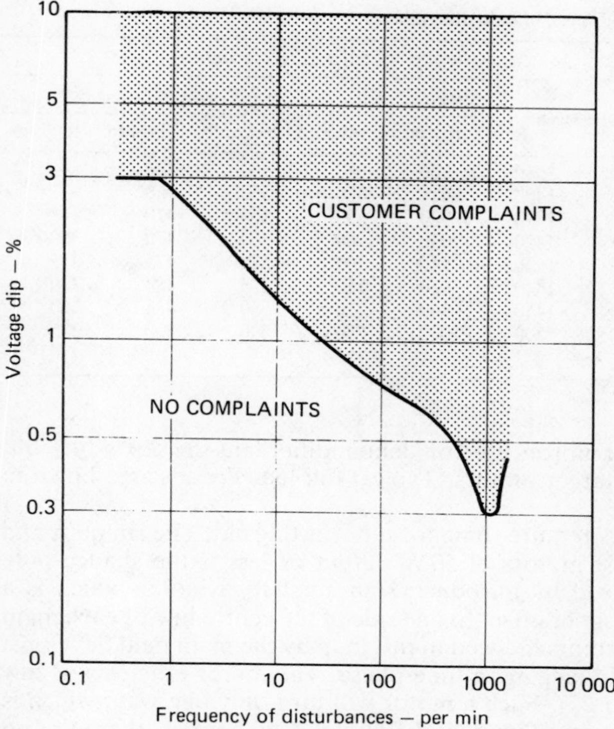

Figure 3.23 Maximum permissible voltage dip on the mains electricity supply varies with frequency of interruption (CENELEC Standard EN 50.006, 1977)[27]

circuits are less pronounced but last for longer. Above 3 kW the motors are normally three-phase[28].

3.8.2 Electric motor drive

Induction motors provide the normal mechanical drive. An induction motor comprises an iron rotor in which is set conducting paths of aluminium or copper, and a stator which contains the field windings. This type of motor is robust, reliable and of low cost. The motor speed is principally a function of the frequency of the electricity supply divided by the number of poles. At no-load the motors run at synchronous speed.

$$\text{Synchronous speed} = \frac{2f \times 60}{p} \text{ rev/min}$$

where f = supply frequency Hz
p = number of poles on the motor

When the motor is loaded the speed falls and introduces a slip between the rotating field and the rotor conductors. This slip generates the rotor currents which react with the rotating field to create torque. In the small

TABLE 3.3 Typical full-load speed of induction motors

kW output	*Number of poles – 50-Hz supply*						
	2	*4*	*6*	*8*	*10*	*12*	*16*
	rev/min	rev/min	rev/min	rev/min	rev/min	rev/min	rev/min
0.1	2700	1380	900	680	550	460	—
0.2	2750	1400	910	680	550	460	—
0.5	2800	1410	920	690	560	470	—
1.0	2825	1420	930	700	560	470	350
2.0	2850	1430	940	700	570	475	355
5.0	2875	1440	950	710	575	480	360
10.0	2900	1450	960	720	580	485	360
Synchronous speed (no load)	3000	1500	1000	750	600	500	375

(Daly, 1979)[17]

fractional-horsepower motors used on dehumidifier fans the slip is 10% but it diminishes for the larger motors. Typical full-load speeds are shown in *Table 3.3*.

Single-phase motors require some form of starting aid. The simplest and the one used for most motors of 50 W output or less is the shaded-pole design. This is achieved by introducing an auxiliary winding which is a closed loop of thick copper offset to one side of the centre line of each main pole, *Figure 3.24*. Currents induced in this loop by the main field develop a rotating magnetic field lagging in time phase. The motor efficiency is low (20 to 30%) (*Figure 3.25*). Such a motor will turn only one way, which is from pole to nearest copper loop. Reliability is high because there are no

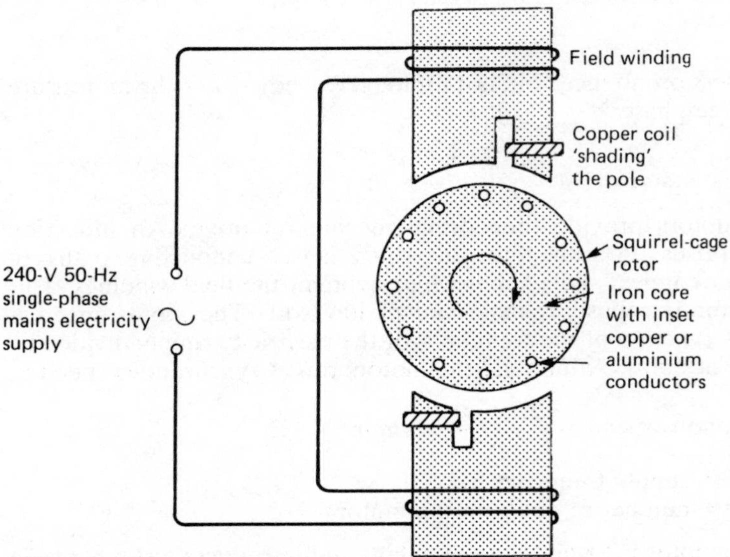

Figure 3.24 Shaded-pole motors are popular for all low-power fan duties. They are simple, low-cost and reliable but inefficient (max 20–50%)

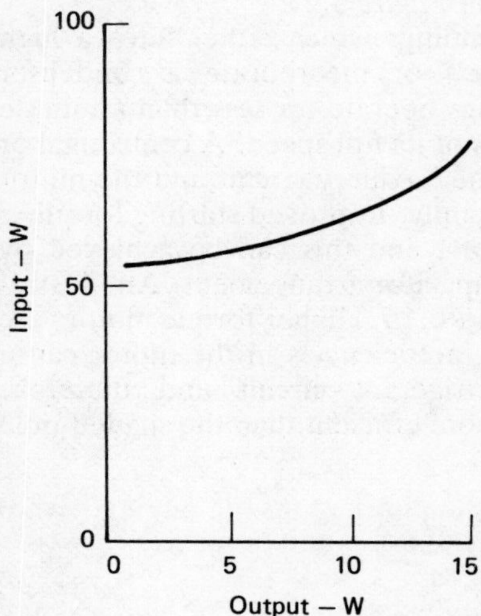

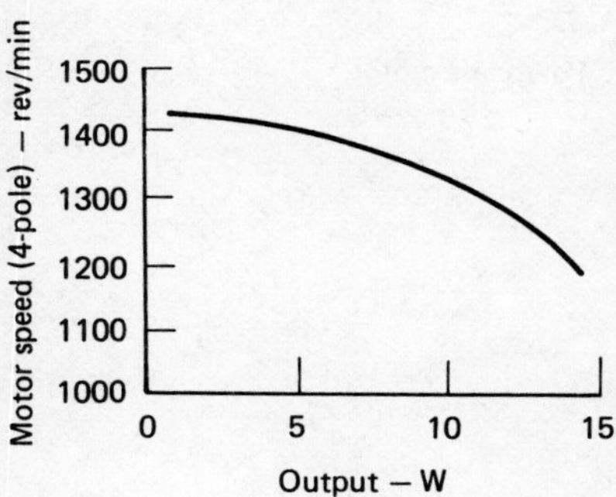

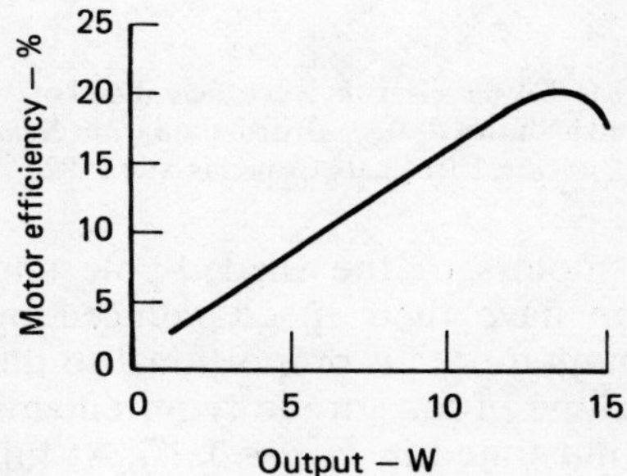

Figure 3.25 **Operating characteristics of a shaded-pole electric motor**

external auxiliary wires and no internal switches. The characteristics of power output and speed are also given in *Figure 3.25*.

Larger motors will have auxiliary windings which either have a high electrical resistance (called 'split-phase') or incorporate a condenser (capacitor start). These auxiliary windings operate for less than a minute while the motor reaches about two-thirds of its full speed. A centrifugal or current controlled switch then isolates the auxiliary circuit and the motor runs up to full speed on its main winding only. Improved starting torque is needed for large single-phase fan motors, and this can be achieved by incorporating a permanent split-phase capacitor arrangement. An illustration of motor efficiencies is given in *Figure 3.26*. Higher torque motors are also needed for the compressor drives. Inefficiencies in the motor cause heat dissipation problems in the refrigerant circuit and therefore compressor motors are normally much more efficient than the shaded-pole type used for fans.

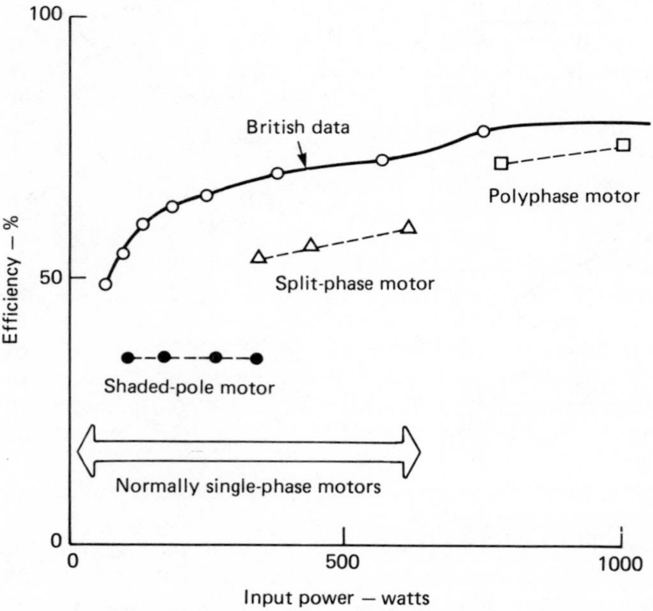

Figure 3.26 Illustrative efficiencies of electric motors (USA data is from less efficient end of US motor range, ASHRAE Fundamentals, 1981, and is shown dotted; British data from *Heat Pumps and Air Conditioning: A Guide to Packaged Systems*, Electricity Council, Nov 1982)

The small-power (>1 kW) induction motors of the shaded-pole and permanent-split-phase capacitor-type can have their speed reduced by lowering the applied voltage. The maximum torque is proportional to the square of the applied voltage. The matching of fan torque requirements with speed with those of the motor are illustrated in *Figure 3.27*. At full voltage the intersecting characteristics are very clear and motor speed clearly defined. At 50% voltage the intersection is less sharp and actual running speed will be less stable. The electric motor is less efficient at part

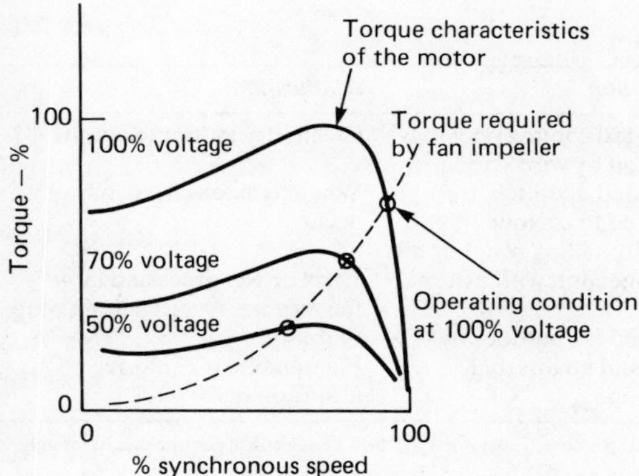

Figure 3.27 Regulation of fan speed by voltage reduction for a shaded-pole motor. Circles show the fan operating condition for each voltage (after Daly, 1979)[17]

speed. This energy loss is dissipated in ordinary motors up to 350 W output by a small rise in motor temperature but motors between 350-1000 W output need to be specially de-rated. Permanent-split-phase capacitor motors are best regulated by control of the main winding voltage alone, leaving the auxiliary winding and capacitor at full voltage. Fan speed control is used in some dehumidifiers to reduce the noise level at night.

Multispeed motors, which contain windings for more than one pole number, are also available for three-phase machines. An external switch selects the required pole numbers to match the speed required.

Electronic control is also available. Thyristor control chops the electricity supply and has an effect similar to lowering the voltage. However, the motor losses can be significantly increased by this form of control unless specifically designed for it. Electronic control of speed can now also be achieved by varying the frequency of the electricity supply to the motor. This works best when the motor is designed to match the controller.

The motor design is also influenced by the environment in which it will be sited. Classifications are based on contamination and temperature. The more contaminated or harsh environments require a more protected motor enclosure, and these are summarized in *Table 3.4*. Drip-proof motors would be desirable in areas where heavy condensation is expected. Heaters can be incorporated into the motor frame to prevent condensation in conditions where very high humidities are expected. Fan motors greater than 1 kW are usually totally enclosed fan cooled (TEFC) to protect the internal parts of the motor from dust. The classification of temperature limits is summarized in *Table 3.5*. Class E is the normal one for Europe and is based on a temperature rise of the motor windings of 75°C above an operating ambient of 40°C. The norm for the USA is Class B which permits slightly higher temperatures. High-temperature dehumidifiers require either a higher temperature limit which is expensive, or separation of the motor from the impeller with the motor sited in a relatively cool zone. A summary of single-phase AC fractional-horsepower motors' characteristics is given in *Table 3.6*.

TABLE 3.4 Types of fan-motor enclosure

Type	*Symbol*	*Description*	*Application*
Screen	SP	Ventilated cooling openings protected by wire screen	Clean, dry indoor locations
Drip-proof	DP	Ventilated openings are protected to exclude vertically-falling water or dirt	Where condensation may occur
Totally enclosed	TE	No connection with external air	Dirty or wet areas and large fan motors. Needs a drain plug
Weatherproof	WP	Designed for outdoor use	Outdoor
Flameproof	FLP	Withstand an internal explosion	Flammable or explosive atmospheres

See: BS 170 The electrical performance of fractional hp motors (generators); BS 2613 The electrical performance of rotating electrical machinery

TABLE 3.5 Temperatures for electric-motor field windings

Class of insulation	*E** °C	*B†* °C	*E* °C	*H* °C
Max temperature rise by resistance	75	80	100	125
Average temperature in 40°C ambient	115	120	140	165
Limiting spot temperature	120	130	155	180
Thermistor thermal protection trip	130	140	160	
Wire enamel	Polyurethane, polyvinyl formal		Polyester	Polyester enamel
Sheet materials	Polyester		Polyamide glass, mica	Silicone elastomers polyamide
Impregnants	Synthetic resins		Polyester or epoxy resins	Silicone resins

*This is the normal class of insulation in Britain.
†This is the normal class of insulation in the USA.

TABLE 3.6 Characteristics of single-phase AC fractional-horsepower electric motors

Type	*Power output* W	*Efficiency* %	*Power factor*	*Starting torque* % full load	*Rated speed* rev/min	*Application*
Shaded-pole	2–200	up to 40	0.5 to 0.67	30–80	875 1300 2600	low-power fans for long life; quiet; compact
Split-phase	40–250	35–50	0.55 to 0.70	90–175	950 1425 2850	fans which are often started; good starting torque
Capacitor start	40–600	35–50	0.55 to 0.70	160–240	950 1425 2850	more expensive very high starting torque, non-adjustable speed
Permanent-split capacitor	20–600	45–60	0.85 to 0.95	30–80	900 1350 2700	direct drive fans; quietest; speed varies under load

(Torrington Manufacturing Co, Swindon, England, 1983)

3.9 Controls

3.9.1 User controls

The main control available to the user is the humidistat. Most domestic dehumidifiers use a low-cost plastics type of humidistat. The length of the strip shortens with decreasing relative humidity. These are not accurate but they are reproducible. Settings are often in terms of 'dryer' rather than relative humidity. Large commercial dehumidifiers use accurate industrial controllers which are much more expensive.

Some machines have a fan speed control. On low fan speed the dehumidifier runs less effectively but will still extract moisture. The noise is much quieter and therefore this option is expected to cater for those who might be disturbed by noise at night.

When dehumidifiers are designed to work at room temperature or cooler, then the evaporator will operate below freezing point. The condensate, as it forms, will therefore freeze to the evaporator. This layer of frost can impair the heat transfer from the air to the evaporator surface and will eventually block the passage of air. Such dehumidifiers are therefore provided with a defrost controller, which interrupts the normal operation of the dehumidifier and melts away the frost. The dehumidifying cycle then restarts (*Figure 3.28*).

Some domestic dehumidifiers have a time clock which stops the normal operation of the dehumidifier each hour. The user can adjust the length of 'defrost' time to match the local need. Such a defrost timer should be set so that all the frost is removed at each defrosting period.

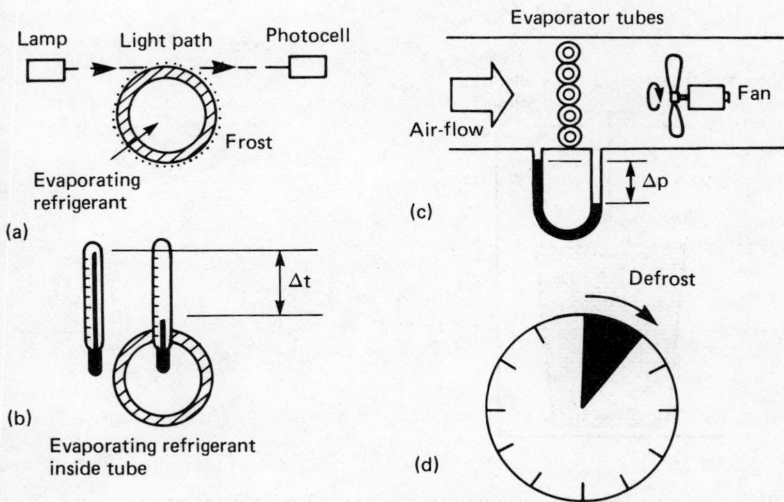

Figure 3.28 Automatic and programmed defrosting techniques. (a) *Optical sensing:* frost will stop light reaching the photocell. (b) *Temperature difference:* frost build-up on the evaporator tube will act as an insulant and the temperature difference air/refrigerant will increase. (c) *Pressure difference:* in ducted systems the presence of frost will increase the air-pressure drop through the evaporator coil. (d) *Time clock:* the simplest method is an adjustable time clock which the owner sets as needed (e.g. defrosts six minutes each hour)

3.9.2 Refrigerant controls

These are controls which are not available to the user. For example, defrosting can be controlled by need rather than by an arbitrary time cycle. The need can be identified by a range of frost sensor devices, *Figure 3.28*. These include optical scanners, pressure-drop detectors across the evaporator air path, and assessment of the temperature difference between evaporator refrigerant and incoming air temperature. When frost is detected and has achieved sufficient thickness, the frost sensor operates in one of two ways. The simplest is to switch off the compressor and leave the fan running continuously. Most dehumidifiers normally work at temperatures well above freezing point and so the room air melts the ice. In very cold conditions or when the defrost time has to be very short, designers can incorporate a hot-gas bypass system. The hot refrigerant is simply pumped around the evaporator loop continuously. The refrigerant circuit is temporarily altered by activating a solenoid-operated bypass valve.

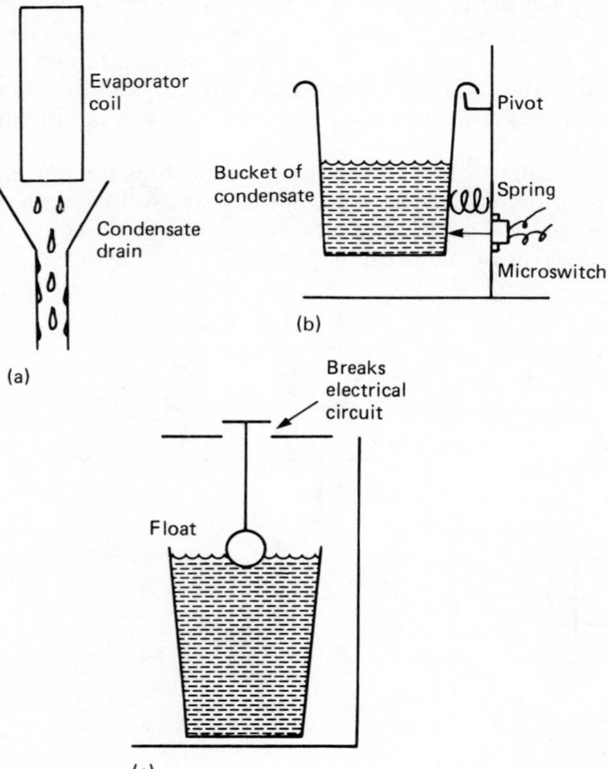

Figure 3.29 Control of condensate. (a) *Plumbed-in to drain:* The collector tray is coupled directly to a drain. All large dehumidifiers used for swimming pools and industrial drying are drained. (b) Pivoted bucket: The domestic bucket collector gives portability to the dehumidifier. It needs an 'off' switch to prevent overflowing. One method is to use a spring which compresses as the bucket fills and eventually operates a microswitch (Westinghouse). (c) *Float cut-off:* Many domestic dehumidifiers use one of a variety of float switches to switch off the machine when the water container is full

Reverse-cycle defrosting, common with heat pumps, is not used because of the possibility of condensation of moisture occurring inappropriately on the heat exchanger normally operating as the condenser.

Compressor motors have a high-temperature cut-out built into the electrical windings. Large dehumidifiers have pressure gauges to show the evaporator and condenser pressures. Large machines usually have a low refrigerant pressure and high-pressure cut-out to protect the compressor. Crankcase oil heaters are used to prevent too much refrigerant diluting the lubricating oil excessively, and oil pressure or level devices can be incorporated.

3.9.3 Recovered-water control

There are two types of water control (*Figure 3.29*). Small domestic machines usually collect the condensate in a bucket and provision is made to switch off the dehumidifier automatically when the bucket is full. The second type, usually reserved for the larger commercial and industrial dehumidifiers, provides for flow directly to a drain. Detail design is important in both types to prevent re-evaporation.

3.10 Noise and vibration

The two main sources of noise are the fan and the compressor.

(a) *Fan noise:* The fan system should be designed for smooth low-resistance air-flow. Particular attention is needed to the inlet conditions. The fan will operate at its quietest when working at its most efficient, and lower or higher flow conditions will increase the noise. There are two terms needed to define the fan noise. The first is the sound power level (SWL) expressed in decibels above a reference of 10^{-12} watts.

$$\text{Sound power level (SWL)} = \frac{\text{sound power in watts}}{10^{-12}\ \text{watts}}\ \text{dB}$$

This sound power is normally considered to be dissipated equally out of the inlet and outlet. Minimum sound power occurs around maximum efficiency. This is shown by way of illustration in *Figure 3.30*.

Sound power SW is proportional to $Q \times (P_t)^a$

where Q = volumetric flow
P_t = total pressure of the fan
a = constant for the fan (typically 2 for centrifugal fans)

Since Q is directly proportional to the fan speed n rev/min, and the fan total pressure is proportional to n^2, we can rewrite

Sound power SW is proportional to $n^{(2a+1)}$
or approximately proportional to n^5

This is illustrated in *Figure 3.31* for a popular forward-curved-bladed centrifugal fan. However, while speed is a critical factor in noise

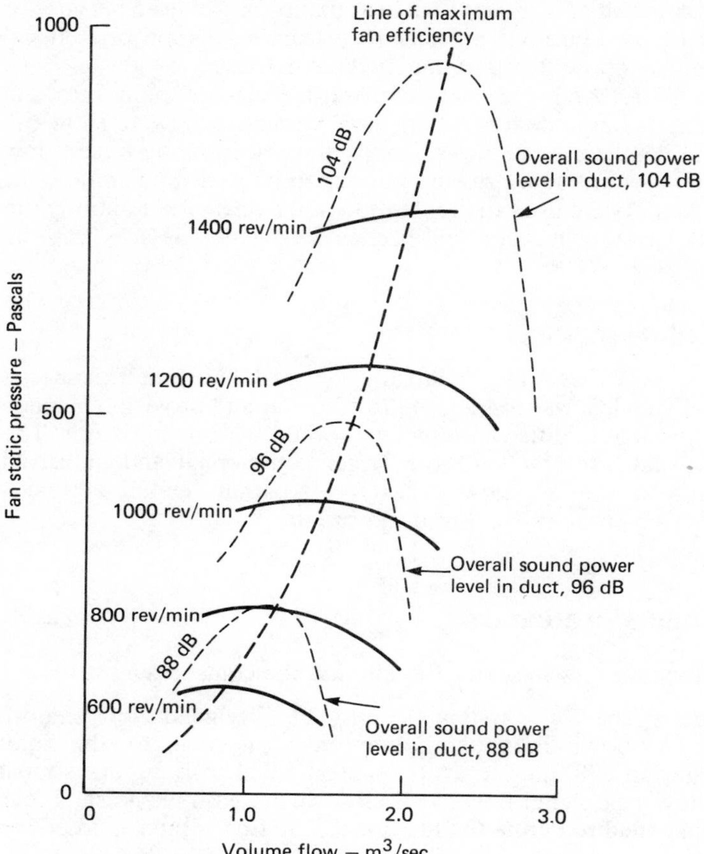

Figure 3.30 Sound power level characteristics are superimposed onto the fan characteristic for different speeds and flows (Sifan Systems Ltd, 1985, Model DBD124, indirect-drive centrifugal fan, impeller 315 mm diam, 315 mm wide, 48 blades)

generation, it must not be used when comparing one type of fan with a different type because the noises generated by two types of fan running at the same speed would be different.

The second factor is the frequency spectrum of the noise. There is international agreement to use standard octave bands whose centre frequencies are 63, 125, 250, 500, 1000, 2000, 4000 and 8000 Hz. The first and last are often omitted because the human ear is relatively insensitive to them.

Sound power spectra differ in character for different types of fan. Centrifugal fans have a high sound power level at the low frequencies of 125 and 250 Hz and this declines rapidly with increasing frequency at the rate of 4–6 dB per octave. Backward-curved blades are more efficient and therefore quieter despite their higher tip speed. However, forward-curved blades are smaller and lighter, and therefore less affected by wheel unbalance. Care should be taken to make sure that the pure tones created

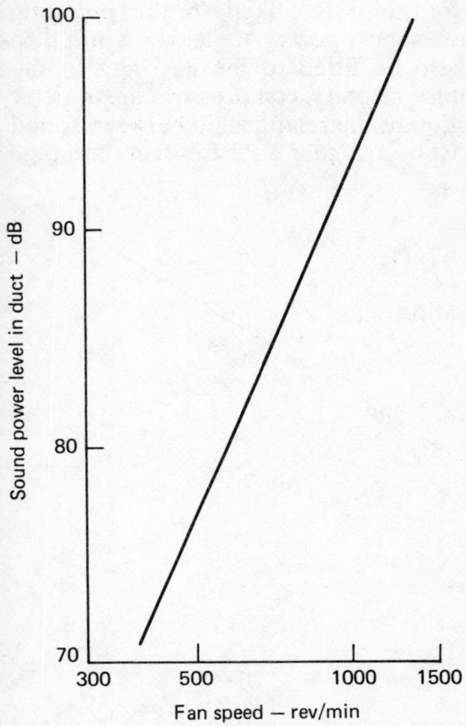

Figure 3.31 Minimum fan noise increases very rapidly with increasing speed (Sifan Systems Ltd, 1985, Model DBD124, indirect-drive centrifugal fan, impeller 315 mm diam, 315 mm wide, 48 blades)

at the blade rotating frequency are not too pronounced because pure tones can be more irritating. Axial fans have broader noise spectra with more noise at higher frequencies (250 and 500 Hz) and less at the lower ones. The noise is normally at its greatest at the blade rotating frequency and has minor peaks at multiples of this. Bearing supports should be placed downstream of the impeller so that the smoothest flow is achieved to the fan[29,30,31].

Calculation procedures and noise attenuation techniques in ducted installations are available in most environmental engineering guides. Fan manufacturers can supply specific data on individual fans.

An earlier technique, called 'sound pressure level' (SPL) measurement is still used for domestic appliances. This is a measurement of the sound pressure level relative to a threshold hearing pressure of 2×10^{-5} N/m^2 and is normally recorded 1 m in front of the air outlet grille. A weighting scale 'A' designed to represent the human response to sound has been shown to correlate well with annoyance. The sound pressure levels therefore represent a listener at that one point and it is measured in units of dBA where 'A' denotes the weighting factor.

(b) *Compressor noise:* Compressor noise is linked to the pulsating discharge of refrigerant through the exhaust ports. A silencer is fitted to muffle this exhaust and one can also be fitted to the gas inlet to the compressor to minimize suction noise. Rotary compressors are quieter than reciprocating ones. An illustration of the relationship between sound power level and machine size is given in *Figure 3.32* for semi-hermetic reciprocating compressors[32].

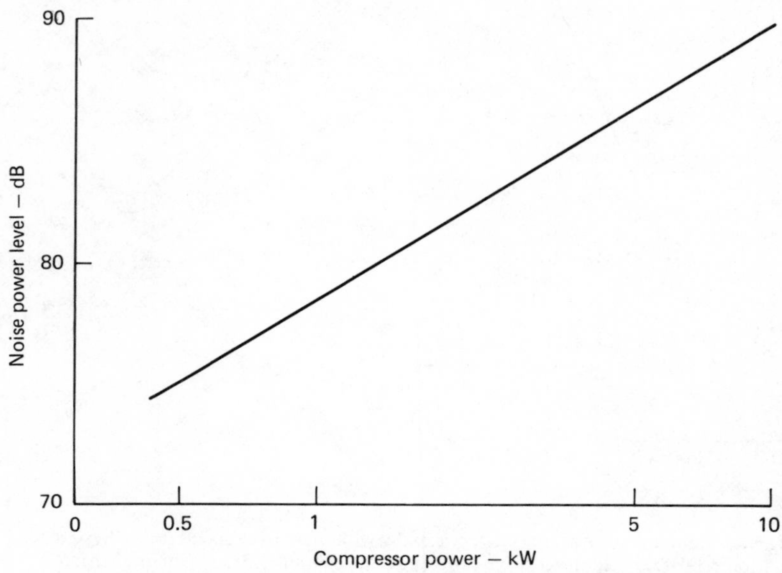

Figure 3.32 Noise power as a function of motor compressor size (semi-hermetic, 4-pole, ± 3 dB) (Preisendantz, 1981)[32]

(c) *Vibration:* Vibration is minimized by factory balancing of the dehumidifier components. In cases where there is an unbalance, for example, in single-cylinder compressors, the compressor can be isolated from the protective case by spring supports. Such designs require buffer stops to allow for inertial shocks during transport and during switch on and off. Vibrations from gas pulses are pronounced at bends in the refrigerant piping, and their frequency is the product of the motor speed and number of machine cylinders. Structural supports and pipe lengths should be checked to ensure that they are well away from the resonant fundamental frequency and the low harmonics of it.

Fan vibration is of two types, radial and in the axial plane. Slim impellers, as in propeller fans, are balanced in the radial sense. Weights are added to counterbalance any uneven running when the impeller is slowly turned, and this is termed 'static' balancing. Wide centrifugal impellers and the long tangential type of fans, however, can be out of balance along the axis as well as radially. These impellers need dynamic balancing which requires them to be run at speed while any unbalanced couples in the plane of the axis are identified (*Figure 3.33*). Failure to do

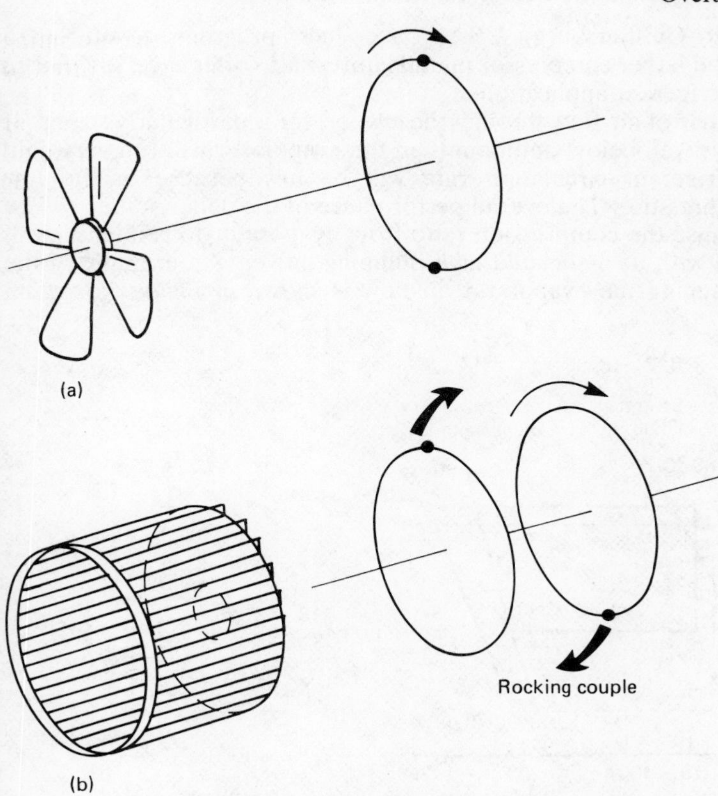

Figure 3.33 Balancing. (a) Slim impellers have only one plane of unbalance, i.e. the radial plane. Static balance, around the axis, is easily achieved by adding a counterbalancing weight. (b) Static balancing is insufficient for wide impellers because of the rocking couple in the plane of the axis. They need dynamic balancing which is done at speed and deals with the rocking couple in the plane of the axis

this will lead to premature bearing wear and consequent fan rattle. Reliance on static balancing alone may make the axial unbalance worse.

3.11 Overall design

Successful design achieves the right balance between qualities the purchaser requires and the cost of providing it. The balance is difficult to predict because the components interact with each other in a complex way not readily calculable manually at reasonable cost. Fortunately, computer modelling of heat pumps and dehumidifiers is now established. Such programs are particularly good at identifying performance trends. Their accuracy is only as good as the accuracy and accessibility of performance characteristics of the circuit components. The use of such programs at the start of new design work is strongly recommended. The Electricity Council Research Centre (ECRC) in Britain, and the National Bureau of

Standards at Gaithersburg, USA, have such programs available to designers. The larger compressor manufacturers also offer excellent design advice on refrigerant applications.

The influence of air-flow through the evaporator is particularly strong. If the air-flow is well below optimum then the evaporator will run very cold and the refrigerant circulation rate will be low because of the low evaporating pressure. The overall performance of the dehumidifier will be low too because the compression ratio from evaporator to condenser will be very high with its associated high pumping power. An example of the effect of changing the evaporator air-flow is shown in *Figure 3.34* from

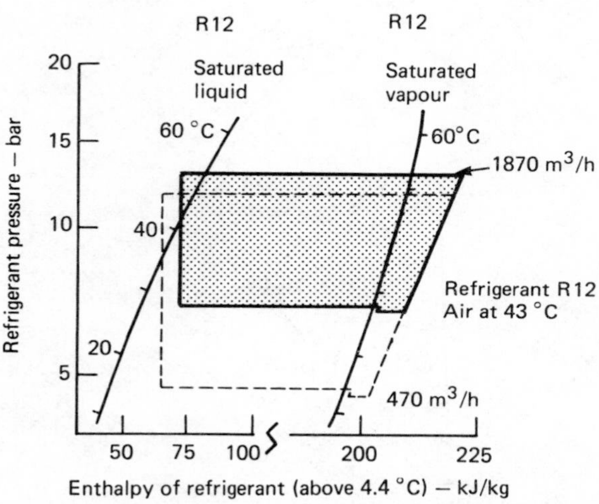

Figure 3.34 Mollier enthalpy diagram illustrating the effect of air-flow through the evaporator (Flikke, Cloud and Hustrulid, 1957)[33]

experimental tests on a grain dryer. Increasing the air-flow through the evaporator by a factor of four almost halves the compression power and even slightly increases the effective cooling duty. This increase also means that the compressor will be circulating more refrigerant around the circuit and therefore, while taking more electricity, will be working at a much higher refrigeration duty[33].

This influence of air flow is modified by the evaporator size and by the relative humidity of the ambient air. Details of nine domestic American machines are plotted in *Figure 3.35* for the standard US test condition of inlet air at 26.7°C and 80% r.h. This illustrates the relationship between performance, air-flow and evaporator surface area for different domestic dehumidifiers. All these units are driven by a 1/8 hp refrigerant compressor. The trend is for the better performance to be associated with the higher air-flows[14].

While high air-flows are generally good, there are two other factors which must also be noted. The first relates to domestic equipment. Noise is the most common complaint in Britain against dehumidifiers. Noise levels increase rapidly with increasing air-flow rate. Special attention must be

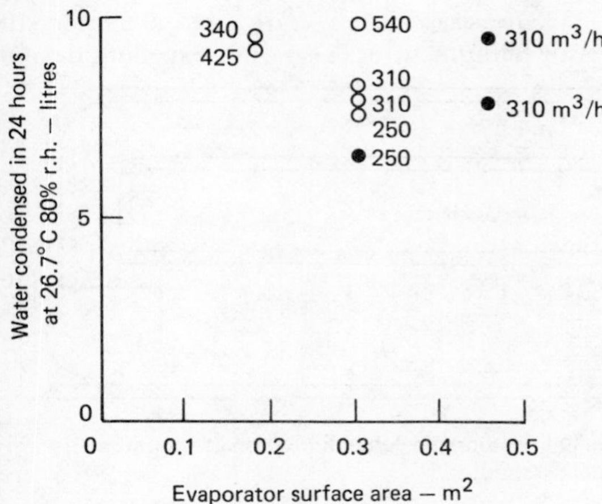

Figure 3.35 Performance characteristics of a range of manufactured dehumidifiers. Smaller surface areas can be compensated by larger air-flows. All machines have a ⅛hp compressor and air-flow m^3/h is given for each machine. O = a bare evaporator, • = a finned evaporator (Peck, 1952)[14]

paid to ensure quiet operation. The quietest machines can be left operating throughout the day and night which means that a smaller powered machine can extract maximum water over the whole day. It also means that the unit can be used at night to take full advantage of the low night-time electric tariff. The second factor relates to industrial drying where the dry air blows through a high pressure drop circuit such as a bed of grain. Studies on grain drying show that while the refrigerant circuit becomes more effective at high flow rates, there is an associated penalty of increasing pumping power. A test rig 1.2 m × 1.2 m square and containing a 0.3-m-deep bed of grain (340 kg corn) (*Figure 3.36*) was used to dry the grain from 25% to 13%. The dehumidifier had a l-kW compressor working on refrigerant R12. A 500-W electric centrifugal compressor was used to provide the air-flow which was varied from 300 m^3/h to almost 2000 m^3/h. Specific drying costs in kWh/kg water extracted was plotted against air-flow to show a minimum at approximately 800 m^3/h for this system. The specific electricity consumption is shown in *Figure 3.37*. Bigger, shallower beds would have a lower pressure drop and a higher optimum air-flow but at an increase in capital cost to provide for the bigger bed.

The actual operating temperature does not have a major effect on the refrigerant cycle. Experiments in the same grain drying rig showed the effect of changing from an air temperature of 43°C to one at 54°C. The chilling capacity of the unit is increased slightly at the higher air temperature because it has a higher evaporator pressure and hence a higher refrigerant recirculating flow. The effect on the refrigerant Mollier diagram is shown in *Figure 3.38*.

The relative importance of the defrost controls is illustrated in *Figure 3.39*[14]. Cold bedroom dehumidification requires defrosting, warehouses may need it occasionally but swimming pools and the higher-temperature industrial process dehumidification do not require it.

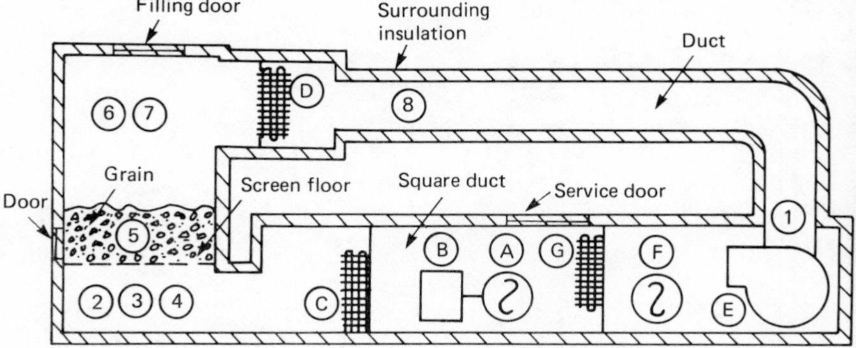

Figure 3.36 Illustration of an experimental grain-drying dehumidifier used to optimize air-flow conditions (Flikke, Cloud and Hustrulid, 1957)[33]

Equipment
A Compressor motor
B Compressor
C Condenser
D Evaporator
E Fan
F Fan motor
G Water-cooled coil

Instrumentation
1 Three thermocouples (averaged)
2 Four thermocouples (averaged)
3 Wet- and dry-bulb thermocouples
4 Relative humidity element
5 Thermocouple probe
6 Four thermocouples (averaged)
7 Wet- and dry-bulb thermocouples
8 Calibrated velometer (air-flow)

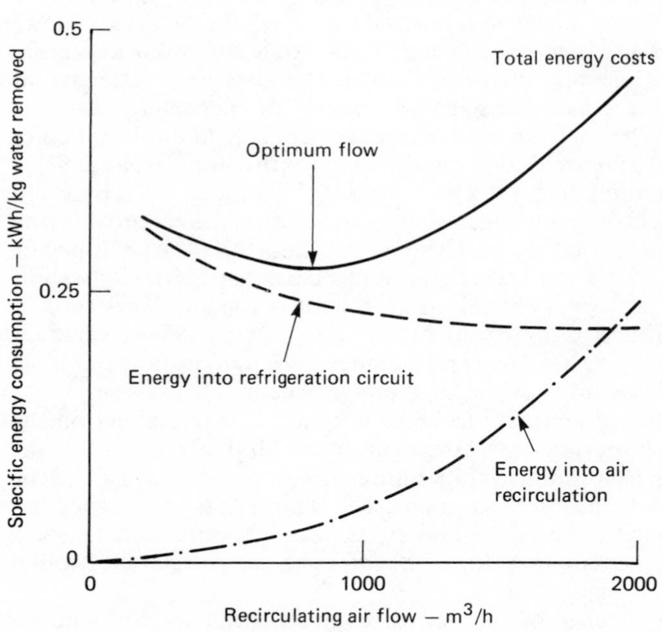

Figure 3.37 An illustration of optimum air-flow for a grain dryer. Bed: 1.2 m × 1.2 m × 0.3 m deep. Material: 340 kg corn. Dryness: from 25% initial to 13%. Refrigerant compressor: 1 kW using R12. Air recirculation: 500-W centrifugal fan (Flikke, Cloud and Hustrulid, 1957)[33]

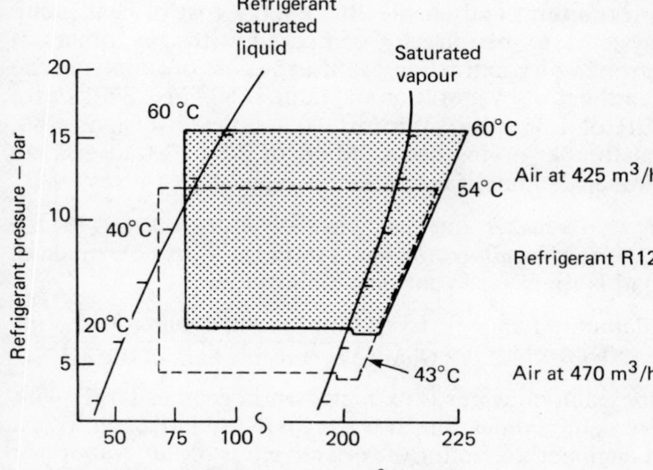

Figure 3.38 Mollier enthalpy diagram illustrating the effect of different air temperatures in the dryer (Flikke, Cloud and Hustrulid, 1957)[33]

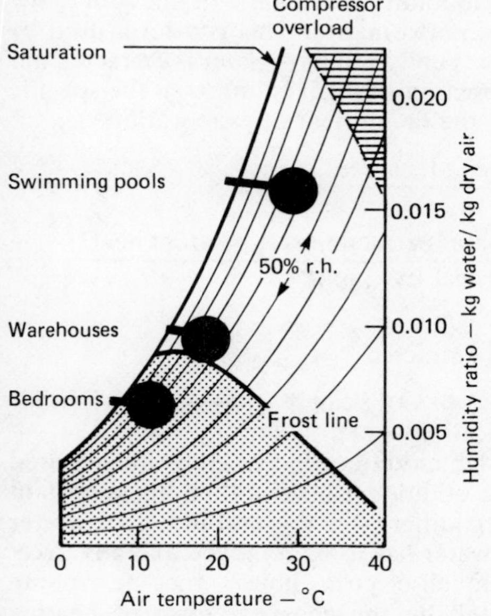

Figure 3.39 Operating conditions for a typical dehumidifier (Peck, 1952)[14]

3.12 Assessment

There are three methods of assessing effectiveness, each having its own particular emphasis.

(1) *Water extracted per unit of electricity*. (Specific moisture extraction rate—SMER). This is the basic index of effectiveness for a dehumidifier. It

is the process engineer's term and enables the energy cost of heat pump dehumidification systems to be directly compared with any other. It expresses the benefit of water extraction against the cost of supplying the electricity. The latent heat of evaporation of water at 80°C is 2300 kJ/litre which gives a SMER of 1.56 litres/kWh for 100% efficient evaporation. Conventional hot-air timber drying has a SMER of 0.8 to 1.0 litres/kWh while heat-pump timber dehumidifiers lie in the range 1 to 4 litres/kWh.

(2) *The ratio of refrigeration load to sensible heat transfer in the evaporator.* This is the refrigeration engineer's term to assess how much of the refrigeration load is spent on latent heat removal.

$$\text{Refrigeration dehumidifying effectiveness} = \frac{\text{Evaporator refrig cooling load}}{\text{Change in sensible heat of the air}}$$

This index is unity when no water is extracted and becomes larger with increasingly effective dehumidification. It is a term in use in Russia. It is a useful refrigeration engineer's term for the effectiveness of the evaporator component rather than the whole system. It has no direct link with the specific moisture extraction rate SMER.

(3) *Coefficient of performance.* (CoP). There is a net gain in sensible heat when dehumidified air leaves the dehumidifier. The ratio of this gain to the electrical input is the coefficient of performance. This is a term used by heating and heat pump engineers. It is unity when no water is extracted but increases with increasing water extraction rates. It is linked to the specific moisture extraction rate SMER by the latent heat of evaporation.

$$\text{CoP} = \frac{\text{net sensible heat out of condenser}}{\text{total electricity in}}$$

$$= \frac{\text{electrical kW input} + \text{water extraction rate} \times \text{latent heat*}}{\text{electrical kW input}}$$

$$= 1 + \text{SMER} \times \text{latent heat}$$

(*neglecting sensible heat in water extracted)

In high humidity and warm conditions CoPs can reach 3–4, though 1–2 is more usual in domestic dehumidification.

This index is useful when both dehumidifiers and heating are required simultaneously. The benefit of the additional heat is then an important advantage for the heat pump dehumidifier. It is a useful index for winter dehumidification in Britain where water has to be removed and any 'free' heat is highly desirable. In an all-electric house the heat-pump dehumidifier operating at night will be the cheapest form of heating although the actual quantity of 'free' heat is small (100 W).

3.13 Codes and guides for design, installation and testing

ACGHI American Conf of Governmental Industrial Hygienists, 650 Glenway Ave, Building D-5, Cincinnati, OH 45211, USA
Threshold limit values for chemical substances and physical agents in the workroom environment, 1983

AFNOR Assoc Française de Normalisation, Paris la Defense, Tour Europe, Cedex 7, 92080 Paris, France

E35-403 (1975). Safety requirements for refrigeration systems of air conditioners

E38-110 (1982). Heat pumps—a model of technical description

AHAM Assoc of Home Appliance Manufacturers, 20 N Wacker Dr, Chicago, IL 60606, USA

AHAM DH-1 (1980). Dehumidifiers (*also* UL 474, 1981)

AMCA Air Movement and Control Assoc, 30 W University Dr, Arlington Heights, IL 6004, USA

AMCA 210/74 (1974). Laboratory methods for testing fans for rating purposes (*also* ASHRAE 51–57 (1975))

ARI Air Conditioning and Refrigeration Institute, 1815 N Ft Myer Dr, Arlington, VA 22209, USA

ARI, 520–78 (1978). Positive displacement refrigerant compressors and condensing units

ARI 759–81 (1981). Thermostatic refrigerant expansion valves

ARI 730–80 (1980). Flow capacity rating and application of suction line filters and filter driers

ASHRAE American Soc of Heating, Refrigerating and Air Conditioning Engineers Inc, 1791 Tullie Circle NE, Atlanta, GA 32329, USA

1. *Fundamentals Guidebook*, 1981
2. *Systems Guidebook*
3. *Equipment Guidebook*

28–78 (1978). Methods of testing flow capacity of refrigerant capillary tubes

23–78 (1978). Methods of testing for rating positive displacement refrigerant compressors

63–79 (1979) Methods of testing liquid line refrigerant driers

17–75 (1975) Methods of testing for capacity rating of thermostatic refrigerant expansion valves (*also* ANSI B60–1–1975)

51–57 (1975). Laboratory methods for testing fans for rating (*also* AMCA 210–74 (1974))

BACAB British Air Conditioning Approvals Board, 30 Millbank, London

BACAB. Interim standard for rating performance and safety of air-to-air and air-to-water heat pumps up to 15 kW nominal output (1982)

BSI British Standards Institution, Linford Wood, Milton Keynes, Bucks MK14 6LE

BS 4788: 1972. Specification for the rating and testing of refrigerated dehumidifiers

BS 2757: 1956. Classification of insulating materials for electrical machinery and apparatus on the basis of thermal stability in service (ISBN 0 580 02664 7)

BS 2048 Part 1: 1961 (revised 1977). Motors for general use

BS 3456 Part 1: 1969. Specification for safety of household and similar electrical appliances. General requirements

BS 4999 Part 20: 1972. General requirements for rotating electrical machines

BS 4609 Part 1: 1970. Enamelled copper conductors (oleo-resinous base with good dielectric properties under humid conditions) (ISBNO 580 06061 6)

BS 6141: 1981. Specification for insulated cables and flexible cords for use in high temperature zones (ISBN 0580 12352 9)

BS 6746: 1976. PVC insulation and sheathing of electrical cables (ISBN 0 580 09473 1) (*also* IEC 540, CENELEC HD 21)

BS 5000: Part 10: 1978. General purpose induction motors (*also* IEC 72)

Part 11: 1973 (revised 1979). Small power electric motors and generators

BS 2626: 1975 (amended 1977). Lubricating oils for refrigerant compressors (ISBN 0 580 08953 3)

BS 848: 1963. Test methods for fans

BS 3456. Specification for safety and household and similar electrical appliances. Section 2.3 1976—Room air conditioners (ISBN 0 580 0934 4) (*also* IEC 378)

BS 2852. Testing of room air conditioners (smaller than 7kW) Part 1: 1982. Cooling performance (ISBN 0 580 12395 2) (*also* ISO 859)

BS 4434 Requirements for refrigeration safety. Part 1: 1980. General (ISBN 0 580 1114 8) (*also* ISO/R/1662)

Part 2: 1976. Particular requirements for small refrigerating systems for use in household appliances (ISBN 0 580 08828 6) (*also* ISO/R/1662)

BS 5491: 1977. Specification for rating and testing unit air conditioners of above 7 kW cooling capacity (ISBN 0 580 09864 8)

CSA Canadian Standards Association, 178 Rexdale Boulevard, Rexdale, Ontario, Canada, M9" 1R3

CSA Standards

C22.2 No 92: 1971. Dehumidifiers

C22.2 No 77: 1970. Motors with inherent overheating protection 1970

C22.2 No 11: 1957. Fractional hp electric motors for other than hazardous locations 1957

C22.2 No 14 1966. Industrial control equipment for use in ordinary (non-hazardous) locations

C22.2 No 21: 1960. Cord sets and power supply cords

C22.2 No 113: 1982. Fans and ventilators

B52: 1965. Mechanical refrigeration code

Z 107.71-M: 1981. Measurement and the rating of noise output of consumer appliances

CENELEC

HD 269–51 Harmonisation of safety requirements for refrigerators and food freezers

CIBS Chartered Institution of Building Services, Delta House, 222 Balham High Road, London, SW12 9BS

1970 Guide

DIN Deutsche Institut für Normung e.V., Berlin 30, W Germany

DIN 622 DK 697. Heuzing, Luftung und Kühlung

1946 T.1 (1979). Raumlufttechnik: Grundlagen (Room ventilation: fundamentals)

T.2 (1979). Raumlufttechnik: Gesundheitstechnische Auforderungen (Room ventilation: technical health principles)

4794 T.1 (1977). Ortsfeste Warmdufterzenger: Allgemeine und Lufttechnische Anforderungen, Prufung

(Stationary fan-assisted air heaters: common requirements and conditions for ventilation, testing)
T.5 (1979). Ortsfeste Warmdufterzenger: Allgemeine und sicherheitstechnische Grundsatze, Aufstellung, Betrieb
(Stationary fan-assisted air heaters: general safety rules, commissioning, operating)
DIN 115 B
57105 T.1a (1977). VDE—Bestimmung für den Betrieb von Starkstromanlagen: Allgemeine Bestimmungen, Teil Anderung (VDE—specification for the operation of electrical power installations, Part 1 General specifications)
DIN 125
42677 T.1 (1966). Oberflachengekühlte Drehstrommotoren mit Kefiglanfer Bauform B5 B10 B14 mit Walzlagern; Aubaumasse und Znordnung der Leistungen
(Totally-enclosed, fan-cooled AC polyphase motors of squirrel-cage design B5 B10 B14 with ball bearings, standard dimensions and relationships for frame sizes and output ratings)
42950 (1964). Kurzzeichen für Bauformen elektrische Maschinen
(Design symbols for rotating electrical machinery)
42973 (1973). Leistungsreihe für elektrische Maschinen: Nemleistungen bei Dauerbetnib
(Rated output values for rotating electrical machinery for continuous duty)
DIN 8900 Part 1: (1980). Anschlussfertige Warmepumpen mit elektrische angetreiben Verdichtern, Begriffe
(Heat pumps: heat-pump units with electric-driven compressors, concepts)
Part 2 (1980). Anschlussfertige Warmepumpen mit elektrisch angetreiben Verdichtern; prufumfang, kennzeichnung
(Heat pumps: heat-pump units with electric-driven compressors, rating conditions, extent of testing, labelling)

HVCA The Heating & Ventilating Contractors' Assoc, London, W2 4JG
Brazing and bronze welding of copper pipework and sheet, 1976
User air conditioning guide for good practice, May 1980
Guide to good practice for domestic heat pumps, Mar 1983
Ductwork (revised) DW 142 (1983)

IEC International Electrotechnical Commission, 1 rue de Varembe, 1211 Geneva 20, Switzerland, 34-01-50 Telex 28872
335-2-1 (1980). Safety of household electrical appliances—general requirements
335-2-2 (1982). Safety of household and similar electrical appliances, particularly requirements for air-to-air electric heat pumps
335-2-24 (1976). Safety of household and similar electrical equipment—refrigerators and freezers
68-2-28 (1968). Guidance for damp heat tests
68-2-10 (1968) Test J Mould growth (3rd edn)
34-1 (1969) Rotating electrical machines
Part 1: Rating and performance (7th edn)
34-9 (1972) Rotating electrical machines
Part 9: Noise limits

34-11 (1978) Rotating electrical machines
Part 11: Built-in thermal protection
378 (1972) Safety requirements for the electrical equipment of room air-conditioners
654-1 (1979) Part 1: Temperature, humidity and barometric pressure
42 Sw Fr

IEE Institution of Electrical Engineers, Savoy Place, London, WC2R OBL
IEE Wiring Regulations: Regulations for electrical installations (15th edn 1981, amended 1983)

NEMA National Electrical Manufacturers' Association, 2101 L St NW Ste 300, Washington DC 20037, USA
Motors and generators NEMA/ANSI/MG 1-1978

NFPA National Fire Protection Association, Batterymarch Park, Quincy, MA 02269, USA
NFPA - 90A Installation of air conditioning and mechanical ventilation systems (1978)

SMAGNA Sheet Metal and Air Conditioning Contractors' National Association 8224 Old Courthouse Road, Vienna, VA 22180, USA
Low pressure duct contruction (1976)

UL Underwriters' Laboratories Inc, 333 Pfingsten Road, Northbrook, IL 60062, USA
UL 474 Dehumidifiers (1983) (AHAM DH-1 1980)
UL 207 Refrigerant containing components and accessories non electrical
UL 1004 Electric motors
UL 984 Hermetic refrigerant motor compressors (1979)
UL 547 Thermal protectors for motors
UL 1020 Thermal cut-offs for use in electrical appliances and components
UL 746C Polymeric materials: use in electrical equipment
UL 62 Flexible cord and fixture wire
UL 181 Factory-made air ducts and connectors (1981)
UL 507 Electric fans (1976)

3.14 Background reading on thermodynamic principles and heat pumps

Ambrose, E.W. *Heat Pumps and Electric Heating*. John Wiley, New York, USA, 1966
Threlkeld, J.L. *Thermal Environmental Engineering*. Prentice Hall, New Jersey, USA, 1970
Wolf, R. *Chauffage et Conditionnement Électriques des Locaux*. Eyrolles, Paris, 1974
Bernier, J. *La Pompe de Chaleur: Mode d'Emploi*. Pyc Edn, Paris, 1979
Reay, D.A. and Macmichael, D.B.A. *Heat Pumps: Design and Application*. Pergamon Press, Oxford, 1979
Heap, R.D. *Heat Pumps*. E. & F.N. Spon, London, 1979
Recknagel-Sprenger. *Manuel Practique du Génie Climatique*. Pyc, Paris, 1980 (Trans from German by J.L. Cauchepin)
McMullen, J.T. and Morgan, R. 'Development of domestic heat pumps'. EEC Final Rep 269-77-1, New Univ of Ulster, 1980

Cube, H.L. von, and Steimle, F. *Heat Pump Technology*. Butterworths, London, 1981 (English edn, E.G.A. Goodall (ed))
McQuiston, F.C. and Parker, J.D. *Heating, Ventilating and Air Conditioning*. John Wiley, New York, USA, 1982
Dicker, C.S. 'Controls for heat pumps'. *Refrign & Air Condg*, **81**, 120–123, 1978
Veyo, S.E. 'An optimised two-capacity advanced electric heat pump'. *ASHRAE Jnl*, 452–48, Nov 1982
Bonne, U., Patan, A., Jacobson, R.D. and Mueller, D.A. 'Electric-driven heat pump systems: simulation and controls'. *ASHRAE trans*, Paper LA-80-5 No 4, **86** (1), 1980
Mueller, D.A. and Bonne, U. 'New heat pump control functions via microelectronics'. Conf on Elec Heat Pump Tech and Appls, Dusseldorf, W. Germany, June 1980
Niederer, D.H. 'Defrosting of air units in central systems'. *ASHRAE trans*, **81** (2), 581–591, 1975
Buick, T.R., McMullan, J.T., Morgan, R. and Murray, R.B. 'Ice detection in heat pumps and coolers'. *Intern Jnl of Energy Res*, **2** 85–98, 1978
Negoro, K. 'The Type KFH-5 dehumidifier' (in Japanese). *Mitsubishi Denki Giho*, **53** (5), 353–356, 1979
Blundell, C.J. 'Optimising heat-exchangers for air-to-air space-heating heat pumps in the United Kingdom'. *Energy Res*, **1**, 69–94, 1977
Brundrett, G.W. and Blundell, C.J. 'An advanced dehumidifier for Britain'. *Htg & Ventg Engr*, 6–9, Nov 1980

3.15 References

1 *ASHRAE Handbook: Fundamentals:* Am Soc of Htg, Refrign & Air Condg Engrs, Atlanta, USA, 1985
2 Jensen, W. 'Kriterien für den Einsatz von Kompressions-warmepumpen in der Industie' ('Criteria for the use of compression heat pumps in industry'). *ASUE*, **6**, 22–28, 1981. Brit Gas trans, T 5893
3 Paul, J. 'Schrauben und Kolbenverdichter im Vergleich'. *Die Kalte und Klimatechnik*, **12**, 1–6, 1981
4 Reichelt, J. 'Working fluid for heat pumps refrigerating and lubricating agents'. *Elektrowarme im Technischen Ausbau, Edition A*, **35**, 65–70, 1977. Elecy Ccl trans, OA 1853: 1982
5 Zylla, R., Tai, K.W., Devotta, S., Watson, F.A. and Holland, F.A. 'Derived thermodynamic data for heat pump systems operating on R22'. *Heat Recovery Systems*, **1** (2), 111–123, 1981
6 Klein, R. 'Screw compressors for applications in heat pump installations'. Heat Pump Conf, Essen, W. Germany, 1977. Elecy Ccl trans, CA 1781: 1979
7 Smith, C.A. 'Compressors for air conditioning'. *Htg & Air Condg Jnl*, 30–37, May 1981
8 Wrede, F. 'Trochoidal compressors as heat pump compressors'. Heat Pump Conf, Essen, W. Germany, 1977. Elecy Ccl trans, OA 1778: 1981
9 Anon. 'Demands on heat pump compressors'. *Danfoss Jnl*, **4**, 12–13, 1982
10 McQuiston, F.C. 'Heat mass and momentum transfer in a parallel-plate dehumidifying exchanger'. *ASHRAE trans*, **82** (2), 87–106, 1976
11 Gogolin, A. 'Mechanical dehumidifiers' (in Russian). *Holod Techn, USSR*, **4**, 18–22, 1960
12 Shaw, A. 'Exploration of air velocity across air conditioning system dehumidifiers: an energy conservation project'. *ASHRAE trans*, Paper 2707, **88** (2), 1982
13 Schulte, D.W. and Howell, R.H. 'The effect of air turbulence on the rate of frost growth on a horizontal flat plate'. *ASHRAE trans*, Paper 2711, **88** (2), 1982
14 Peck, F.G. 'Mechanical dehumidifiers come of age'. *Refrign Engg*, **60** (9), 956–958, 1952
15 Kays, W.M. and London, A.L. *Compact Heat Exchangers*. National Press, Palo Alto, California, USA, 1955
16 Kawalczewsk, J.J. 'Performance of refrigeration systems with fixed restriction operating under variable evaporator and condenser conditions'. *Jnl of Refrign*, **4** (6), 122–128, 1961
17 Daly, B.B. *Woods' Practical Guide to Fan Engineering*. Woods of Colchester, 1979
18 Chartered Institution of Building Services. *Design Guide 1970*. CIBS, London, 1971
19 Kenny, R.J. 'Fans and blowers'. *Machine Design*, **40** (6), 152–173, 1968
20 Weaver, G.C. (ed). *Electric Motors Handbook*. Design Engr, London, 1968

21 Electricity Council. *Electrical Services in Buildings*. Elecy Ccl, London, 1972
22 Fink, D.G. and Wayne-Beaty, H. *Standard Handbook for Electrical Engineers*. McGraw-Hill, USA, 1978
23 Say, M.G. *Electrical Engineers' Reference Book*, 13th edn. Newnes-Butterworths, London, 1977
24 Bell, J.C. and Hester, I.R. 'Electric motors. An overview of electric motors, speed control, power factor and other characteristics'. *Htg, Piping & Air Condg*, 51–56, Dec 1981
25 Zigler, R. 'Motor speed modulation of air-conditioning and heat-pump systems'. *Intern Jnl of Refrign*, **3** (4), 196–204, 1980
26 Anon. 'Netzruckwirkungen beim Anlauf von Warmepumpenheizungen in Einfamilien und Kleinen Mehrfamilienhausern' ('Network reaction to heat pump heating in single family and small blocks of flats'). *Elektrizitätsverwertung*, **56** (5), 91–100, 1981
27 VDEW. 'Connecting heat pumps to public low voltage supply systems'. Note for Technische Anschlussbedingungen (Technical Rules for connections to the supply network), May 1981. Elecy Ccl trans, OA 2480: 1981
28 Egli, F. von, and Kunzler, D. 'Anlaufstrommessungen von Warmepumpen und Auswirkungen auf das Netz' ('Measurement of the starting current used by heat pumps and its effect on mains power supplies'). *Bull Assoc Suisse Electr*, **72** (16), 885–888, 1981
29 Daly, B.B. 'Noise level in fans'. *Instn of Htg and Ventn Engrs Jnl*, 29–44, May 1958
30 Goldman, R.B. and Maling, G.C. 'Noise from small centrifugal fans'. *Noise Control*, USA, 26–29, Nov 1955
31 Peistrup, C.F. and Wesler, J.E. 'Noise of ventilating fans'. *Jnl of the Acoustical Soc of Am*, 322–325, Mar 1953
32 Preisendanz, K. 'Schall in der Kalte Luft und Heiztechnik'. *Die Kalte und Klimatechnik*, **34** (1), 6–12, 1981
33 Flikke, A.M., Cloud, H.A. and Hustrulid, A. 'Grain drying by heat pump'. *Agricl Engg*, 592–597, Aug 1957

Chapter 4

Domestic applications of dehumidifiers

4.1 The market

Dampness is Britain's major housing problem, affecting two million homes seriously and even more houses less seriously (*Table 4.1*). About two-thirds of this problem is attributed simply to condensation inside the house.

Careful local authority surveys confirm the general pattern. The Newcastle survey covering more than 600 dwellings found that 30% of dwellings experienced dampness. Private, rented, unfurnished accommodation had the highest incidence (49%), while only 14% of owner-occupied dwellings reported it. Bedrooms were most affected (45%), kitchens less so (26%), with living-rooms and bathrooms noted in only 16% of the reports.

TABLE 4.1 Dampness is one of Britain's major problems
(One in four of Britain's houses has a damp problem)

	Owner occupier (million)		*Private rented* (million)		*Local authority* (million)		*Total* (million)	
No damp	7.7	82%	1.3	52%	3.5	67%	12.5	73%
Slight damp	1.2	13%	0.5	19%	0.8	16%	2.5	15%
Severe damp	0.4	5%	0.7	28%	0.9	17%	2.0	12%
	9.3		2.5		5.2		17.0	

Data from 1976 *English House Condition Survey* sampled from random survey of 7000 houses (Cornish, 1983)

Three major factors were highlighted. Condensation problems were highest in the poorly-insulated dwellings. They were also higher if the dwelling was exposed. Detached and end-terrace dwellings were more affected by damp than mid-terraced houses of the same construction. Family size was the third factor. The incidence of dampness increased rapidly with family size (*Figure 4.1*).

Personal space also had an influence. Houses with only one occupant did not experience dampness. One-person households in smaller flats and maisonettes did. This characteristic appeared to be a general one because less dampness was reported by similar-sized families who had more rooms.

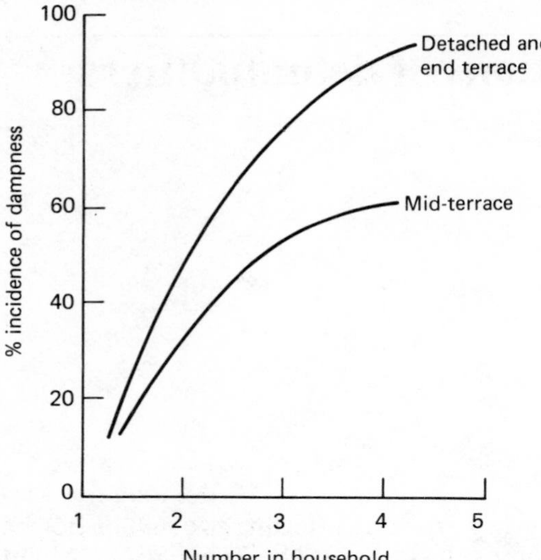

Figure 4.1 Family size and degree of exposure also affect the probability of experiencing dampness in the home (Preston, Stephens and Brundrett, 1979)

The conclusion was that dampness did not appear to be due to action or inaction by the tenants, but had been affected by the increasing fuel costs in houses designed for an earlier period. Almost two-thirds of the damp dwellings were below the recommended minimum temperatures proposed in the Parker Morris guidelines.

An exploratory survey of one week's complaints of dampness supplied by five local authorities in England and Wales analysed the 269 complaints they received. The majority were linked to condensation, with the older houses associated with a higher number of complaints. The rooms affected most were kitchens (80%), bedrooms (77%), living-rooms (68%) and bathrooms (61%). Other dampness complaints were about rising damp and rain penetration, and these building defects were more common in the older, pre-1939 buildings. From the tenants who replied to specific questions, two-thirds dried clothes indoors in winter and 20% used a paraffin or bottled-gas room heater.

The reasons for condensation are complex and interactive but include low levels of space heating, poor thermal insulation, more use of hot water for showers and washing, less use of absorbent materials in the house and lower ventilation rates due to weatherstripping. While the cure for future homes is controlled ventilation and high levels of thermal insulation, dehumidifiers are a convenient and effective cure for existing homes. Several million are already in homes in USA and Japan and it is surprising that so few are used in Britain.

Research into quantifying the moisture generated within a home is rare but estimates suggest approximately equal amounts from the combined respiration and perspiration from the occupants and from cooking. This, together with moisture from washing, makes a total for five persons of

TABLE 4.2 Moisture generated in the home

Metabolic water vapour (breath and perspiration)	
5 persons asleep × 8 hours	1.5 kg
2 persons active × 16 hours	1.7
Cooking	3.0
Bathing, dish washing, etc	1.0
	7.2 kg
Additional sources:	
Clothes washing	0.5
Clothes drying	5.0
Paraffin heater (if used)	1.7
	7.2 kg
Combined total	14.4 kg

BS 5250: 1975 *The control of condensation*

7 kg/day. This can be doubled if clothes are dried in the home and even more if flueless paraffin or bottled-gas heaters are employed (*Table 4.2*).

The coldest free surfaces in any house are usually the glass in the windows, although cold-water pipes and cisterns can be equally as cold. Condensation on glass is not normally a problem, provided that the water is regularly mopped up from the window sill. Conditions for this are shown in *Figure 4.2*. However, the next coldest surface is usually the insides of the external corners of the upstairs bedrooms because bedrooms tend to run at

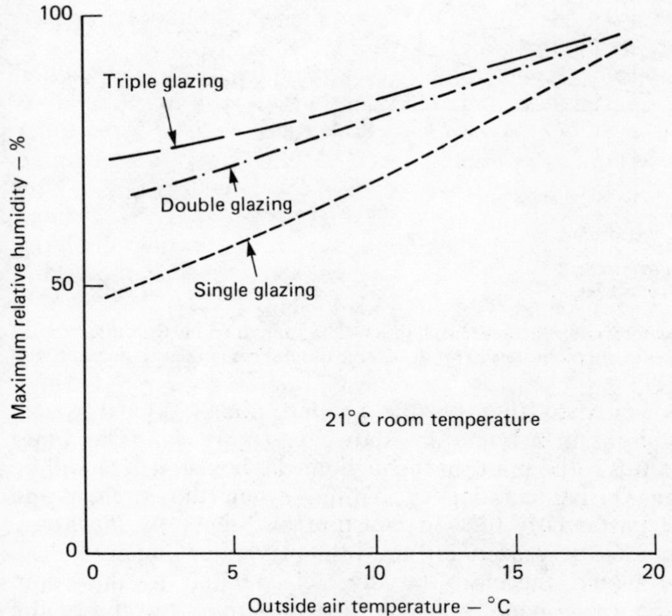

Figure 4.2 Maximum relative humidity for rooms with glazing (dewpoint condition on the inner window surface)

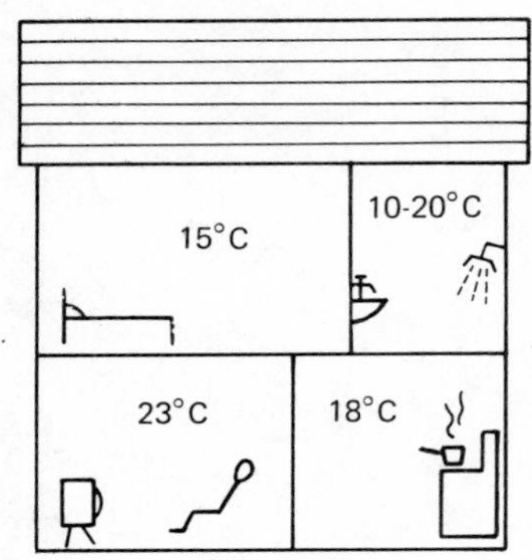

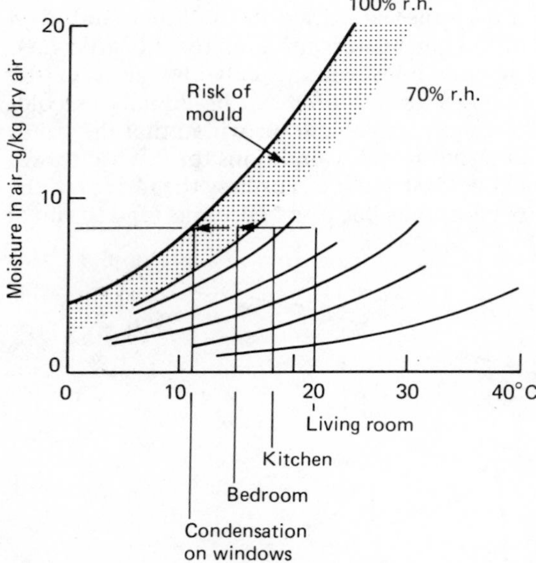

Figure 4.3 While the water vapour pressure in a house will be approximately the same everywhere, differences in temperature will produce large differences in relative humidity

a temperature lower than that on the ground floor. Typical winter temperature conditions in a home are shown in *Figure 4.3*. The water vapour pressure tends to be uniform throughout the house. There will be exceptions to this during cooking or bathing when the kitchen and bathroom will be particularly high in moisture but generally the house would be expected to be reasonably uniform in vapour pressure. The relative humidity would therefore be inversely related to the room temperature. In the warm living room the relative humidity would be the lowest while in the coldest room, most probably the bedroom, it would be the highest. Since dehumidifiers work best at high relative humidities, the

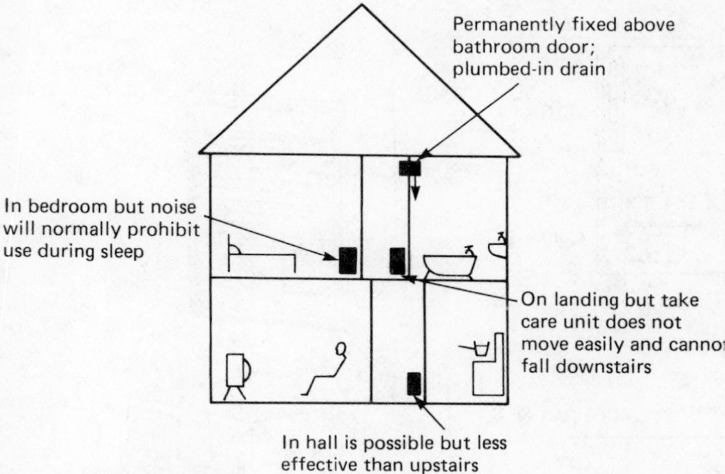

Figure 4.4 Preferred sites for the dehumidifier (it will work best in the dampest condition)

best site is either in the damp room itself or near to it, such as on the upstairs landing in a house (*Figure 4.4*).

The biggest benefits from dehumidifiers would therefore be:

(1) In private unfurnished dwellings and, to a slightly lesser extent, in local authority and private furnished dwellings for let. Private sector households experiencing dampness problems would benefit but the survey suggests that the proportion of families experiencing dampness is low.

(2) In dwellings where the personal space is low, i.e. when buildings are occupied at or over their design occupancy. Large families in ordinary houses are the best examples.

(3) In dwellings which are exposed by virtue of either their location or their surroundings. Detached houses have four outside walls and would therefore be exposed. Corner top-floor flats in high-rise buildings are also exposed because of the high wind speeds they receive and because of their relatively large exterior surface.

(4) In dwellings where moisture generation is high. This would include dwellings where clothes are regularly dried indoors or where bottled-gas or paraffin heaters are used. While dehumidifiers can remove the moisture generated by portable flueless heaters, care must be taken to ensure that the ventilation is adequate to prevent asphyxiation by carbon dioxide.

4.2 Domestic dehumidifiers

The availability of domestic dehumidifiers has been growing during the 1980s, with manufacturers and importing agencies competing to supply the specialist retailers. Some electricity boards now stock the units. Annual

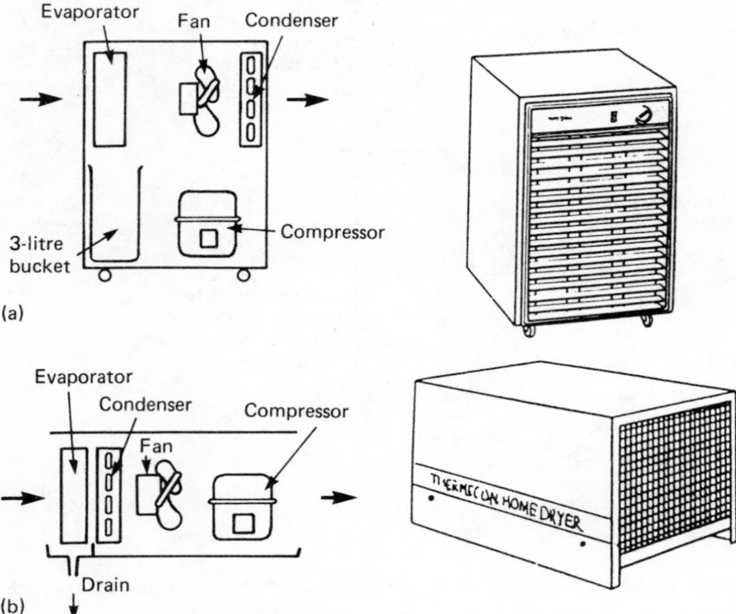

Figure 4.5 The two types of domestic dehumidifier installation, free-standing and plumbed-in. (a) Most common arrangement for the free-standing domestic dehumidifier (courtesy of Haydons Ltd). (b) Most common arrangement for built-in domestic dehumidifier (courtesy of Thermecon Ltd)

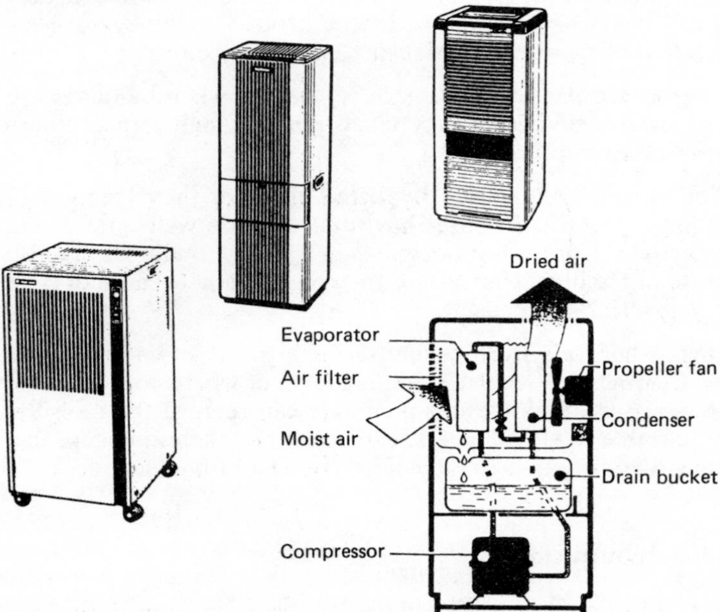

Figure 4.6 Domestic dehumidifiers are available in a wide variety of sizes and shapes (courtesy of National, Japan)

sales in Britain are 20000 per year and the majority of these are manufactured here in the UK.

The most common unit is the 200 W free-standing dehumidifier of the type illustrated in *Figure 4.5(a)*. Typically 25 kg in weight, it is 500 mm in height and 300 mm × 300 mm in plan, and contains within it a three-litre water tank which needs to be emptied regularly. Physically smaller machines can be made if they do not need an internal water container but are meant to be coupled directly to a drain. Such a layout is illustrated in *Figure 4.5(b)*. There is a growing range of sizes and shapes of all these domestic units and a selection from a major Japanese manufacturer is illustrated in *Figure 4.6*.

All the machines use the refrigerant vapour compression cycle. The most popular refrigerant circuit is illustrated in *Figure 4.7*. Operation in the

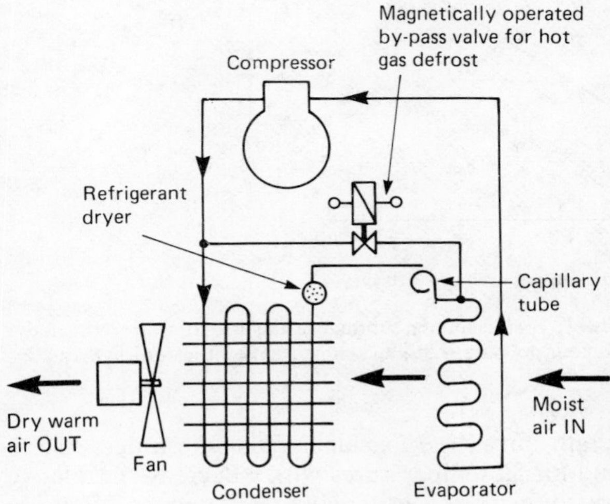

Figure 4.7 Basic refrigerant circuit for a small dehumidifier (courtesy of Dantherm)

home means that a defrost cycle is essential because dehumidification could be required between 10 and 20°C and frost will certainly form on the evaporator at the lower ambient temperature of 10°C. The hot gas bypass directs the hot compressed refrigerant vapour directly into the evaporator whenever defrosting is required. There are alternative methods of defrosting, for example by switching off the compressor and using direct electric heaters to warm up the evaporator.

In its normal operation the refrigerant compressor draws the refrigerant vapour from the evaporator, thus cooling the evaporator. When the temperature of the evaporator falls below the dewpoint of the air passing through it, then dehumidification starts. The latent heat of water absorbed by the evaporator is released through the condenser to the room as sensible heat. The dehumidifier is unique in translating the latent heat of water vapour into sensible heat and hence providing more background heating than electricity consumed. It works as a small heat pump.

$$\text{Coefficient of performance (CoP)} = \frac{\text{Useful heat supplied}}{\text{Electricity used}}$$

This coefficient increases as more moisture is extracted for each unit of electricity. The conventional index of effectiveness for a dehumidifier is litres of water extracted for each kWh of electricity used. This can be converted to CoP from the knowledge of the latent heat of the evaporation. This relationship is illustrated in *Figure 4.8*.

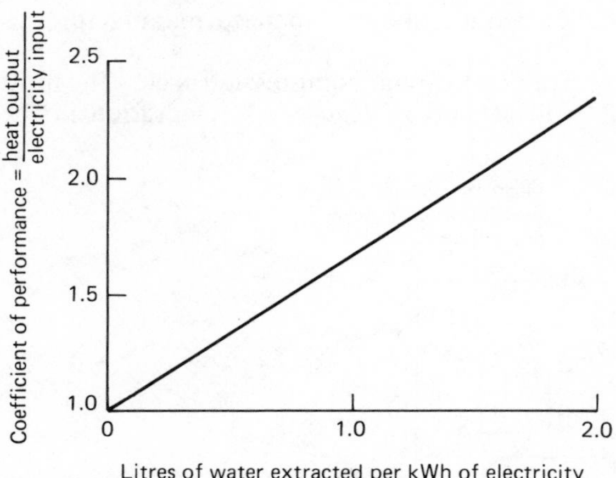

Figure 4.8 The relationship between coefficient of performance and litres of water extracted per kWh of electricity (water vapour pressure ~20 mb, assumed constant, error less than 2% for dewpoints from 5 to 20°C)

The water extraction rate for all the machines falls with a decrease in ambient temperature, and for all temperatures with a decrease in relative humidity. Typical performance curves for three domestic dehumidifiers are illustrated in *Figure 4.9* for a range of relative humidities from 70% to 100% and for room temperatures from 5 to 20°C. When selecting a machine, take care to note its temperature sensitivity. Listed water extraction rates in the sales literature are often at the maximum operating temperatures and relative humidities.

There is also a wide variation in effectiveness of water extraction between the different dehumidifiers. Two examples, expressed in forms of CoP, are illustrated in *Figure 4.10*. An important factor in determining the effectiveness of a dehumidifier is the air flow through it. An empirical relationship between water extraction and air flow through the dehumidifier is shown in *Figure 4.11*. This data is taken from 11 American dehumidifiers which each used a 1/8 hp compressor. Unfortunately, a potential drawback with high air-flows is that they are associated with noisier machines.

In dehumidifiers made in Europe or America the bulk of the noise comes from the fan and the associated air movement. The larger air-flows are associated with much noisier machines, and also with larger compressors, but the compressor's contribution to overall noise is usually

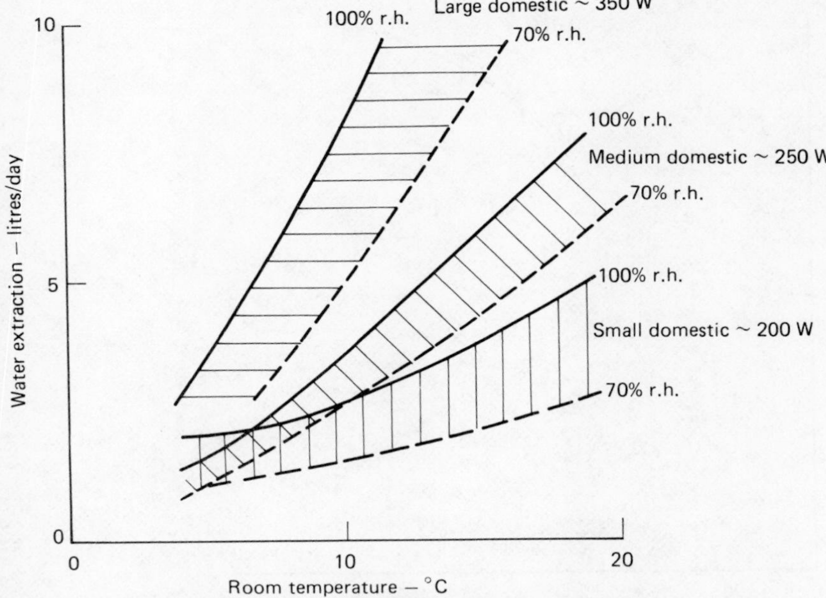

Figure 4.9 Machines differ in their performance and sensitivity to temperature

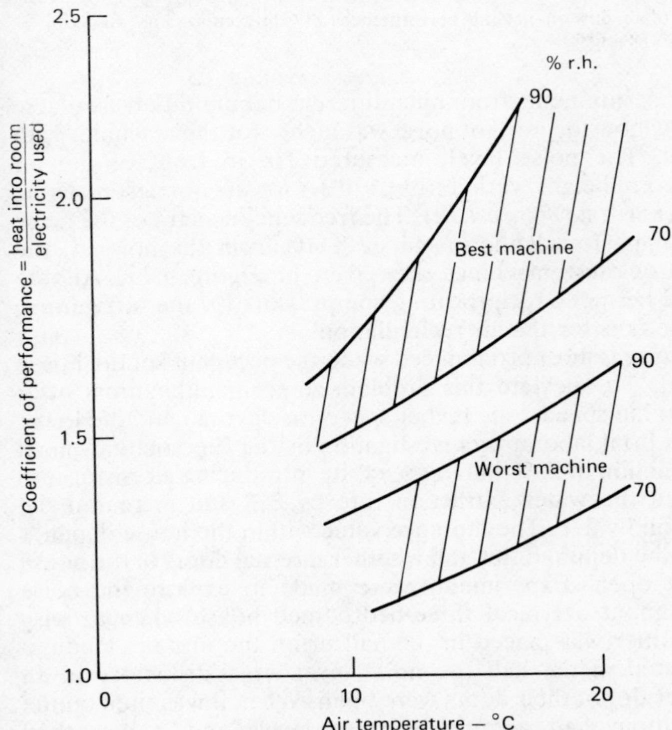

Figure 4.10 Machine effectiveness varies widely between equipments

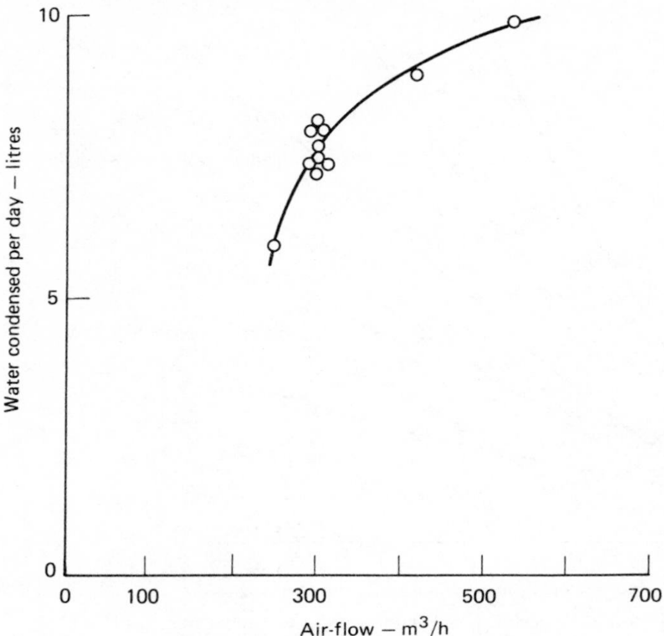

Figure 4.11 Influence of air-flow on machine performance (all ⅛hp compressors; all taking 230W; all at 26.7°C (80°F) and 80% r.h.)

small. Acoustic measurements from nine different dehumidifiers available in Britain did show how the level of noise was higher for the machines with a bigger air-flow. The noise level, measured 1m in front of the air discharge and at 1.2m height, varied from 40dBA for the quietest machine to 56dBA for the noisiest (*Figure 4.12*). The frequency spectra of the noise were of similar shape for all the machines. Data from the noisiest, the average and the quietest machines are given in *Figure 4.13.* All the dehumidifiers had hermetic reciprocating compressors for the refrigerant, and propeller-type fans for the air recirculation.

Dehumidifier noise is most pronounced when the occupants of the house have gone to bed. To alleviate this problem some manufacturers offer machines with two fan speeds, the higher speed for daytime and the lower speed for night. A brief laboratory investigation by the Electricity Council showed that a reduction of 30% in fan speed, by introducing a resistor into its circuit, lowered the water extraction rate by 8% and increased the energy consumption by 2%. The nuisance value within the house depends upon the siting of the dehumidifier and whether internal doors in the house are closed or left open. Experiments were made to explore the noise distribution throughout a typical three-bedroomed house when a noisy (51dBA) dehumidifier was placed in the hall or on the upstairs landing. When it was located in the hall the noise level was satisfactory in all bedrooms, whether or not their doors were open. When it was sited on the landing one bedroom had acceptable noise levels and it was then satisfactory only when that bedroom's door was closed. The results of these

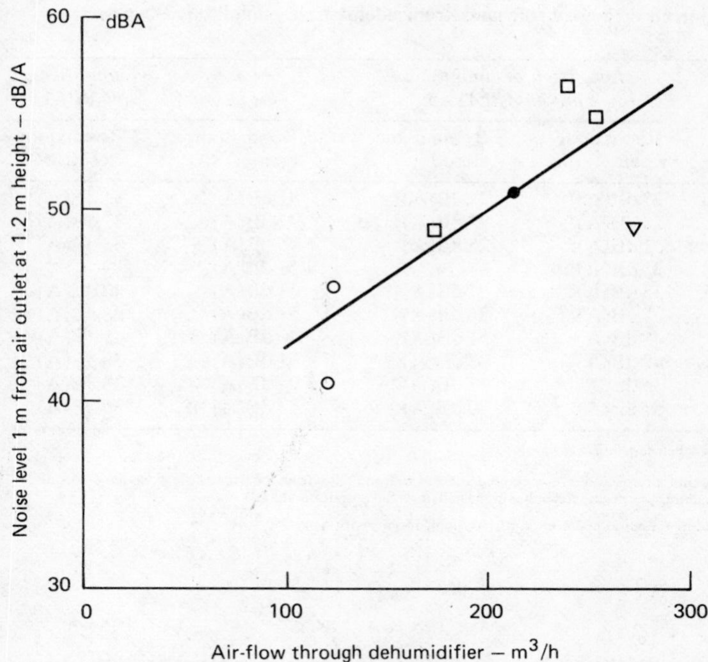

Figure 4.12 The relationship between noise and air-flow (nine models; regression coefficient 0.81). Compressor ratings (hp): O ⅙, ▽ ⅕ X ¼, □⅓

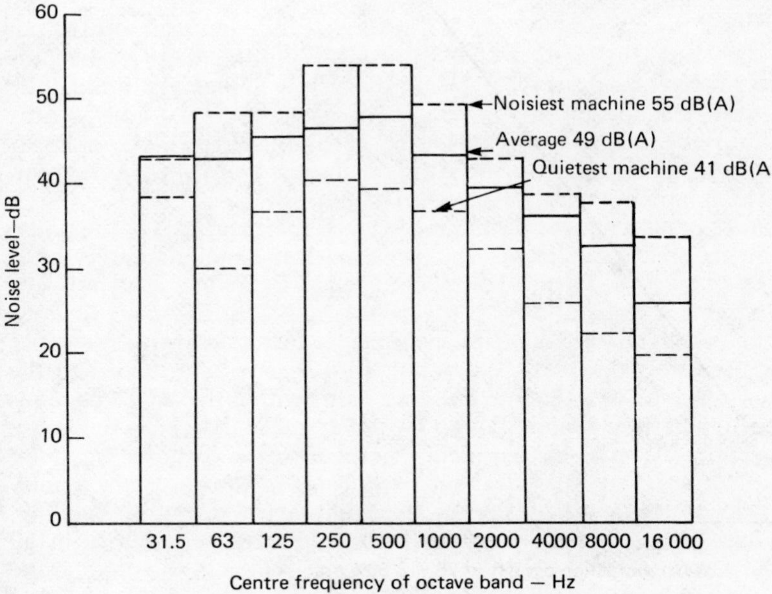

Figure 4.13 Noise spectra from three domestic dehumidifiers

TABLE 4.3 Experiments on noise disturbance from a domestic dehumidifier: 3-bedroom semi-detached

Room	*Noise from dehumidifier in hall dB(A)*		*Noise from dehumidifier on upstairs landing dB(A)*	
	Room door open	Room door closed	Room door open	Room door closed
Bedroom 1	27 dB(A)*	22 dB(A)*	41 dB(A)	31 dB(A)*
2	28 dB(A)*	23 dB(A)*	47 dB(A)	37 dB(A)
3	31 dB(A)*	25 dB(A)*	46 dB(A)	33 dB(A)
Landing	35 dB(A)*	—	51 dB(A)	—
Upstairs toilet	33 dB(A)*	27 dB(A)*	51 dB(A)	40 dB(A)
Bathroom	35 dB(A)	26 dB(A)*	51 dB(A)	38 dB(A)
Hall	48 dB(A)	51 dB(A)†	40 dB(A)	41 dB(A)†
Living room	42 dB(A)	32 dB(A)*	31 dB(A)*	30 dB(A)*
Dining room	35 dB(A)*	31 dB(A)*	29 dB(A)*	28 dB(A)*
Kitchen	50 dB(A)	40 dB(A)	34 dB(A)*	30 dB(A)*

*acceptable values †kitchen and lounge doors closed

The noise from this dehumidifier was 51 dB(A) measured at 1.2 m high and 1.0 m from the front of the machine. Only one dehumidifier was used and this was positioned either in the hall or on the upstairs landing.

Maximum permissible rating for noise: bedroom 31 dB(A); living room 36 dB(A)

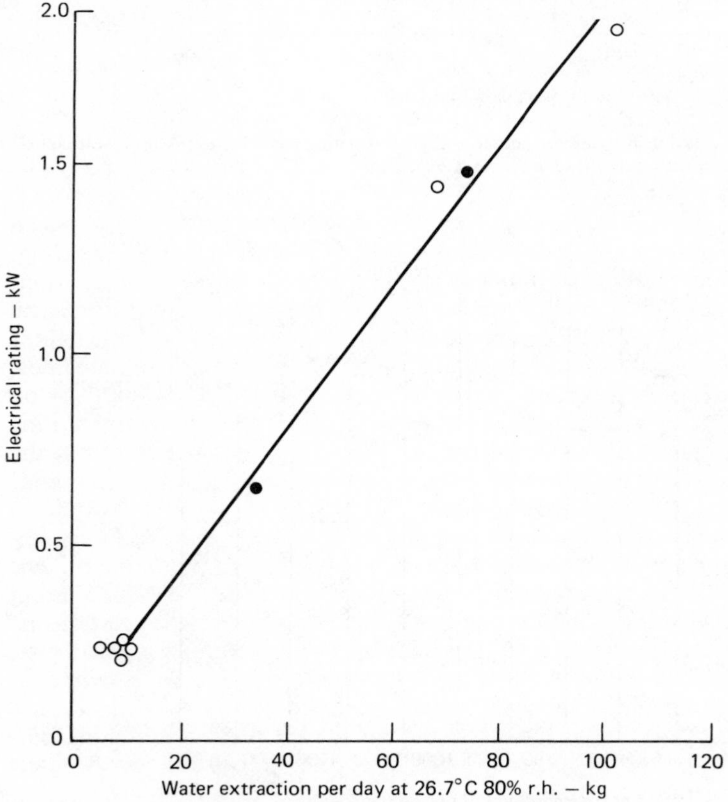

Figure 4.14 The relationship between electrical rating and moisture removal (O = American machines, ● = British machines)

TABLE 4.4 Checklist for selecting a domestic dehumidifier

Q 1. *Portable or fixed?*
Most portable machines can be coupled to the drain but such machines are physically larger than the 'fixed' ones which do not have provision for a bucket.

Q 2. *What physical size?*
Check dimensions and air-flow route in view of likely site. Most machines are of similar physical size regardless of electrical properties.

Q 3. *How much water do I extract?*
Plan on 1 litre/person/day at 10°C 70% r.h.

Q 4. *Do I need a humidistat?*
Yes, if left unattended for long periods of several days.

Q 5. *Do I need an automatic cut off?*
Not necessary for the 'fixed' ones, essential for portable models if left unattended for longer than a day, to prevent the bucket overfilling.

Q 6. *Do I need a defrost cycle?*
Yes, when used for all British house bedrooms.

Q 7. *Will the noise disturb me?*
Yes, all machines are too noisy to use in the bedroom during sleep. Some machines have a two-speed fan which is valuable where noise is sensitive.

Q 8. *What is the guarantee?*
1 year for most machines with an extra period on from 1–4 years for the refrigerant cycle.

Q 9. *What are the service arrangements?*
Check with each supplier.

Q 10. *How much do machines cost?*
Prices vary between £150 and £350.

---

tests are summarized in *Table 4.3*. Care is also needed if the unit is placed directly on a suspended floor because resonant vibration can be irritating. Soft pads under the feet of the dehumidifier help to reduce this vibration.

Japanese dehumidifiers are smaller in both electrical forms and physical dimensions. They tend to be approximately 150 W and to be both lighter and much quieter than conventional European and American machines. There is also the trend in Japan towards using the rotating-piston compressor which is smaller and has less vibration than the reciprocating compressor. It is also insensitive to liquid refrigerant entering the compressor and can therefore offer the designer hope of good performance and reliability at small pressure ratios.

While the bulk of dehumidifiers are clearly designed for the ordinary size of house, most manufacturers make a wide range of equipment. The customer in a very large house then can choose between installing either several small dehumidifiers or one large one. There is a clear relationship between the electrical rating of a machine and its moisture extraction rate, as is illustrated in *Figure 4.14*. It is customary to provide at least one air change per hour in the space in which the dehumidifier is sited. Typical moisture generation rates in the home have already been detailed in *Table 4.2*. A checklist to help prospective users of dehumidifiers to select machines appropriate to their needs is given in *Table 4.4*.

There is also a miniature domestic dehumidifier which works on the basis of a deliquescent dessicant. Calcium chloride has a strong affinity

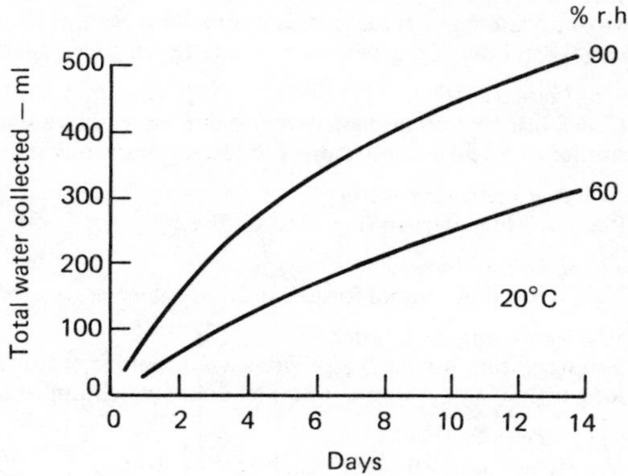

Figure 4.15 Small containers of deliquescent salts can be used to dehumidify well-fitting cupboards or tool boxes. The salt can be regenerated by heating the solution

for water vapour and will eventually dissolve itself and form a salt solution. Packets of such salts are sold together with a plastics container to hold the solution (*Figure 4.15*). Such devices extract a very small amount of moisture (3.5 ml/day) and are thrown away when dissolved. They are valuable in protecting the contents of small cupboards with tightly-fitting doors. Even smaller are the sachets of silica gel which often protect delicate electronic equipment while in transit through tropical countries. However, such methods are not recommended in spaces greater than 30 m^3.

4.3 User experience

Two surveys have recorded family experience in the use of dehumidifiers, the first being conducted by the Electricity Council in conjunction with Doulton Wallguard Ltd. From 150 purchasers of dehumidifiers over the previous three years, 82 took part in a questionnaire interview (*Table 4.5*). Dampness, mould or condensation were the reasons why people bought the dehumidifiers. The room in which the dehumidifier was most frequently sited was the bedroom (32%), followed by the hall, living-room and landing. Satisfaction was high, with 89% of purchasers satisfied. Over half of the families hardly ever moved the dehumidifier, and in most houses the water container was emptied every few days. The worst feature of the machine was their noise disturbance, while their best feature was that they cured the dampness.

The second survey comprised trials on three different sizes of dehumidifier which were conducted by the Building Research Station (BRS) and the Electricity Council in conjunction with tenants of the Inverclyde District Council and with the full support of that council. The Electricity Council loaned the dehumidifiers to the householders. The householders' responses to similar questions show similar replies—

TABLE 4.5 Surveys of households with a dehumidifier

	Local authority[(1)]	*Private purchasers*[(2)]	
Family size: adults	2.0	2.4	
children	1.4	0.5	
Problem:	2 damp rooms	Condensation troubles	61%
	1.8 rooms with mould	Damp	27%
		Condensation and damp	7%
		Mould and mildew	5%
In which room is the dehumidifier used?			
Living	4%		14%
Bedroom	96%		32%
Kitchen	0		11%
Bathroom	0		0
Hall	0		23%
Landing	0		10%
Is it moved about?	Yes 16%	Moved a lot	13%
	No 84%	Occasionally	31%
		Hardly ever	36%
		Never	20%
Satisfaction	Yes 84%	Very satisfied	47%
	No 16%	Quite satisfied	42%
		Not sure	3%
		Not very satisfied	7%
		Not at all satisfied	1%
Bad features	Yes: 56% said noise	Yes: 55% said noise	
		13% said difficult to move	
Frequency of emptying bucket		Twice a day	4%
		Daily	23%
		Every 2–3 days	13%
		Every 3–5 days	17%
		Weekly	19%
		Two-weekly	5%
		Monthly	2%

(1) BRS survey of 25 households in local authority flats, February 1983.
(2) Electricity Council survey in co-operation with Doulton Wallguard; 82 purchasers of dehumidifiers, February 1982.

satisfaction was very high (84%), most people did not move the machine around, and noise was the biggest undesirable feature of the machines.

4.4 Future trends

Domestic dehumidifiers are already becoming lighter, smaller, more transportable and more attractive. The appreciation of the importance of reducing noise in the home, particularly during the night, is now influencing the designs towards quieter units. There is already a British design (Andrews) which works successfully on a natural convection air flow so that there is only the very low noise from the compressor. Further technical advances include the use of the rotating-piston compressor to improve efficiency, reduce cost and noise and enhance reliability despite that reliability already being very good. They also include the use of an air/air heat-exchanger to improve the effectiveness of the cycle and to make the performance less sensitive to ambient entering relative humidity. One British company (Mons Precision Services Co-operative Ltd, Sheffield) has already produced a model and are actively selling it. Its performance is one-third better than the conventional units. The principles which apply to dehumidifiers will be discussed in detail in the general review of the future in Chapter 9.

The market for a domestic dehumidifier is potentially enormous in the mild temperature winter climate of Britain, the northern European coast and the cooler parts of the Mediterranean. It is also particularly useful in combatting dampness in unoccupied property, including spare rooms, second houses, caravans and boats. It is essentially for the whole of the present building stock.

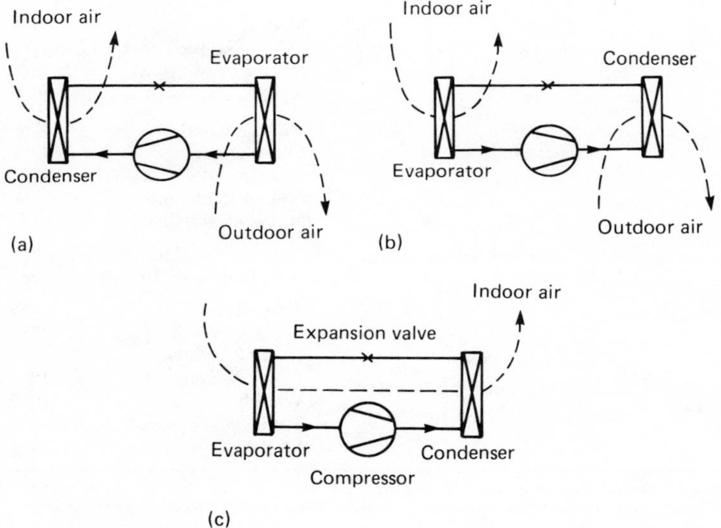

Figure 4.16 Three-function heat-pump air conditioners are popular in Japan. They can provide heating in winter, cooling in summer and dehumidification in spring and autumn. (a) Heating cycle (indoor air over condenser). (b) Cooling cycle (indoor air over evaporator). (c) Dehumidifier cycle (indoor air over evaporator then condenser; no outdoor air)

There is not likely to be a market for dehumidifiers in new homes in Britain, which are incorporating mechanical ventilation systems with heat recovery. Such systems not only control dampness, they also give quite excellent indoor climates, and obviate the need for dehumidifiers.

The situation is different for damper climates, such as that in Japan. Where summer conditions require air conditioning, the air-conditioning units are now being designed for 'three-season operation'. In summer they provide conventional cooling (*Figure 4.16*), while in winter they convert to an air-source heat pump by reversing the cycle and using the outdoor heat exchanger as an evaporator to provide a heat source. In spring and autumn there are often cool damp spells when some heating and dehumidification are needed, and during this period the air-conditioning unit can be switched into a simple dehumidification role.

4.5 Standards and guides

4.5.1 BS 4788: 1972. Specification for rating and testing of refrigerated dehumidifiers (British Standards Institution, Milton Keynes). Table 4.6 and Figure 4.17.

The refrigeration, heating and air-conditioning industry Standards Committee supervized the preparation of this British Standard which defines five standard tests for three classes of dehumidifier. The classes are based on design operating temperatures of 5°, 15° and 35°C. The five tests are:

(1) *Design rating*. This is the condensate extracted per day at one of the three specified design temperatures and a relative humidity of 50%. The rating is based on at least six hours' running, starting after one hour's operation. Recommended units are kg/day.

(2) *Maximum operating conditions*. After two hours' operation at 110% of design voltage the unit has to restart satisfactorily after a three-minute break and run for a further hour. The test is repeated at 90% design voltage. The operating temperatures are defined in *Table 4.5* but are dry-bulb temperatures of 30°C for machines designed for 5°C and 15°C and 52°C for the 35°C unit.

TABLE 4.6 BS4788: 1972 Specification for rating and testing of refrigerated dehumidifiers
(for full details please refer to the actual standard specification)

Classification	*A*	*B*	*C*
1. *Design rating*			
Dry-bulb temperature °C	5°C	15°C	35°C
Wet-bulb temperature °C	1.4°C	9.7°C	26.2°C
Relative humidity*	50%	50%	50%
Units of condensate extraction	kg/24h	kg/24h	kg/24h
2. *Maximum operating conditions*			
Dry-bulb temperature	30°C	30°C	52°C
Wet-bulb temperature	20°C	20°C	32°C
Relative humidity	39%	39%	25%
3. *Freeze-up conditions*			
Dry-bulb temperature	5°C	5°C	20°C
Wet-bulb temperature	2.9°C	2.9°C	15.5°C
Relative humidity	70%	70%	62%
4. *Sweat test*			
Dry-bulb temperature	5°C	15°C	35°C
Wet-bulb temperature	4.7°C	14.5°C	34.9°C
Relative humidity	95%	95%	99%
5. *Condensate disposal*	No drips with 5° tilt on unit		

*The relative humidity values are not given in the standard–these values assume that 'wet-bulb' is 'sling wet-bulb'

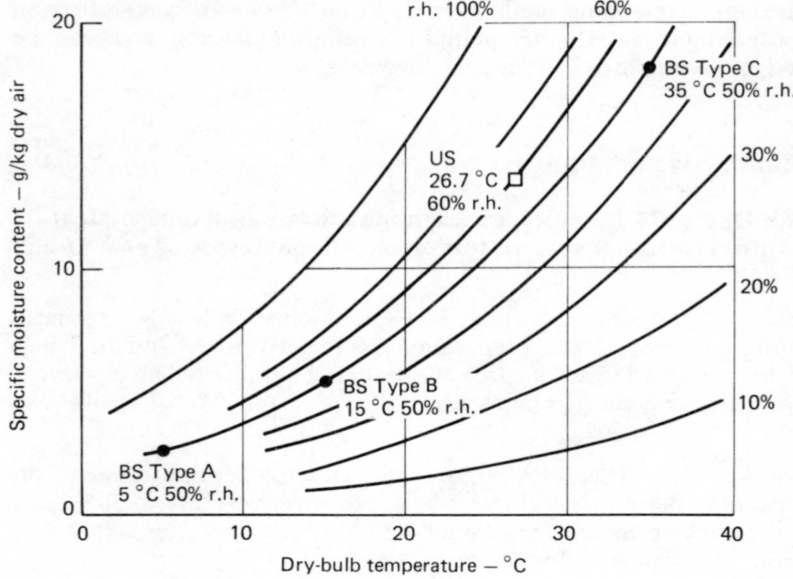

Figure 4.17 Standard rating conditions for domestic dehumidifiers in Britain and the USA

(3) *Freeze-up conditions.* If no defrosting cycle is used then the dehumidifier should not have ice on the evaporator heat-exchanger after twelve hours' operation at the freezing conditions specified for each machine type. If there is a defrost then the refrigeration cycle should operate for at least 90% of the time and no ice should remain at the end of each cycle.

(4) *Enclosure sweat test.* This is designed to avoid unplanned water flow. The dehumidifier should not drip water or blow droplets under the worse of these test conditions.

(5) *Condensate disposal.* This is designed to ensure that the drainage is adequate, even if the dehumidifier is tilted 5° away from the vertical.

The dehumidifier should have a nameplate identifying its type. This standard is not widely known and in practice it is not used by manufacturers. BS 3456: 1973, *The testing and approval of household electrical appliances*, covers general safety matters.

4.5.2 American National Standard B149.1: 1972, AHAM DH-1. Dehumidifiers. (Assoc of Home Appliance Manufacturers, Chicago, USA) Table 4.7.

This American standard applies to self-contained electrically-operated, mechanically-refrigerated dehumidifiers, and it has four requirements:

(1) *Standard rating.* This is the condensate collected in 24 hours at 26.7°C and 60% r.h. ambient. The test must last at least six hours. The recommended units are pints per 24 hours.

(2) *Maximum operating conditions*. This is 32.2°C (90°F) 50% r.h. at 110% of rated voltage. The dehumidifier is run for two hours, switched off for two minutes and then run for a further hour. This test is also run at 90% of the rated voltage.

(3) *Low-temperature test*. The conditions are 18.3°C (65°F) 60% r.h. If there is no provision for defrost, the dehumidifier must run for at least eight hours without ice formation. If there is a defrost cycle then the refrigeration system must operate for at least 50% of the time and no ice must be left at the end of each cycle.

TABLE 4.7 American National Standard B149.1–1972; AHAM DH-1 Dehumidifiers (issued by the Association of Home Appliance Manufacturers, USA)

1. *Standard rating**	
Dry-bulb temperature °C (°F)	26.7°C (80°F)
Relative humidity	60%
Units	pints/24 hours
2. *Maximum operating condition*	
Dry-bulb temperature °C (°F)	32.2°C (90°F)
Relative humidity	50%
3. *Low temperature-test*	
(8 hours with no ice at end)	
Dry-bulb temperature °C (°F)	18.3°C (65°F)
Relative humidity	60%
4. *Production units*	
Not less than	92% of prototype rating

*The rating can be derived at other temperatures from the following:

$$\text{Rating lb/day} = C_t + 0.025\, C_t\,(80 - r_t) + 0.022\, C_t\,(60 - H_c)$$

$$\text{where } C_t = \frac{\text{condensate actually collected (lb)} \times 24}{\text{duration of test period} \times 1.04}$$

T_t = average dry-bulb temperature °F
H_c = average relative humidity corrected for barometric pressure according to the formula

$$H_c = H_t[1 + 0.0063(29.921 - B]$$

where H_t = average r.h. for the test
B = average barometric pressure in inches of mercury

(4) *Production units*. Samples from the production line must not fall below 92% of the rated performance.

This standard is accepted and quoted by all American manufacturers.

4.5.3 Underwriters' Laboratories: Dehumidifiers; standard for safety. Underwriters' Laboratory USA Report UL 474, June 1973, amended March 1974.

This standard is complementary to the AHAM National US Performance Standard. The rating condition is identical at 26.7°C dry-bulb temperature 60% r.h., but the dehumidifiers have to work safely at 40°C dry-bulb temperature and 34% r.h.

4.5.4 Canadian Standards Association: C22.2 No 92-1971. Dehumidifiers

This is the Canadian safety standard for mechanical refrigeration indoor dehumidifiers with a cooling capacity not exceeding 10.5 kW (3 tons) of refrigeration. It includes requirements for the electrical features of the equipment and for the safety of the refrigerating systems. The test conditions are specified at 35°C ambient dry-bulb and 23.9°C wet-bulb (40% r.h.).

4.5.5 US Energy Policy and Conservation Act 1975: Public Law 94-163

The US Department of Energy is the administrator of this law which prescribes energy efficiency improvements required in equipment. Dehumidifiers are not a high priority item but a 19% improvement target over 1972 has been prescribed. This requires present US equipment to extract 1.105 litres/kWh compared with the 1972 base figure of 0.929/kWh.

4.5.6 Capacity selection guide

The American manufacturers share a capacity selection guide to cater for dehumidification during warm and humid outdoor conditions. This is presented in *Table 4.8*. This shows the design rating of dehumidifier needed to cure the condition described. There is a second US guide which suggests that domestic dehumidifiers will maintain satisfactory levels of humidity in an enclosed space when the air flow rate and placement of the dehumidifier permit the entire air volume of the space to be moved through the dehumidifier once an hour.

There are no guides for use in Britain but a figure of 1 litre/24 hours per person, extracted at 10°C 70% r.h. ambient should be adequate until better guidance can be given. Divide the American ratings by four to estimate water extraction rates at 10°C 70% r.h.

TABLE 4.8 Dehumidifier selection guide for warm and humid outdoor conditions
(guidelines used in USA for summer use)

Condition without dehumidification	*Area of room in m²*			
	50	*100*	*150*	*200*
Moderately damp —				
space feels damp and has musty odour only in humid weather	5.1 litres/24h	7.1 litres/24h	9.2 litres/24h	11.2 litres/24h
Very damp —				
space always feels damp and has musty odour. Damp spots show on walls and floor	6.1 litres/24h	8.6 litres/24h	11.2 litres/24h	13.8 litres/24h
Wet —				
space feels and smells wet. Walls or floor sweat or seepage present	7.1 litres/24h	10.2 litres/24h	13.2 litres/24h	16.3 litres/24h

This table shows the size of dehumidifier recommended to combat dampness in rooms when the outdoor climate is warm and humid. These values relate to extraction rates at 26.7°C 60% r.h. They are USA guidelines and are not appropriate for indoor conditions in Britain in winter.

4.6 Further reading on condensation and domestic dehumidifiers

4.6.1 Condensation

Her Majesty's Stationery Office. *Condensation in Dwellings.* HMSO, London, 1970

McDonald, D.P. 'Condensation: a conference report'. *Inste of Htg & Ventn Engrs Jnl*, **38**, 29–36, 1970

Day, B. and Burberry, P. 'Condensation in buildings'. *Architects' Jnl*, 1149–1159, May 1971

Building Research Establishment. 'Prevention of condensation'. *BRE Digest* 91 (2nd series), 1968

Croome, D.J. and Sherratt, A.F.C. (eds) 'Condensation in buildings'. *Applied Science*, London, 1972

Kenwood, H.R. 'Dampness in houses'. *Public Health Jnl*, **5**, 247–250, 1983

Willock, D.A. 'Condensation in dwellings'. *Housing Monthly*, 14–18, Nov/Dec 1977

Smith, J.M., Blome, C.E., Hauser, H., Eades, A. and Hite, S.C. *Research in Home Humidity Control.* Purdue Univ Engg Sta Res Series 106, 1948

British Standards Institution. *Basic Data for the Design of Buildings: the Control of Condensation.* BS 5250: 1975

Atkinson, G. 'Water, water'. *Building.* 40–41, 14 Aug 1981

Preston, G.K., Stephens, C.J. and Brundrett, G.W. 'The Newcastle Condensation Survey'. BSER & T, **2** (2), 93–99, 1981

Consumers' Guide. 'Condensation'. *Handyman WHICH*? 292–294, May 1981

Wild, A. and Pate, T. 'Condensation and mould growth in dwellings'. *PSA Constn* (**35**), June 1981

Richardson, S.A. *Protecting Buildings.* David & Charles, Newton Abbot, 1977

Sanders, C.H. 'Condensation and its treatment'. *Bldg Techy & Managet*, **18** (11), 1980

Cornish, J.P. and Sanders, C.H. 'Condensation and mould growth in dwellings'. 7th Nat Bldg Maint Conf, 16 pp, London, Nov 1982

Kooi, I.V. and Knorr, K.Th. 'The temperature and humidity in houses'. *Klimaatbeheersing*, **2** (10), 490–496, 1973. Elecy Ccl trans, OA 1966: 1982

Sanders, C.H. and Cornish, J.P. 'Dampness complaints'. *BRE News*, **58**, 2–3, 1982

Sanders, C.H. and Cornish, J.P. 'Dampness: one week's complaints in five local authorities in England and Wales'. *BRE Rep*, HMSO, 1982

Gratwick, R.T. *Dampness in Buildings.* Crosby Lockwood, London, 1966

Royal Institute of Chartered Surveyors. *Condensation Problems: New and Existing Buildings.* RICS, London, 1979

Cornish, P. 'Condensation and mould growth'. *Bldg Servs Jnl*, 75, Sept 1984

Byrd, R.H. 'Condensation in terrace housing: causes and cures'. *Bldg Servs Engg Res and Techy*, **6**, No 3, 109–116, 1985

4.6.2 Domestic dehumidifiers

Alsing, E.C. 'The dehumidifier in today's home'. *Refrign Engg*, **61** (2), 157–159, 1953

Brundrett, G.W. 'Moisture control in buildings: opportunities for a heat pump dehumidifier'. CIB Intern Sem, Dubrovnik, Yugoslavia, 1977

Peck, F.G. 'Mechanical dehumidifiers come of age'. *Refrign Engg*, **60** (9) 956–958, 1952

Brundrett, G.W. and Blundell, C.J. 'An advanced dehumidifier for Britain'. *Htg & Veng Engr*, 6–7, Nov, 1980

Brundrett, G.W. 'Advanced dehumidifiers for moisture control'. *Bldg Res & Prac*, 98–101, Mar/Apr 1981

British Standards Institution, BS 4788: *Specification for Rating and Testing of Refrigerated Dehumidifiers.* BSI, London, 1972

Underwriters' Laboratories. *Dehumidifiers: Standards for Safety.* Underwriters' Labs, (USA), UL Standard 474, 3rd edn, Jun 1973

Assoc of Home Appliance Manufacturers. 'Dehumidifiers'. NASI-AHAM B149.1 1972-DW 1, AHAM, Chicago, USA, 1972

Am Soc of Htg, Refrign and Air Condg Engrs. 'Room air conditioners and dehumidifiers'. In *ASHRAE Handbook:* Equipment 1983, Chap 41, ASHRAE, Atlanta, USA, 1979

Brundrett, G.W. 'Controlling moisture in the home'. First Intern Cong on Bldg Energy Managet, Oporto, Portugal, May 1980

Electricity Council, *Electric Heat Pumps*, 1983. Heat Pump & Air Conditg Bureau, 30 Millbank, London, SW1P 4RD

Skeet, P. 'High humidity—extraction of moisture the answer'. *Do-It-Yourself Magazine*, 27 Feb 1983

Galbraith, G.H. and Brundrett, G.W. 'Dehumidifiers in houses at Greenock, Scotland'. *Htg & Ventg Engr*, 27–30, Apr/May 1984

Brundrett, G.W. 'A guide to packaged dehumidifiers'. Memo by Elecy Ccl Res Cen, Capenhurst, ECRC/M1871, 1984

Sanders, C.H. 'Domestic dehumidifiers'. *Bldg Servs Jnl*, 93, Sept 1985

Chapter 5

Swimming-pool dehumidification

5.1 Background

The starting point for the building service engineer in the design of a swimming pool is the water temperature. This varies according to the intended use and has risen in recent years. Therapeutic pools, usually associated with hospitals or health centres, operate at between 29 and 35°C. Conventional pleasure pools operate at between 24 and 27°C. The tendency in public pools is to operate at the highest temperature because attendance at pools declines at the lowest temperature. Competitive swimming and training pools operate at 22 to 24°C.

Humidity control is traditionally achieved by dilution with fresh air. Design targets are 50–60% r.h. The air temperature is chosen to be 1 or 2°C above the water temperature. This meets the comfort requirements of the pool-side swimming and ensures that natural convection currents rising from the pool surface are inhibited. Fresh air is also needed to provide pleasure and comfortable conditions for the bather (20 to 45 m^3/h/person). The amount needed for humidity control usually dominates that required for comfort, therefore the designer uses the highest of the two values, which is moisture control[1–6].

In 1950 half of the major pools in Britain used fixed ventilation rates of between 2 and 16 a.c.h. Private pools had no planned ventilation other than by opening a window. Today most people have 3 to 4 a.c.h[1]. Recommended ventilation rates are ill-defined. The Ministry of Housing and Local Government Design Bulletin Number 4[7] recommends 2 to 3 a.c.h. The professional Building Services Guide (CIBS Book B, 1970)[8] recommends 72 $m^3/h/m^2$ plus a margin of 20% for wetted pool surrounds. Another British guide[1] recommends 60 $m^3/h/m^2$ recirculation air-flow of which 25% should be fresh air. A German guide (RWE)[9] recommends a ventilation rate of 30 $m^3/h/m^2$ normally and 15 $m^3/h/m^2$ when the outdoor temperature drops below 0°C.

The constant evaporation of water from a pool to the air extracts heat from the pool. A heat supply is provided to meet this evaporative loss, and from time to time the pool water is drained away and replaced. The energy cost of this is high but normally it is done only once a year.

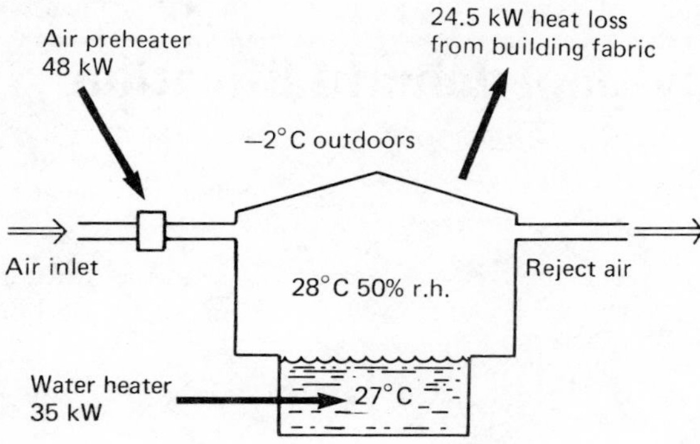

Heat balance for 145 m² swimming pool

	Design day power	% total
Ventilation for moisture control: 4720 m³/h	48.0 kW	44.0
Water heating to combat evaporation: 50.4 kg/h	35.0 kW	33.0
Heat loss through the building fabric 28°C indoor, −2°C outdoor	24.5 kW	23.0
Total	107.5 kW	100.0
Energy needed to heat pool water through 1°C	290 kWh	

Figure 5.1 Illustration of heat losses in a medium-sized swimming pool (Harrison, 1975)[10]

The building envelope itself loses heat to the outside. This is a function of the exposure, the amount, orientation and type of glass installed, and the thermal transmittance of the walls, roof and floor.

The design requirements of a medium-sized indoor swimming pool are illustrated in *Figure 5.1*[10]. This shows that almost 80% of the design requirements are associated with moisture control, partly through preheating the fresh incoming air used to replace discarded moisture laden air and partly to compensate for the evaporative losses from the pool surface. The potential benefits of electrical dehumidification are therefore immense[11–13]. The dehumidifier not only provides heating with a heat-pump coefficient of performance (CoP) of around 2.0 but it also eliminates the need for the ventilation to control moisture. No fresh-air ventilation is needed during the unoccupied period and only that for odour control during occupancy.

5.2 Evaporation

Dalton was an English physicist who, in the nineteenth century, explored the factors influencing evaporation rates[14]. He proposed the basic law which is used today.

evaporation/m^2 of surface = k x (vapour pressure difference between pool water surface and pool air)

The factor is a function of the air velocity. In the succeeding two centuries many researchers have introduced their own version of 'k' and there is still no agreement on its value for a swimming pool. There are two reasons for this:

(1) The wetted surface area is not known. The actual wetted surface is always greater than the pool water surface. This is attributed partly to the bodies of the bathers themselves and partly to ripples and splashing and dropping onto the surrounding walking areas. Children have a more pronounced effect on evaporation than adults because of their enthusiastic splashing. However, there is better agreement between authors on the evaporation rate during unoccupied hours when this factor is not applicable.

TABLE 5.1 Different guides to the evaporation constant k

Daltons's evaporation law may be stated:

$$\text{evaporation g/m}^2\text{h} = \text{k.}\left[\begin{matrix}\text{saturated vapour press}\\ \text{of liquid}\end{matrix} - \begin{matrix}\text{vapour press}\\ \text{in air}\end{matrix}\right] \text{millibar}$$

The following table gives different authors figures for the value of k

Author	*Type*	*Year*	*Evaporation constant k*
Dalton	Experimental	1802	20 for still air 32 for brisk movement
Carrier	Experimental	1929	13.4 (1 + 0.85v)
Powell and Griffiths	Experimental	1935	$11.6 (1 + 6v^{0.85})$
Gettman	Guide	1969	13.4
CIBS Guide	Professional guide for Britain	1970	9.6–15.1 low value for still air higher value for 0.25 m/s
Milbank	Experimental	1975	8.5–16.1
VDI 2089	Professional guide for Germany	1977	13 for private pools 28 for normal pools 35 for wave-machine pools
Villain	Experimental–adopted as French Government guide	1977	10 for calm water 10 + 84 n for occupied pools where n = people/m^2 pool; $n_{max} = 0.2$
ASHRAE Applications	Professional guide for USA	1978	14.4 for air speeds up to 0.15 m/s
Reeker	Measurement	1978	6.9 unoccupied 12.8 occupied
RWE*	Electric utility design guide for private and hotel pools	1983/4	4.5–5.6 for unoccupied pool 9 for 1 person to 40 m^2 pool 11.2 for 1 person to 20 m^2 pool 17.8 for 1 person to 10 m^2 pool

*Recommended for use for private pools

(2) The local air flow is influenced by bathers' activities. Air-flow measurements, when they are taken in a pool, are recorded in an unoccupied pool. The boundary layer conditions are stable and constant. An occupied pool has much activity and this breaks up the boundary layer which is half a m thick and enhances local heat and mass transfer. It takes minutes for the layer to re-establish.

Different relationships are listed in *Table 5.1*[15–24]. There is agreement that the lowest evaporation constant, which would correspond to an unoccupied pool, is between 8 and 10. There is less unanimity in the factor for the occupied pool. The German and French recommendations favour 25–28[20,21]. The relations linking evaporation to population are summarized in *Figure 5.2*. The German electricity utility RWE has much experience with swimming pools. Its recommendations for private or hotel pools follow the french trend but at a lower value. This would be expected from the type of use which would favour quiet adult use. This RWE relationship is recommended for private pools[24].

New techniques are continuously coming forward to cover the pool surface during unoccupied periods. These are strongly recommended in principle but at present they are available for only small/medium-sized pools where the sheer bulk of the wet cover is still handleable (*Figure 5.3*).

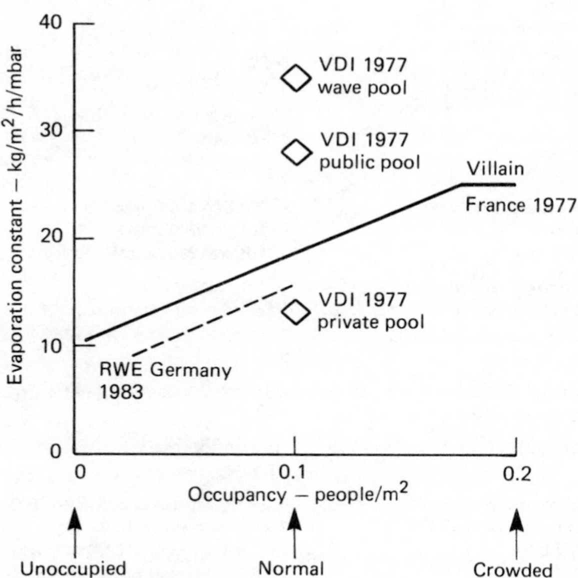

Figure 5.2 Change in the evaporation constant k for different pool occupancies

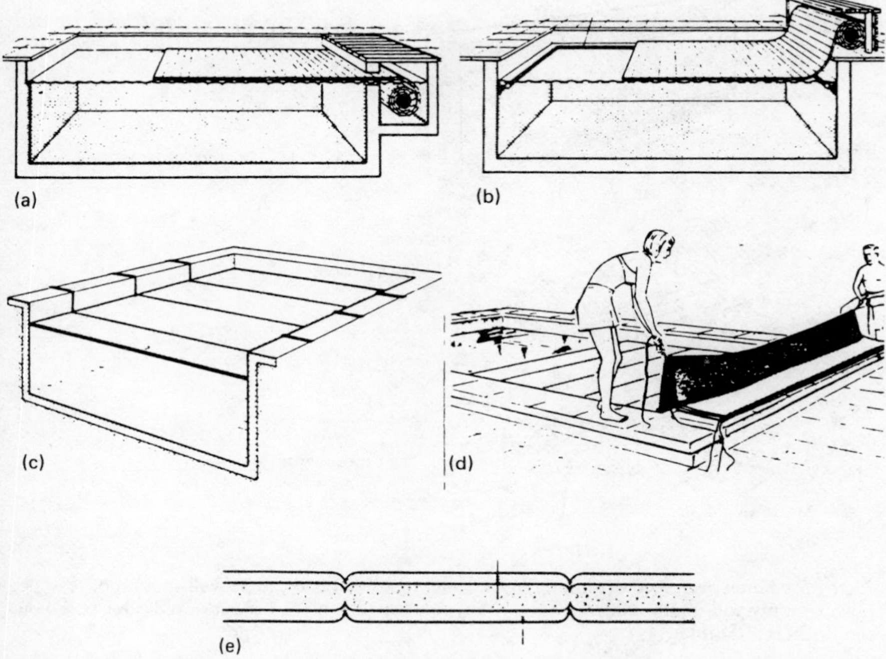

Figure 5.3 Pool covers inhibit evaporation, but they must be kept clean. (a) Submerged roller cover. (b) Poolside roller cover. (c) Flotation cover. (d) Manual withdrawal of flotation shutter. (e) Construction of flotation cover—a tough protective cover with aerated interior (RWE, 1974)

New flotation types now being offered rest on the pool floor until needed, when compressed air is injected and the cover floats to the surface. Care is needed to ensure that pool hygiene is unaffected by the covers. Covering techniques save energy by reducing evaporation but they do not influence the size of the dehumidifier needed for the occupied period.

5.3 Pool dehumidifier

The electric heat-pump dehumidifier can be used in a variety of ways to recover the latent heat of evaporation of the water vapour and return the energy to either the pool water or air or both. This means that the ventilation requirements will also be reduced to those needed for contamination control and comfort.

In the simplest case usually used in the smaller pools the dehumidifier will be mounted in the pool hall and will simply recycle the pool air, dehumidifying it and then reheating it. There is a range of attractively styled units, *Figure 5.4*.

The larger pool will usually have a full-ducted air supply designed to keep the glazing condensation-free. The packaged dehumidifiers are available in a large range of sizes and can return the heat either to the air or

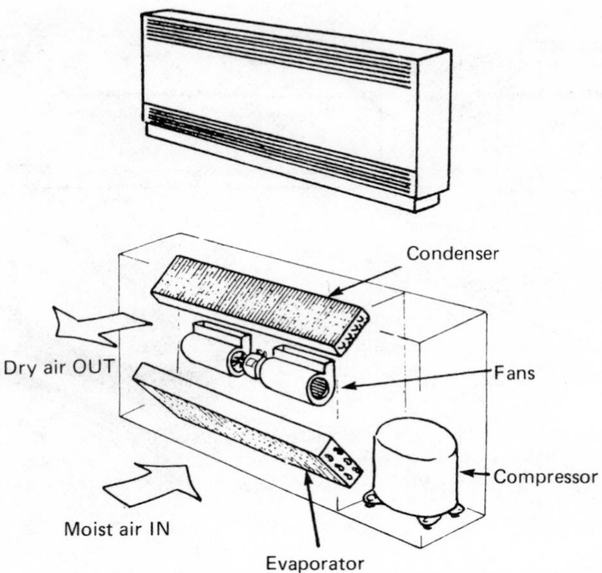

Figure 5.4 Small packaged dehumidifiers are self-contained and can be wall-mounted. A power supply and small-diameter water drain pipe are the only services needed (illus based on the Fritherm, Germany)

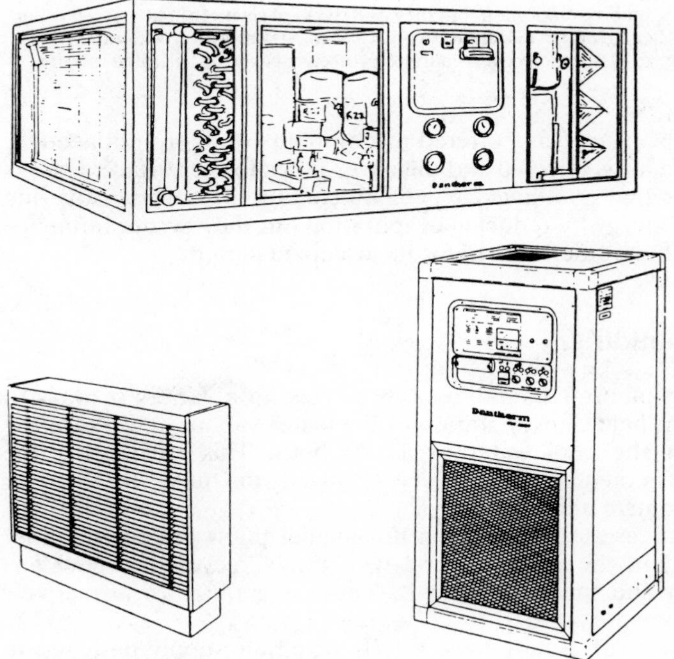

Figure 5.5 There is a wide range of packaged dehumidifiers specially designed for swimming pools (courtesy of Dantherm)

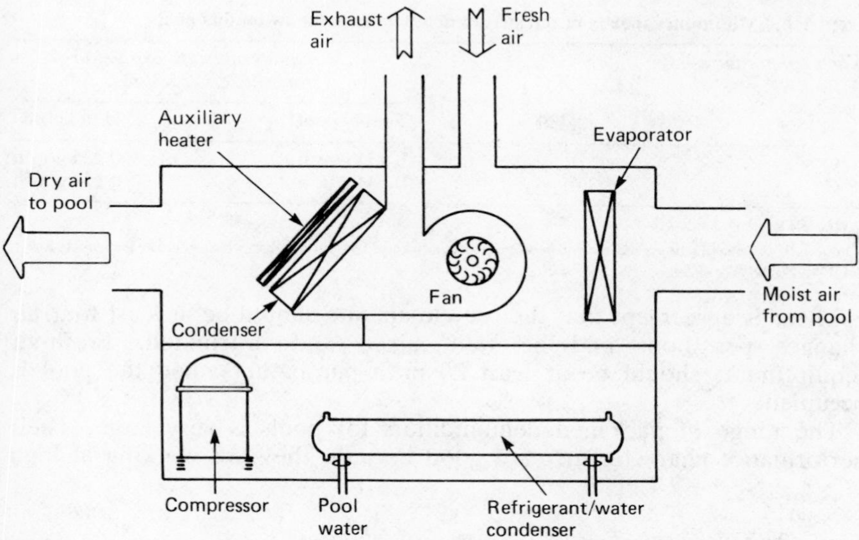

Figure 5.6 A packaged dehumidifier for medium-sized swimming pools can dry the air and supply some heat to the pool water through a separate water/refrigerant condenser

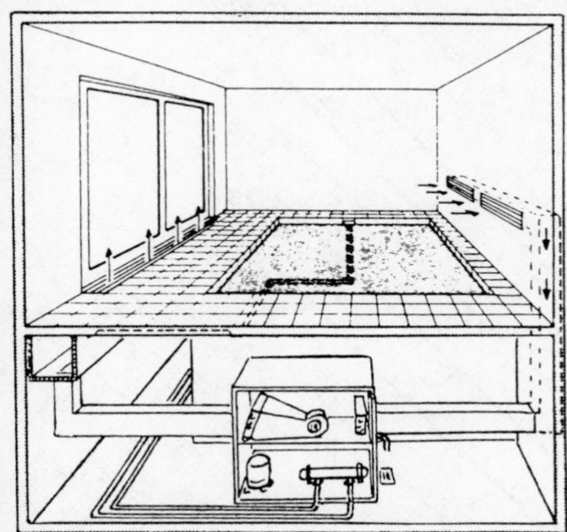

Figure 5.7 Typical illustration of small hotel swimming pool, 32 m^2 water, 70 m^2 hall (RWE, 1983)

to the pool water directly (*Figure 5.5*). A schematic illustration is given in *Figure 5.6* and a typical layout for a small hotel pool is shown in *Figure 5.7*.

German experience suggests that the occupancy for a private house pool will be one person for 40 m^2 of pool surface, while a hotel pool will have one person for 10 m^2 of pool surface. These conditions, for an air temperature of 28°C and a relative humidity of 55%, leads to the RWE sizing recommendation given in *Table 5.2*. British manufacturers recommend much smaller design loads which are appropriate for cool pool water temperatures.

TABLE 5.2 Minimum capacity of refrigerant dehumidifiers for swimming pools

Water temperature	*Minimum moisture extraction rates at 28°C 55% r.h.*	
	Family pool*	Hotel pool
26°C	0.13 kg/m²h	0.22 kg/m²h
28°C	0.14 kg/m²h	0.25 kg/m²h

(RWE, W Germany, 1983/84)

*Caution: British manufacturers recommend between 0.04 kg/m²h and 0.06 kg/m²h, values which would be inadequate for water temperatures ~ 26°C.

There is agreement that the recycle air rate should be at least four air changes per hour and be well mixed and distributed. Fresh-air requirements should be at least 20 m³/h per bather when the pool is occupied.

The range of packaged dehumidifiers for pools is very large. Their performance characteristics are good because they are working at high

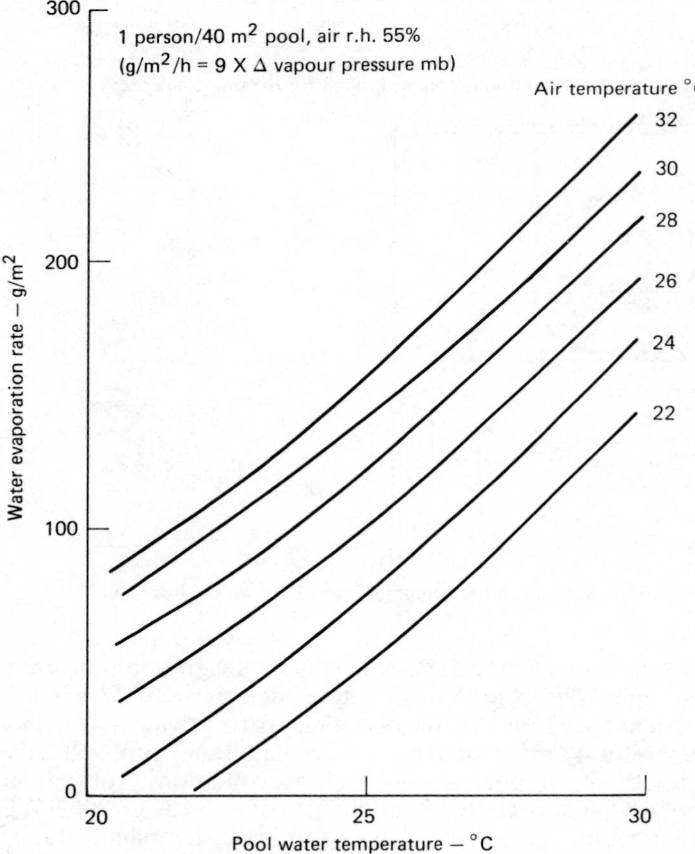

Figure 5.8 Evaporation rates for a home indoor swimming pool (double the values for a hotel pool with one person/10 m²) (RWE, 1983/4)

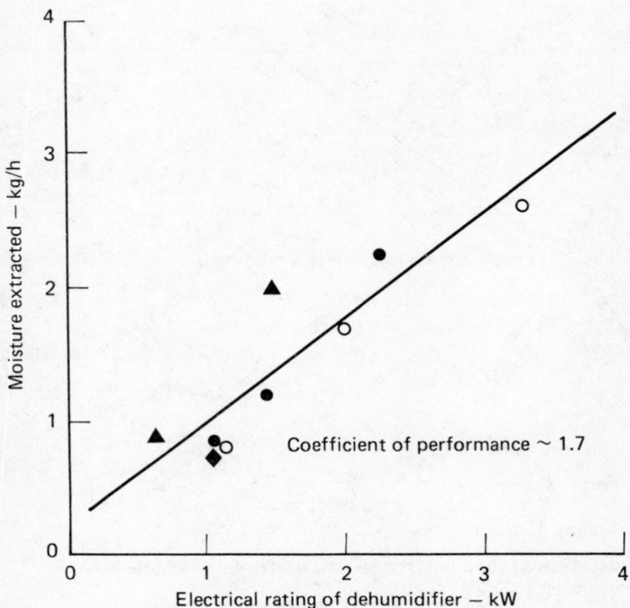

Figure 5.9 Illustrative relationship between moisture extraction rate and electrical size of small domestic pool dehumidifier (most points represent inlet air at 27°C 60% r.h., except those shown O which are rated at 30°C 60% r.h.)

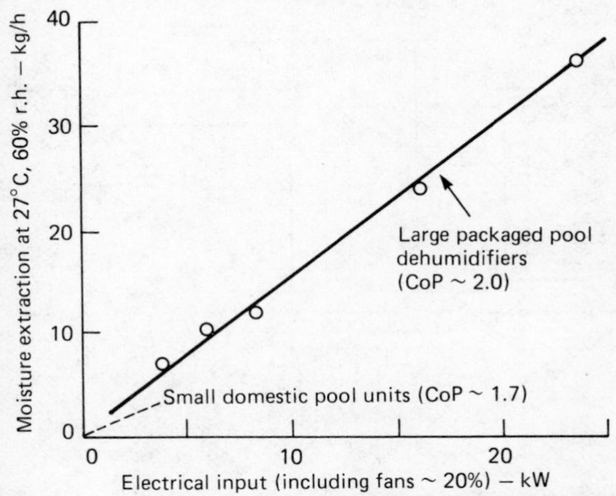

Figure 5.10 An illustration of the moisture extraction rate as a function of electrical size of the dehumidifier (CoP ~ 2.0) (data from Walkair trade catalogues, 1983)

ambient relative humidities. The larger machines are usually more effective than the smaller but CoP are typically 1.7 to 2.0.

Sizing of the dehumidifier for non-standard water- and air-temperature conditions can be determined from data given in *Figure 5.8*. These determine the evaporation rate for a quiet domestic pool, and the values should be doubled for hotel use.

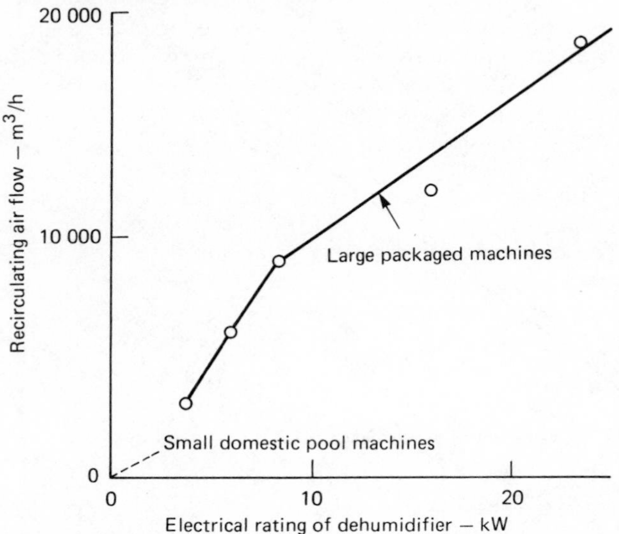

Figure 5.11 Air recirculation rate as a function of the electrical size of the dehumidifier (check: air-flow should give at least 4 a.c.h.)

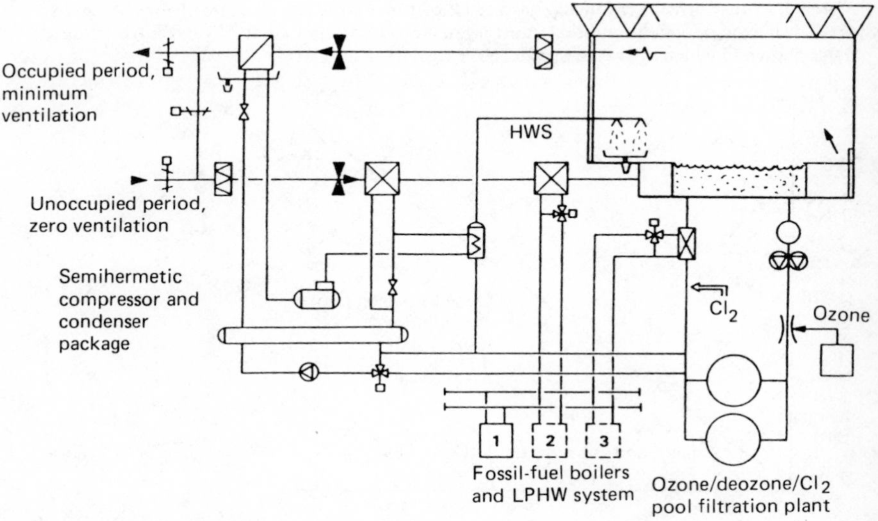

Figure 5.12 Conventional layout of a dehumidifier swimming pool (Braham, 1981)[13]

The electrical rating of the dehumidifier can be estimated approximately from the manufacture's data supplied in *Figure 5.9* for small machines and *Figure 5.10* for larger ones. All but the very smallest machines require three-phase electrical supply.

Check calculations on the air flow should show that the pool hall has at least four air changes per hour. Manufacturers' data on air flow are given in *Figure 5.11* for a range of dehumidifiers.

In large public pools the energy consumption can be reduced to less than 25% of that in a conventional pool. Improved management techniques of using better ventilation control and variable fresh-air flows can reduce the savings even further. One illustration is shown in *Figure 5.12*. The fresh-air requirement is matched to the occupants' need and can be switched off completely when the pool is unoccupied. The dehumidifier is split between the two air streams with the evaporator coil in the pool extract and the condenser in the pool air supply. The condenser is split so that in warm outdoor conditions the dehumidifier can heat the pool water directly. A reheater battery is placed immediately before the air inlet to the pool to top up any shortcomings in cold weather. Specialist professional advice is required for the large integrated pools.

5.4 Future trends

Advances in heat-recovery techniques now mean that the dehumidifier can be combined with a heat-recovery circuit to improve the effectiveness of the system even more. The heat-recovery circuit is usually of the 'run round' recirculating brine type, an illustration of which is shown in *Figure 5.13*. The heating analysis chart for such a system is shown in *Figure 5.14*. The combination of heat recovery, normal solar gains and lighting energy can provide the bulk of the heating needed. Heat-pipe heat-exchangers will also serve this function, provided that the supply and extract ducting are sufficiently close together. A commercial scheme is illustrated in *Figure 5.15*.

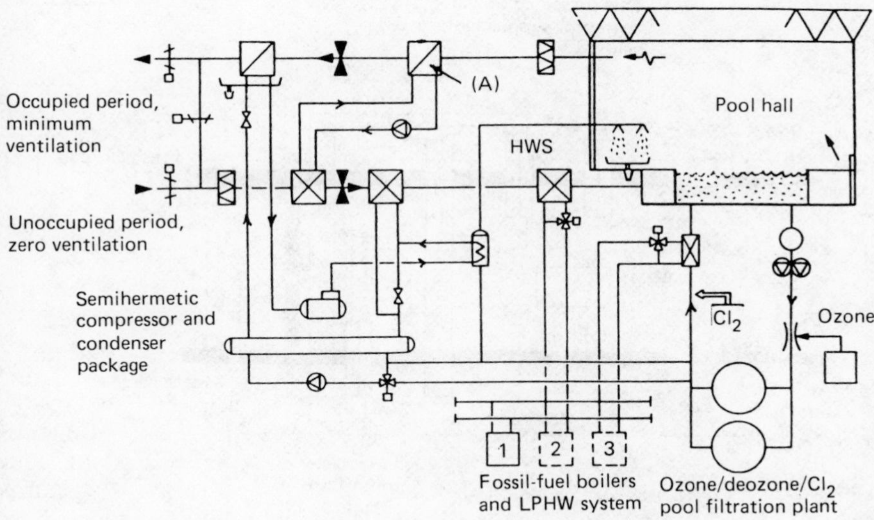

Figure 5.13 To enhance performance, the advanced dehumidifier system incorporates an additional heat transfer loop (A) which takes heat from the outgoing air to heat the incoming fresh air (Braham, 1981)[13]

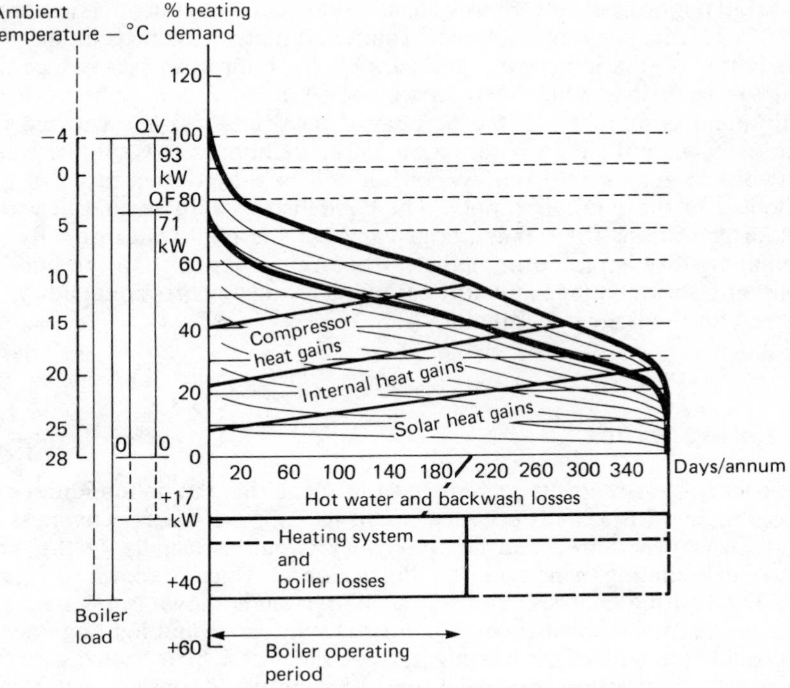

Figure 5.14 Heating analysis chart for the advanced dehumidifier. The area under the degree day curve represents energy (Braham, 1981)[13]

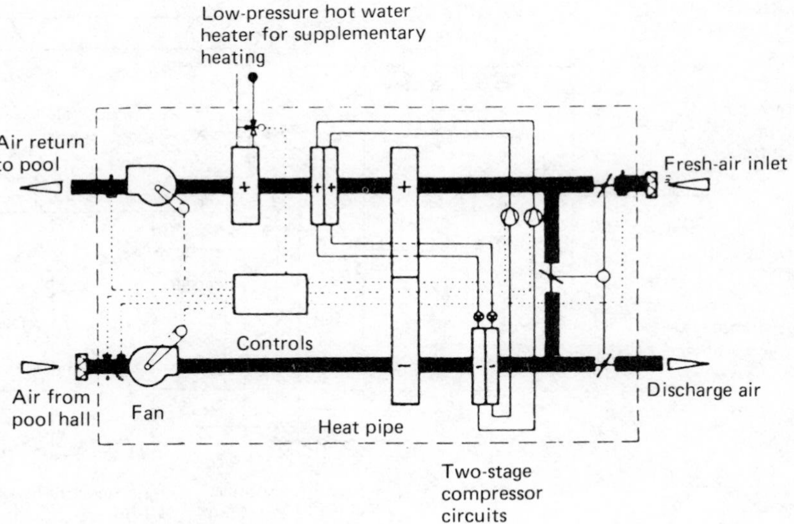

Figure 5.15 Significant improvements in performance are possible when a heat-pipe exchanger is linked across the airstream to reinforce the dehumidifier (courtesy of Fritherm, Germany)

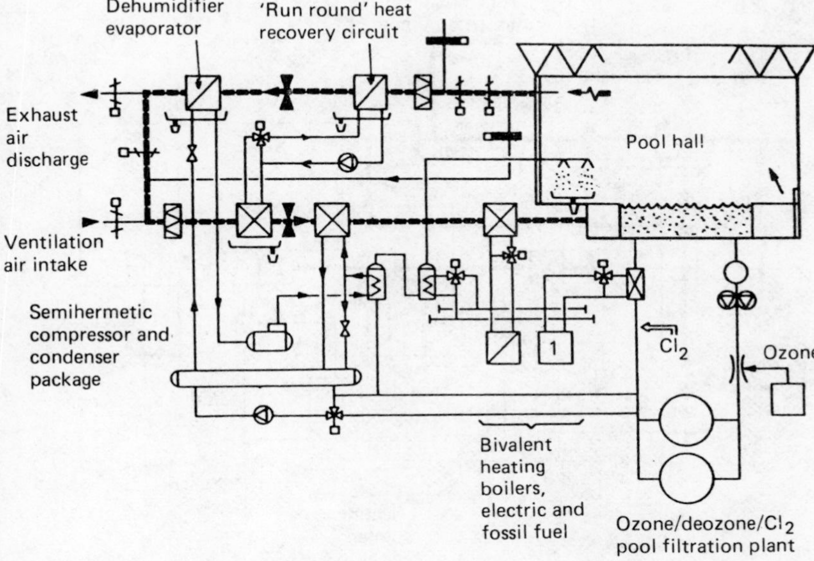

Figure 5.16 The pool dehumidifier in normal use during the occupied period

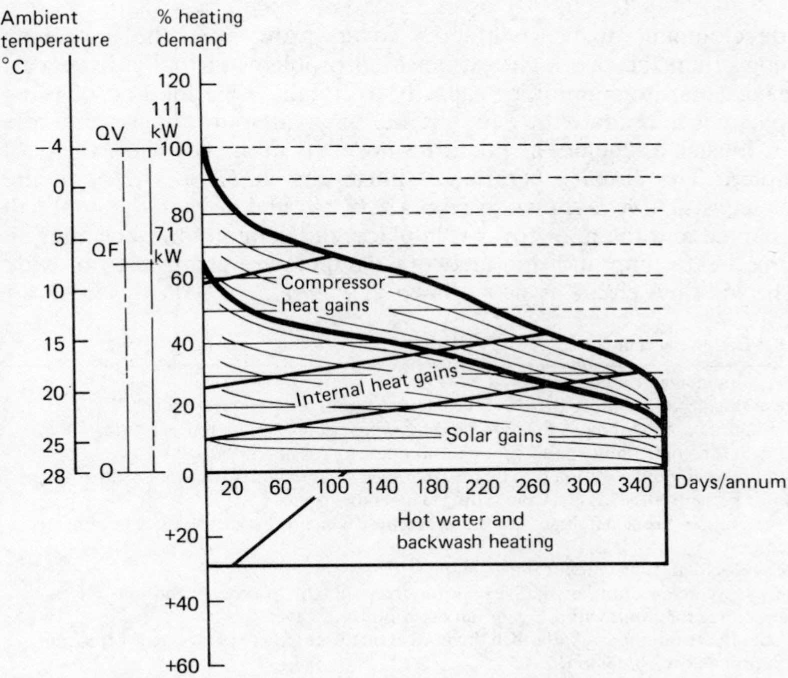

Figure 5.17 Heating analysis chart for the daytime operation of the dehumidifier (13 hours occupied). The area under the degree day curve represents energy

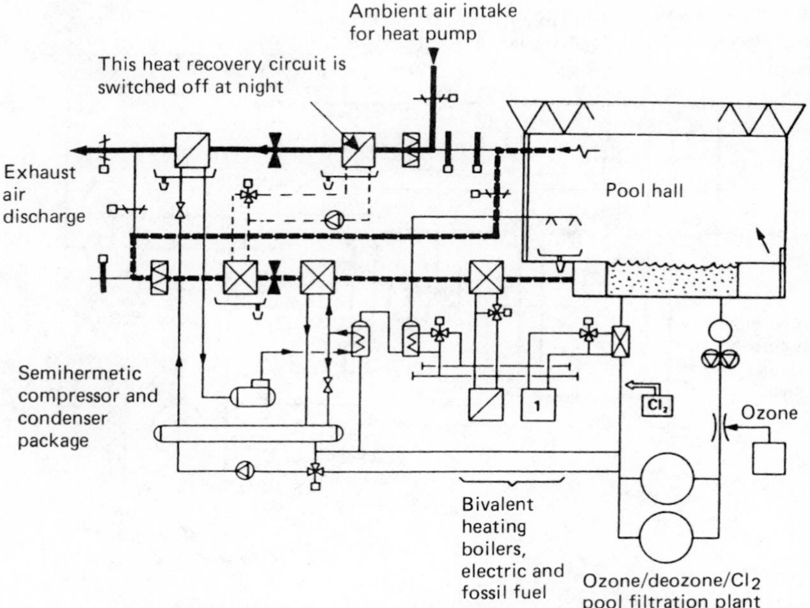

Figure 5.18 Electric dehumidifier in use as an air-source heat pump at night. Pool covers inhibit evaporation and no fresh-air mechanical ventilation is provided (Braham, 1981)[13]

As development in overnight pool covers grows with the improving technology then the overnight evaporation problems virtually disappear. This leaves spare dehumidifier capacity overnight. One method of using this capacity is to operate the dehumidifier in an air-source heat-pump role at night. In such a scheme the pool runs normally in the day while the pool is occupied. The circuit operation is illustrated in *Figure 5.16* and the energy analysis curve is shown in *Figure 5.17*. At night, when the pool hall is unoccupied and the pool cover is in place, the dehumidifier becomes an air-source heat-pump and the ductwork dampers are changed to provide this. The air flow circuit is now shown in *Figure 5.18* with the fresh air

TABLE 5.3 Design procedure

1. Select suitable water temperature—say 27°C.
2. Choose the air temperature to be 1–2°C above the pool temperature—say 28°C.
3. Using figure 9, select the evaporation rate/m^2 appropriate to these temperatures—e.g. 140 g/m^2h for single family pools (double this quantity for hotel pools).
4. Multiply the unit evaporation rate by the pool surface area, i.e. 20 m^2 pool = 20 × 140 = 2.8 kg of moisture/h. This gives the required machine capacity.
5. Check manufacturers' catalogues to find a machine which will extract 2.8 kg of moisture per hour at 28°C 55% r.h.
6. Check recycle-air flow-rate for the machine selected.
7. Will this give at least four air changes/hour in the pool hall? If not, try another manufacturer for a unit with a bigger fan capability.
8. Estimate likely number of bathers in the pool at one time. Make provision for fresh-air ventilation ~20 m^3/h/person.
9. Examine the practicality of a pool cover to inhibit evaporation when unoccupied.
10. When the pool is commissioned check and, if necessary, reset the controlling humidistat.

going through the evaporator heat-exchanger but not into the pool hall. It returns directly to the outside. The heating analysis chart in *Figure 5.19* illustrates the energy implications. The air-source heat-pump mode of the dehumidifier can provide the bulk of the fabric heat loss. Such a scheme is particularly favourable for countries such as Britain with a time of day tariff which offers substantial price reductions for night time energy.

The refrigerant condenser of the dehumidifier can also be used to provide underfloor heating of the pool surround. A schematic illustration is shown in *Figure 5.20*. A summary of the progressive steps which can be taken to reduce the energy in swimming pools is summarized in *Figure 5.21*.

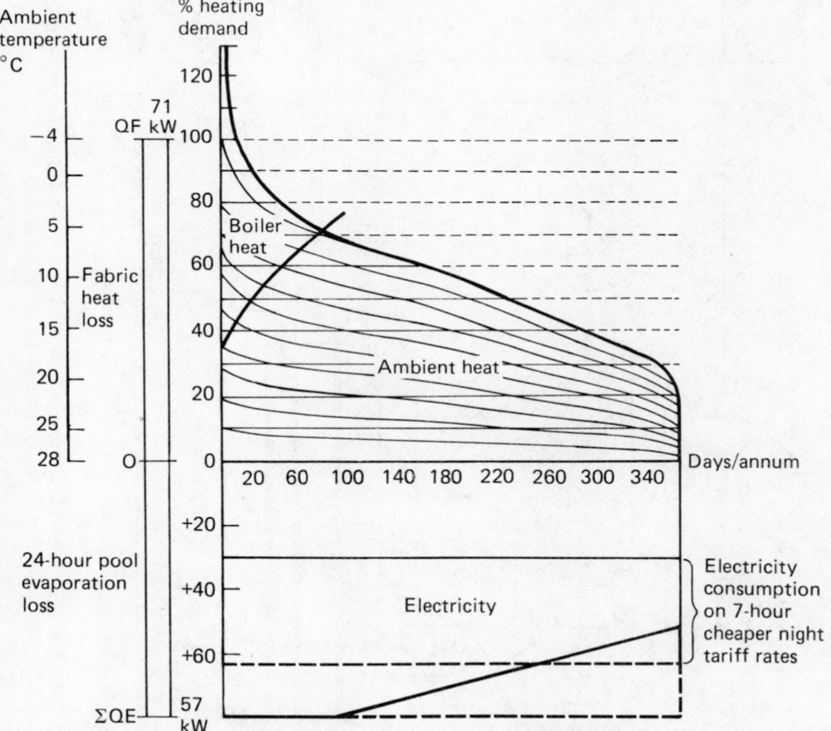

Figure 5.19 Heating energy analysis chart for the night-time operation of the dehumidifier in the air-source heat-pump mode (11 hours unoccupied). The area under the degree day curve represents energy

Further developments on a combined heat and power scheme to provide an independent, self-contained pool are being explored. Much of the electrical load is of an all-year-round nature to provide the lighting and the pumps. If a gas-driven heat-pump can reliably provide the dehumidification then there is scope for a high load factor for such equipment.

Finally there is research in progress on the effect of flow distribution within the pool hall on evaporation, which if implemented, could influence the dehumidifier sizing procedures.

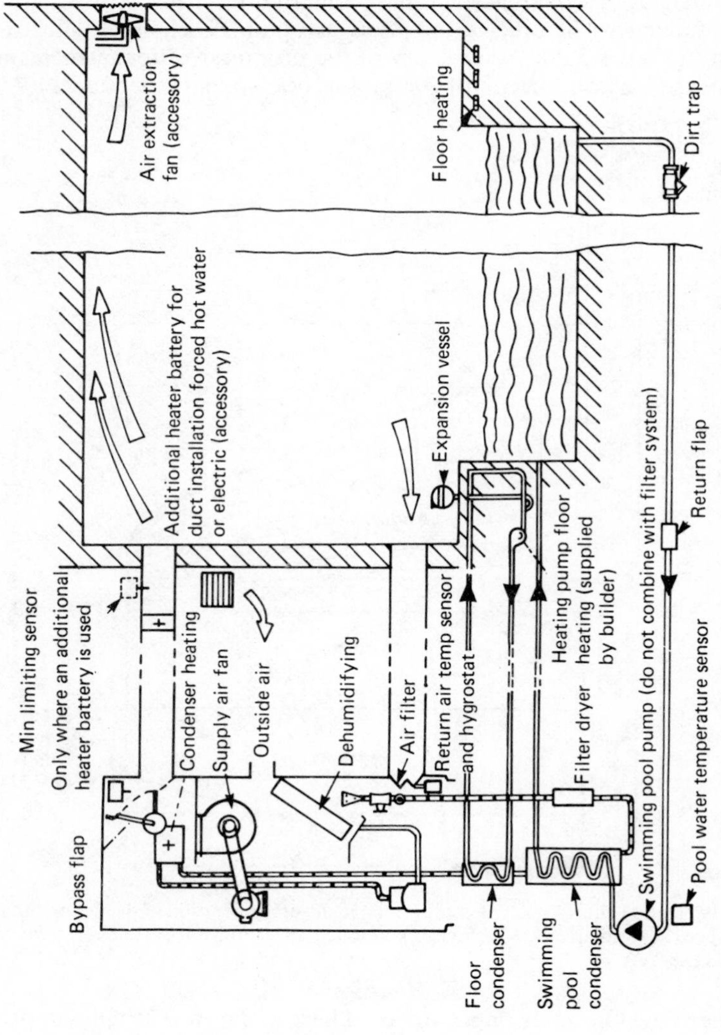

Figure 5.20 The refrigerant condenser of the dehumidifier can be used to heat the pool air, to provide underfloor heating and to heat the pool water (courtesy of Fritherm, Germany)

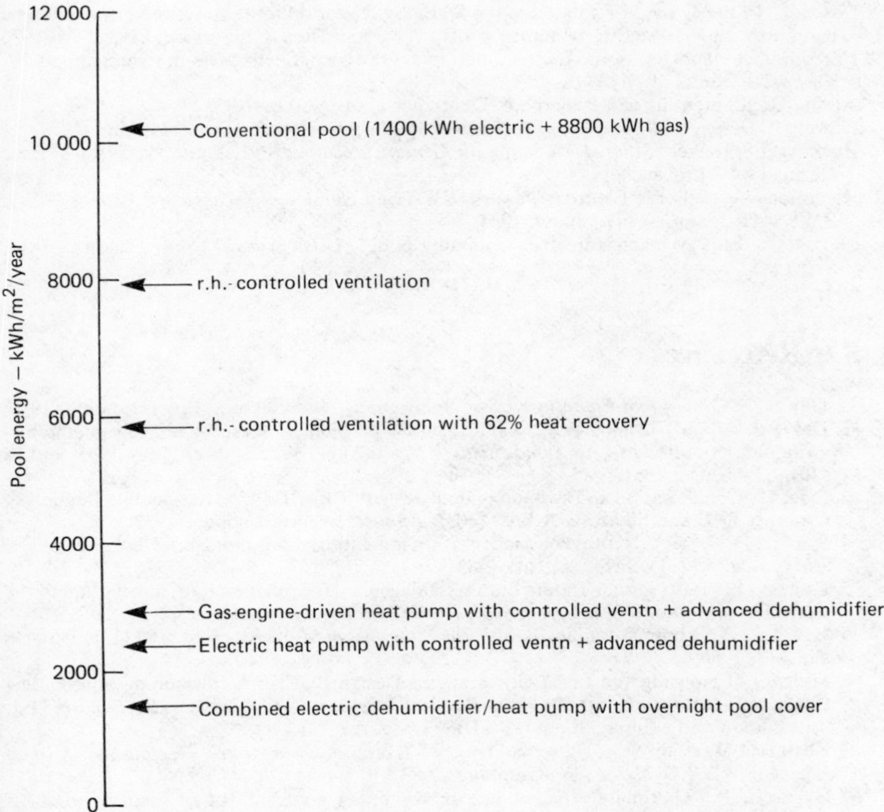

Figure 5.21 Progressive improvements in reducing energy in pools (Braham, 1981)[13]

5.5 Further reading on pool design

Fabian, D. *Moderne Schwimmstatten Welt.* Carl Schunemann, Bremen, W. Germany, 1958

Holt, J.S.C. 'Some aspects of swimming pool design'. Htg & Ventg Res Assoc, Tech Note No 10, Apr 1962

Garden, G.K. 'Indoor swimming pools'. Nat Res Col of Canada, UDC 725.74, Nov 1966

Institute of Baths Management. *Swimming pools.* Design Guide No 1, including Suppliers Register, 1967

Savidge, R. *The Modern Swimming Pool.* Bldg Cen Trust, 1970

Swimming Pool & Allied Trades Assoc. *Standards for swimming pools: Design, Construction, Filtration & Heating*, 1971

Anon. 'Thermal environment for indoor swimming pools'. Htg & Ventg Res Assoc, Tech Note No 28, Mar 1972

Fleischer, H. *Schwimmbecken Wirtschaftlich Planen und Bauen.* Heinz-Joachim Drager Verlag, Stuttgart, W. Germany, 1972

Kappler, H.P. *Das Private Schwimmbad.* Bau Verlag GmbH, W. Berlin, 1972

Sports Council. 'Public indoor swimming pools'. TUS Bull No. 1, HMSO, 1973

Perkins, P.H. 'Swimming pools. A treatise on the planning, layout, design and construction, including water treatment and other services'. *Applied Science*, London, 1975

Loyd, S. 'In the swim. An annotated bibliography of world literature on the environmental conditions and services in swimming pools'. Bldg Servs Res & Inf Assoc, LB 105/76, 1976

Braham, G.D. and Johnson, A.J. 'A guide to energy cost effectiveness in swimming pools'. Elecy Ccl Guide, 1977

Anon. 'Richtlinien für den Baderbau'. Deutscher Sportbund ev, 1977

Dawes, J. *Design and Planning of Swimming Pools.* Architectural Press, London, 1979

Recknagel-Sprenger, *Manuel Practique du Génie Climatique.* Pyc, Paris, 1980 (trans. from German by J.L. Cauchepin)

Rheinisch-Westfalisches Elektrizitätswerk. *RWE Bau-Handbuch Technischer Ausbau 1983/4.* RWE AG, Essen, W. Germany, 1983

Martin, T. 'Energy management in swimming pools'. CIBS Annual Conf, Reading, 8–14, Mar 1983

5.6 References

1 Dawes, J. *Design and Planning of Swimming Pools.* Architectural Press, London, 1979

2 Daly, R.E. and Bishop, W.P. 'Condensation problem is solved with new method of swimming pool design'. *Air Condg, Htg & Ventn Engr*, **58** (5), 81–88, May 1961, and **58** (10), 63–66, Oct 1961

3 Doe, L. 'Condensation and swimming pool design'. Paper II: 'Condensation in buildings'. Croome, D.J. and Sherratt, A.F.C. (eds), *Applied Science*, London, 1972

4 Synder, D.H. 'How to prevent condensation in heating a swimming pool'. *Htg, Piping & Air Condg*, **35** (11), 127–128, Nov 1983

5 Duggen, U. 'Beitrag zum Thema Luftungsanlagen in Hallenbadern'. ('Contribution to the subject of ventilation in indoor pools') *Klima und Kalte Ingenieur*, **2** 47–50, 1975

6 Heathen, P. 'Indoor swimming pools'. *Jnl of the Inst of Municipal Engrs*, **87** (12), 395–416 and 442, 1960

7 Ministry of Housing and Local Government. Design Bull No 4, 'Swimming pools'. 1964

8 Chartered Institution of Building Service Engineers. *Guidebook B*, Section B2: 'Installation and equipment guide', CIBS, London, 1970

9 Rheinisch-Westfalisches Elektrizitätswerk. *RWE Bau-Handbuch Technisher Ausbau 1983/4.* RWE AG, Essen, W. Germany, 1983

10 Harrison, P. 'Thermally efficient indoor swimming pools'. Dept of the Environment Constn Note 18, 1976

11 Anon. 'Les économies d'énergie dans les "1000" piscines'. Une étude entreprise par le Centre Scientifique et Technique du Bâtiment pour le Secretariat d'État à la Heunesse et aux Sports, 1977

12 Villain, J. 'L'hygrothermique des piscines et la recherche d'économies d'énergie'. *Le Moniteur des Travaux Publics et du Bâtiment* (France), **11**, 109–112, 21 Mar 1977. ('Hygrothermal conditions in swimming pools and research into energy saving'. Elecy Ccl trans, OA 2541: 1982)

13 Braham, G.D. 'The energy factor'. 51st Ann Conf of the Inste of Baths & Recreational Managet, Sept 1981

14 Dalton, J. 'Experimental essays on the constitution of mixed gases'. *Memoirs and Proceedings of the Manchester Literary and Philosophical Society*, **5**, 535–602, 1802

15 Carrier, W.H. 'The control of humidity and temperature as applied to manufacturing processes and human comfort'. *Htg, Piping & Air Condg*, **1** (7), 535–543, 1929

16 Powell, R.W. and Griffiths, E. 'The evaporation of water from plane and cylindrical surfaces'. Inst of Cheml Engrs, trans, **13**, 175–198, 1935

17 Gettman, H. 'On the ventilation of swimming baths' (in German) *Warme Luftungs und Gesundheitstechnik, 259–269, Dec 1965*

18 Chartered Institution of Building Service Engineers. *Guidebook A*, Section A10: 'Moisture problems'. CIBS, London, 1970

19 Milbank, N.O. 'Energy consumption in swimming pool halls'. BRE Current Paper 40/75, Apr 1975

20 VD1. German Standard for Swimming Pools, VD1 2089, 1976

21 Villain, J. As ref 12

22 ASHRAE. *Applications Hdbk*, Chap 4: 'Places of assembly'. Am Soc of Htg, Refrign and Air Condg Engrs, Atlanta, USA, 1982

23 Reeker, J. 'Water evaporation in indoor swimming pools: the results of practical tests'. *Klima und Kalte Ingenieur*, **6** (1), 29–33, 1978
24 RWE AG. As ref 9
25 Lurie, M. and Michailoff, N. 'Die Verdunstung von Wasser aus offenen Oberflachen Gesundheits Ingenieur'. **59** (21), 289–294, 1936
26 Leve, K. 'Beitrag zur Frage der Wasserverdunstung'. *Warme und Kaltetechnik*. **44** (11), 161–167, 1942
27 Dienelt, H. 'Untersuchungen zur Wasserverdunstung an offen Oberflachen'. *Luft und Kaltetechnik*, 149–159, 1967
28 Probert, D. 'Inhibition of evaporation'. *Applied Energy*, **3**, 257–266, 1977
29 Biasin, K. and Krumme, W. 'Evaporation in an indoor swimming pool'. *Electrowarme in Technischen Ausbau*, Edition A, **32**, 115–129, May 1974. Elecy Ccl trans, OA 976: 1975
30 Godfrey, J.A., Milbank, N.O. and Woodhouse, D.K. 'Local authority covered pools case studies of some design aspects'. *Official Architecture and Planning*, **33**, (1), 57–64, 1970
31 Bobel, A. 'Vaihingen indoor swimming pool serviced exclusively by a heat pump'. *Heizung, Luftung, Haustechnik*, **25** (5), 153–158, May, 1974. Elecy Ccl trans, OA 944: 1975
32 Anon. 'Heat pump for swimming pool'. *Bldg Res & Prac*, 124, Mar/Apr 1981
33 Martin, T. 'Energy management in swimming pools'. CIBS Ann Conf, Reading, 8–14 Mar 1983
34 Linnell, C. 'Combined heat and power can slash fuel bills'. *Natural Gas*, 22–23, Sept/Oct 1984

Chapter 6

Industrial dehumidification

6.1 Introduction

There are three types of industrial dehumidification. In increasing complexity and difficulty these are:

(1) *Casual drying and condensation avoidance.* This is simply a heavy-duty version of a conventional packaged dehumidifier. There is often a

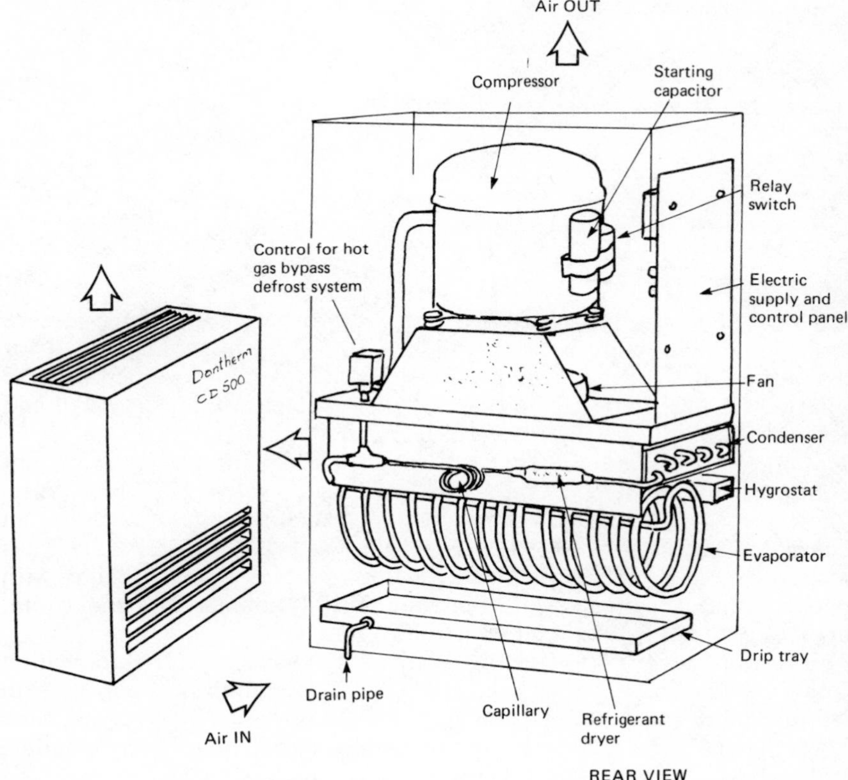

Figure 6.1 A small domestic/industrial dehumidifier (courtesy of Dantherm)

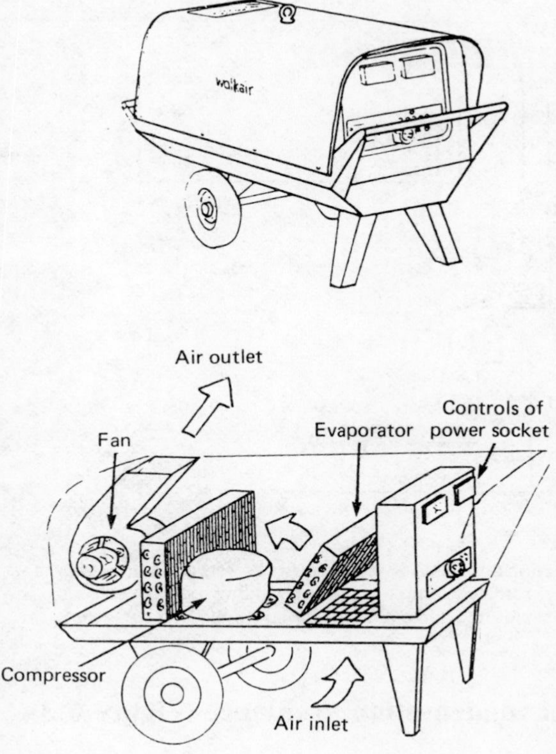

Figure 6.2 A readily-transportable industrial dehumidifier (based on the Dantherm unit)

dual-voltage motor for versatility and safety where lower voltages are available. Construction is robust and often lifting eyes are provided for easy lifting and rugged wheels for convenient transportation. These dehumidifiers are expected to operate at room temperature. A small and medium-sized unit are illustrated in *Figure 6.1* and *6.2*.

(2) *Controlled humidity*. A whole variety of tasks and processes do not require drying but they do require a controlled relative humidity. At its simplest this could be a conventional packaged dehumidifier with an accurate industrial-process type of humidity controller. More usually it has to operate at a specific temperature too and often can be an air chiller with specific duties designed into it to provide sensible chilling for a cool room, together with controlled relative humidity.

(3) *Process drying*. This is a new and growing area where dehumidification equipment is specifically designed into a drying system. It is usually large in size and often has to operate at high temperatures to keep drying time short. There is a range of drying cycles and their corresponding applications.

Let us examine these areas in more detail.

Figure 6.3 Avoidance of condensation and damp in industry. (a) Preservation of stored metallic parts. (b) Small specially-protected zone, e.g. storing welding rods. (c) Dry-air curtain around chilled injection moulds to avoid condensation spotting

6.2 Casual drying and condensation avoidance (Figure 6.3)

Corrosion problems have long been associated with warm, damp conditions. The application of plastics-coated cocooning to military equipment seals it against much of the external air and enables small dehumidifiers to maintain a dry atmosphere (<60% r.h.) inside the equipment[2]. This allows the equipment to be kept rust-free so that it can be brought into commission very quickly. The most widespread early application was naval warships and the result was so successful that it is now a standard technique. The equipment is very similar to ordinary domestic or industrial low-temperature dehumidifiers but with a wider range of ambient operating temperatures. The technique has been applied to farming equipment and to small pleasure boats.

The same technique is now being applied to semi-automated warehouses[3] storing metallic products. The warehouse is sealed from infiltration as far as is practicable and a battery of strategically-sited dehumidifiers control the moisture. Staff workstations are sited at one end of the building and these spots are comfortably heated by local radiation heaters. The air temperature inside the building is cool but dry. This saves much space heating energy. These dehumidifiers are large but operate around conventional room temperature. Siting is the major practical problem and suitable roof reinforcement is needed for an unobtrusive roof mounting.

Avoidance of condensation inside the refrigerant circuit is the reason why refrigerant gases are dried so carefully during manufacture[4].

However, the dewpoint requirements are so low that only dessicant drying is practicable. Extra-dry gases are particularly valued by refrigeration engineers because if condensation droplets occur within the refrigerant circuit they are highly likely to freeze and the ice may block delicate pipes or control valves. This could lead either to malfunction or at least poor performance. Similar arguments apply to compressed air but this subject is treated separately in the book.

Dehumidification also has a special place in avoiding condensation during cooling operations[5]. The Maryland Plastic Company (USA) makes a wide variety of custom-moulded products ranging from medical and electronics components to disposable cutlery. Most of these products are fashioned on high-speed injection-moulding machines. Within each moulding machine the plastics material is melted, injected into a mould, chilled and ejected in finished form. For most plastics products it is important that the material hardens as quickly as possible. To achieve this the moulds are refrigerated from −4 to −7°C. In humid summer conditions moisture condenses on the cold surface of the mould to form droplets which create local distortion in the plastics component and make it difficult for the two halves of the mould to meet correctly. The traditional method of avoiding the summer problem is to raise the mould temperature. Unfortunately this lengthens the cooling time, lowers the quality of the component and slows down the production rate. The more satisfactory solution now deployed uses an air curtain around the moulds. This air is dehumidified and reheated to supply air at 0.3 m/s 43°C and 20% r.h. This simple action restored both productivity and quality even in peak summer conditions.

6.3 Controlled humidity (Figure 6.4)

Controlled humidity is required in a wide variety of applications, (*Table 6.1*). At normal temperatures this will necessitate the provision of both

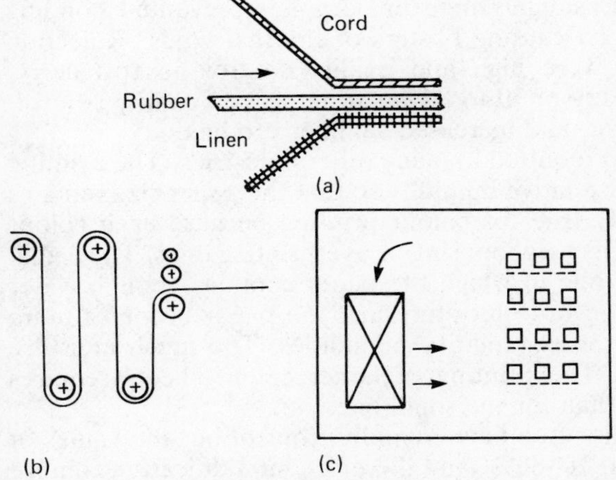

Figure 6.4 Controlled humidity for industry. (a) Quality control during manufacture, e.g. of composite rubber products. (b) Product uniformity, e.g. in printing where colour registration must be exact. (c) Specialist food storage, e.g. to prevent mould

TABLE 6.1 Moisture conditions for manufacturing industries

Product		*Recommended relative humidity—%* (0 10 20 30 40 50 60 70 80 90 100)
Cotton manufacturing	spinning	
	combing	
	warping	
	weaving	
Wool manufacturing	combing	
	carding	
	weaving	
	spinning worsted[1]	
Tea packaging		
Electrical switchgear manufacture		
Cereal packaging		
Lithographic printing[2]		
Pharmaceutical packaging		
Transformer winding		

[1]Varies with type of wool
[2]Tighter tolerance is required for large sheets

dehumidification and humidification equipment. At low temperature the vapour pressure will be below ambient and only *de*humidification will be needed. At high temperatures and high design humidities then only humidification may be needed.

An early factory application involved the mass production of rubber drive belts[6]. The process involved the permanent combination of three elements. A tension member made of high-strength rayon cord was set in a firm rubber base which, in its turn, provided the compression grip in the pulley. The whole composition was then wrapped in a coated fabric to provide a tough wearing surface. High relative humidities in summer within the factory created a variety of problems. It affected the length of the tension cord, and occasionally moisture droplets prevented bonding adhesion within the belt by causing blisters or internal voids. Rejection rates within the factory were high and quality control unsatisfactory. Controlled relative humidity of 70 to 80% r.h. improved quality control, reduced wastage by a third, and increased summer productivity.

Humidity control is also required in many other industries. The printing industry requires constant relative humidity so that the paper size remains stable. This is particularly true for colour printing because each colour must register exactly with its neighbouring or overprinting ones. The actual value chosen is normally one in which the paper contains enough water content to be flexible. Too little moisture and the paper becomes more rigid, and actually brittle at low relative humidities. Too much moisture and mould will develop. The printing of larger colour sheets requires greater humidity control than for the small ones.

Cotton and woolen mills often have humidity control but the values of relative humidity are high, 70–80%, and therefore humidification is more common. The actual value varies with the different stages of production. At some stages the relative humidity is high to avoid electrostatic problems.

Humidity control is essential also in flour milling and in the tobacco industry. In flour milling, too low a relative humidity creates dust clouds and raises the risk of an explosion. At high relative humidity the flour will take up a high moisture content which makes it more likely to deteriorate.

Production of antibiotics necessitates very low relative humidity because the shelf life of the drugs is limited by high r.h.[7,8]. Originally the whole packaging room was kept at 15% r.h. but newer techniques supply dry air (3% r.h.) specifically to the filling machine. These values are too low for normal refrigerant dehumidification, and dessicants, either solids or liquids, are used.

Controlled humidity is also essential for food storage. Most perishable foods will develop mould problems if the relative humidity is greater than 80%. This fine sensitivity is illustrated in *Figure 6.5* with respect to stored

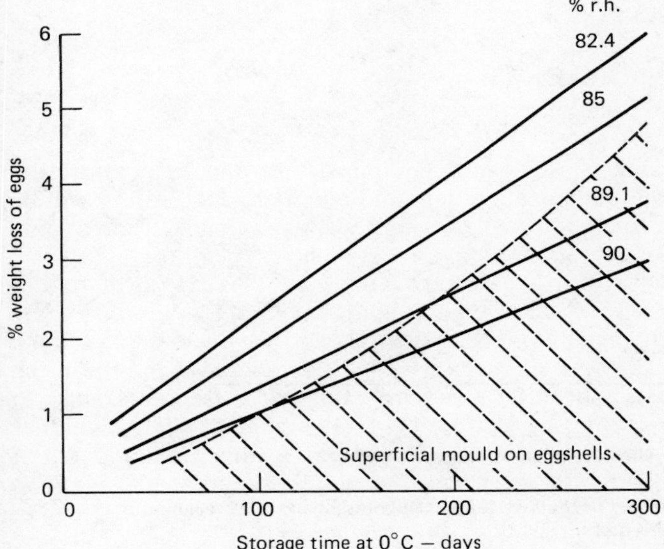

Figure 6.5 The sensitivity of eggs to different relative humidities (DSIR, 1949)[9]

eggs[9]. The time taken for superficial mould to develop was almost doubled by lowering the relative humidity from 90% to 89%. This mould did not affect the flavour of the egg and could be removed, but this cleaning process would be an added cost. Prevention of the mould is much more economic. Mould can occur at lower relative humidities on some foodstuffs. Peanuts are considered safe from mould damage below 65% r.h. (*Figure 6.6*)[10]. Mould-free storage life could be doubled from that at 80% r.h. 20°C by either lowering the relative humidity by ten percentage points or lowering the temperature to 10°C at 80% r.h. However, the storage problem is complex. Drier conditions favour insects, and insect damage occurs if insects can penetrate the container. Early experiments on stored peanuts showed the advantage of strong, multiwall paper containers compared with the conventional canvas or cotton bags (*Table 6.2*).

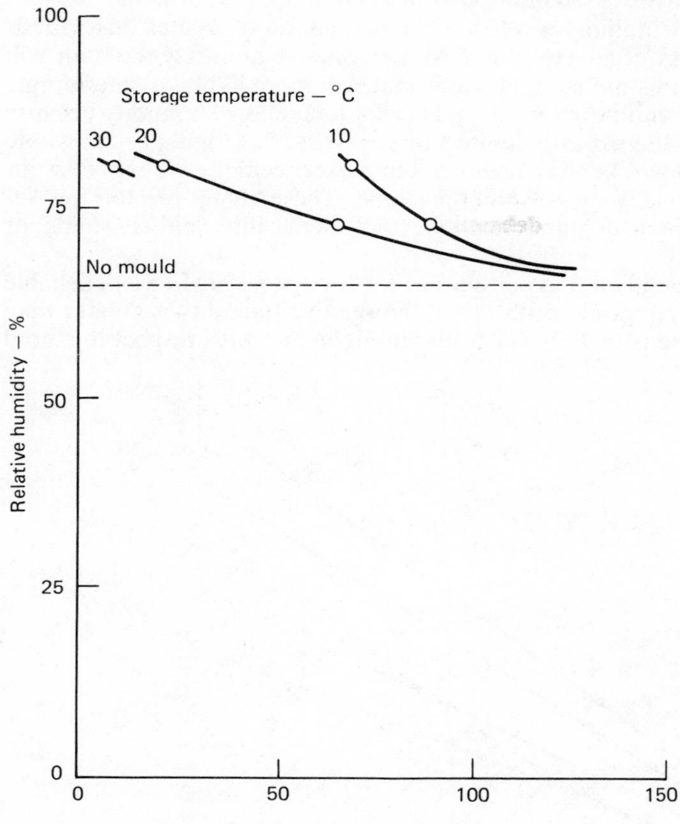

Figure 6.6 The sensitivity of peanuts to storage temperature and relative humidity (Thompson, Cecil and Woodruff, 1951)[10]

TABLE 6.2 Experiments in storing peanuts

Type of bag	*Canvas*		*Cotton*		*Multiwall paper*	
Average ambient relative humidity	63%	80%	63%	80%	63%	80%
Insects found/bag	hundreds	17	165	8	6	1
Insect damage in bag	100%	4%	60%	1%	1%	0
Mouldy nuts in bag	nil	100%	nil	98%	nil	49%

(Thompson, Cecil and Woodruff, 1951)[10].

The 63% r.h. storage room was a dry barn with abundant insects. The 80% r.h. room was a basement whose r.h. varied from 70 to 80%. Temperatures were not controlled.

However, if the relative humidity is lower, then the fresh-looking produce dehydrates and can become tough, discoloured and unattractive. The speed at which dehydration occurs is a function of the difference in vapour pressure between the moist plant or meat and the ambient. This difference can be minimized by storing at a lower temperature in a controlled relative humidity. The storage temperature must be above the freezing point for the produce and this freezing point varies widely for different foods. They are all below the freezing point of water. Below freezing point ice crystals are likely to form slowly and damage the plant cell structure of the food. Recommended values developed by experience are listed in *Table 6.1*. These are not critical for short-time storage but are essential for longest storage. This duration is a function of storage temperature. Toffee, for example, should be stored at 50% r.h. At higher humidities (~65% r.h.) the toffee would become sticky at 20°C within a few days, but at 5°C the same deterioration would take several weeks. Tolerance to humidity control is therefore much wider at lower temperatures.

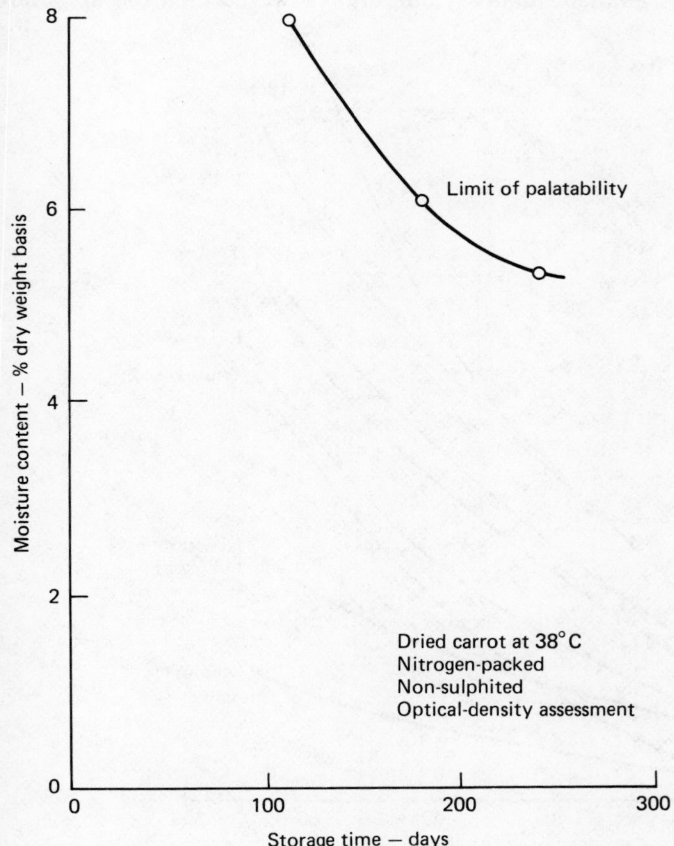

Figure 6.7 The rate of browning of dried food increases exponentially with increasing moisture content (Legault *et al*, 1947)[11]

Moisture control is also essential in dried-food storage. The rate of browning of dried food increases exponentially with increasing moisture content[11]. Experiments on dried carrots showed how the storage time decreased with increasing moisture. This relationship is illustrated for the maximum storage life in *Figure 6.7*. Flavour deteriorates in a similar relationship.

The equipment needed to chill and control humidity in a warehouse is of a special design to ensure that humidity control and cooling can occur simultaneously. This normally means a large surface area evaporator heat-exchanger. A highly-rated, very-low-temperature evaporator would be of lower capital cost but would tend to overdry the products stored.

6.4 Drying cycles

Many common materials absorb water, and the amount absorbed is related to the ambient relative humidity. Typical relationships are illustrated in *Figure 6.8*[4]. If the ambient relative humidity is lowered then the material

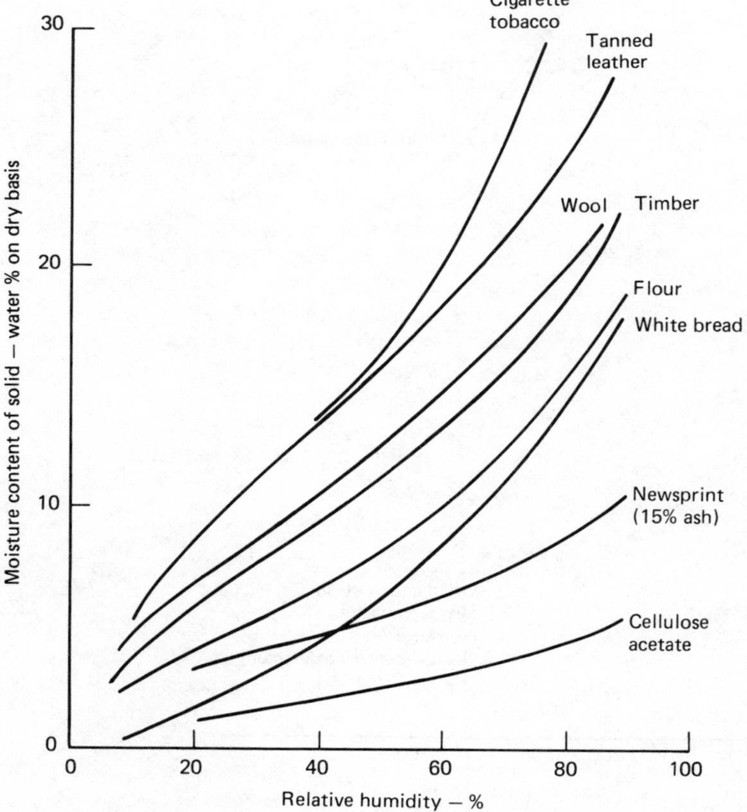

Figure 6.8 Equilibrium moisture content of common materials at 24°C (*ASHRAE Applications*, 1982)[4]

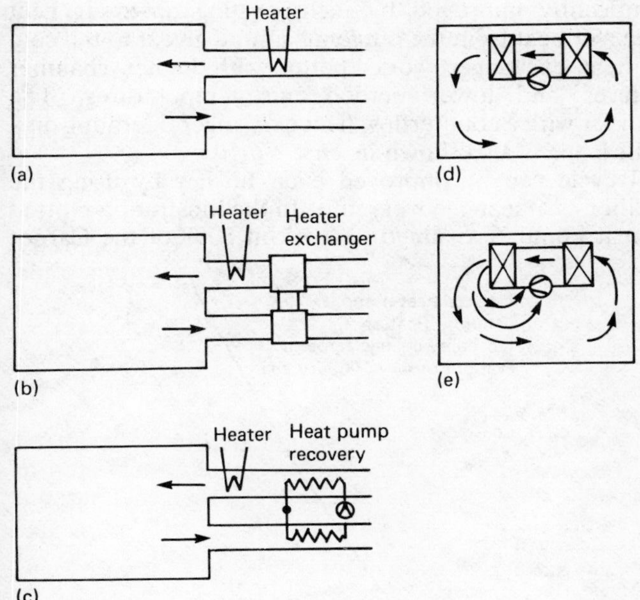

Figure 6.9 Drying techniques. (a) Hot-air drying. (b) Hot-air drying with heat recovery. (c) Hot-air drying with heat-pump heat recovery. (d) Heat-pump dehumidification with direct flow through the evaporator and condenser. (e) Heat-pump dehumidifier with bypass

will lose water until it is in equilibrium with the new lower r.h. This is the basis of the industrial drying process for solids. The most common technique of lowering r.h. is to increase the temperature of the ambient air. The energy cost of this method is high and two new applications of heat-pump dehumidifiers are being developed (*Figure 6.9*). The first is to use the dehumidifier as a heat-recovery unit. The evaporator is placed in the hot moist air rejection duct of the drying chamber and returns much of the latent and sensible heat back to the incoming fresh air. This technique is particularly appropriate for improving existing hot-air drying chambers. The second technique is to incorporate the dehumidifier within the drying chamber and constantly extract moisture to create the desired dryness in the chamber.

In practice, the energy penalty for drying is a complex function not only of psychrometrics, but also of the heat losses through the drying chamber. These chamber losses are strongly influenced by permissible operating temperatures, thermal insulation, infiltration and duration of the drying cycle. For simplicity we will restrict discussion to the psychrometrics of the recycling air. The subject has been thoroughly explored by Geeraert for the Belgian National Electroheat Laboratory, LABORELEC. His report[12] forms the basis of this section.

The effectiveness of conventional hot-air drying is low but insensitive to relative humidity within the drying chamber (*Figure 6.10*)[12]. In this calculation, losses through the chamber walls and any preheating of the solids are ignored. Outdoor air is at 10°C. The performance of hot-air dryers can be significantly improved by incorporating air-to-air heat exchangers which recover heat from the outgoing air and give it to the cold incoming air. The heat exchanger works better with higher chamber operating temperatures and lower outdoor air temperatures. The effectiveness of the dryer with a counterflow heat exchanger operating on a 5°K temperature difference is also shown in *Figure 6.10*.

This conventional cycle can be improved even further by using the heat-pump dehumidifier as a heat-recovery unit. In the illustration plotted in *Figure 6.10* the heat pump is assumed to work at 50% of the Carnot

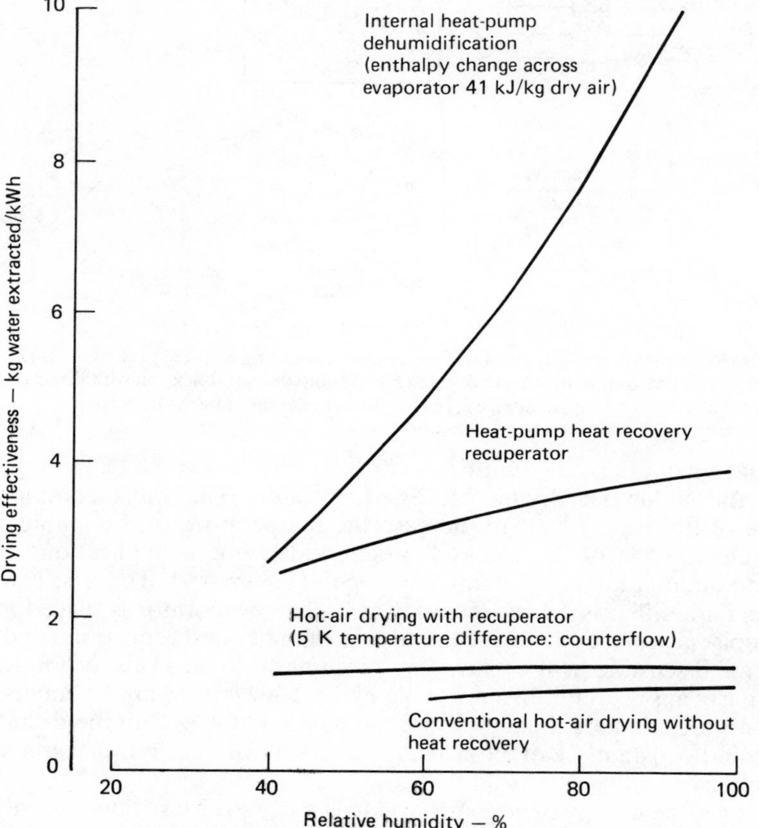

Figure 6.10 Theoretical assessment of drying effectiveness, neglecting losses through chamber walls and heating of the solids. 40°C drying chamber, 10°C outdoor temperature (after Geeraert, 1975)[12]

efficiency. Its effectiveness is three or four times that of the conventional dryer but it is now sensitive to the relative humidity in the chamber. The heat pump can extract much more latent heat, and hence moisture, at the higher relative humidities.

Finally, we have the internal heat pump dehumidifier. This unit goes inside the drying chamber and no fresh-air is necessary. Assuming that the heat loss from the drying chamber equals the electrical input to the

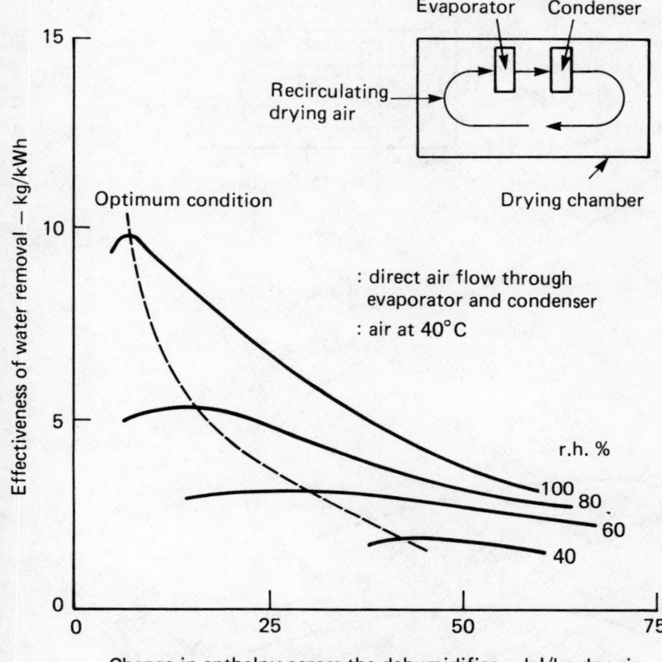

Figure 6.11 Theoretical effectiveness of dehumidification at different relative humidities when the air-flow is straight through the evaporator and the condenser and electrical input power equals chamber heat loss (Geeraert, 1975)[12]

dehumidifier, then the effectiveness of the internal dehumidifier is shown in *Figure 6.10.* While similar in effectiveness to the heat-recovery dehumidifier at 40% r.h., the internal dehumidifier reaches very high levels of effectiveness (10 kg of water/kWh) at high relative humidities (~95% r.h.).

This analysis was then extended further by Geeraert who investigated how the drying effectiveness was influenced by the enthalpy change in the moist air when it passed across the refrigerant evaporator. This is shown in *Figure 6.11*[12]. The optimum enthalpy change varies with relative humidity, increasing for lower relative humidities. Manufacturers often design for an enthalpy change of around 10 to 20 KJ/kg dry air. This is optimum for the very high relative humidities but not for the lower ones. Even further improvements could be made if the condenser could be operated at constant temperatures. This could be achieved by recycling more air around the condenser unit. The benefits are illustrated in *Figure 6.12*[12].

Laboratory measurements on commercially-available industrial dehumidifiers show a wide range of effectiveness. A selection is illustrated in *Figure 6.13*[12].

New studies are examining the application of the air cycle heat pump to drying[13]. Theoretical analyses of a sub-atmospheric pressure Brayton-cycle dehumidifying circuit show that the energy requirements of a conventional

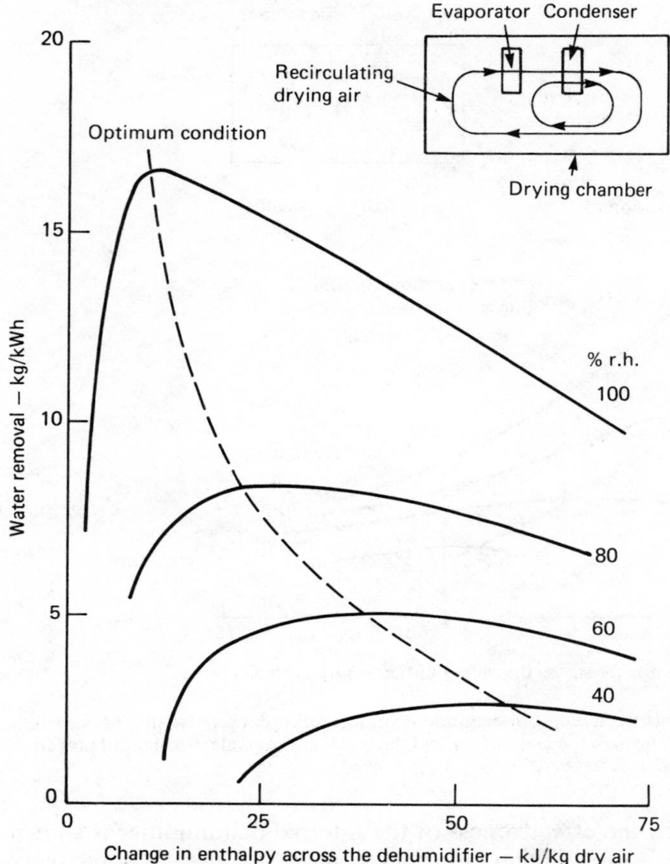

Figure 6.12 Theoretical effectiveness of dehumidification at different relative humidities when the condenser operates at constant temperature (by air recirculation) (Geeraert, 1975)[12]

hot-air dryer could be reduced by an order of magnitude. In this cycle (*Figure 6.14*) air is expanded to sub-atmospheric pressure through a turbine. Adiabatic expansion of this air provides some of the power required to drive the system. The remainder of the power needed is provided electrically by a motor drive. The air cooled by this expansion is heated in the heat-exchanger by the moist gas rejected from the dryer. The heated air is then compressed to ambient pressure in the compressor, which further increases the air temperature to the desired value before it enters the dryer.

This cycle is inferior to the conventional reverse Rankine refrigerant one for heat load applications which are essentially at constant source and constant sink temperatures. However, as the required process temperature increases, and with non-isothermal source and sink heat transfer, the Brayton-cycle performance approaches, and can exceed, the Rankine cycle. The critical factors for any practical application are working

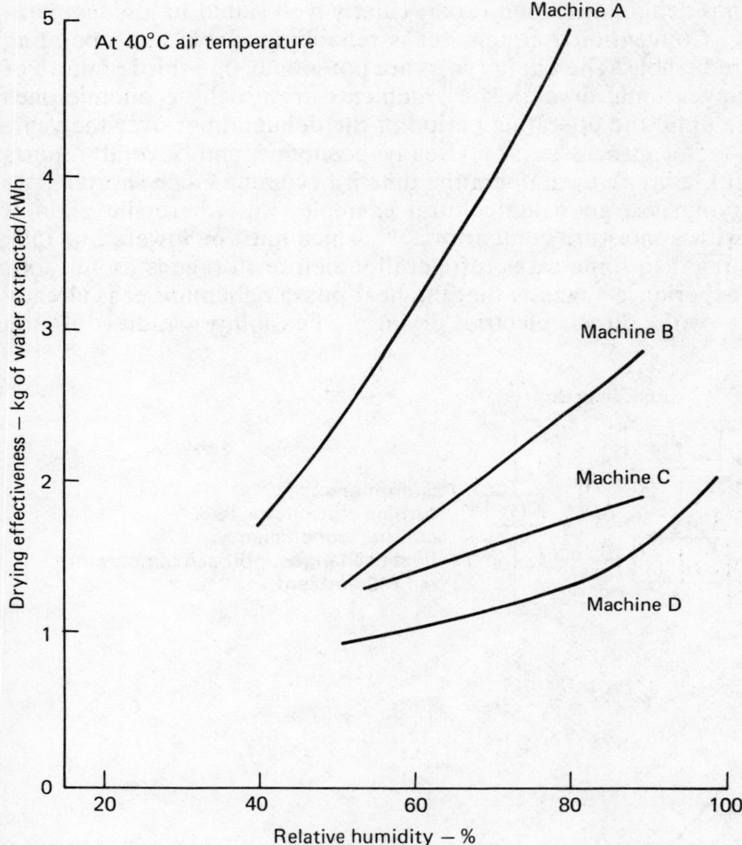

Figure 6.13 Performance characteristics of present-day vapour compression dehumidifier equipment (Geeraert, 1975)[12]

temperatures, turbine and compressor efficiencies, and heat-exchanger temperature differences. Feasibility studies show the relationship between coefficient of performance and operating temperatures (*Figure 6.14*)[13].

6.5 Drying applications

While no exact data exist, reasonable estimates suggest that thirty million tonnes of water are removed from manufactured products in Britain each year. Most of this is done by hot-air dryers whose efficiency depends much upon the drying rate required and the maximum permitted drying temperatures. Thermally sensitive operations such as the drying of pharmaceutical tablet coatings operate at around 7% while batch fluidized-bed drying of food additives can be 20%. Brick-drying chambers operate around 65% efficient.

Heat-pump dehumidification is particularly well suited to low temperature drying. Conventional equipment is reliably available and operating costs are predictable. The energy costs are potentially one-third of those of the best conventional dryers. The arguments are usually economic ones which hinge upon the operating period of the dehumidifier over the year. High load-factor processes are already economic and several reports suggest that the break-even operating time is becoming much shorter[10,11].

Grain drying is a good agricultural example, i.e. where the grain is harvested with a moisture content of 25% which must be lowered to 15% for safe storage. In some cases refrigeration before storage is useful, too. American experience suggests that the heat-pump dehumidifier is already competitive with direct electric drying[10]. Feasibility studies of the

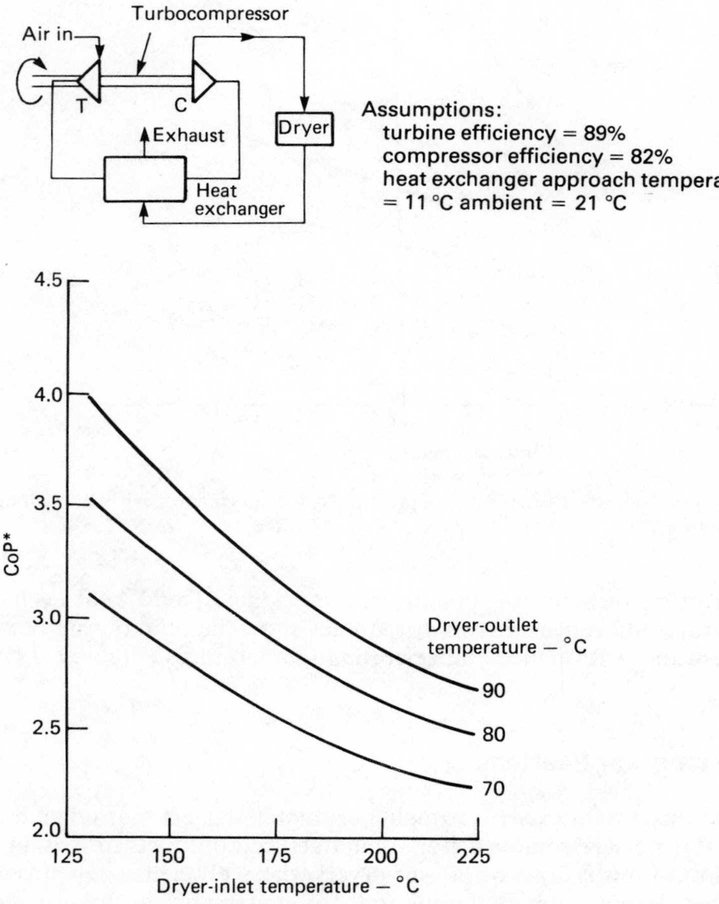

Figure 6.14 Sub-atmospheric Brayton-cycle dehumidifier (Iles, 1980)[13]

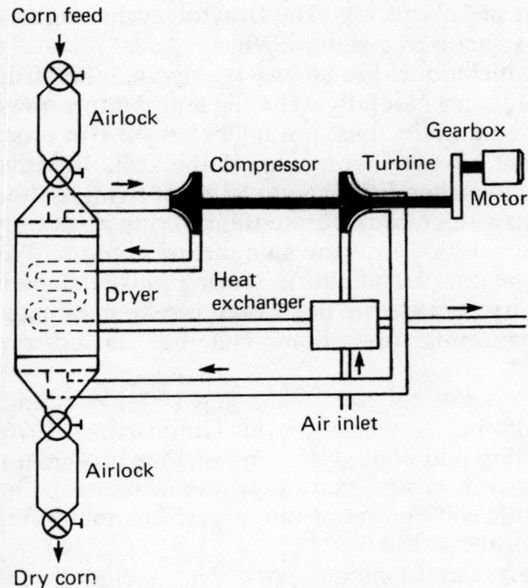

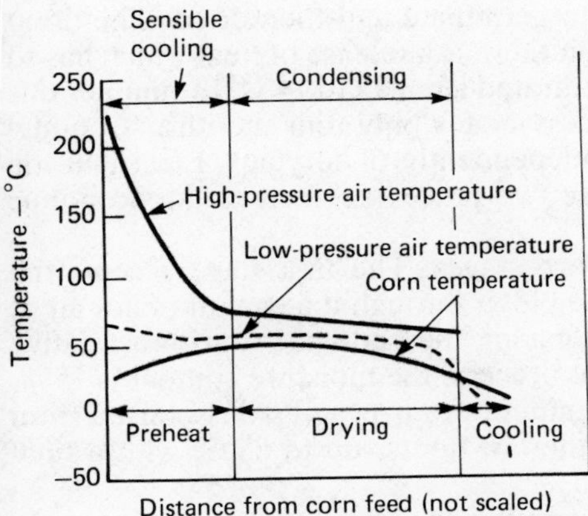

Figure 6.15 Schematic representation of an air-cycle corn dryer (Iles, 1980)[13]

application of the Brayton air cycle are also looking attractive (*Figure 6.15*)[13]. In this process the corn first enters an air lock whence it is fed into a drying chamber and preheated by the outgoing air. Then it enters the main body of the dryer where on passing through a plate heat exchanger, it becomes heated. Finally, the dry corn drops through the cold inlet air (from the turbine) which chills it and preheats the incoming air. The corn is then discharged cool and dry through the bottom air lock.

Energy comparisons show conventional hot air (90°C) convection dryers would extract 0.6 kg of water for each kWh while slow low-temperature air drying would be more effective at 1.0kg/kWh. The Brayton cycle operated at 0.25 bar and 50°C would extract 6.0kg water/kWh.

Other specialist food-drying techniques are being developed. Salted fish, for example, needs to be dried very carefully. The air temperature must not exceed 26°C and its relative humidity must not fall below 40% in order to prevent unwelcome cooking or case-hardening of the fish. Relative humidities above 76% for heavily-salted fish or 80 to 85% for lightly-salted fish would not dry it. Fish processors often operate their drying plant only in the winter months when the outdoor air is low in moisture content. The drying plant is then a simple heater. Dehumidifier drying makes all-year operation possible with economy because the fish stored can be minimized and the manpower and marketing operations can be carried out continuously over the year[16].

Two prototype tea-drying installations of 250–kW and 160–kW ratings have been operated successfully in Samtredia (Soviet Union) since 1976. They have provided both heating and cooling for one of four production lines and the scheme has been so successful that the whole factory is being converted. When completed this will be one of the largest dehumidifying plants (1.55MW electrical)[17] in the world.

French and West German development work has included the application of heat pumps for malt drying for the brewing industry[18,19,20] (*Figure 6.16*). The present process is very energy intensive. Barley is harvested, prepared and allowed to germinate and then dried. The dried product is malt. During germination there is a release of heat which has to be removed by the circulation of saturated air at 12 to 14°C. In summer this requires refrigeration which is necessary for only four months. 'Cooling' was therefore considered quite independently of 'drying'. Électricité de France successfully integrated these two processes to create an economic energy-efficient system.

A traditional drying cycle has two stages. The first stage accepts the barley at 45% moisture content and blows through it a stream of hot air at 60°C. The temperature of the air leaving the bed is 28°C with a relative humidity of 98%. At the end of the process, the moisture content is 15%. During the second stage, the air temperature is progressively raised from 60°C to 80°C, and finally, during the last hours, up to 85°C, with a final moisture content of the malt of 4.5%.

Integration of the existing refrigeration facilities into the drying cycle enables the heat recovered to be used as a low-cost preheat for the conventional type of hot-air convection drying. The bulk of the energy required still comes from the fossil-fired burners which heat the air. An experimental ammonia-based plant was installed in the Brazey en Plaine plant of the Chevalier-Martin Malthouses in 1976. Two 132–kW electric compressors gave coefficients of performance of 4.8 at 50°C condensation and 25°C evaporation temperatures and 6.6 at 30°C condensation with 5.5°C evaporation temperature. In terms of the complete drying cycle the heat pump preheat increases the effectiveness of the cycle from 0.35kg/kWh for single-bed drying or 0.5 for double-bed drying to 0.6kg/kWh. It is economic where refrigeration is used for temperature control during germination. Similar arguments apply to rice drying[21]. The economic arguments vary according to relative prices of energy.

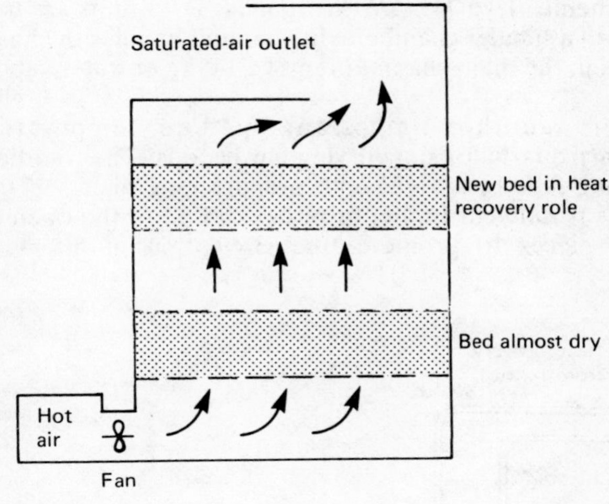

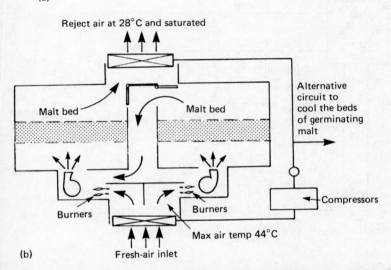

Figure 6.16 The cooling equipment for the germinating malt beds can be used for heat recovery in the drying operation. (a) Double-floor malt-drying kiln. (b) Heat-pump recovery in malt drying (Guyon, 1980)[18]

Consideration should be given to the integration of both heat recovery and dehumidification into malt drying[22] (*Figure 6.17*).

Higher-temperature applications are also being developed. Manufactured woollen items of clothing are often washed three times during the various stages of cleaning, drying and pre-shrinking. Speedy, effective drying by using high-temperature dehumidifiers operating at 50°C has been achieved at Kangol Wear Ltd[23], a woollen-goods manufacturer in Cumbria (UK). Not only was the product of better and more uniform quality but also the drying costs were reduced by 75%. Drying time was 78% of the original convective scheme. Two 7½–kW Westair HPD 75 units are used in one chamber while in a smaller chamber a further unit handles the hanks of yarn. The two units in the main chamber remove 145 kg of water vapour in 4½ hours.

Timber drying is another important medium-temperature application[1,14,23–6], particularly for slow-drying hardwoods. The traditional method, after having felled the tree, is to prepare long planks 27 mm thick and to stack this freshly-cut timber in piles exposed to the open air and with separation pieces to promote free circulation of air. Four

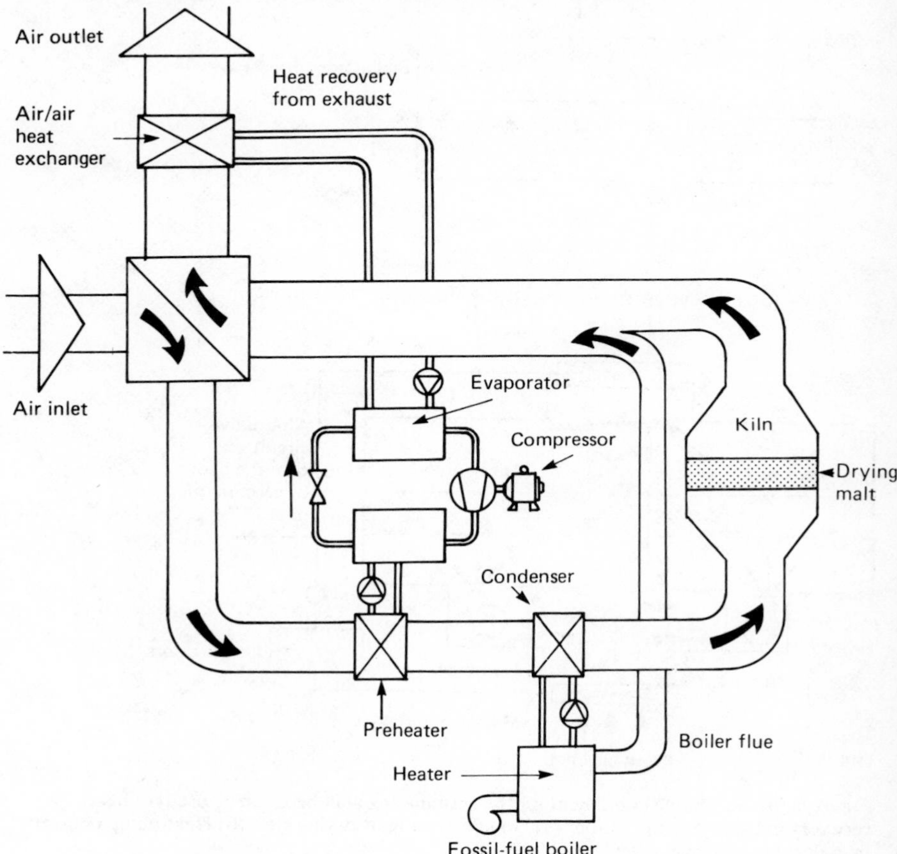

Figure 6.17 Malt-drying kiln with heat recovery and dehumidification (Mann, 1982)[22]

drawbacks to this conventional approach are unpredictability, high capital investment in stocks, poor quality-control and the risk of 'blueing' due to attack by micro-organisms. Its main advantages are low energy cost and usually gentle drying which does not lead to splitting. Two alternatives are the hot convection dryer and the heat-pump humidifier, approaches which are illustrated in *Figure 6.18*[25]. The split condenser on the dehumidifier enables the temperature to be controlled independently of the dehumidification load on the evaporator. The dehumidifiers are available in a range

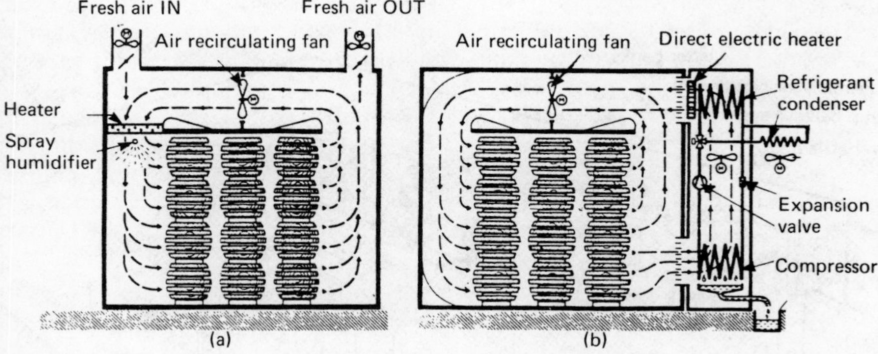

Figure 6.18 Two approaches to timber drying. (a) Conventional hot-air convection drying. (b) Low-energy heat-pump dehumidifier cycle (Hess, 1980)[25]

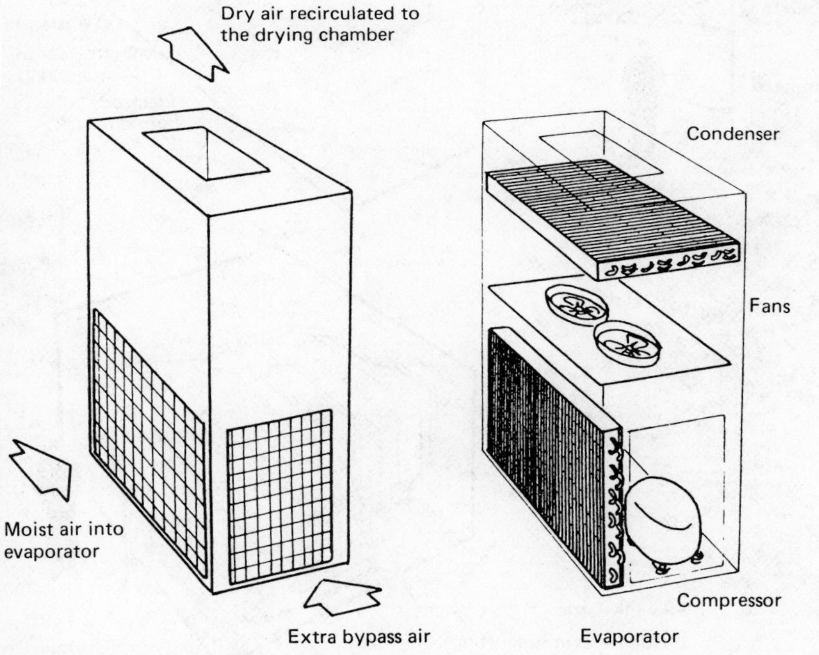

Figure 6.19 Illustrative layout of a timber dryer

of sizes. The construction of a small, free-standing unit is shown in *Figure 6.19*. The drying kiln is usually arranged as in *Figure 6.20*.

Oak weighs 700 kg/m^3 when dry. Before felling, the timber will have a moist content of about 80 to 90% by weight. In the form of freshly-cut or split planks, oak will have a moisture content of 55 to 65%, but when it is air-dried, the moisture will be down to 13 to 19% and the wood is considered seasoned. Approximately 330 litres of water are removed from each cubic metre of cut timber.

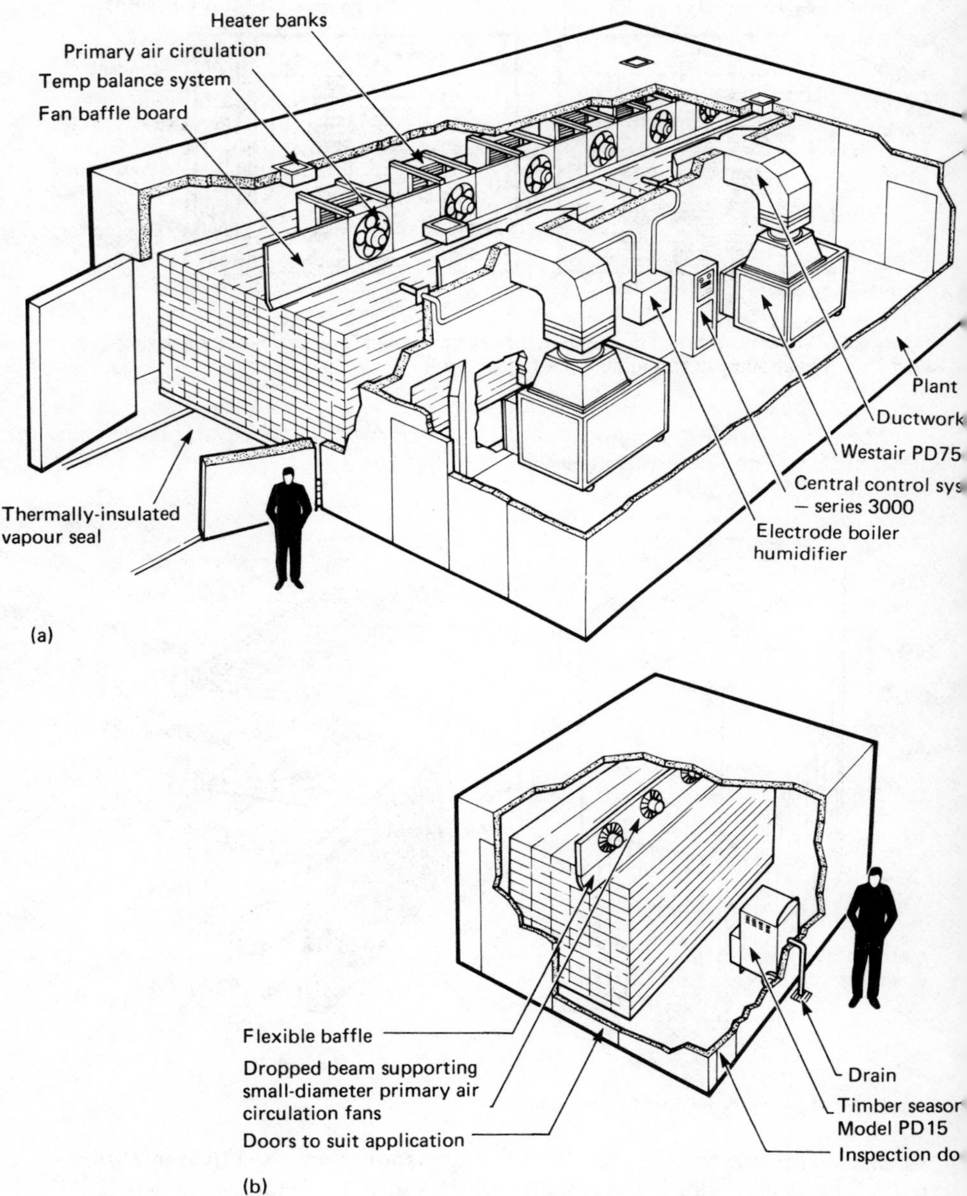

Figure 6.20 Timber-drying kilns can be large and system-designed, or small and using free-standing dehumidifiers. (a) A typical Airscrew Howden timber-drying system. (b) A small kiln containing a single free-standing Airscrew Howden (courtesy of Airscrew Howden, 1985)

Commercial medium-temperature dehumidifiers are now available. A French example uses an 18 kW (electrical) compressor, Uraken UB25, in association with a 412 m^3 thermally-insulated and sealed cell[24]. The volume occupied by the timber stack is 210 m^3 of which 70 m^3 is timber. A large recirculation fan can create sixty air changes an hour inside the empty cell. The temperature and humidity conditions follow the manufacturer's recommended pattern, and this is complemented by embedding a dozen moisture probes in the wood. The whole cycle takes from 50 to 55 days and the uniformity along the lengths of the timber is high. There is a small change in moisture content across the grain of the planks but this reaches complete uniformity within eight days after the end of the drying cycle. The energy effectiveness of dehumidification declines as the timber dries. This is illustrated in *Figure 6.21*[12].

The French had a particularly sensitive application for the final timber. The oak is used to make the barrels in which wine is stored. The micro-organisms within the wood contribute to the complex process of ageing and maturing the wines and spirits. Some of these enzymes are destroyed above 40°C and therefore a medium-temperature dehumidifier dryer is preferred.

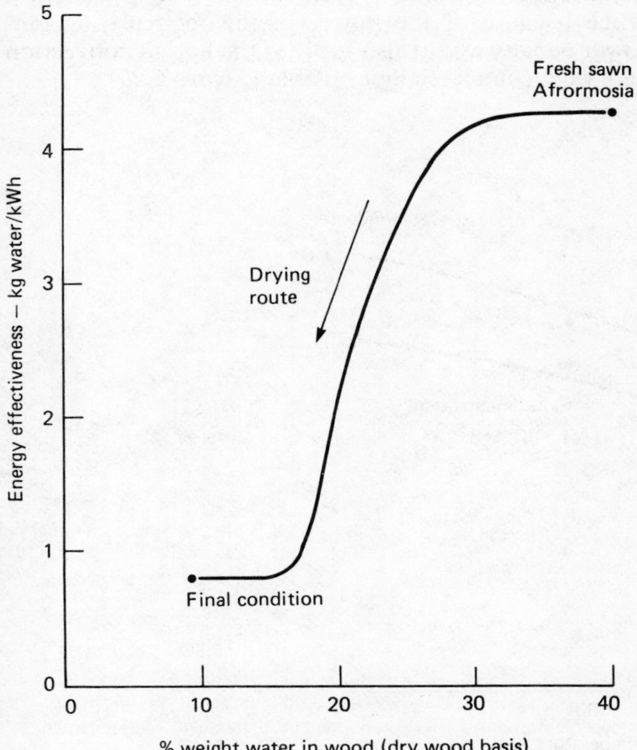

Figure 6.21 Hardwood drying by dehumidification at 40°C (Geeraert, 1975)[12]

Energy comparisons have been made between hot convection drying and heat-pump dehumidification. Conventional convection drying, using a steam boiler fired by scrap chippings and sawdust, removed 0.75 kg of water per kWh. This energy was simply used in the recirculating fans. Heat-pump dehumidification used much lower fan power and with the heat pump resulted in one kg of water being removed for one kWh. The energy comparison becomes even more in favour of the heat pump if fuel is actually purchased for the convection drying. Maintenance costs are believed to be high for conventional drying because of the hot and acid environment inside the dryer which necessitates frequent coats of the protective paint. Some protective coating is needed on the evaporator heat exchanger of the heat-pump dehumidifier but as the operating temperature is low the chemical activity is correspondingly low[27–29].

Similar experiences were reported from Germany[30]. Drying oak at 45°C took six weeks compared with three weeks at 60°C. The effectiveness of drying was reflected by 0.8 kg of water being removed for each kWh consumed, compared with 0.15 kg for conventional convection dryers.

More recent research by the Electricity Council has shown the benefits of going to even higher temperature operation[26]. Laboratory results on prototype high-temperature dehumidifiers show that over three kg of water can be extracted per kWh of electrical energy going to the compressor at an ambient of 60% r.h. 80°C (*Figure 6.22*)[26]. This value will be lowered in practice because of the power of the recirculating fan. However, the fan power penalty would also apply to the hot-air convection dryer. Such dryers are now commercially available (*Figure 6.20*).

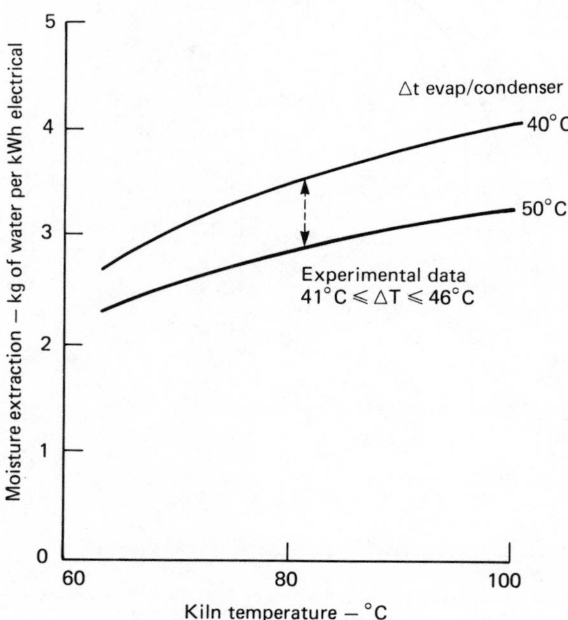

Figure 6.22 Timber-drying can be achieved at low energy cost (Lawton, 1981)[26]

Électricité de France have experimented with even higher operating temperatures for dehumidifier units[30]. In 1978 a plaster-block manufacturing company PIC, at Bray-sur-Seine, installed three sets of high-temperature dehumidifiers. Each set comprised two COMEF compressors, one a 30–kW 6 CF 80 and the other a 45–kW 8 CF 80 unit. The recycling air fan power was 50 kW. The refrigerant was R12 B1 and the designed refrigerating operating temperature was 120°C maximum. The drying tunnel, which was 35 m long × 3 m wide × 2 m high, dried 900 blocks per day (*Figure 6.23*)[30]. The application was attractive, partly because of the energy saving and partly because of the high annual load factor (6000 hours). After six months of difficulty, the refrigerant was leaking from failed joints and the lubricating oil was acidic. When the refrigerant circuits were emptied and refilled with R114 in two machines and R12 in the third, the system then worked satisfactorily. Drying effectiveness was 2.7 kg of water for each kWh used, a cost saving of 40%.

In 1979 Électricité de France designed a new medium-temperature dehumidifying dryer at a plaster-block factory, PREMACO, at Ste Mère

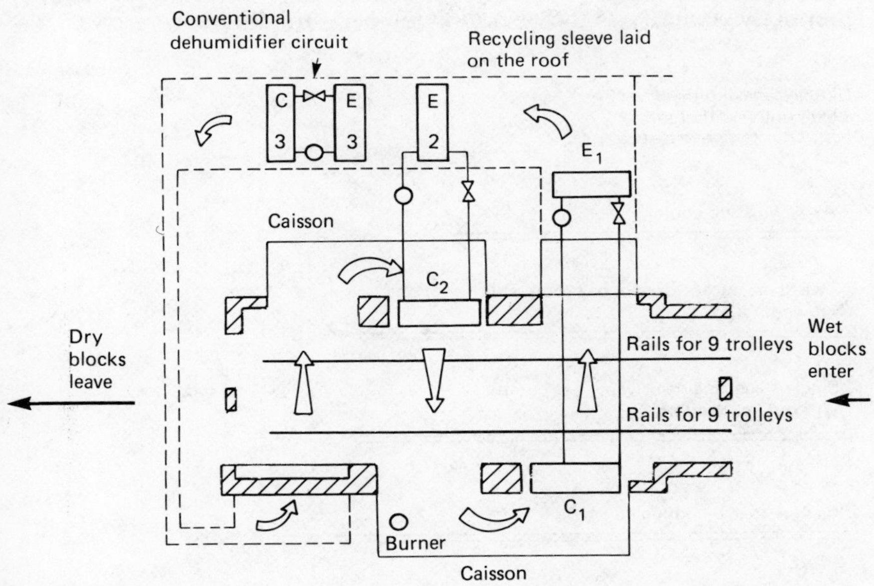

Figure 6.23 Illustrative plan of the plaster-block drying line at PIC, Bray-sur-Seine, France (Gauthier, Legoff and Bassac, 1980)[30]
Drying cycle
Plaster blocks—enter wet, right, move to left to leave dried
Air cycle—at extraction point from kiln the air passes over three heat-pump evaporator batteries E_1, E_2, E_3, to dehumidify the air
—the dry air is reheated by the condenser of the third heat pump and enters the dry end of the kiln as the blocks are about to leave
—this air, now moistened a little, is reheated by the condenser C_2 and recirculated over the intermediate zone of the kiln
—having absorbed more moisture, the air is reheated by condenser C_1 and recirculates around the incoming wet plaster blocks

Église, Manche, where at 3700 plaster blocks/day, production was four times that of the first factory.

Three heat pumps were used. Total compressor power was 270 kW and a further recirculation fan power was 100 kW. Condensation temperature for the refrigerant was 60°C to avoid the high-temperature problems of the first prototype. Flakt Industrie built the units and guaranteed a drying effectiveness of 4 kg water/kWh. While the capital cost was double that of a conventional convective dryer, the energy savings meant an economic payback time of two years.

6.6 Future trends

Two possible improvements are presently being explored, the first being an improvement in system design. Most dehumidifiers operate on a single compression cycle. The effectiveness of the refrigerant cycle falls with increasing temperature difference between evaporation and condensation. Two or more stages of compression become increasingly effective thermodynamically as the operating temperature difference grows.

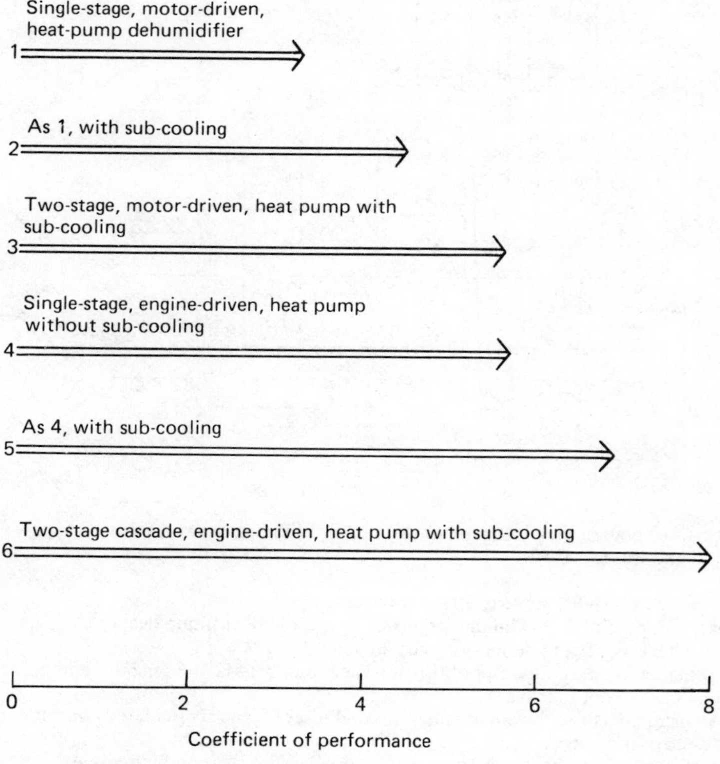

Figure 6.24 Feasibility study of barley drying at 66°C, 5% r.h. (Perry, 1981)[32]

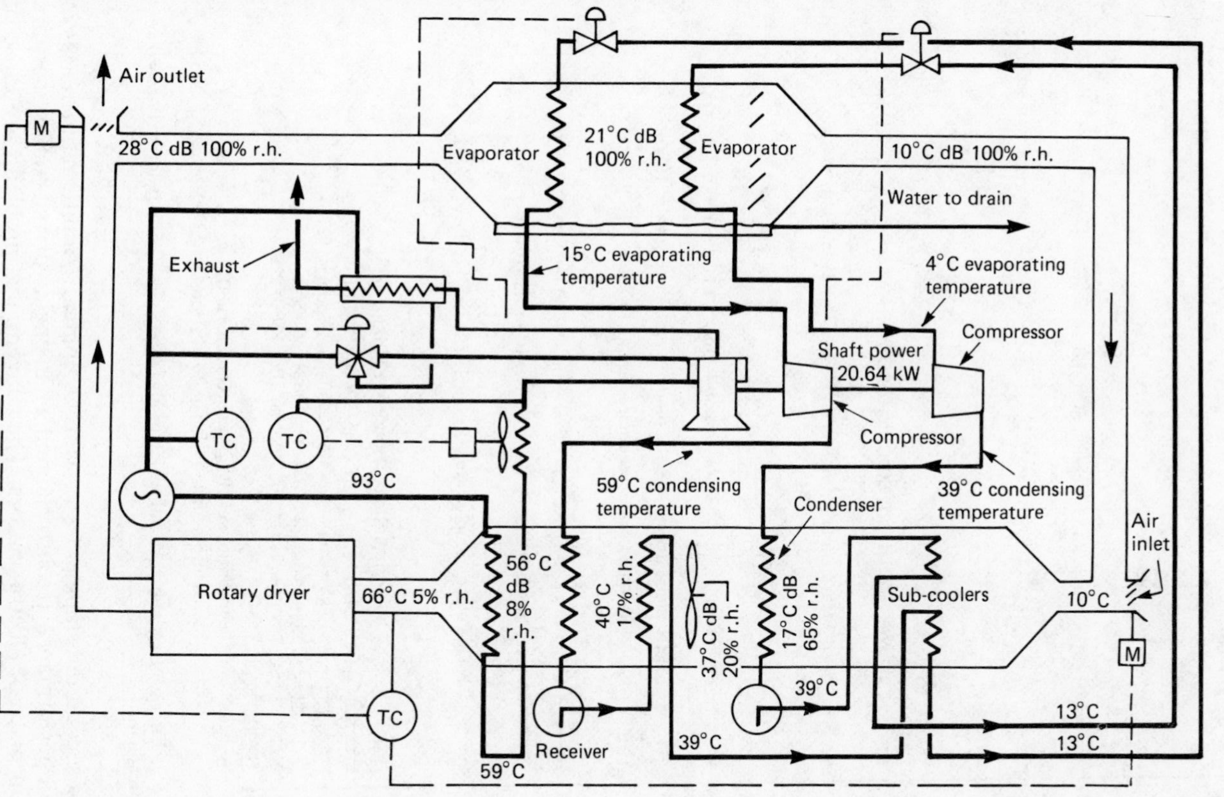

Figure 6.25 Circuit diagram for the two-stage cascade engine-driven heat pump with sub-cooling (Cop ~ 8; option 6 in *Figure 6.24*) (Perry, 1981)[32]

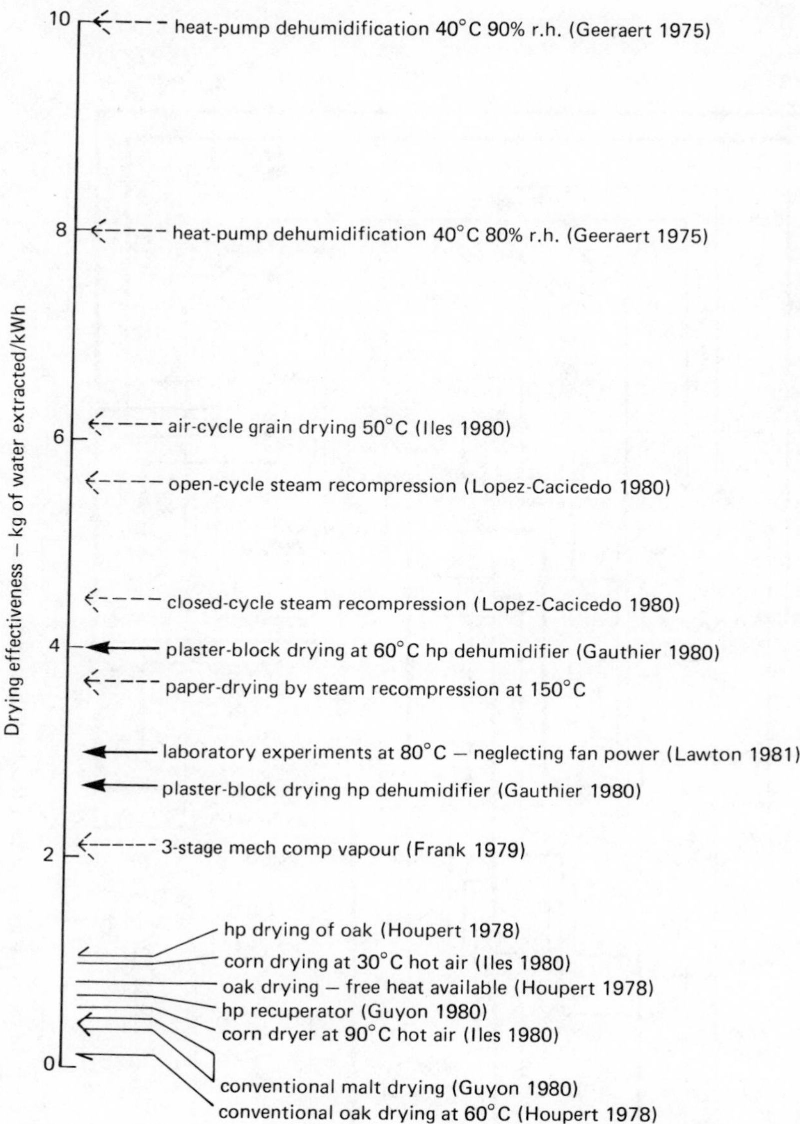

Figure 6.26 Energy effectiveness of industrial drying (solid lines = actual; dotted lines = theoretical data)

The second development area is in equipment. Additional increases in overall performance are also claimed when engine-driven compressors are used in place of electric motors. The conventional problems are those of leaking seals at the motor/compressor interface and the cost of maintenance and standby equipment for breakdowns. Work is now in progress to produce a relatively quiet, low-maintenance, reliable engine and to develop an effective seal for the compressor drive shaft. A feasibility study, using barley-drying as an example, has shown the potential benefits of this increasing complexity. Six options which were considered are displayed in *Figure 6.24*[32]. Overall coefficients of performance at 66°C varied from 3.0 for the simplest system to 8.0 for the most advanced. The circuit arrangement of the most comprehensive scheme is illustrated in *Figure 6.25*[32]. Such a system deserves particular care on the control philosophy.

A summary of the different views and experiences of dehumidifier drying are presented in *Figure 6.26*. The solid lines show the drying effectiveness reported from practical measurements in the laboratory or in the factory. The dotted lines show the potential effectiveness estimated by the researchers or designers.

However, the most active research is directed at the drying operations between 100 and 200°C. This would cover almost all known drying needs. These temperatures pose serious chemical degradation problems for the refrigerants. The steam itself then becomes an attractive working fluid and air is excluded. This leads to mechanical steam recompression cycles replacing dehumidification for many operations. The cycle is illustrated in *Figure 6.27*[31]. Superheated steam enters the dryer at 150°C and evaporates X kg of water from the material being dried and leaves the dryer at 110°C. The major portion of this steam is recirculated over the outside of a heat exchanger but X kg are bypassed to the compressor. These X kg are compressed to a temperature of 180°C and circulated to the inside of the same heat exchanger. This can reheat the major steam flow up to 150°C before it returns to the dryer for another cycle. The water evaporated is therefore available at 170°C to preheat the incoming feed. Practical

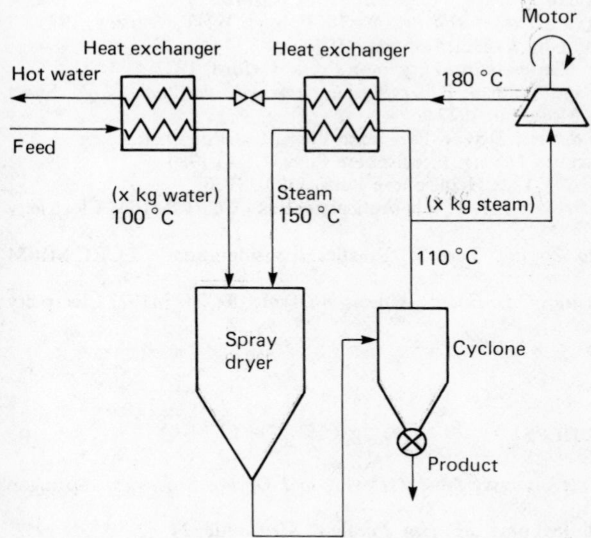

Figure 6.27 A high-temperature (150°C) open-cycle steam recompression dryer (Lopez-Cacicedo, 1980)[31]

problems to be overcome are fouling, air ingress and steam escape, and their effect on both compression and heat exchange. Superheating during compression can be solved by condensate injection and the new screw compressors appear well-suited to this role. Potential savings in primary energy are 55%, assuming an electrical generation efficiency of 30%.

6.7 Further reading on industrial drying processes

Foxwell, G.E. (ed). *The Efficient Use of Fuel.* HMSO, 1942

Lurie, M.J. *Suszlinge Dieko, Gosudarstwiennoje Energeticzeskoje.* Izdatielstwo Moskwa-Leningrad, USSR, 1948

Loesecke, H.W. von. *Drying and Dehydration of Foods.* Reinhold, New York, 1955

Razons, P. *Théorie et Pratique du Séchage Industriel.* Paris, 1955

Kroll, K. *Trockner und Trocknungsverfahren (Drying and Drying Processes).* Springer Verlag, W. Berlin, 1978

Smolsky, B.M. *External Heat and Mass Transfer in Convective Drying Processes.* 1zd Gosunversite, Minsk, USSR, 1961

Krischer, O. *Die Wissenschaftlichen Grundlagen der Trocknungstechnik.* Springer Verlag, W. Berlin, 1963

Dascalescu, A. *Le Séchage et ses Applications Industrielles (Drying and its Industrial Applications).* Dunod, Paris, 1969 (Originally in Romanian, 1964)

Vanevek, V., Prbohlav, R. and Markvart, M. *Fluidised Bed Drying.* L. Hill, London, 1965

Villiere, A. *Séchage des Bois (Drying of Wood).* Dunod, Paris, 1966

Luikov, A.V. *Heat and Mass Transfer in Capillary Porous Bodies.* Pergamon Press, Oxford, 1966

Treybal, E.R. *Mass Transfer Operations.* McGraw-Hill, USA, 1968

Williams-Gardner, A. *Industrial Drying.* L. Hill, London, 1971

Nonhebel, G. and Moss, A.A.H. *Drying of Solids in the Chemical Industry.* Butterworths, London, 1971

Gavelin, G. (ed). *Drying of Paper and Paperboard.* Lockwood, 1972

Keey, R.B. *Drying Principles and Practice.* Pergamon Press, Oxford, 1972

Strumillo, C. *Principles of Drying Theory and Practice* (in Polish). WNT, Warsaw, 1975

Masters, K. *Spray Drying*, 2nd edn. L. Hill, London, 1976

Reay, D.A. *Industrial Energy Conservation.* Pergamon Press, Oxford, 1977

Schlunder, E.U., Martin, H. and Gunmel, P. *Drying Fundamentals and Technology.* Short course notes. McGill Univ, Montreal, 1977

Keey, R.B. *Introduction to Industrial Dryers.* Pergamon Press, Oxford, 1978

Mujumdar, A.S. (ed). *Advances in Drying.* Hemisphere Pubs, USA, 1980

Mujumdar, A.S. (ed). *Drying '80.* **1**, **2**, Hemisphere Pubs, USA, 1980

Strumillo, C. *Introduction to Drying.* Part 1: 'Theoretical aspects'. ECRC/M1624 Electricity Council, 1982

Strumillo, C. *Introduction to Drying.* Part 2: 'Practical considerations'. ECRC/M1624 Electricity Council, 1982

Strumillo, C. and Lopez-Cacicedo, C.L. *Energy Aspects in Drying.* ECRC/M1577 Electricity Council, 1983

6.8 Industrial references

1 Kroll, K. *Trockner und Trocknungsverfahren (Drying and Drying Processes).* Springer Verlag, W. Berlin, 1978

2 Gates, A.A. 'The mothball fleet pays off'. *Htg, Piping & Air Condg*, **24**, 42–95, Jly 1952

3 NEEB Warehouse, North Eastern Electricity Board, Carliol House, Newcastle upon Tyne, Tyne and Wear

4 *ASHRAE Handbook Applications*, 1982. Am Soc of Htg, Refrign & Air Condg, Atlanta, USA, 1982

5 Niess, R.C. 'Industrial heat-pump applications for waste heat recovery'. *Elektrowärme im Technischen Ausbau* Edition A **38**, A 4/5, 295–300, 1982
6 Davidson, W.G. 'A better V-belt is made with humidity control'. *Refrign Engg*, **60** (11) 1186–1187, 1952
7 Anon. 'Humidity control necessary for production of antibiotic drugs'. *Refrign Engg*, **81**, 180 and 198, Feb 1973
8 Caprio, A.A. Dryomatic advertisement. *ASHRAE Jnl*, Jan 1983
9 Moran, T. and Bate-Smith, E.G. 'Storage of eggs at different humidities'. *Modern Refrign,* **52**, 195–196, 1949
10 Thompson, H., Cecil, S.R. and Woodruff, J.G. *Storage of Edible Peanuts.* Univ of Georgia Experimental Sta Bull No 268, Mar 1951, 43 pages
11 Legault, R.R. 'Browning of dehydrated vegetables'. *Indusl & Engg Chemy*, **39**, (10), 1294–1299, 1947
12 Geeraert, B. 'La deshumidification de l'air et le séchage par pompe à chaleur' ('Dehumidification of air and drying by heat pump'). Rep 8.1127.f.G2.BG.Cr, Apr 1975. Laboratoire National Belge d'Électrothermie et d'Électrochimie, LABORELEC, Brussels, Belgium, 61 pp
13 Iles, T., 'The Brayton-cycle heat pump for industrial process applications'. *Elektrowärme im Technischen Ausban*, Edition A, **38**, A 4/5, 285–294, 1980
14 Hodgett, D.L. 'Efficient drying using heat pumps'. *Cheml Engr*, 510–522, Jly/Aug 1976
15 Ayers, D.L., Doering, O.C., Foster, G.H. and Hogan, M.R. 'Development and testing of a heat pump for low-temperature grain drying'. *Elektrowärme im Technischen Ausban*, Edition A, **38**, A 4/5, 275–280, 1980
16 Passey, C. 'Proprietary coordinated heat pump system for saving energy in drying heat labile materials'. *Drying '80: Developments in Drying.* **1**, 314–319, (A.S. Majumdar, ed), Hemisphere Pubs, USA, 1980
17 Filkov, V.M. and Yankov, V.S. 'A survey of heat pump research in the USSR'. World Energy Conf Working Party Paper, 1979. Elecy Ccl trans, OA 2275, 1979
18 Guyon, J. 'Example of the application of the heat pump incorporated in the malt drying process'. PAC Industrie' Electricité de France Pub No 14, 1–15, 1980. Elecy Ccl trans, OA 2369, 1980
19 Dickopp, A. 'Heat pumps for process heating: investigation of the comparative cost effectiveness of gas and electrically powered heat pumps and heat exchangers for a malt kiln'. Rep to Enkon Conf, Nuremberg, W. Germany, 1981. Elecy Ccl trans, OA 3123, 1983
20 Anon. 'Information relating to the demonstration of a 3.5 MW heat pump system for energy recovery from the malt drying process'. Doc. in German from the Friedrich Weissheimer Malt Factory, Gelsenkirchen, W. Germany, 1982. Elecy Ccl trans, OA 3122, 1983
21 Singh, P.P., Wang, C.Y. and Zuritz, C. 'A numerical approach to simulate rice drying'. *Drying '80: Developments in Drying.* **1**, 227–229, (A.S. Majumdar, ed), Hemisphere Pubs, USA, 1980
22 Mann, E.W. 'The possibilities of using heat pumps in drying and evaporation'. *Elektrowärme International*, Edition B, **40**, 3/4, 177–181, 1982. Elecy Ccl trans, OA 2641, 1983
23 Electricity Council Industrial Case History. 'Electric heat pump drying'. EC Doc 4403, 1983
24 Houpert, J.M. 'Artificial drying of timber by dehumidification'. Paper presented by Comité Français d'Électrothermie, Bordeaux, 1978. Elecy Ccl trans, OA 2217, 1978
25 Hess, H. 'Warmepumpenanwendung in der Holztrochung' ('Use of heat pumps in drying timber'). *Elektrowärme im Tecnischen Ausban*, Edition A, **38**, A 4/5, 270–274, 1980
26 Lawton, J. 'Closed and open cycle heat pumps for drying'. Symp No 3, NW Branch of the Institn of Cheml Engrs. *'Heat pumps: energy savers for the process industries'*. Salford, Apr 1981
27 Schikorr, G. 'Corrosion of metals in wooden casings'. *Werkstoff und Korrosion*, **12** (1), 1–10, 1961. Elecy Ccl trans, OA 1822, 1982
28 Sandermann, W. and Rothkamm, M. 'The determination of pH values in timber and the practical importance of this data'. *Holz als Roh- und Werkstoff*, (FRG), **17** (11) 433–440, 1959. Elecy Ccl trans, OA 1824, 1982
29 Sandermann, W., Gerhardt, U. and Weissman, G. 'Investigations of volatile organic acids in various species of wood'. *Holz als Roh- und Werkstoff*, (FRG), **28** (2), 59–67, 1970. Elecy Ccl trans, OA 1823, 1982

30 Gauthier, R., Legoff, R. and Bassac, C. 'System of drying plaster blocks using a heat pump'. *Drying '80:* **2**, A.S. Mujumdar (ed), Hemisphere Pubs, USA, 1980
31 Lopez-Cacicedo, C. 'Application possibilities for heat pumps in the higher temperature range'. *Elektrowarme im Technischen Ausbau*, Edition A, **38**, A 4/5, 281–284, 1980
32 Perry, E.J. 'Drying by cascaded heat pumps'. Inst of Refrign Mtg, Oct 1981 8 pp
33 Villiere, A. *Séchage des Bois (Drying of Wood)*. Dunod, Paris, 1966
34 Mathewson, J.S. *The Air Seasoning of Wood.* Dept of Agri Tech Bull 174, Washington, USA, Apr 1930
35 Hodgett, D. 'Dehumidifying evaporator for high-temperature heat pumps'. Intern Inste of Refrign, Commissions B1, B2, E1, Yugoslavia, 1977
36 Tai, K.W., Devotta, S., Watson, F.A. and Holland, F.A. 'The potential for heat pumps in drying and dehumidification systems'. *Energy Res*, **6**, 333–340, 1982
37 Oliver, T.N. 'Process drying with a dehumidifying heat pump'. *Intern Symp on Indusl Appls of Heat Pumps*, Mar 1982. BHRA 74–88
38 Curis, O. and Laine, J.D. 'Gas motors driving heat pumps in the malting industry'. *Intern Symp on Indusl Appls of Heat Pumps*, Mar 1982. BHRA 99–45

Chapter 7

Food and flowers

7.1 Plant growing

Dehumidifiers have had little role until recently in the growing process of plants. In most cases water is plentiful and a dehydrating environment would be potentially harmful. While this is still true there is one potential role for dehumidifiers to operate in advanced greenhouses at night.

Traditionally, greenhouses in Britain have been made of loosely-assembled panes of single glass. Air infiltration has been high and at night the combination of infiltration with condensation on the single glazing means that high internal relative humidities are avoided. The large area of glass radiating to the cold night sky forms a dewpoint dehumidifier.

New advanced greenhouses are very different in construction. They have double-skinned walls and roof and are relatively airtight so that controlled atmosphere techniques, such as carbon dioxide enrichment, can be undertaken economically. The heat loss is almost halved. However, in addition to saving space-heating energy, this insulation increases the plant canopy temperature and prevents condensation on the glass. This means that the relative humidities will be higher than previously. While the increase in plant temperature is beneficial, there is an increased risk to the crop of Fulvia infections due to the much higher relative humidities. If condensation occurs on the plants themselves than Botrytis can develop and spread.

The increasing demand for very high standards of uniformity in produce throws an even greater importance on crop yield. In today's intensive growing, just one defective plant creates a non-uniformity, and the subsequent asymmetric growth of adjacent plants makes them substandard.

The new dehumidifier role is therefore one of plant protection at night. Its purpose is to lower the relative humidity to 90% r.h. The refrigerant dehumidifiers are particularly efficient at such high relative humidities and a heating coefficient of performance between 2 and 3 would be expected. The dehumidifier would therefore remove excessive moisture and provide background night-time heating[1] (*Figure 7.1*).

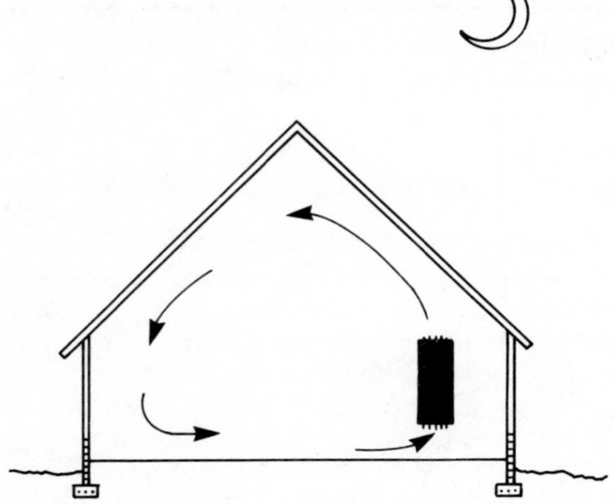

Figure 7.1 Schematic illustration of a dehumidifier in a greenhouse. Night-time operation prevents condensation on the crops

The development potential is large for such a heat-pump dehumidifier to be able to behave as an air-source heat-pump heater, or as a dehumidifier, or with a reverse-cycle operation as a summer cooling unit[2].

Dehumidifiers could also be used to protect plants such as roses which are particularly sensitive to disease at high relative humidities. Late afternoon/early evening is the danger period when condensation may occur[3]. Some care will be needed if dehumidification is applied to soft-stemmed flowers such as gerberas and freesias. Such plants, when young and tender or when growing under weak winter light, can suffer collapse of the stem tissue behind the head if the relative humidity falls quickly[4].

Care will also be needed to some fumigation or fungical treatments. Sulphur dioxide fumigation is twenty times more effective at 96% r.h. than at 75% r.h.[5]. However, in petal blight on chrysanthemums (*Itersonilia perplexans*) the recommended treatment to eliminate the fungus is to lower the relative humidity and spray with Zineb at the coloured bud stage[6].

TABLE 7.1 Preferred relative humidity for house plants (Condar, USA)

	Relative humidity	
30–45% r.h.	*45–60% r.h.*	*60%+ r.h.*
Agapanthus	Achimenes	Azalea
Aspidistra	African violets	Camellia
Cacti	Amaryllis	Cyclamen
Century plant	Asparagus fern	Brake fern
Chenille plant	Begonia	
Chrysanthemums	Episcia	
Crocus	Fuschia	
Daffodils	Gardenia	
Hydrangea	Hyacinth	
Tulips	Spider plant	

There are suggestions that some flowers respond best to those conditions which are found in their native habitat. Plants such as ferns enjoy wet conditions and would welcome high relative humidities; cacti favour dry conditions. Suggestions for preferred plant relative humidities are given in *Table 1*[7].

7.2 Storage of fresh plant-derived food and flowers

Dehumidification is important in food storage but it is in association with refrigeration[8–11]. The humidification problem is therefore one of correctly sizing the refrigerant evaporator coil to operate at the correct dewpoint temperature to meet both the refrigeration and moisture control duties.

All produce continues to carry on some form of metabolic processes even when cut from the root or branch of the plant. The most important of these is respiration by which the oxygen of the air is chemically combined with carbon from the plant tissue, chiefly in the form of sugars, to form various decomposition products which lead ultimately to carbon dioxide and water vapour. Illustrations of respiration rates for perishable

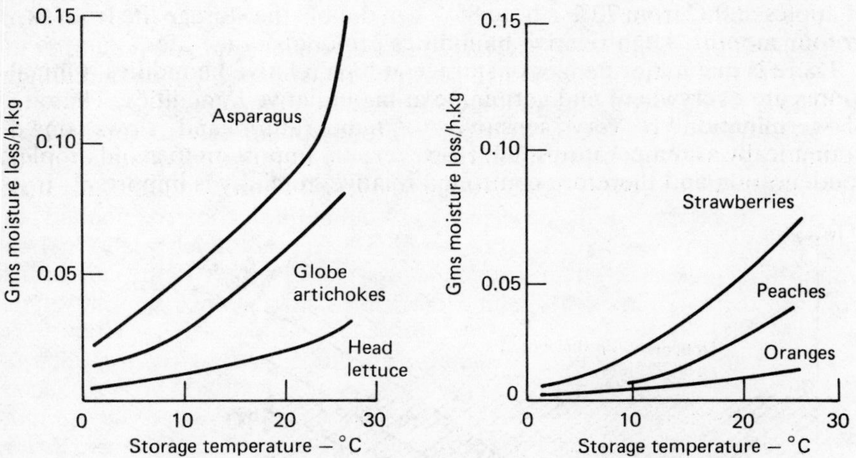

Figure 7.2 Respiration rate of stored perishable vegetables and fruits (based on carbon dioxide release rate) (Lutz and Hardenburg, 1968)[12]

vegetables and fruits are given for different temperatures in *Figure 7.2*[12]. Values of respiration vary from 0.01 g moisture loss/h kg for oranges stored at 25°C to 0.1 g moisture loss/h kg for asparagus.

The process can be grossly simplified to the oxidation of hexose sugar:

$$\text{sugar} + \text{oxygen} = \text{carbon dioxide} + \text{water vapour} + \text{energy}$$
$$C_6H_{12} + 6O_2 = CO_2 + 6H_2O + \text{energy}$$

which in mass terms represents:

$$192\text{ g} + 192\text{ g} = 284\text{ g} + 108\text{ g} + 673\text{ kg cal}$$

The energy is released in the form of heat. Once the sugar is consumed the produce dies.

This chemical reaction rate is governed by temperature, and up to 40°C will double or triple with every 10°C rise in temperature. The recognized way of maximizing storage life is therefore to store the produce at the coolest practicable temperature above its freezing point. The moisture and carbon dioxide generated has to be removed to maintain a dry and safe atmosphere.

Appearance, texture and flavour are also important in determining storage life. Most plants are 80 to 90% by weight water. This water slowly evaporates to the environment. Evaporation from living tissue is termed 'transpiration'. All plants can lose some of their water without visibly changing their attractiveness but eventually the produce will look wilted and shrivelled. The weight loss at which the produce becomes unacceptable to the customer varies widely with the commodity. Grapes lose their appearance when only 1% of water is lost, apples when 5 to 7% is lost, and flowers when they lose 10 to 15%. The rate of water loss is normally proportional to the difference in water vapour pressure between the water in the plant and that in the ambient atmosphere. Drier atmospheres mean faster water loss[13–15]. The influence of this on apples can be seen in *Figure 7.3*[16]. Increasing the relative humidity in a warehouse of apples at 0°C from 70% r.h. to 85% can double the storage life from two to four months. High relative humidities prolong storage life.

There is one major danger of storage at high relative humidities. Fungal spores are everywhere and germinate at high relative humidities. The rate of germination is very sensitive to temperature and slows down dramatically as temperatures fall. However, it is important to avoid droplet condensation and therefore controlled relative humidity is important. It is

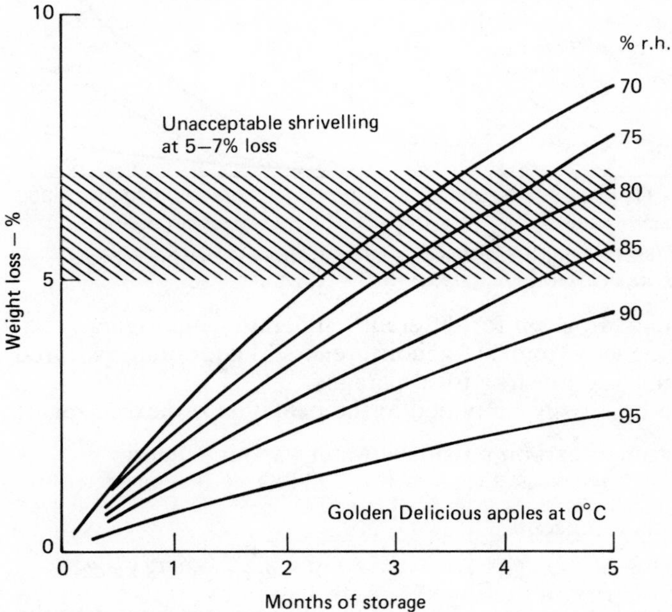

Figure 7.3 The storage of apples in different relative humidities (Christopher *et al*, 1948)[16]

TABLE 7.2 Illustrative conditions for storage*

Product	*Temp °C*	*Recommended relative humidity—%* (scale 0, 20, 40, 60, 80, 100)
Fish	0°C	↔
Green vegetables	0°C	↔
Fresh beef	0°C	◆
Poultry	0°C	◆
Eggs	−1°C	↔
Cheese	5°C	↔
Fur and fabrics	4°C	↔
Hard toffee	20°C	◆
Chocolate	20°C	◆
Grain	15°C	↔

*For specific products, consult the specialist publications, e.g. Christensen, C.M. (ed.), *Storage of cereal grains and their products*, Am. Ass. Cereal Chem Inc, 1974; Lutz, J.M. and Hardenburg, R.E., US Dept of Agric. *Agric. Handbook 66: Commercial storage of fruits, vegetables, florist and nursery stock*, 1968; *ASHRAE Handbook:* Applications, 1985.

also essential to have uniform temperature conditions within the whole warehouse. Unusually warm areas will dehydrate more rapidly and unusually cold areas may suffer from condensation or even frost damage.

Two exceptions to the general rules are nuts and onion sets[17]. All nuts except chestnuts should be stored at 60 to 80% r.h. Chestnuts need special protective packaging to avoid going very hard. Onion sets need 65 to 70% r.h. at 0°C for long-term storage. Higher relative humidities dispose onions to root growth and rot.

General recommendations are listed in *Table 7.2* but refer to specialist guides for more detailed recommendations and achievable storage times; for example, Lutz and Hardenburg, US Department of Agriculture, 1968[12].

7.3 Storage of grain and seed

Cereal grains and plant seeds deserve special attention because they are stored in vast quantity and for long periods. This section reviews the critical factors of moisture content and temperature. The actual drying operations are considered separately in the section on industrial drying.

Seeds are considered first because they are the most sensitive. The essential factor is whether they will germinate and grow. Over time the proportion of seed which actually germinates will decline and those seeds that do may do so with less vigour. The two factors which most influence the seed viability are temperature and moisture content. The moisture content of seed is a function of the ambient relative humidity (*Figure 7.4*)[18]. Very crudely each reduction of 10% in ambient relative humidity from 70% to 10% r.h. will double the storage life[19]. Below 10% r.h. germination may decline because of the autoxidation of the seed lipids but commercial storage does not run at such dry conditions. Similarly, between 0 and 40°C each 5°C rise in seed temperature halves the storage life. A given storage life can therefore be achieved by a variety of combinations of temperature and ambient relative humidity. The economic storage

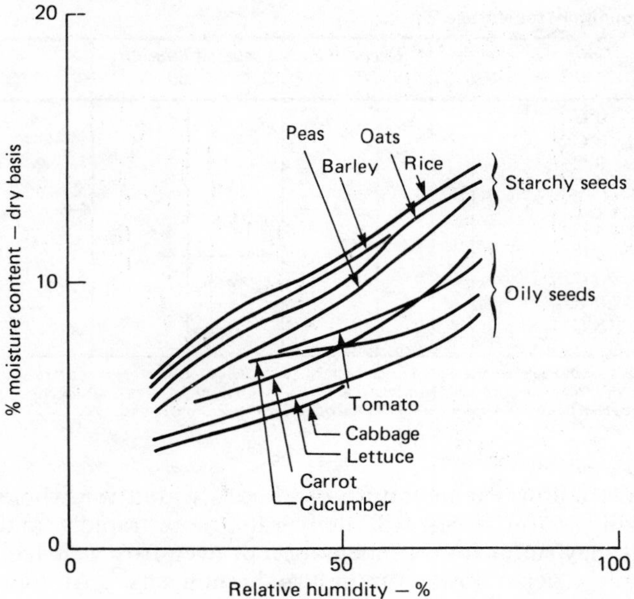

Figure 7.4 Adsorption isotherms for seeds at 25°C (Howe, 1972)[18]

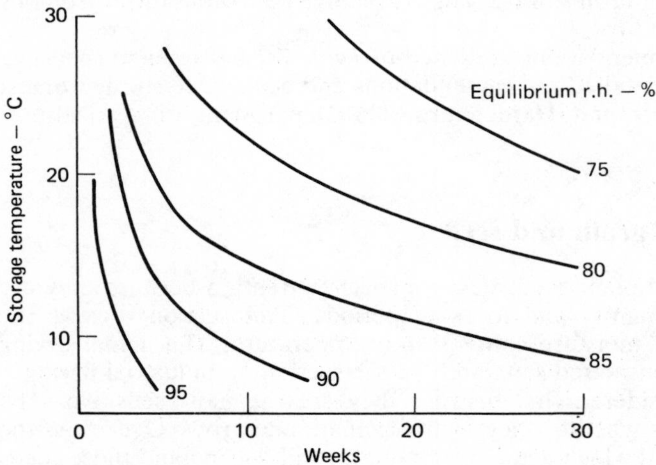

Figure 7.5 Maximum storage period for barley to keep viability at 95% (Burell, 1974)[20]

conditions therefore depend upon the relative costs of dehumidification, refrigeration and insulation, taken together with the risk of spoilage at high relative humidities and the practical advantages of having the grain flowing easily as it does at lower relative humidities.

Barley, once it has germinated, becomes the source of malt for our brewing industry. Commercial standards require at least 95% germination. The relationship between storage temperature and ambient relative humidity and viability is illustrated in *Figure 7.5*[20]. It is also essential to avoid mould because of the off flavours which could be introduced into beer.

The progressive loss of germination with time has been studied for a wide variety of seeds. A representative illustration for onion seed is shown in *Figure 7.6*[21].

The storage of grain destined for foodstuff is not concerned with germination but with attractive appearance and absence of contaminants. The two spoilage routes are invasion by fungi or infestation by insects. Both of these problems are strongly influenced by temperature and moisture. We will examine the microflora first[22,23].

Fungal activity results in:

1 a decrease in viability,
2 discolouration,
3 possible production of harmful mycotoxins,
4 heating and
5 mustiness and unpalatability.

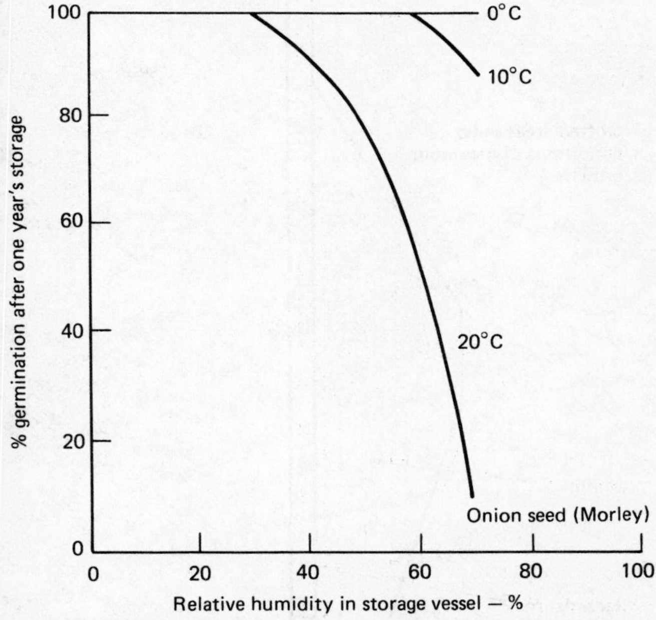

Figure 7.6 The influence of temperature and relative humidity on the viability of stored onion seed (Gane, 1948)[21]

The spores of the hundred thousand different kinds of fungi are continuously around us. More than 150 have been reported from cereal grains and these are always present in high concentration around grain warehouses and mills. They have to be accepted as a natural hazard and the storage conditions have to ensure that they do not prosper.

The common field fungi *Alternaria, Gladosporium, Fusarium* and *Holminthosporium* require very high moisture contents to grow. This would be in equilibrium with relative humidities of between 90 and 100%

and therefore unlikely to be found indoors[8]. The danger lies with the storage fungi which develops on materials which are in equilibrium with relative humidities of 70–90%. These comprise five group species of *Aspergillus* and several species of *Penicillium*. The two group species usually associated with the start of such deterioration are *A. restrictus* and *A. glaucus* which can grow in atmospheres 70% r.h. at temperatures of between 0 and 45°C but with an optimum 30 to 35°C. *Penicillium* tends to grow better at lower temperatures, −5°C to 40°C with an optimum of 20 to 25°C. *Penicillium* also requires equilibrium relative humidities greater than 80 or 90%.

Correct storage requires an equilibrium relative humidity below 70%. Particular problems can arise when grains already contaminated are

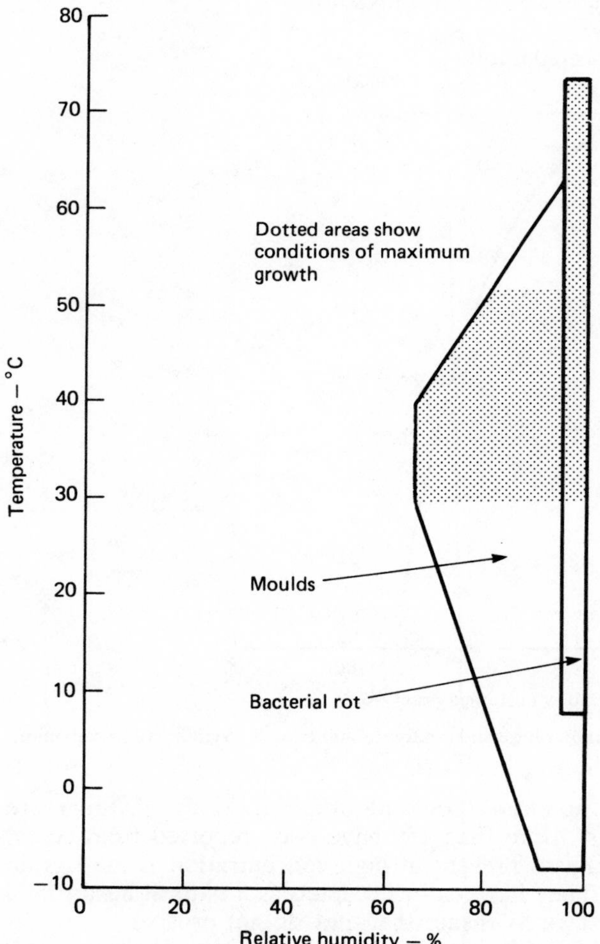

Figure 7.7 Conditions under which mould and bacterial rot occur (based on data from Semenicek, 1954)[24]

stored. One of the metabolytes of mould growth in moisture. Once a fungal invasion starts then it can generate local heat and moisture. This temperature rise can favour more rapid growth and the higher moisture content can encourage other moulds to propagate. Surveys have shown that grain can be stored at 5 to 10°C with 15% (75% r.h.) moisture content for nine months to a year without damage. However, if the same grain had been moderately or heavily invaded by storage fungi, the fungi may grow and create extensive spoilage within six months.

As the fungi develop, any insect population eventually declines. However, often associated with the mouldy grain, there are grain-infesting mites which can migrate to clean grain, taking with them the spores which in turn infect the clean grain.

Bacterial infection requires free water to be available, i.e. a moisture content of material in equilibrium with a relative humidity of 100%. Thermophylic bacteria can raise the temperature to around 70 to 75°C. However, by this stage, the grain is spoiled beyond use for food.

The danger zone for risk of fungal problems is shown in *Figure 7.7*[24]. This can be related back to the more conventional index of moisture content by means of the moisture equilibrium relationship shown in *Figure 7.4*.

Moisture and temperature are also critical in determining whether insects survive and prosper. The activity level of insects is determined by the ambient temperature. Few eggs are laid below 15°C, and hatching and larvae development around this temperature is very slow. Dormancy normally occurs below 7°C. Most grain-damaging insects are of subtropical origin and do not hibernate. Dormancy prevents the insects from feeding and at low temperatures they die from starvation. The upper temperature limit for the reproduction of most grain pests is 35°C and the adults are short-lived at this temperature (*Figure 7.8*)[25].

The most likely temperature zone for insect attack falls between 20 and 35°C. Within this band the determining factor is moisture content, and this content is a function of the relative humidity of the storage atmosphere. In general, increasing grain moisture favours a rapid increase in the number of insects. However, as discussed earlier, there is a critical moisture point at which fungi develop and destroy the insects, except for those which feed on the fungi.

The most persistent insect is the flour beetle, which can develop in very dry grain provided that there is plenty of fine dust present. Experiments show that the grain has to be very dry before breeding ceases, and temperature is the dominant factor (*Figure 7.9*)[26].

Weevils are more sensitive to the moisture of the grain. Reproduction stops in grain below 10% moisture (dry basis) and adults soon die in drier grain. The results on experiments with granary weevils are shown in *Figure 7.10*. Rice weevils behave in a very similar way. The critical moisture content for weevil development is 12 to 13% moisture (dry basis).

Bulk grain with a thriving insect population has one further disadvantage—it can become hot. In large storage vessels insects can generate local metabolic heat faster than the heat can dissipate. This results in hot spots, which at first favour the more rapid breeding of the insects. The moisture generated by the insect metabolism can then

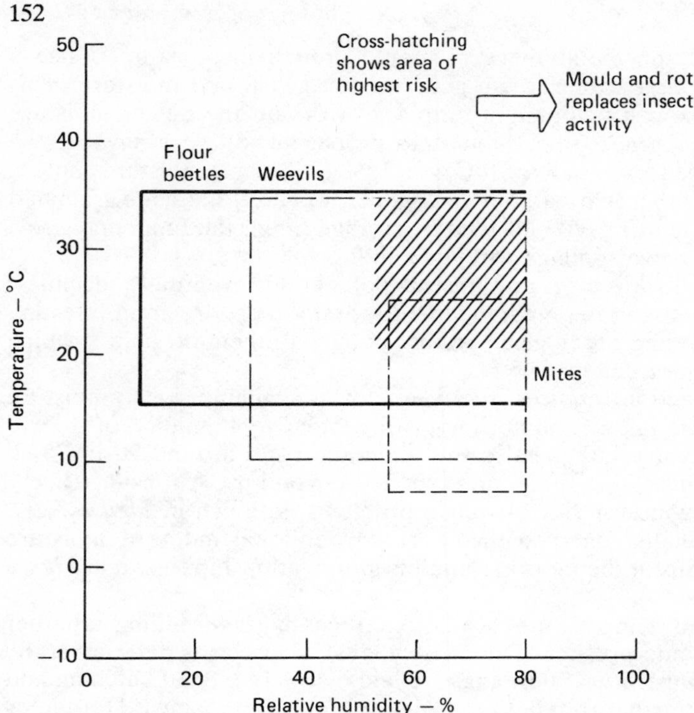

Figure 7.8 Conditions for insect activity in stored grain (based on data from Cotton and Wilbur, 1974)[25]

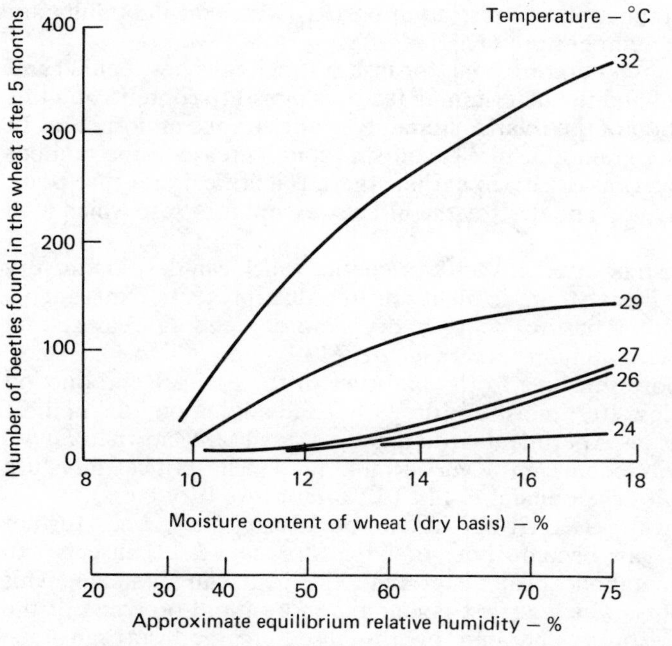

Figure 7.9 Beetle abundance under different conditions of temperature and moisture. (25 pairs of beetles were introduced at the start of the test) (Cotton, 1963)[26]

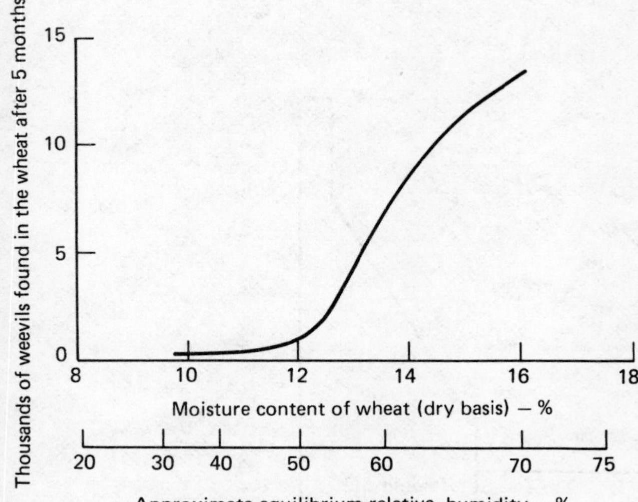

Figure 7.10 The development of granary weevils in wheat (50 pairs of beetles were introduced at the start of the test) (Cotton, 1963)[26]

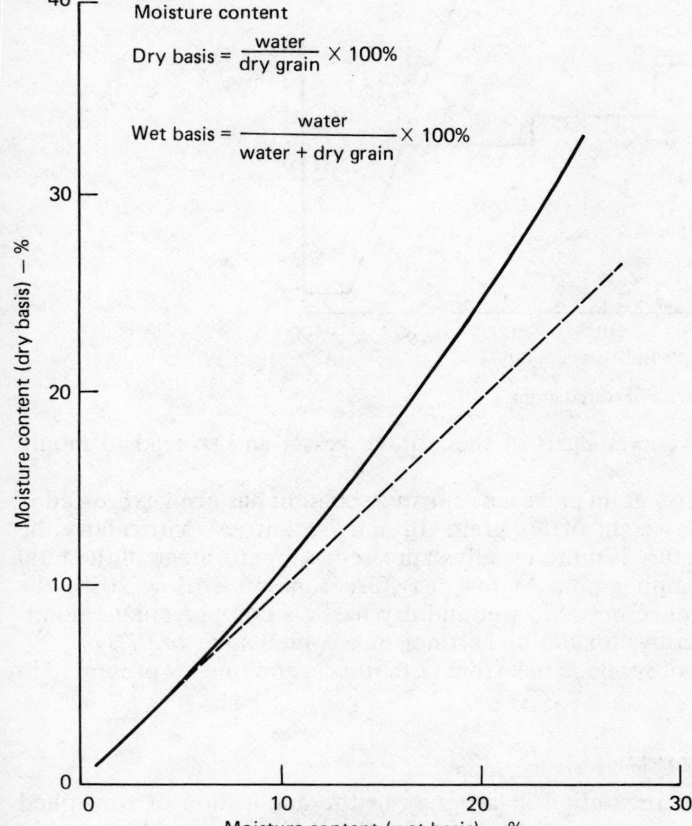

Figure 7.11 Relationship between moisture content expressed on the basis of wet or dry weight

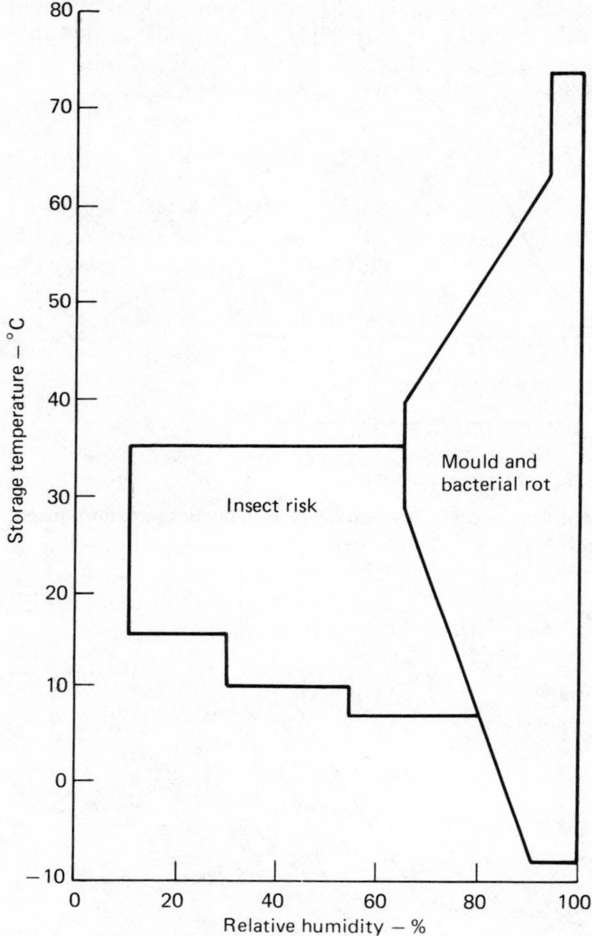

Figure 7.12 Spoilage risk of stored grain

condense in the cooler parts of the storage vessel and so lead to mould damage.

In this section on grain and seed, moisture content has been expressed in terms of the dry weight of the grain. In many countries, particularly the USA, grain moisture is more usually expressed as a percentage of the total weight of the damp grain. At low moisture contents (below 10%) the maximum difference between wet and dry bases is one percentage point. The difference grows for the higher moisture contents (*Figure 7.11*).

The summary of spoilage risk from both insects and fungi is presented in *Figure 7.12*.

7.4 Future trends

There is a major revolution in progress in the application of controlled atmospheres for plant growth, transport, storage and sales. The trend in

Britain is away from the multiplicity of small local independent growers selling through a wholesale market, and towards scientifically-controlled large-scale intensive growing, through specially-designed chilled transport, to carefully-controlled storage areas for subsequent sale through high-volume supermarket outlets.

The control of humidity in the transport and storage of fresh produce is already achieved by the correct size and type of refrigeration chillers. The active area of research is in the growing stage. The new double-glazed greenhouses are sealed and there may be positive benefits of lower relative humidities to enhance transpiration and the flow of nutrients through the plant. This would be a positive benefit if found to be significant and one which would complement the use of the dehumidifier for plant protection by lowering the relative humidity at night to prevent plant spoilage by fungal attack. Such equipment would have the possibility of operating as a modest-sized heat-pump heater or chiller as required. While such a machine would be ineffective in size in the peak summer condition, it could be beneficial during the early spring or late autumn when crop prices are at their highest.

There are also experiments in progress in France to explore the benefit of a small dehumidifier in large-scale grain storage. Large silos of grain (40 000 kg) are particularly sensitive to uneven temperatures and much thought goes into the storage-bin design and operation to maintain an even temperature. If a temperature gradient occurs, then, since the vapour pressure in the store is approximately uniform and constant, there will be an inverse effect on relative humidity. The cool spots will be at a higher relative humidity than the hot spots. Damp problems may then occur in these cool areas. One possible cure is to place a refrigerant evaporator inside the grain bin above the grain, to lower the vapour pressure by dehumidification.

7.5 Further reading

Allen, R.C. 'Temperature and humidity requirements for the storage of dahlia roots'. *Am Soc for Hortl Sci, Proc*, **35**, 770–773, 1938

Barton, L.V. 'Relation of certain air temperatures and humidities to viability of seeds'. Boyce Thompson Inste Contrib, **12**, 85–102, 1941

Barton, L.V. 'Effect of temperature and moisture on the viability of stored lettuce, onion and tomato seed'. Boyce Thompson Inste Contrib, **23**, 285–290, 1966

Boswell, V.R., Toole, E.H., Toole, V.K. and Fisher, D.F. 'A study of rapid deterioration of vegetable seed and methods for its prevention'. Dept of Agri Tech Bull 708, Washington, USA, Apr 1940

Cooke, F.M. 'Humidity control of seed storage areas'. Missouri Seedsmen Assoc, short course. *Seedsmen Proc*, 29–37, 1966

Electricity Council. 'Vegetable conditioning and storage — potatoes'. Tech Inf, AGR 8–1, 1981

Electricity Council. 'Vegetable conditioning and storage — onions'. Tech Inf, AGR 8–2, 1981

Electricity Council. 'Vegetable conditioning and storage — red beetroot'. Tech Inf, AGR 8–3, 1981

Electricity Council. 'Vegetable conditioning and storage — winter white cabbage'. Tech Inf, AGR 8–4, 1982

Farm Buildings Inf Centre. 'Buildings for grain storage'. Farm Bldgs Inf Cen, Kenilworth, 1982

Hass, A. 'Dehumidification in seed storage'. *Seedsmens Digest*, **12** (8), 8, 10, 11, 32, 33, 1961
James, E. *An Annotated Bibliography on Seed Storage and Deterioration.* A review of 20th century literature reported in foreign languages. Dept of Agri, ARS, 34–15–2, Washington, USA, 1963
Justice, O.L. and Bass, L.N. *Principles of Practices of Seed Storage.* Castle House Pubs, London, 1979
McLean, K.A. *Drying and Storing Combinable Crops.* Farming Press Ltd, 1980
Rocha, F.F. 'Interaction of moisture content and temperature on onion seed viability'. *Am Soc for Hortl Sci, Proc*, **73**, 385–389, 1959
Rockland, L.B. 'Water activity and storage stability'. *Food Techy*, **23**, 11–21, 1969
Snow, D., Crichton, M.H.G. and Wright, N.C. *Mould Deterioration of Feedingstuffs in Relation to Humidity of Storage.* Part 1: 'The growth of moulds at low humidities'. Ann of Appld Biol, **31**, 102–110, 1944. Part 2: 'The water uptake of feedingstuffs at different humidities'. Ann of Appld Biol, **31**, 111–116, 1944

7.6 References

1 Bailey, B.J. 'Limiting the relative humidity in insulated greenhouses at night'. *Acta Hort*, **148**, 1–11, 1983
2 Weir, J.A.C. 'Bivalent heating systems applied to greenhouses in the UK'. Unipede Conf: Bivalen systems, Killarney, Eire, Sept 1983
3 Anon. Grower Guide No 9: *Roses under Glass.* Grower Bks, London, 1980
4 Anon. Grower Guide No 11: *Quality in Cut Flowers.* Grower Bks, London, 1980
5 Coney, H.M. and Uota, M. 'Effect of concentration, exposure time, temperature and relative humidity on the toxicity of sulphur dioxide to the spores of *Botrytis cinerea*'. *Phytopathology*, **S1**, 815–819, 1961
6 Walls, I. *Modern Greenhouse Methods: Flowers and Plants.* F. Muller, London, 1982
7 Condar Manufacturing, USA, 1985
8 Mann, G. 'The control of relative humidity in cold stores'. Inste of Refrign, *Proc*, **50**, 177–191, London, 1954
9 Browne, M.W. 'Humidity and air circulation in cold storage'. *Refrign*, USA, **63**, 140–143, 1922.
10 Platenius, H., Jamison, F.S. and Thompson, H.C. 'Studies on cold storage and vegetables'. Cornell Univ Agricl Experl Sta, Bull No 602, 1934
11 Brooks, J. 'Humidity control in egg storage'. Inste of Refrign, *Proc*, **48**, 94–97, 1951/2
12 Lutz, J.M. and Hardenburg, R.E. 'The commercial storage of fruits, vegetables and florist and nursery stocks'. Agri Hdbk 66, Dept of Agri, Washington, USA, 1968
13 Hitchcock, A.E. and Zimmerman, P.W. 'Effect of chemicals, temperature and humidity on the lasting qualities of cut flowers'. *Am Jnl of Bot*, **16**, 433–440, 1929
14 Berg, L. van den, and Lentz, C.P. 'Effect of temperature, relative humidity and atmospheric composition on changes in quality of carrots during storage'. *Food Techy*, USA, 20, 954–957, 1966
15 Smith, W.H. 'Evaporation of water from apples in relation to temperature and atmospheric humidity'. *Ann of Appd Biol*, **20**, 220–235, 1933
16 Christopher, E.P., Pieniazek, S.A., Shutak, V. and McElroy, L. 'Transpiration of apples in cold storage'. Am Soc for Hortcl Sci, *Proc*, **51**, 114–118, 1948
17 Anon. Grower Guide No 2: *Onion Storage.* Grower Bks, London, 1979
18 Howe, R.W. *Seed Biology.* (T.T. Kozlowski, ed), **3**, Chap 4: Academic Press, New York, 1972
19 Harrington, J.F. 'Thumb rules for drying seed'. *Crops and Soils.* **13**, 16–17, USA, 1960
20 Burrell, J.J. Chap 12, 449–480, 'Aeration', *Storage of Cereal Grains and their Products.* (C.M. Christensen, ed), Am Assoc of Cereal Chem, St Paul, Minnesota, USA, 1974
21 Gane, R. 'The effect of temperature, water content and composition of the atmosphere on the viability of carrot, onion and parsnip seed in storage'. *Jnl of Agricl Sci*, **38**, 84–89, 1948
22 Harrington, J.F. Chap 3: 'Seed storage and longevity'. *Seed Biology.* (T.T. Kozlowski, ed), **3**, Academic Press, New York, 1972
23 Christensen, C.M. (ed), *Storage of Cereal Grains and their Products.* Am Assoc of Cereal Chemy, St. Paul, Minnesota, USA, 1974
24 Semenicek, G. Chap 3: 'Microflora', 97–151, *Storage of Cereal Grains and their Products.*

(J. Anderson and A.W. Alcock, eds), Am Assoc of Cereal Chem, St Paul, Minnesota, USA, 1954

25 Cotton, R.T. and Wilbur, D.A. Chap 4, 'Insects' pp.193–231 in *Storage of cereal grains and their products*. (C.M. Christensen, ed.), Am Assoc of Cereal Chem, St. Paul, Minnesota, USA, 1974

26 Cotton, R.T. *Pests of Stored Grain and Grain Products*. Burgess Pubg Co, Minneapolis, USA, 1963

Chapter 8

Compressed air and other gases

8.1 Introduction

Two factors are encouraging factory managers to consider drying their compressed air before circulating it throughout the factory air lines. The first is the growing realization of the cost of compressed air. Wasteful practices such as leaving air-line valves slightly open to ensure speedy water drainage are expensive. The second factor is the recognition of the importance of quality control in the products and processes in which the compressed air is used, and the benefit which dry air creates.

When water precipitates it can have the following effects:

(1) Reduction in performance of the air-driven tools and machines. This can be caused by washing away the lubricant or by ice build-up in the outlet ports.
(2) Increased cost of maintenance of the tools. This is attributed to the lack of adequate lubrication.
(3) Production losses due to plant breakdown.
(4) Formation of corrosion and eventually scale in the distribution pipework leading to higher pipework flow resistance and prematurely-blocked filters.
(5) Increased costs to replace and repair piping.
(6) Sensitivity to cold weather, particularly if pipes run outside.
(7) Malfunctions in instrumentation and control system due to the corroding and blocking effect of rust and water droplets.
(8) Impaired finishing processes, particularly paint spraying.
(9) Product contamination as in air-gauging techniques where the measuring head is inserted into the machined components.

This chapter will show how such drying may be achieved.

8.2 Psychrometrics

The act of compressing moist air reduces its volume and increases its temperature. Dalton's law of partial pressures declares that in a mixture of perfect gases each gas exerts the same pressure as it would if it alone occupied the vessel. The same is approximately true for a mixture of vapours which do not interact. The mass of the vapour needed to saturate a given space is independent of the other occupants of the space and depends only upon the ambient temperature.

The amount of water vapour entering the compressor is a function of the ambient temperature, pressure and relative humidity. The amount which can be retained in the compressed air after compression is simply related to the temperature which determines the saturation vapour pressure, and hence the maximum amount of water vapour per unit volume, and to the final volume which determines the quantity.

The partial pressure of air at 1 bar is $(1 - \frac{\%\text{r.h.}}{100} \times P_1)$ bar

where P1 = saturation vapour pressure in bar at ambient temperature T_1

Following compression to 7 bar and a temperature of T_2 the partial pressure of the air becomes $(7 - P_2)$ bar

where P_2 = saturation vapour pressure in bar at T_2

The amount of water remaining after compression of free air at 1m^3/h is

$$W_2 \text{ g/h} = (\text{saturation g/m}^3 \text{ water at } T_2) \times \frac{(1 - \frac{\%\text{r.h.}}{100} P_1)}{7 - P_2} \times \frac{T_2{}^\circ\text{K}}{T_1{}^\circ\text{K}}$$

The weight of water entering the compressor is for each cubic metre of free air/h

$$W_1 \text{ g/h} = (\text{saturation g/m}^3 \text{ at } T_1) \times \frac{\%\text{r.h.}}{100}$$

The condensate/hour = W_1/hour − W_2/hour

In practical terms we can consider an air compressor drawing air at 60% r.h. and 20°C at the rate of 3000 m^3/h.

For saturated air at 20°C the weight of water/m^3 is 17.25 g and the water vapour pressure is 0.0233 bar.

If this air is compressed to 7 bar and cooled to 35°C then it will become saturated at 35°C. Saturated air at 35°C can hold 39.55 g/m^3 and has a water vapour partial pressure of 0.0422 bar.

$$\text{The amount of water entering the compressor} = \frac{60\%}{100} \times 17.25 \times 3000 \text{ g/h}$$
$$= 31050 \text{ g/h}$$

The amount of water leaving the after-cooler, saturated at 35°C, is

$$39.55 \times \frac{(1 - \frac{60}{100} \times 0.0233)}{(7 - 0.0422)} \times \frac{(273 + 35)}{(273 + 20)}$$

$= 17700$ g/h

i.e. condensate $= 31050 - 17700 = 13400$ g/h

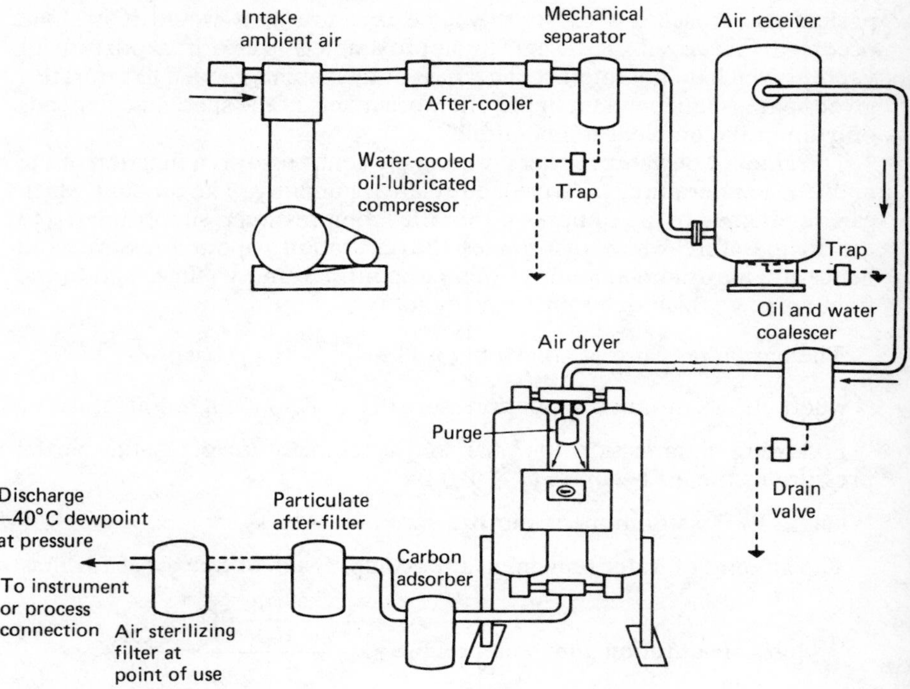

Figure 8.1 Typical layout of a compressed-air drying system (courtesy of Pall Pneumatics)

and the amount of water still flowing through the system is 17700 g/m^3. A significant proportion (~85%) is removed by a refrigerant dryer down to 2°C dewpoint or over 99% of it by the use of a desiccant dryer (dewpoint −40°C or −70°C).

A schematic layout of a compressed-air supply is shown in *Figure 8.1*. For continuously-operated equipment the air receiver is normally sized to be the volume discharged by the compressor in one minute. It can be positioned either before or after the dryer. The dryer is a desiccant type if dewpoints below 2°C are required, or a refrigerant type for dewpoints of between 2 and 10°C.

Air is drawn into the compressor, compressed typically to between 7 and 10 bar, and then cooled to 30 to 35°C in the after-cooler. The quality of moisture entering the system depends upon the temperature and relative humidity of the ambient air. The amount leaving the after-cooler depends principally upon the after-cooler temperature. The relative quantities are illustrated in *Figure 8.2*.

The compressed air goes through the air receiver and is then filtered to remove oil and water droplets. The quantity and type of contaminants associated with different types of compressor are shown in *Figure 8.3*. The compressed air is then dried and, if necessary, deodorized in a carbon bed if it is to be used in a sensitive area, such as food processing, and then finally filtered before distribution.

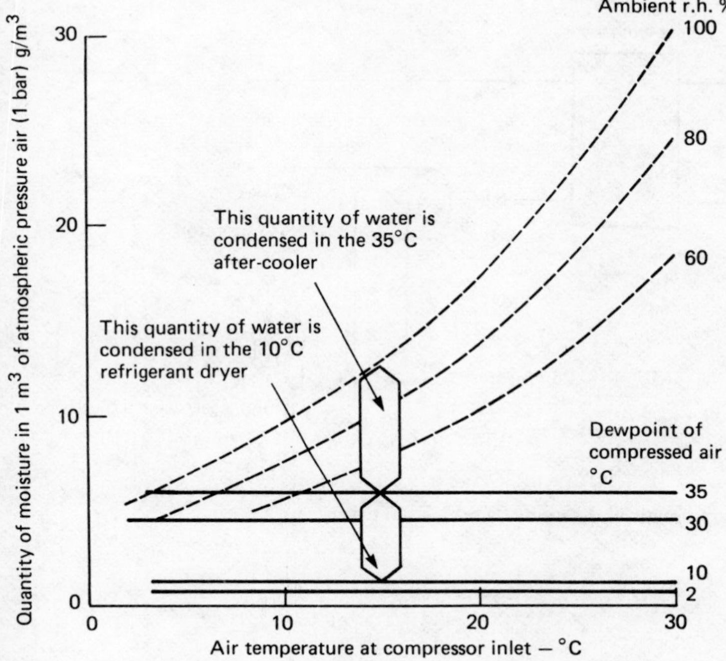

Figure 8.2 Approximate quantities of water to be removed from air compressed to 7 bar and then cooled to either 35°C or 30°C dewpoint and subsequently down to 10°C or 2°C by refrigerant dryer. Any further drying would have to be by desiccant techniques

Air quality from compressors	Contaminants: Water		Oil		Dirt
Compressor type	Liquid	Vapour	Liquid	Vapour	
Oil-lube reciprocating	●	●	●	●	●
Oil-lube screw	●	●	●	●	●
Oil-free reciprocating	●	●			●
Oil-free screw	●	●			●
Centrifugal	●	●			●

Figure 8.3 Contaminants from different types of compressor (courtesy of Pall Pneumatics, 1984)

Let us now consider the two major dehumidifying routes, refrigeration and desiccation.

8.3 Refrigerant dehumidification

The principle of the refrigerant dehumidifier for drying compressed air is slightly different from that described for conventional dehumidification in Chapter 2. In conventional air drying it is often an advantage to have the air outlet both hot and dry and therefore the refrigerant condenser is

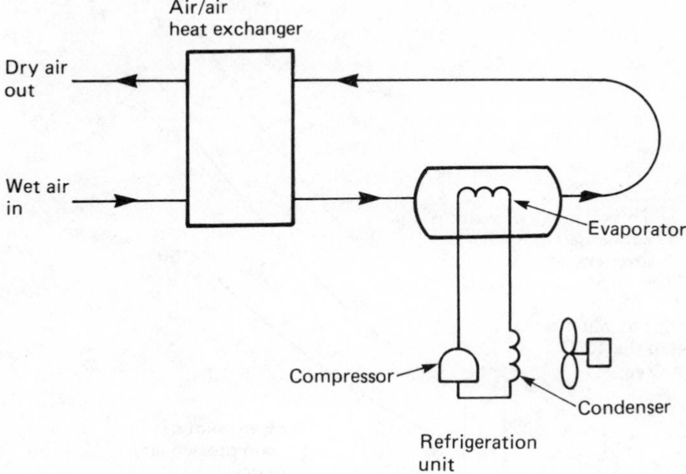

Figure 8.4 Diagrammatic illustration of a refrigerant dryer

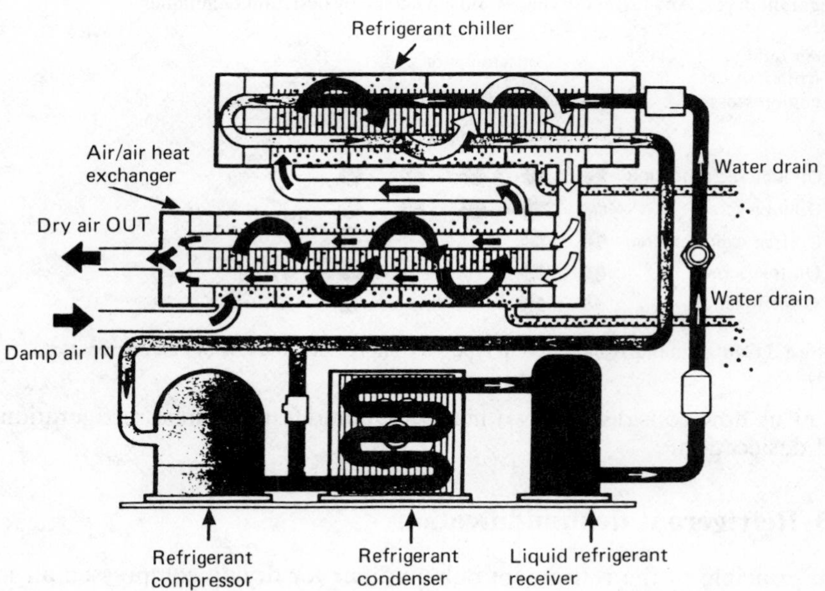

Figure 8.5 A refrigerant-type compressed-air dryer using a copper air-to-air heat-exchanger (courtesy of Broomwade)

mounted in the outlet of the airstream. In the case of compresed air the customer does not want his air heated but rather slightly cooled. An efficient refrigerant cycle for this purpose therefore incorporates an air-to-air heat exchanger but excludes the refrigerant condenser as this is cooled separately by ambient air (*Figure 8.4*).

Warm saturated air enters the dehumidifier air-to-air heat exchanger where it is cooled down. Some of its moisture will condense to drain. The cooled air is drawn through the evaporator of the refrigeration plant and cooled further, releasing more moisture down to a dewpoint temperature of 2°C. This cold, dry air is then returned to the other side of the air-to-air heat exchanger to chill the incoming air. This layout means that the system is very effective because a significant amount of water extraction can occur in the air-to-air heat exchanger. It also means that the dry outlet air will leave at a slightly cooler temperature than it entered the dehumidifier.

The refrigerant condenser can be air cooled, as shown in *Figure 8.5*, or water cooled.

An illustration of a practical layout is shown in *Figure 8.5*. There is little pressure difference across the air-to-air heat exchanger tubes and therefore no great strength is required within the tubes. The outer containment shell caters for the stresses created by the high working pressure of the compressed air. A more detailed view of how a shell/tube heat exchanger can be used for both air-to-air and refrigerant-to-air heat transfer is illustrated in *Figure 8.6*.

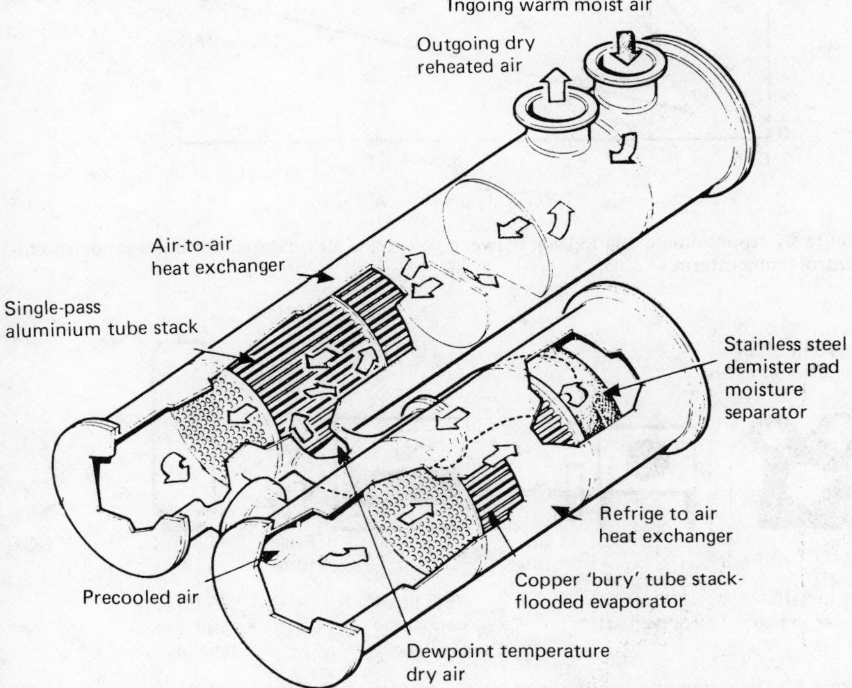

Figure 8.6 Cut-away view of a split refrigerant-type compressed-air dryer (courtesy of Denco Air Ltd)

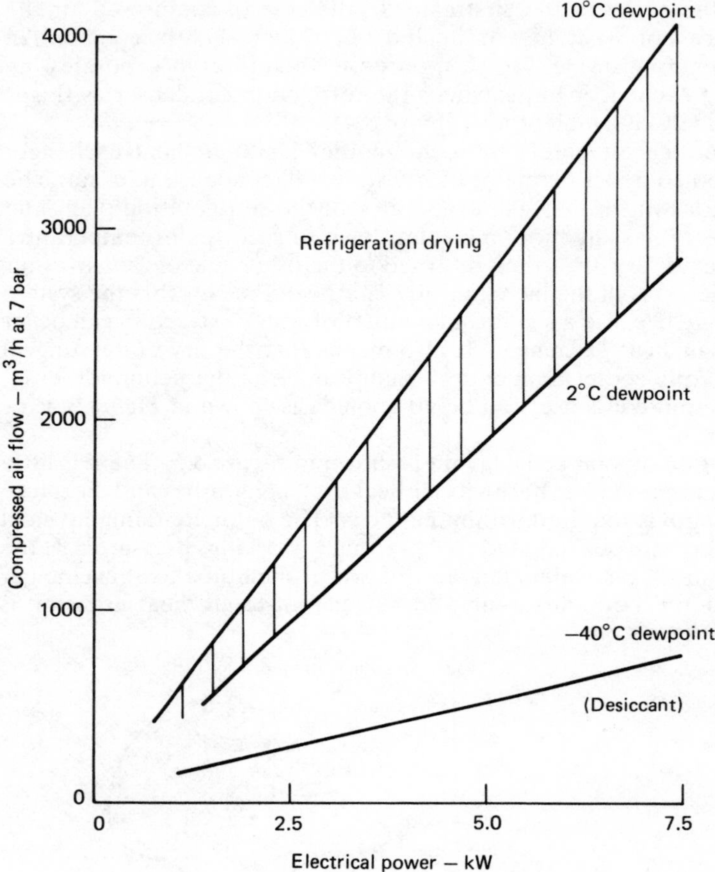

Figure 8.7 Approximate relationship between power and air treatment for different dewpoint control temperatures

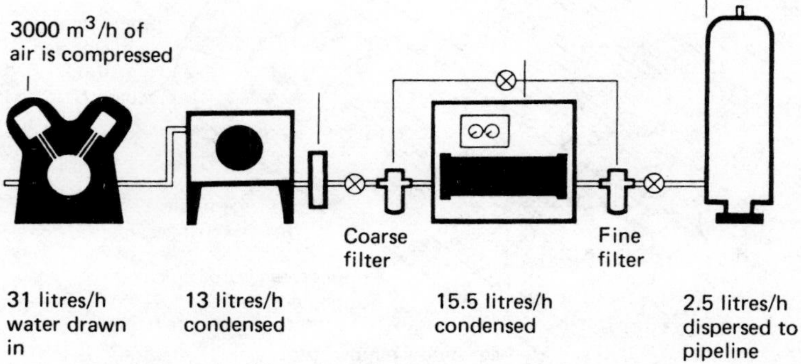

Figure 8.8 Diagrammatic illustration of refrigerant-drying of compressed air. The working conditions are: inlet air 60% r.h. 20°C 3000 m^3/h; supply pressure 7 bar; intercooler air temperature outlet 35°C; refrigerant dryer 2°C dewpoint

Approximate power requirements for a range of flows and dewpoint conditions are given in *Figure 8.7.* These have been rounded off from equipment performance data supplied by the manufacturer. Typical water extraction rates are illustrated in *Figure 8.8.*

Refrigerant dehumidifiers work on a continuous basis only when the heat transfer surfaces operate above freezing point. In these circumstances the cycle runs all the time and the condensate drains away continuously. Lower dewpoint-temperature operation is possible but would involve a defrosting cycle of the evaporator. This would necessitate either a break in dehumidification or a duplicate refrigerant plant. Neither of these additional techniques is normally practicable in terms of operation and expense.

8.4 Desiccant dryers

Desiccant dryers are essential for very low dewpoint air and are invariably used in practice for dewpoints below 2°C where ice problems complicate the operation of the refrigerant dryers. A dewpoint of −40°C is the normal design criterion for desiccant dryers, although manufacturers offer −70°C as a standard option.

There are two types of desiccant dryer, identified as 'heat-reactivated' or 'heatless'. In principle they share the same drying operation. Moist air is blown through a bed of hygroscopic solids. As the solids take up moisture from the air their drying ability declines till eventually, as the maximum permitted dewpoint is reached, the bed has to be taken out of the circuit and reactivated. This means that a duplicate drying circuit has to be provided for the air while this reactivation takes place. However, the practical implementation of the principle is different in the two cases, and we will now consider them separately.

The electrically-heated reactivated desiccant dryer contains a highly-absorbent solid such as silica gel. Electrically-heated plates are spread within the cylinder because the thermal conductivity of the packed desiccant is poor. This is illustrated in *Figure 8.9.* Moist air enters the top of the vessel and flows through the packed bed, and the temperature of the desiccant rises as moisture is adsorbed. After about four hours the bed has a safety margin of only 10 to 20% dry material at the base and the air circuit is transferred to the second identical bed. The original bed is depressurized and then supplied with 2 to 6% of the air flow from the outlet of the second drying bed now in service. When expanded down to atmospheric pressure this dry air has a dewpoint of around −70°C. This air is blown through the original bed in counterflow to the initial air supply and simultaneously the electric heater in the bed is switched on. These heaters are designed to operate at around 150°C. The desiccant cannot retain its moisture at high temperature and so as it heats up it releases the water vapour into the dry purge air. The maximum water-holding capacity of silica gel is illustrated in *Figure 8.10.* The drying cycle takes about three hours of heating and a further hour to cool down to an acceptable operating temperature. The cycle then restarts. Typical layout and operating cycle are illustrated in *Figure 8.11.* The drying chamber operates

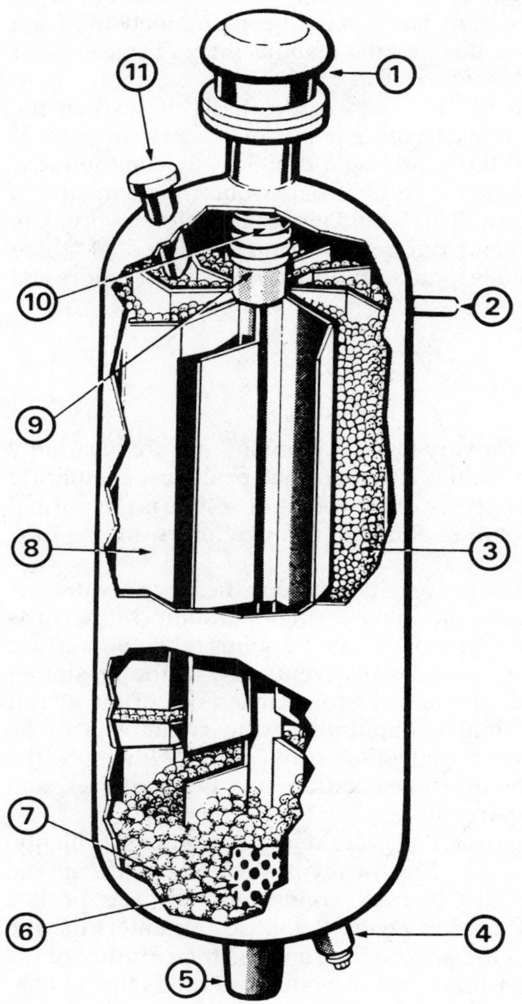

Figure 8.9 Exploded view of an electrically-reactivated desiccant dryer (courtesy of Pall Pneumatics)

1 Heater
2 Chamber inlet
3 Desiccant
4 Desiccant drain
5 Chamber outlet
6 Perforated stainless steel screen
7 Tubular bed support and gas diffuser
8 heat-conducting fins
9 Heater tube
10 Expansion bellows
11 Desiccant filler extends into vessel to prevent overfill

at working pressure for the compressed air while the regenerating chamber is at atmospheric pressure.

If the moisture load is variable then the fixed time-clock operation, designed for the maximum moisture load, could be wasteful of reactivation energy. Manufacturers therefore offer automatic controls which initiate changeover whenever it is needed. A moisture sensor is placed 10 to 15%

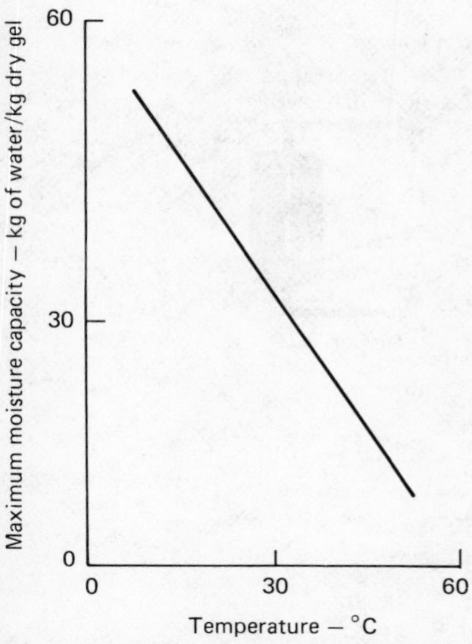

Figure 8.10 Illustration of change in maximum moisture-holding capacity with temperature for silica gel (data is only illustrative; consult manufacturer's data for precise values)

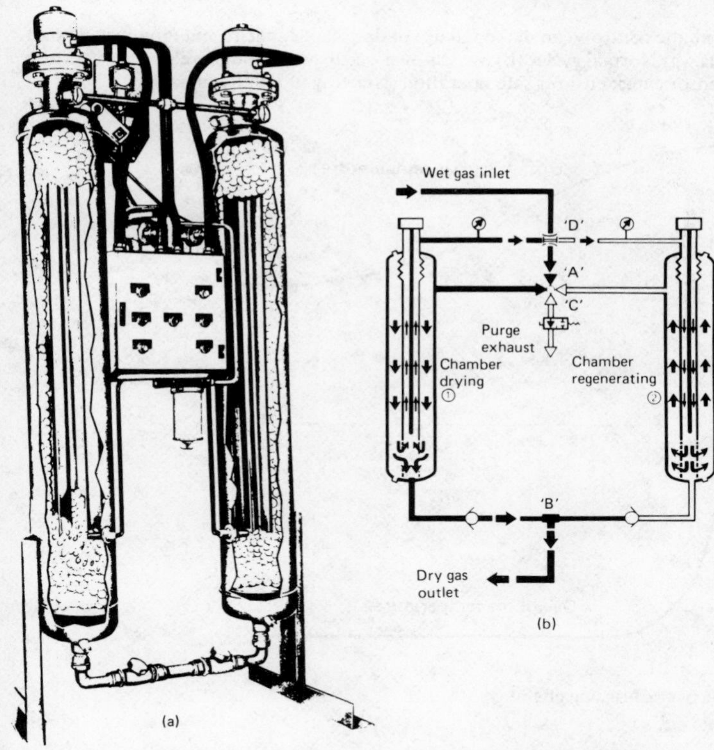

Figure 8.11 A heat-reactivated desiccant dryer (courtesy of Pall Pneumatics)

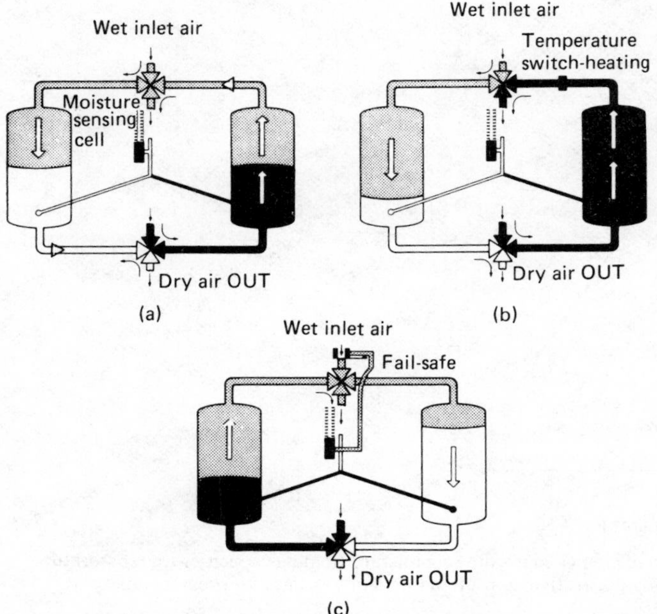

Figure 8.12 Automatic controls can make full use of desiccant capacity and minimize wasted drying operations. (a) Normal cycle. (b) Switch-over occurs when moisture reaches sensor. (c) Automatic sensor check ensures safe operation (courtesy of Pall Pneumatics)

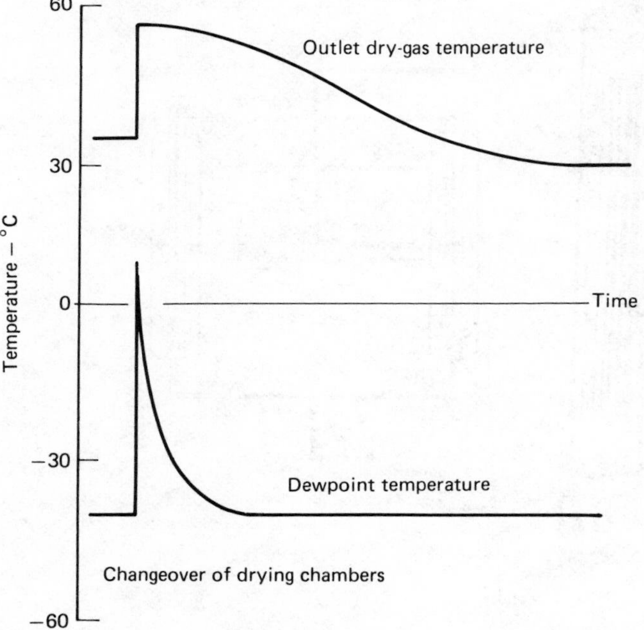

Figure 8.13 Illustration of 'heat bump' on heat-reactivated desiccant dryers

above the bottom of the bed. When this shows the presence of rising moisture the changeover is started. The 10 to 15% of bed is the safety margin. Such an automatic system is shown in *Figure 8.12.* This has one additional feature and that is a fail/safe cycle. Moist air is regularly sent to the sensor and the sensor response is monitored. If it fails to respond to this check then the cycle operation is immediately returned to time-clock operation.

There is one practical, albeit transient, characteristic of heat-reactivated desiccant dryers. This is the 'heat bump' which occurs on changeover. On changeover the reactivated bed is still hot, although cooling when the moist air enters. The rise in temperature as moisture is adsorbed means that the bed does not act as a perfect dryer but permits a temporary rise in both actual temperature and dewpoint. This transient phenomenon is called the 'heat bump', and is illustrated in *Figure 8.13*.

For very large volume flows, for example in chemical engineering processes, the electric heaters can be put into the air supply and the purge air is not bled from the pressure side of the dryer but is provided

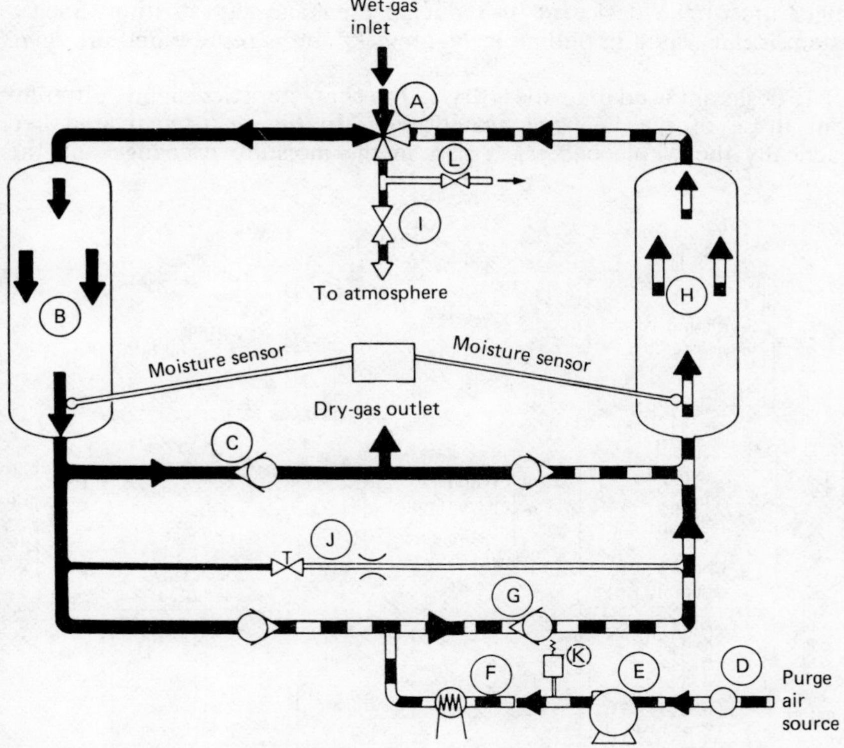

Figure 8.14 Schematic illustration of regeneration without using process gas (courtesy of Pall Pneumatics)

A: wet inlet gas
B: drying chamber
C: outlet check valve
D: suction filter/silencer
E: purge blower
F: electric heater
G: purge check valve
H: heated reactivation of desiccant

independently from a low-pressure Rootes blower. The same technique can be applied when expensive or dangerous gases are being dried and it would not be appropriate to purge such gas through the reactivating bed and to waste. The cycle is illustrated in *Figure 8.14*.

Heatless dryers use the heat of adsorption itself to provide the energy of evaporation during regeneration. In these dryers only the top 2 to 3% of the bed is actively involved in moisture transfer, the rest of the column behaving as a thermal regenerator running about 10°C above the inlet air temperature. This means that the drying time per cylinder is usually restricted to five minutes. Once this is completed the cylinder is depressurized and very dry air expanded from the dry air outlet of the working drying cylinder blown through the bed for four-and-a-half minutes. The final half minute is used to repressurize the cylinder in anticipation of the next drying cycle within it. Purge gas continues to flow while the system is being pressurized until the pressure rises to that of the system. The purge is then stopped. The inlet gas is then switched over to the regenerated bed. Repressurization before switchover ensures that the desiccant will not be jolted by inrushing downward gas. This ensures a longer life of the desiccant by reducing breakage and attrition. Such a system is illustrated in outline in *Figure 8.15* and is represented in *Figure 8.16*.

The desiccant used in heatless dryers has characteristics slightly different from those of the heat-reactivated type. In the heat-reactivated bed practically the whole bed takes part in the moisture exchange and the

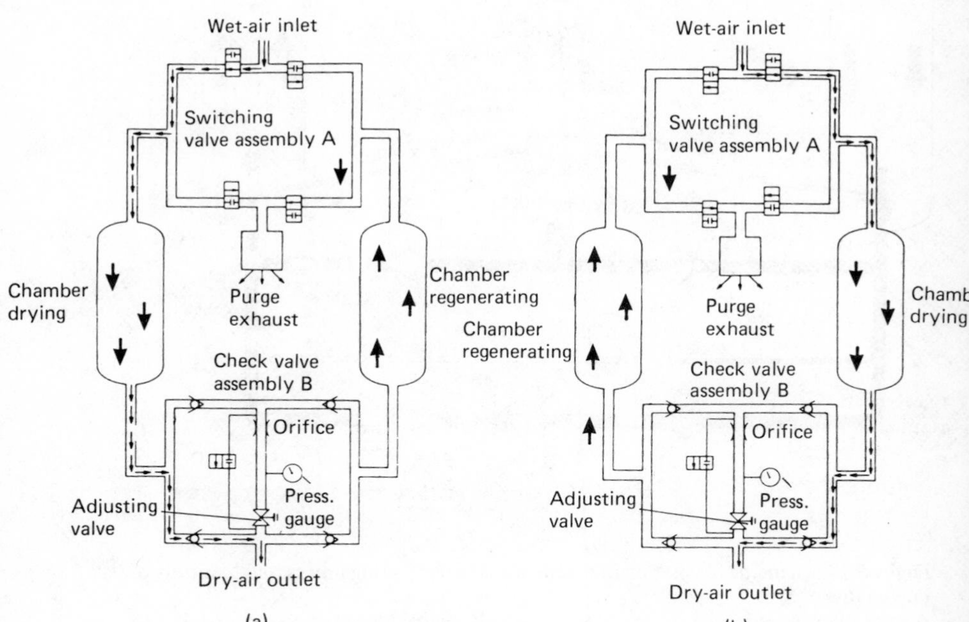

Figure 8.15 A heatless type of desiccant compressed-air dryer. (a) Drying in the left-hand chamber, and (b) drying in the right-hand chamber (courtesy of Pall Pneumatics)

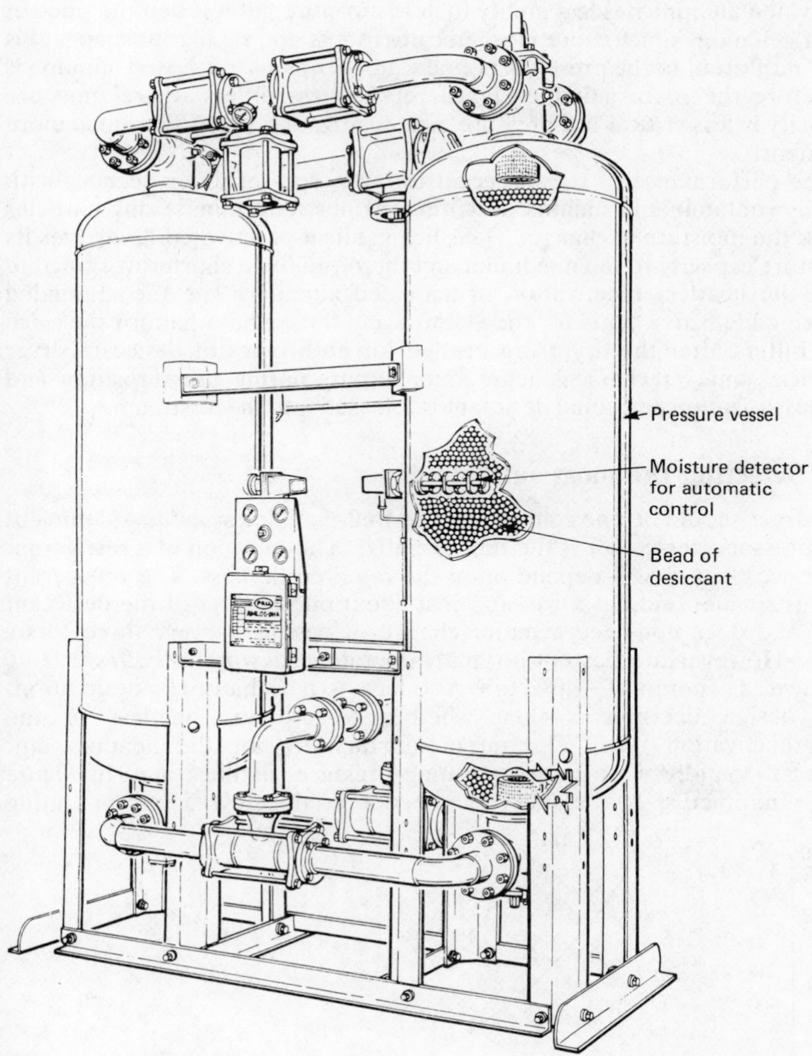

Figure 8.16 Desiccant compressed-air dryers comprise two cylinders, one to dry while the other bed is reactivated (heatless type). A: pressure vessel; B: moisture detector for automatic control; C: beads of desiccant (courtesy of Pall Pneumatics)

complete cycle time is typically eight hours. Maximum moisture retention by the desiccant is therefore very important. In the heatless dryer only a small part of the bed actively takes part in the moisture transfer. However, the cycle time is normally only 10 minutes. This means it recycles fifty times more often than the heat-reactivated version. Silica gel has a very large moisture-adsorbing capability but this is offset by its extreme degradation on exposure to moisture droplets and by its mechanical friability. It is therefore appropriate for the heat-reactivated dryer.

Activated alumina has less ability to hold moisture but it is half the price of silica gel and is much more mechanically robust and regular in shape. It is also indifferent to the presence of fine water droplets. Activated alumina is therefore the more suitable choice for heatless dryers where moisture capacity is less critical but pressure/depressurization cycles are much more frequent.

The performance of the desiccant in both types of dryer declines with age as contaminants such as dust, fine oil mist and minute dirt particles block the moisture exchange. The silica gel heat-reactivated dryer uses its moisture capacity to the maximum and therefore has a shorter working life than the heatless reactivation of activated alumina. The recommended working life is five years for the alumina and three-and-a-half for the silica gel. Filters after the dryer are needed for both types of desiccant dryer because some mechanical degradation occurs during pressurization and depressurization and some desiccant is released into the airstream.

8.5 Selecting the most suitable dryer

The dryer should be one component in a well-matched system. An efficient compressor after-cooler is the first essential. The selection of a refrigerant or desiccant type will depend upon the required dryness. The refrigerant type is smaller and has a running cost about one quarter of the desiccant type and does not need a major change of desiccant every three to six years. However, it does not normally operate at dewpoints below 2°C.

Lower dewpoints of −40°C to −70°C have to be achieved by desiccation. The design decision is then whether to use the heatless or the heat-reactivation type. The purge air quantity for the heatless unit increases rapidly with lower operating pressure, as illustrated in *Figure 8.17*. In practice heatless dryers are not used below 5 bar operating

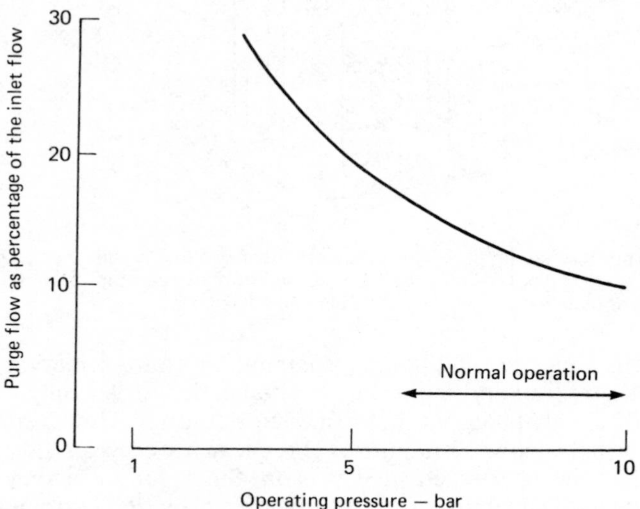

Figure 8.17 Heatless desiccant dryers become less effective at lower operating pressures (data from Pall Pneumatics)

TABLE 8.1 Comparison of the three methods for drying compressed gas

Factor	*Refrigeration*	*Heat-reactivated desiccant*	*Heatless desiccant*
Minimum dewpoint	10°C to 2°C	−40°C to −70°C	−40°C to −70°C
Continuity of low dewpoint	Yes	No, small increase on changeover	Yes
Sensitivity to overload	High	High	Low
Operating costs	Low (service + electricity)	Silica gel at £5/kg, renewed at 3–4 yrs	Activated alumina at £3/kg, removed at 5 yrs
Plant complexity	High	Medium	Low
Purge gas	None	Low	High
Use of downstream carbon adsorber	Yes	Not practicable	Yes
Suitable for Class I Fire Safety	Yes	No	Yes
Size	Smallest	Medium	Largest
Dust created during drying	No	Yes	Yes
Sensitivity to contamination	Low	High	Medium

pressure. The heat-reactivated dryers are very sensitive to inlet temperature conditions and to the possibility of water droplets destroying the silica gel. The heatless type is less sensitive to occasional overload conditions of moisture. In practice, if all other factors are the same, then a heatless dryer will be physically smaller and cheaper to run at high pressure (7 to 10 bar) when the inlet air temperature is above 35°C, and the heat-reactivated dryer more suitable for temperatures below 35°C.

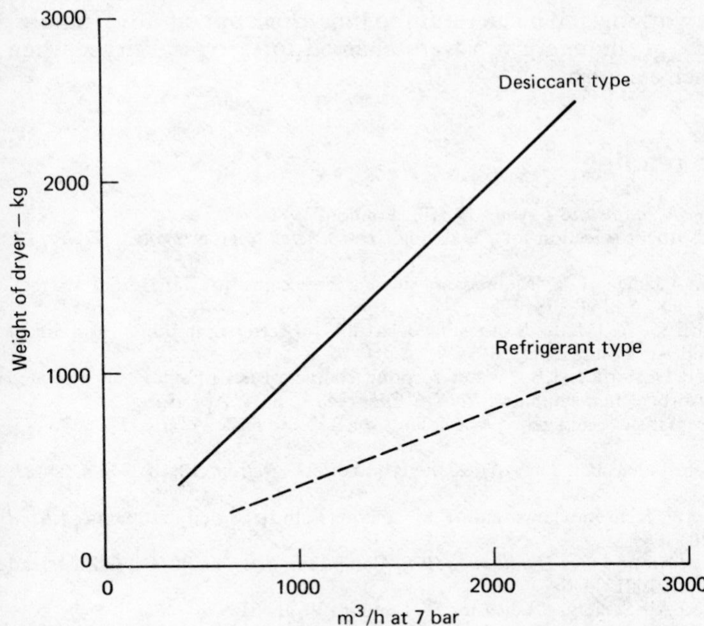

Figure 8.18 Approximate relationship between weight of dryer and air-flow

A list of characteristics of the three dryers, refrigerating, heat reactivated desiccant and heatless desiccant, are listed in *Table 8.1*. Approximate weights of such units are illustrated in *Figure 8.18*.

8.6 Future trends

Compressed-air dryers are an essential requirement for high-quality air supplies. They must be used in association with after-coolers and filters.

For the simplest service, refrigeration dehumidification can reach dewpoints down to 2°C on a continuous basis. It is economical. Recent advances have included the incorporation of air-to-air heat recovery heat exchangers for more effective operation. Further progress will include all the improvements which are being incorporated into conventional refrigeration machinery. This will be the progressive incorporation of electronic controls for speed control of the compressor and for automatic monitoring of the normal operation of the plant with built-in fault diagnosis routines.

Only the desiccant dryer can operate down to −40°C dewpoint. Advances in technology are basically an improving desiccant in terms of controlled size, robustness and moisture-holding capacity. While this is highly developed for moisture removal in air, there are growing numbers of special desiccants for different gases. The major advance in economy has been the automatic cycling time. This saves energy through unnecessary pressurization/depressurization cycles and the loss of purge air if the regeneration occurs only when needed. The embedded moisture detector achieves this. Such a detector can have built-in check measures to make sure it is working and it can return to time-clock operation on failure. Savings of 40% of the energy cost are claimed for a typical dryer when operated on such a control.

8.7 Further reading

Williams-Gardner, A. *Industrial Drying*. L. Hill, London, 1971

Colley, C.R. 'Adsorbent selection for gas drying'. *Brit Cheml Engg & Process Techy*, **17**, 229–233, 1972

Dunne, S.R. and Clancy, T.J. 'Methods of testing desiccants for refrigerant drying'. *ASHRAE trans*, **90** 1A, 164–178, 1984

ASHRAE Standard 35–76. 'Methods of testing desiccants for refrigerant drying'. Am Soc of Htg, Refrign and Air Condg Engrs, 1976

Walker, W.O. and Hostettler, J.B. 'Water sorption characteristics of silica gel, activated alumina anhydrous calcium sulphate'. *Refrign Engg*, USA, p 34, Apr 1956

Mays, R.L. 'Molecular sieve and gel type desiccants for R12 and R22'. *ASHRAE Jnl*, 73–75, Aug 1962

Walker, W.O. 'Latest ideas in the use of desiccants and driers'. *Refrign Serv & Contg*, 24–27, USA, Aug 1963

Fleming, J.B., Getty, R.J. and Townsend, F.M. 'Drying with fixed bed desiccants'. *Cheml Engg*, 71, 69–76, 1964

CAGI. *Compressed Air and Gas Handbook, 1979*. Compd Air and Gas Inste, 122 East 42nd St, NY, New York 10017, USA

British Compressed Air Society, 8 Leicester St, London WC2H 7BN

Electricity Council. 'Electrical methods for drying compressed air'. Elecy Ccl Tech Inf Sheet IND 14, 1975

Warrior, J.R. and Wood, M.J. 'Molecular sieve drying'. *Cheml Process Engg*, **50** (10), 97–102, 1969

Getty, R.J. and Armstrong, W.P. 'Drying air with activated alumina under adiabatic conditions'. *Indusl & Engg Chemy Process Design & Dev*, **3** (1), 60–68

Rouse, M. 'Characteristics of sorbent materials'. *ASHRAE trans*, **81**, 608–614, 1975

Chapter 9

Future trends

9.1 Introduction

Research and development work is laying the path for even better dehumidification. Some of the work is aimed directly at dehumidification itself although much more is aimed at improving heat pump technology which will help dehumidification as a byproduct. There is also complementary work on solar devices which explore cooling and dehumidification[1].

The development route of the present refrigerant and absorption dehumidification cycle is becoming clear, although the timing is uncertain. Novel cycles and more fundamental approaches are more speculative.

For convenience the trends will be reviewed in terms of development of the present units, the possibilities of new techniques and finally the spread of dehumidifiers into the market.

9.2 Development of the present refrigerant dehumidifiers

Research activity in this refrigerant technology is the most active. The small-sized popular domestic dehumidifier is changing, due partly to the scaling up of production from batch to continous flow. This necessitates much more intensive product evaluation because changes are very expensive to introduce once production has started. The growing interest in energy efficiency, even if only at statutory level as in the USA, has produced improved designs. At the other end of the size spectrum in very large-scale dehumidification schemes, growing design expertise enables one-off high-budget projects to be tackled with confidence.

Let us see how the component parts of the cycle are developing.

(a) Compressors

Small, hermetically-sealed compressor units are increasingly following the Japanese preference for a rotary-piston design. The absence of a suction valve together with a lower suction superheat, leads to a higher efficiency

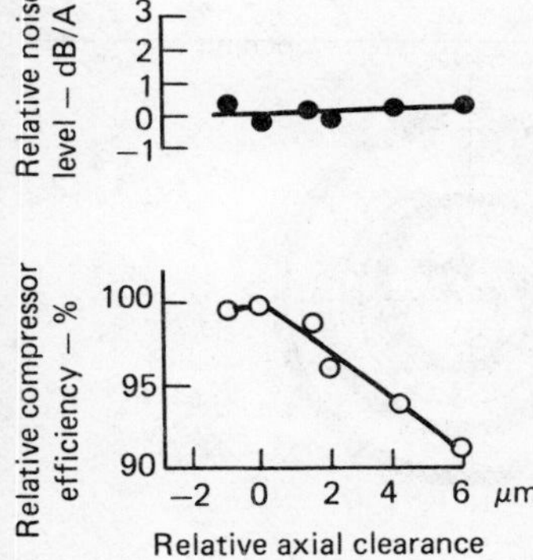

Figure 9.1 Change in noise emission and compressor efficiency with different axial clearances in a rolling-piston compressor (Asami, Ishijima and Tanaka, 1982)[2]

than for the reciprocating type. This higher efficiency is obtained with a smaller number of moving parts and much less dynamic imbalance. The result is a smaller, quieter, cheaper and more reliable compressor. The critical factor for rotary-piston design is end-leakage of gas which can occur if the axial clearance is too large. Such axial clearance, while having little effect on noise, does rapidly lead to a reduction in efficiency. *Figure 9.1*[2]. Fortunately the new standards in production engineering mean that very close working tolerances can be consistently manufactured and such compressors are now well proven.

The reciprocating type of compressor has been more effective for larger compressors (greater than 1 kW). However, in 1982 Hitachi introduced an orbiting-scroll compressor which retained many of the advantages of the rotary-piston type and was more efficient than the reciprocating. These relationships are illustrated in *Figure 9.2*[3,4]. The orbiting-scroll compressor requires two similar scrolls, one fixed and one orbiting (not rotating). The orbiting scroll traps the low-pressure refrigerant gas and compresses it to a central discharge port. The cycle is illustrated in *Figure 9.3*. The cross-section of such a compressor is shown in *Figure 9.4*.

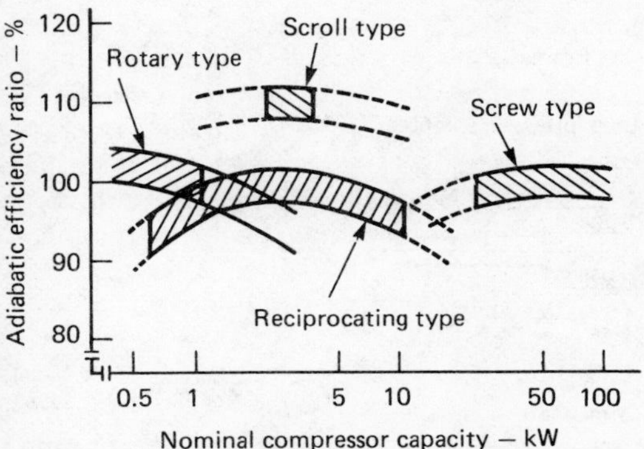

Figure 9.2 Performance comparisons of different types of refrigerant compressors relative to the reciprocating type (Matsuo *et al*, 1984)[3]

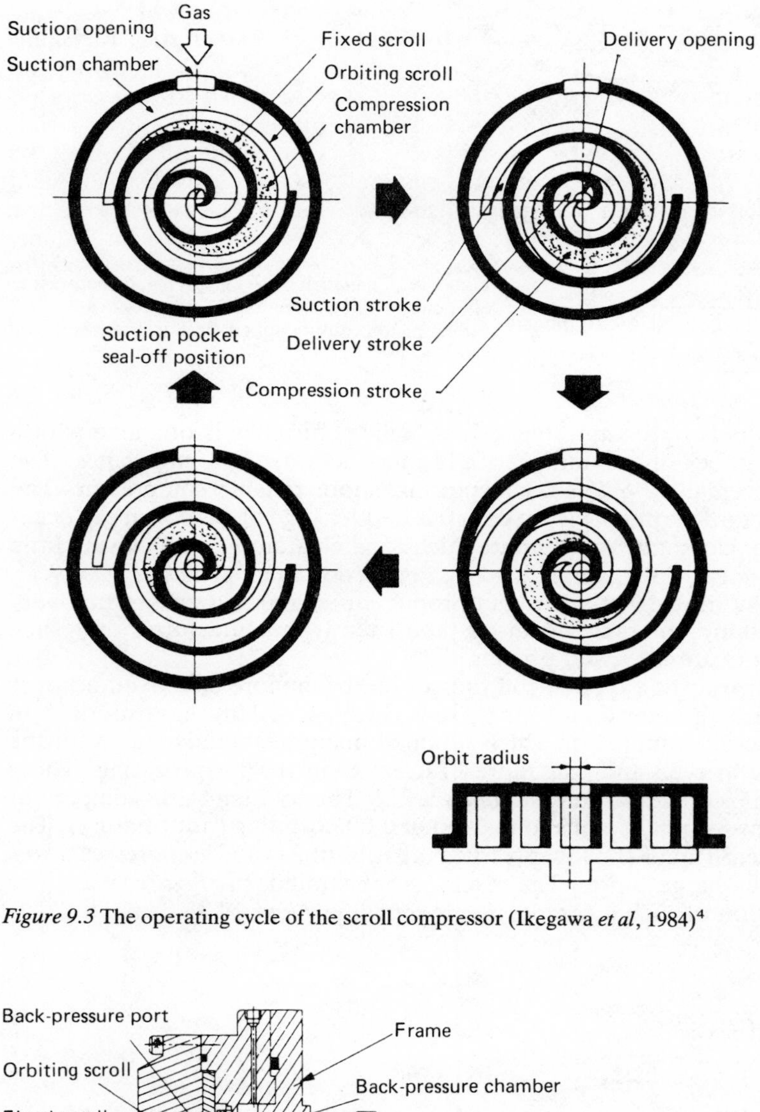

Gas
Suction opening
Suction chamber
Fixed scroll
Orbiting scroll
Compression chamber
Delivery opening
Suction stroke
Delivery stroke
Compression stroke
Suction pocket seal-off position
Orbit radius

Figure 9.3 The operating cycle of the scroll compressor (Ikegawa *et al*, 1984)[4]

Back-pressure port
Orbiting scroll
Fixed scroll
Discharge
Suction
Frame
Back-pressure chamber
Motor
Crankshaft

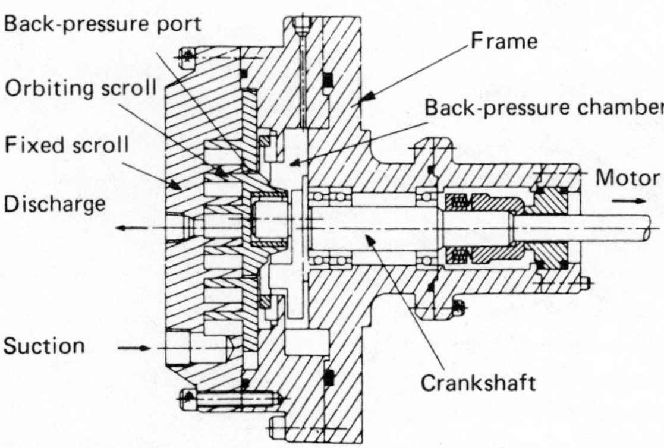

Figure 9.4 Section of an orbiting scroll compressor (Ikegawa *et al*, 1984)[4]

Competition is expected from the Wankel compressor which is being developed by Neumag[5] which has a high output for a given size. Resonant piston compressors are also possible contenders because they rely on free pistons and have the advantage of a variable stroke. Such compressors are being developed by Exxon Enterprises and Mechanical Technology USA[6].

Compressor speed control is now becoming more common. It offers the advantage of load matching and eliminates or reduces the frequent start/stop cycles which are stressful and wearing. Pole-switching electric motors have been technically available for many years. This usually enables the motor speed to be halved by going from two-pole operation to four-pole operation. Recent research has revived the concept of pole amplitude modulation to enable two speeds to be available to the designer in motor drives from 1 kW to 10 MW[7].

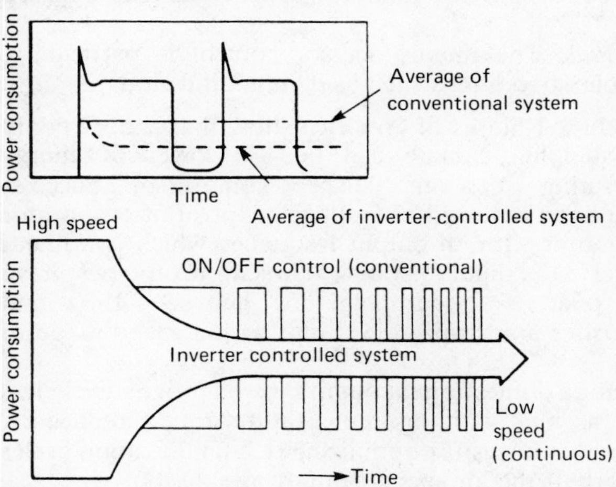

Figure 9.5 Variable-speed compressors use less energy at part load (Toshiba, 1986)[8]

The availability of low-cost, high-current, high-voltage solid-state electronic circuit components has grown since they were first marketed in 1979. This has enabled variable-frequency power supplies to be built to give an efficient variable-speed compressor motor. These drives have several advantages.

(i) *Improves the efficiency*. The elimination of frequent stop/start means that the power consumption is much less than a conventional system for a given duty. Efficiency is particularly high at the lower speeds where most equipment would be expected to operate for most of its working life. *Figure 9.5*[8].

(ii) *Increases reliability*. The variable-speed operation keeps motor windings consistently cooler than the conventional machines and keeps the bearings continuously lubricated.

(iii) *Eliminates the high starting current surges*. The compressor can start up at low frequency (20 Hz) and a microprocessor-controlled current sensor can regulate the current in a gentle fashion (*Figure 9.6*).

(iv) *Proportional control*. The variable frequency drive means that proportional control becomes readily achievable. The compressor speed

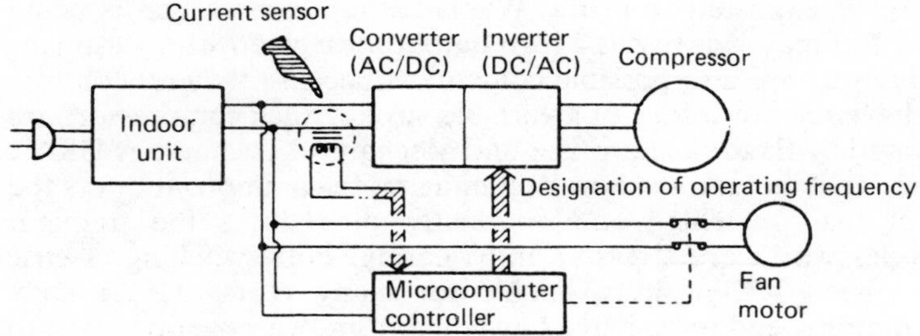

Figure 9.6 The variable-frequency compressor drive can be controlled on start-up to keep the maximum current to a preset value (Toshiba, 1986)[8]

range can vary from 1800 rev/min (40% load) to 7200 rev/min (120% design load).
(v) *Development potential.* The microprocessor control is particularly suited to optimize complex operations such as dehumidification.

Experiments in the United States of America show that a heat pump operating in the Philadelphia climate can be 8% lower in energy requirements when operating with a variable-speed compressor[9]. Successful field trials have also been reported of feedback control of evaporator pressure using an AC motor with an output frequency which is a linear function of a low-level DC input signal[10]. Hitachi prototypes have operated successfully over a speed range of between 1800 and 5400 rev/min[3]. Toshiba offer a mass-produced unit with a speed range of 1800 to 7200 rev/min.

A sensitivity analysis for a domestic heat pump showed progressively less energy saving benefit as the working temperature range reduced[11]. However, the potential advantages for optimizing dehumidification cycles are very good, particularly if the air speed can be variable too.

There is one further development in compressor philosophy. Rotary compressors are insensitive to droplets of refrigeration; therefore they can incorporate a novel type of compressor cooling based on the injection of liquid refrigerant at the outlet port. This reduces the outlet enthalpy and increases the mass flow rate through the compressor. One leading compressor manufacturer, Toshiba, already incorporates the technique into its standard equipment. This results in a very efficient cycle and is particularly valuable at heavy loads, *Figure 9.7*[8].

Compressor drives are nearly always electrical. In the small motor sizes this leads to a reliable, hermetically-sealed construction. Motor efficiency is already outstandingly high for such small motors but thicker motor winding stacks, better steels, and carefully matched split-phase capacitor control gear can increase motor efficiencies even further. Experiments showing the interaction between motor winding, stack thickness and capacitor size are illustrated in *Figure 9.8*[12].

In the larger sizes the inherent reliability and efficiency of electric drives still predominates. However, as the refrigerant cycle applications move away from simple cooling duties towards heating and dehumidification, so fossil-fuel-fired engines are being more seriously considered. The main advantage is the addition of the waste heat from the engine to the heating

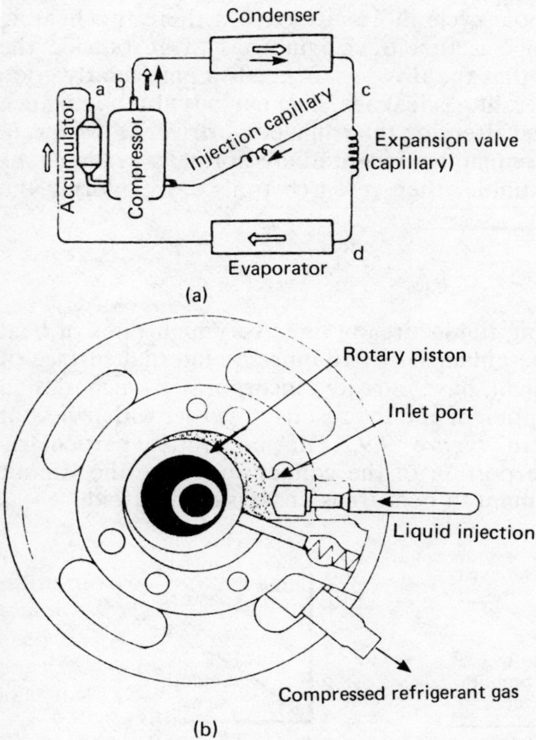

Figure 9.7 Rotary compressors are insensitive to droplets of refrigerant. Liquid injection for enhanced efficiency is now a standard procedure in Toshiba equipment. (a) Refrigerating cycle for injection-type rotary compressor. (b) Refrigerating cycle for injection-type rotary compressor. (b) Section of inlet port to compressor (Toshiba, 1986)[8]

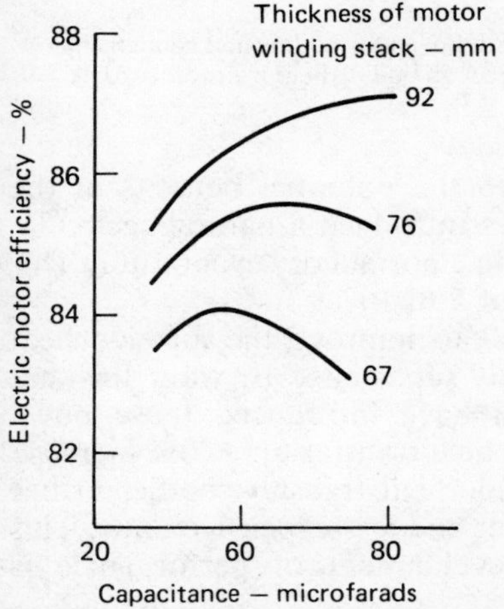

Figure 9.8 Motor efficiency, for the small permanent-split capacitor compressor, varies with both motor stack thickness and capacitor size (Kandpal, 1978)[12]

process. This makes the whole cycle more attractive if there is a heating need. The main disadvantage is that the engine has to be outside the compressor and this means that the drive shaft needs a particularly good gas seal to avoid high refrigerant gas leakage. The engines also need much more maintenance and skilled attention than an electric drive. However, in large-scale applications where maintenance staff are normally available, as in a swimming pool for example, then research trials are exploring the feasibility of such drives.

(b) Heat exchangers

While boiling and condensing fluids already offer very high rates of heat transfer, these values can be enhanced by ribbing the internal surface of the refrigerant tubes. Hitachi have already incorporated such design improvements into their equipment and the results, together with a view of the tube, are illustrated in *Figure 9.9*. The benefit is particularly pronounced at the entrance portion of the condenser where the vapour quality is dry. The improvement in heat transfer is over threefold.

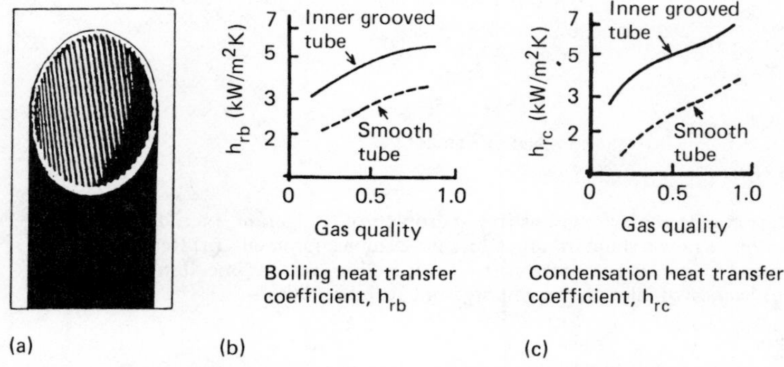

Figure 9.9 Ribbed internal surface promotes heat transfer even for boiling and condensing processes. (a) The ribbed refrigerant pipe. (b) The effect on boiling heat transfer. (c) The effect on condensing heat transfer (Matsuo *et al*, 1984)[3]

Renewed research has also started into the potential benefits of the flooded evaporator (*Figure 9.10*). Bubbles introduce a natural recirculation rate some five to eight times the flow in a normal dry evaporator. This can result in an increase in performance of 5 to 10%[13].

Similarly, finning has been widely used to improve the air side heat transfer. Plain fins have been progressively superseded by wavy fins and now by slit convex louvre fins. Hitachi have introduced these novel configurations and claim a 70% increase in heat transfer for a 40% increase in pressure drop[3]. In ten years, the air side heat transfer coefficient has doubled, and this has led to smaller, lighter and less expensive units. This particular fin layout and the steady development of performance is illustrated in *Figure 9.11*.

Water-repellant surface coatings have been tried to induce droplet water condensation on the heat exchanger. This was aimed at avoiding a thick

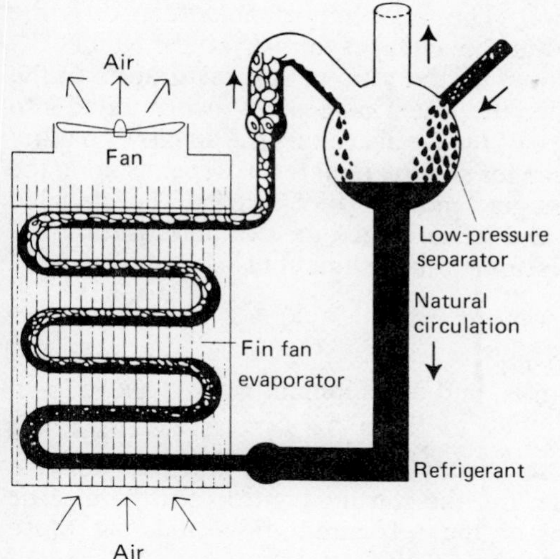

Figure 9.10 Renewed research is examining the benefits of the flooded evaporator. Bubbles introduce a natural recirculation rate some five to eight times the flow in a normal dry evaporator and increase performance by 5 to 10% (University of Trondheim, 1985)[13]

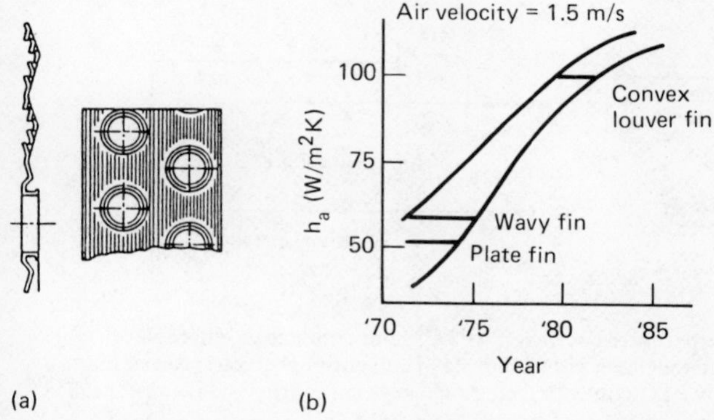

Figure 9.11 The air side heat transfer has improved with wavy, and now slit wavy, fins. (a) Advanced type of slit wavy fin. (b) Progression in performance of finned heat exchangers. h_a = air side heat transfer coefficient (Matsuo *et al*, 1984)[3]

water film coating and promoting rapid water drain. Field experience suggests that the life of such coatings is not long. More recent experiments are investigating hygroscopic surfaces to promote condensation.

Frost build up on the evaporator surface is a common occurrence in domestic dehumidifiers operating in normal British bedroom temperatures (~10 to 15°C). Sublimation of the water vapour to ice on the evaporator surface is then the main process of dehumidification. Research studies are actively exploring the phenomenon and suggest that icing dehumidification follows physical principles quite different from those of conventional vapour-to-water dehumidification. The most important difference is the insensitivity of the frost build-up to changes in Reynolds Number[14]. Crystal growth is largely influenced by the ratio of supersaturation of the heat of sublimation released when the water molecule is incorporated into the crystal lattice[15]. The presence of the ice also alters the air-flow quantity and route through the heat exchanger and the final result depends upon the interaction of fan heat exchanger and ice blockage[16]. The detailed measurements of ice build-up and its influence on dehumidification are being studied at the Building Research Establishment in Scotland[17].

(c) Controls

There are three families of controls, and development work is active in all of them.

The first type includes those controls which are essential for the successful operation of the cycle, i.e. the starting controls for the electric compressor motor, the control of the refrigerant flow and, for those dehumidifiers designed to operate below 10°C, a defrost cycle.

The starter control for a single-phase electric motor provides current to an auxiliary starter winding until the motor is rotating and the auxiliary winding can be switched out. Starting relays are conventionally used to activate this winding (*Figure 9.12*). However, there is a new type of

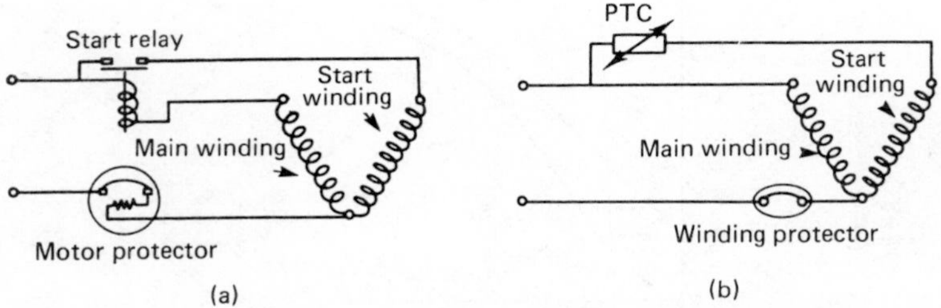

Figure 9.12 New positive temperature coefficient (PTC) semi-conductors can replace electromagnetically-operated mechanical switches. (a) Conventional electrical system for single-phase motors. (b) New PTC-controlled electrical system (courtesy of Danfoss, 1981)[19]

semi-conductor switch which has a positive temperature coefficient (PTC)[19]. When cold, the device has a low electrical resistance and permits current to pass. Once the motor has started the resistance of the semi-conductor rises and its resistance increases, allowing only sufficient current to keep it hot. The resistance characteristic of such a device is shown in *Figure 9.13*. It has no moving parts and therefore has great reliability, is independent of voltage fluctuations and cannot chatter to create radio or television interference.

Refrigerant control for small dehumidifiers (<1 kW) is based upon the pressure drop through a length of capillary pipe. The theory for such control is based on adiabatic operation and much practical experience is usually needed for an optimum choice. Research is now exploring the non-adiabatic characteristics of such a capillary to assess the influence of

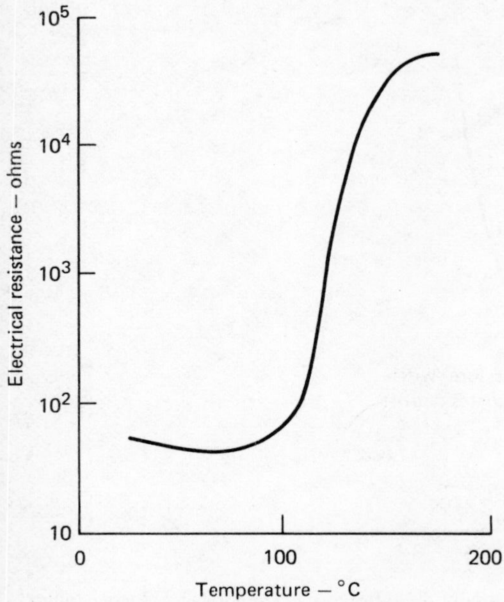

Figure 9.13 Electrical resistance as a function of temperature for a positive temperature coefficient (PTC) semiconductor (courtesy of Danfoss)[19]

different heat flows from the capillary[18]. Larger dehumidifiers invariably use controlled-expansion valves which directly control the flow to give the desired superheat. While such a control can be accurately set for any one condition, it is difficult to maintain the same degree of control over widely different ambient conditions. Work is in progress to develop a microprocessor-controlled, electrically-actuated expansion valve[3]. This could lead to more efficient operation over a wide range of conditions. The microprocessor would inspect the inlet air temperature and relative humidity and then adjust the refrigerant conditions to the optimum. As variable-speed motor drives develop, an advanced microprocessor could optimize compressor and fan speed too. Such developments require low-cost, reliable pressure, and temperature and relative humidity sensors, and work is in progress.

Defrost controls are essential for many dehumidifiers. Standardized time-clock operation works reliably but has to be set for the worst likely condition. Experimental and theoretical studies are in progress to understand the importance of the ice on the overall performance of the evaporator. Work originally undertaken for air source heat pumps has a strong potential application in dehumidification. The effect of ice blockage on the temperature difference between ambient and refrigerant in the evaporator is illustrated in *Figure 9.14*[20]. The refrigeration duty is not affected until approximately 60% of the evaporator is blocked with ice. Pressure switches which detect changes in air-flow can be used to initiate defrost. Microprocessor controls are already available which have a defrost algorithm to permit, initiate and terminate the defrost operation. The

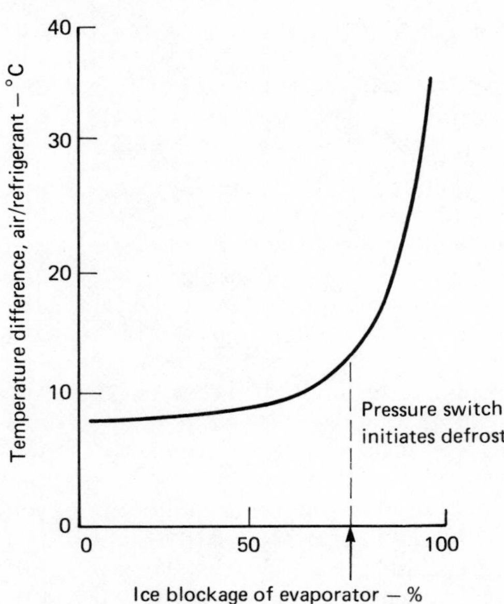

Figure 9.14 Illustrative air/refrigerant temperature difference in evaporator coil as ice builds up (Bonne and Mueller, 1981)[20]

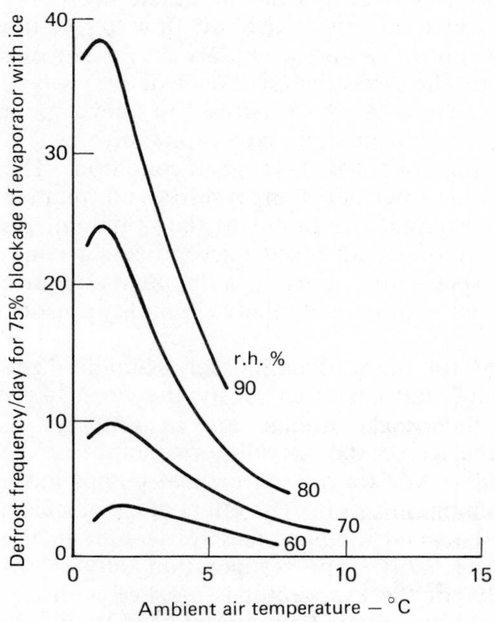

Figure 9.15 Established operating characteristics of a particular machine can be used to initiate defrost cycles (Bonne and Mueller, 1981)[20]

initiation stage can be further refined by using known characteristics of appraisal of such cycles has been made by Honeywell[21] and is illustrated in *Figure 9.15*. Microprocessor control can use the dehumidifier's operating characteristic and determine the number of desirable defrosts each day in accordance with the ambient air temperature and relative humidity.

The second family of controls comprises the protective ones which ensure that the equipment is operating within its design conditions. If a fault develops then an appropriate sensor should detect a deviation from normal and close down the unit before any major damage is done. Such controls include high- and low-pressure switches for the refrigerant, high and low temperature sensors and time delays to ensure the correct sequence of events. Excessive compressor motor power, reduction in air flow, loss of refrigerant and expansion valve failure can result in excessive compressor discharge temperature. Inadequate discharge temperatures can be caused by total loss of refrigerant, compressor contactor failure, internal high pressure by-passing or internal overload operation. Temperature cut-outs are now widely used in the motor windings of even the smallest compressor motors. Positive Temperature Coefficient (PTC) semiconductors are also becoming available in an ever-widening range of switching temperatures and can be used as a temperature safety cut-out.

The third and most recent family of controls comprises the system logic ones. These involve microprocessor integration of several sensors over time and examine the whole operation of the cycle. It removes one of the irritating failure routes where the cycle operates within its design limits but ineffectively because it is locked into a repeated defrost cycle, for example.

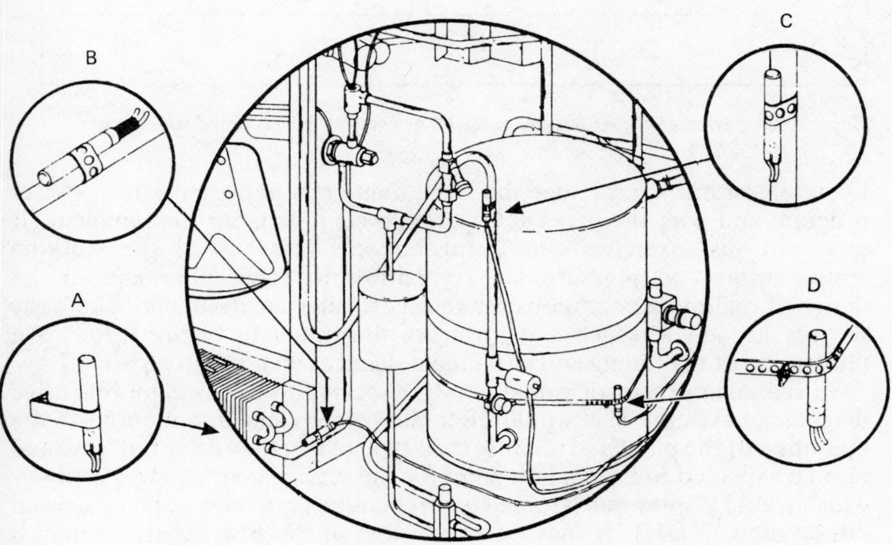

Figure 9.16 Basic sensors for microprocessor control[20]. A: inlet air temperature; B: refrigerant temperature entering the evaporator; C: refrigerant discharge temperature from the compressor; D: compressor crankcase oil temperature

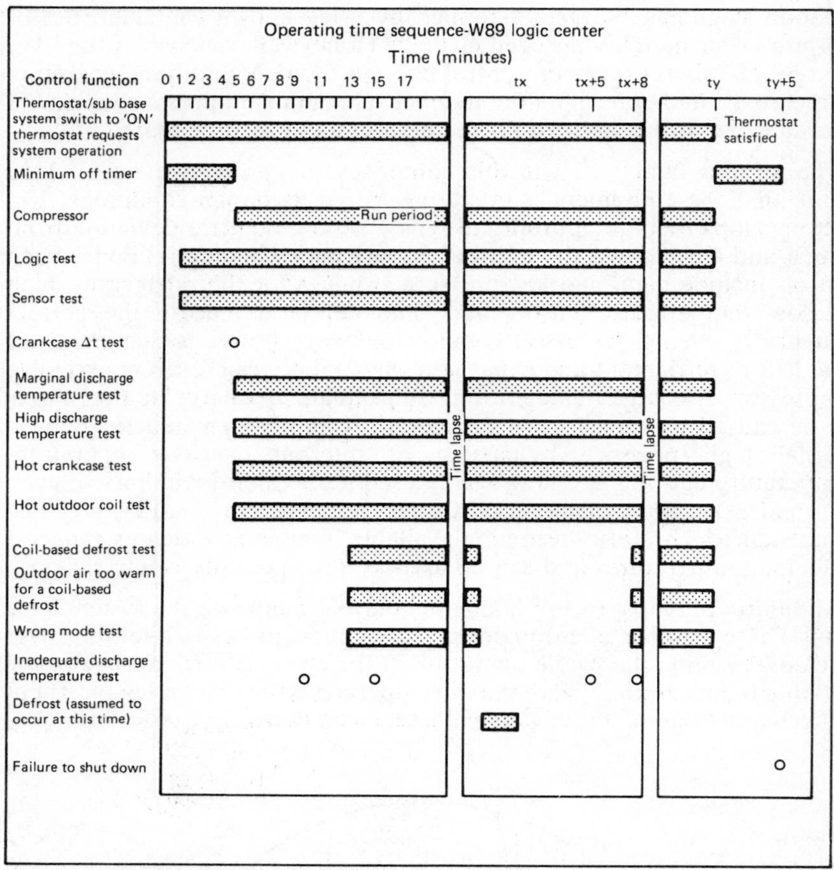

Figure 9.17 Operating time sequences for the Honeywell W89 microprocessor control[22]

Logic algorithms check that the dehumidifier is performing to a preset program and with the expected operating conditions for that ambient. It does not just examine one factor but ensures that all the working temperatures and pressure are compatible to each other and to the designed operating conditions for that particular environment. The basic sensors needed for such a control are illustrated in *Figure 9.16*[20]. An illustration of the timing and checking sequences is shown in *Figure 9.17*[22].

Such a microprocessor would also be expected to have a comprehensive diagnostics system. This would offer the owner clear information on the operation of the plant and identify fault types when they occurred. It would also be expected to have a link point for the service man's system analyser which would display much more comprehensive data on request to a visual display unit (VDU). It may be practicable in the near future to hold a record of the last day's operating conditions so that the service man can identify the fault pattern and confirm the diagnosis. Such a control would also be valuable at the delicate commissioning stage for the larger-scale dehumidifiers which cannot always be delivered as one factory-built package.

(d) Fans

Accurately-moulded plastics blades for low noise are now available. Simple variable-speed controllers are very readily applied to fans because of the decreasing torque requirement at lower speed. New, more powerful, permanent magnet motors using samarium/cobalt material offer high torque possibilities at low cost and with simple speed control[23].

(e) Humidistats

There is very active research in accurate, low-cost, relative-humidity sensing. The biggest potential market is for carburation in the motor industry but successful development could be used to help dehumidifiers. One recognized domestic problem is fouling of the sensor by grease or fat if the sensor operates in a kitchen where frying or deep-fat cooking takes place. One innovation to combat this is the self-cleaning humidistat. This is designed to operate every few hours at a very high temperature and burn off the minute deposition of fat. This regular self-cleaning cycle prevents accumulation of deposits[24].

(f) Advanced cycles

The existing refrigerant cycles use single-stage compressors. The performance of a compressor is very dependent upon the temperature range between the evaporator and condenser. Two improvements which would reduce the inefficiency are multistage or cascade compression and a planned use of sub-cooling of the refrigerant. The combination of such techniques will almost double the effectiveness, albeit at the expense of a more complex engineering installation. The complexity would probably be worthwhile on large-scale plant[25].

Additional improvements can also be made by more careful consideration of the air circuit through the dehumidifier. For all air-flows, except those actually saturated with water vapour, the refrigeration cooling of the evaporator has to chill the air to its dewpoint and then extract the water. If the relative humidity of the incoming air is low, then the bulk of the refrigeration is spent chilling the air to its dewpoint, leaving very little for dehumidification. This is why the performance of dehumidifiers usually falls dramatically with lowering inlet relative humidity. The incorporation of an air-to-air heat exchanger can improve the cycle. The inlet air to the dehumidifier first passes over a chilled heat exchanger. This cools the air to below its dewpoint and the first stage of dehumidification occurs. The cool air then passes through the evaporator and is chilled and dehumidified further. The very cold air is then returned through the air-to-air heat exchanger to chill the incoming air. Efficiency of water extraction is doubled and the dehumidifying capacity of a given compressor can be tripled[26]. The cycle is illustrated in *Figure 9.18*. Much of the dehumidification occurs within the air-to-air heat exchanger itself and the refrigerant

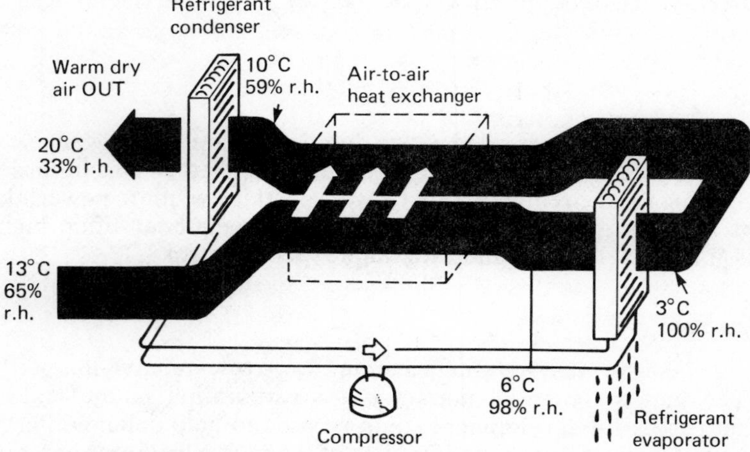

Figure 9.18 A geared dehumidifier incorporating an air/air heat exchanger for optimum effectiveness (Brundrett and Blundell, 1980)[26]

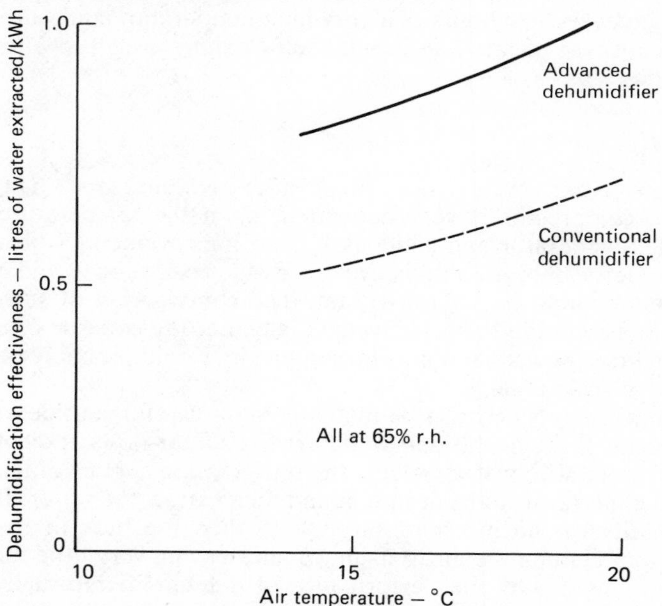

Figure 9.19 The improved effectiveness of a geared dehumidifier (data from Mons Precision Services (Co-op) Ltd, Sheffield, 1985)

evaporator normally sees only saturated air. This means that finned evaporators can be used instead of plain tubes. The whole cycle is much less sensitive to the ambient relative humidity than a conventional unit. The major drawback has been the availability of low-cost air-to-air heat exchangers.

One manufacturer now offers such an advanced dehumidifier and its effectiveness is much better than the conventional units (*Figure 9.19*).

Recent Japanese research by Toshiba has led to a very low cost moulded-plastics air-to-air heat exchanger being marketed for mechanical ventilation units. Research is in progress to apply the same technology to produce a heat exchanger for the advanced dehumidifier. The technique of air-to-air heat recovery is becoming used in large-scale swimming-pool dehumidifiers in which a secondary fluid runs through a heat exchanger in the other airstream. This procedure is termed a 'run-round coil'.

(g) Refrigerants

Present-day refrigerants used in dehumidifiers are normally the pure single halocarbon compounds. They have simple properties and boil and condense at constant temperatures. They are particularly well suited to refrigeration where the main purpose is to maintain a product at a constant and low temperature. The fluids are called 'azeotropic'. In dehumidification a constant temperature evaporation cannot give the best heat transfer. A counterflow heat exchange technique using a refrigerant which boils over a range of temperature is theoretically thermodynamically better[27]. This is normally termed the 'Lorenz cycle' and the fluids or mixtures of fluids which boil and condense over a temperature range are termed 'non-azeotropic' or, at the risk of verbal misunderstanding, a 'zeotropic' fluid. Experiments suggest 40% extra capacity when using an R13 B1/R 152a mixture[28]. At lower evaporating temperatures the higher boiling point R 152a begins to collect preferentially in the accumulator and allows the circuit to become richer in R13 B1.

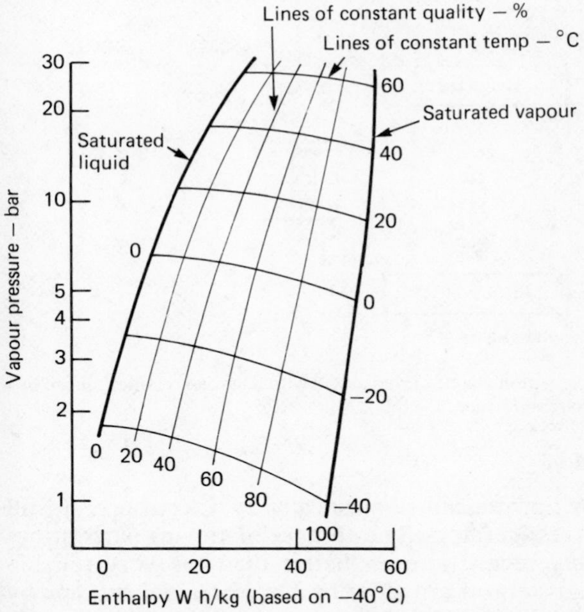

Figure 9.20 Non-azeotropic mixtures do not boil and condense at constant temperature. The enthalpy diagram illustrates the saturated liquid line (bubble point) and the saturated vapour line (dewpoint) of a 70%/30% mixture of R13B1/R152A (Connon and Drew, 1984)[29]

This change in working fluid allows the system to maintain a higher pressure than if the conventional fluid R22 was used. The complexity of the changing refrigerant composition poses two special types of problem. The first is the practical engineering to ensure counterflow operation of the air and the refrigerant, and the rather special role of the accumulator to accept the redundant component. The second is the control difficulty of dealing with a working fluid whose properties change with the ambient temperature. At present the chemical companies are preparing thermodynamic data sheets for mixtures of favoured fluids. However, it is unlikely to be in general commercial use until microprocessor control can take full advantage of the potential benefits. An illustration of the pressure enthalpy diagram for one favoured mixture is given in *Figure 9.20*. The 'saturated liquid' line represents the stage at which bubbles occur and for such fluids this is sometimes referred to as the dewpoint for the vapour. The two-phase region between the two is of varying composition. The vapour is richer in the more volatile R13 B1 while the liquid is correspondingly richer in R 152a[29-33].

Kruse[30] has extended the concept even further and proposes external control of the refrigerant in the circuit by storing the refrigerant in a heated rectifier. This is illustrated in *Figure 9.21*. The composition of the refrigerant in the circuit will then be controlled by the rectifier temperature.

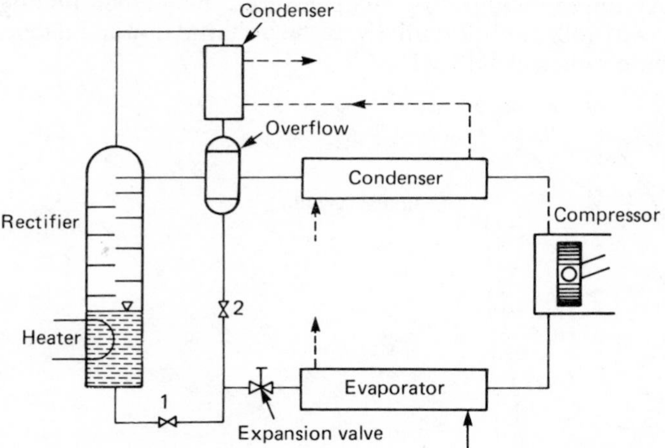

Figure 9.21 The refrigerant composition can be varied at will with a heated rectifier placed in the non-azeotropic refrigerant circuit (Kruse, 1981)[30]

(h) Absorption refrigeration

Absorption refrigeration, introduced domestically by Electrolux, is still commonly used for small refrigerators. The absence of moving parts brings silence, and the reliability record is even better than the very reliable compressor type. These advantages are offset by a higher initial cost and by a running efficiency about half of that with a compressor. Occasionally very large scale absorption plants are built but there is usually a special reason, such as the availability of industrial waste heat.

In the last five years interest has revived in absorption techniques for two complementary reasons. The first is for an air-conditioning unit and the second is for a more efficient heater. The concept of the air-conditioning chiller is to combine a solar panel with the cooling load[1]. Normal absorption chemical pairs require very high temperatures for regeneration. Solar studies are searching for chemical pairs which can be regenerated at temperatures around 90°C which can be reached by solar collectors. When the sun shines strongly, then the building will need cooling and the absorber refrigeration will work at its best. The feasibility of a solar-driven refrigerator grows as the working regenerator temperature becomes lower. Yazaki, a Japanese pioneer, already offers a small lithium bromide/water absorber which can be regenerated at 88°C[35]. The onset of crystallization limits the attainable concentration and therefore the efficiency. Water, the refrigerant, exerts a very low vapour pressure and the whole cycle is therefore sub-atmospheric pressure[36].

An example of a closed-type forced-flow solar regenerator for dehumidification is illustrated in *Figure 9.22*[37].

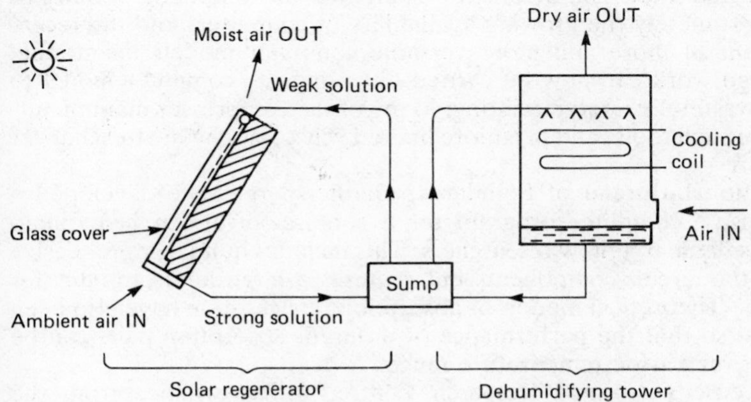

Figure 9.22 Closed-type forced-flow solar regenerator using a liquid absorbent (Gandhidasan, 1983)[37]

The second aim of absorption research is to enhance the output of fossil-fired boilers used for space heating. The coefficients of performance are very low, ~1.2, compared with 2.5 for an electric compressor refrigerant type but much better than achieved simply by burning the fuel. Lithium bromide and water cannot be used because of the risk of water freezing. The mixture of ammonia and water is a very attractive thermodynamic pair but its working pressure is very high (20 bar at 50°C) and there is concern over the possible hazard of keeping a significant quantity of toxic ammonia inside the building. Ammonia is also corrosive to copper and this increases production costs. One current favourite is the mixture of the readily available refrigerant R22 with tetra ethylene dimethyl ether E181. While less effective than ammonia in performance, it is non-explosive and non-toxic and therefore is much more attractive to the user. It does require a high circulation ratio of solution[38,39]. Theoretical modelling of the characteristics of the mixtures are also in progress for computer simulation of performance[40].

Research is already exploring whether or not small fossil-fired absorber dehumidifiers could form a useful kitchen cooler/dehumidifier/water heater. A gas heater could, for example, regenerate the absorber at high temperature and the hot flue gases would still be valuable for space or water heating. If or when the larger size of absorption units become mass produced and of low cost, then there could be a spate of multifunction units which offer either cooling or dehumidification and heating. If low-temperature regenerators become practicable then small absorption units could be driven from a gas-fired domestic hot-water heater and provide a very dry airing cupboard while preheating the water.

(i) Computer-aided design

The drawback of all refrigerant circuit design is that the components are interactive and their characteristics change as the operating conditions change. Fortunately the growing availability of computers and the recent development of more and more versatile computer models means that much design work can now be carried out using the computer model to eliminate wasteful prototype testing. Many of the compressor manufacturers now use such tools, and in a more limited way so do the heat-exchanger manufacturers.

The National Bureau of Standards, Gaithersberg, have developed a comprehensive computer program for a compressor-driven heat pump which is available to fellow researchers. This includes quite comprehensive details of the circuit components but requires a large minicomputer for operation[40]. Theoretical models of absorption refrigeration have also been constructed so that the performance of different absorption pairs can be examined over a wide temperature range[39].

The Electricity Council Research Centre, with assistance from the National Bureau of Standards, has produced a computer model devoted to all forms of compressor-driven refrigerant dehumidifiers, using a wide range of refrigerants operating over a temperature range of 0 to 120°C. The outline of this program, which can also include the geared air-to-air heat exchanger, is illustrated in *Figure 9.23*[26].

The main purpose of these models is to explore the sensitivity of any design to changes in the physical factors. The air-flow can be increased or decreased, the compressor size can be changed with respect to the heat-exchanger duties, and the air side conditions of temperature and humidity can be altered at will. Trend lines can then be speedily identified and the important design factors identified. The models are an aid rather than a design. To date they are not accurate in predicting performance but they are accurate in identifying sensitivity. The use of such predictive techniques is growing. The major limitation is the absence of published information of the more detailed aspects of a manufacturer's product. Manufacturers are still reluctant, for commercial reasons, to disclose too much information on their products even if they possess it.

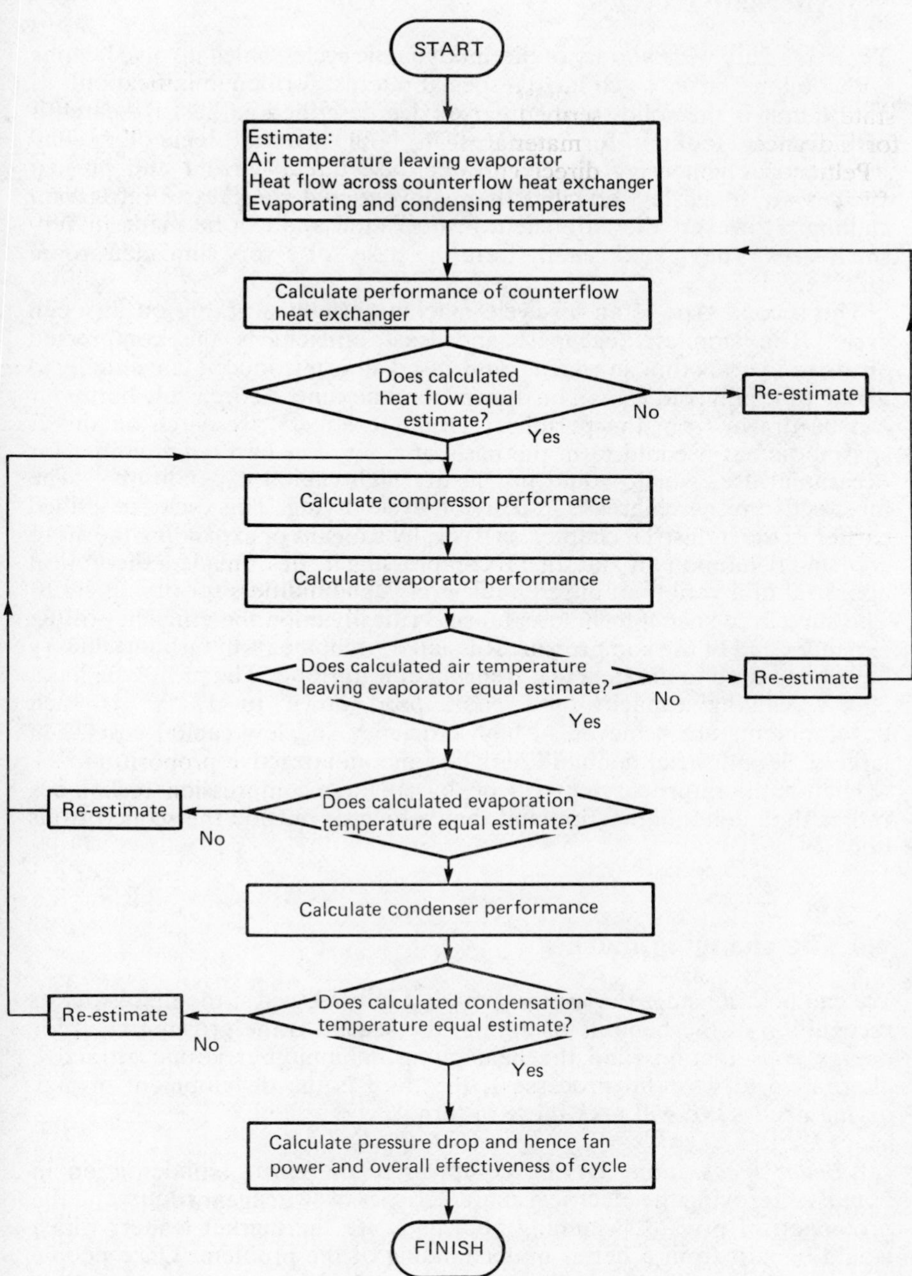

Figure 9.23 Logic diagram for computer-aided design program (Brundrett and Blundell, 1980)[26]

9.3 Alternative cycles

There is a very wide variety of thermodynamic cycles which involve heating and cooling but only two have a special interest for dehumidification.

The first is the solid-state Peltier device described earlier. Research is still actively looking for advances in both material technology and production engineering. Peltier devices use direct current and present devices are much less efficient than conventional compressor/refrigerant chilling. However, they are silent in operation and can be made in very small sizes. They could readily form the basis for a very slim silent room unit[41].

The second type is an air-cycle machine usually working on an open cycle. The simplest, cheapest and least efficient is the compressed air-driven vortex tube in which compressed air is introduced tangentially to a long tube and cold air can be drawn from the central core while hotter air can be drawn from the periphery (Ranque effect). Research on this is spasmodic but it could form the basis of a very low cost dehumidifier for occasional use, which would not justify high capital expenditure[42]. The most active research area is in Brayton-cycle drying. This cycle, described earlier in the industrial chapter, is basically a means of expanding the air to cool and dehumidify it and then recompressing it. Iles[43] made a theoretical appraisal of a variety of different air-cycle dehumidifiers for drying grain. The success of such a technique hinges critically upon the efficiency of the expander and of the compressor. Russian developments in turbomachinery have been used to create a fast-freezing unit for food. The prototype has a 30-kW chilling capacity and cools food down to 173°K. If such developments are achieved at high efficiency and low capital cost, then large-scale industrial dehumidifiers become an attractive proposition.

High-temperature drying will be by steam recompression techniques rather than dehumidification and that subject is outside the scope of this book.

9.4 The changing market

We can best consider the growing market in three ways: the first is better recognition of the benefits of drying; the second is the growing need for energy conservation (and the heat pump dehumidifier is one attractive alternative to wasteful processes); the third is the development of new drying needs. We will take these in turn.

(a) *Better recognition*. Drying compressed air, curing condensation in homes, improving the electrical characteristics of switchgear rooms and the protection of private swimming pool halls are the market leaders which would benefit from a better understanding of the problem. Once people can trace their problems back to a surplus of moisture, then the dehumidifier is used and with success. Eight large Carlyle SF60 20-kW compressors are in readiness to cure all dampness problems in the new 2000-MW high-voltage direct-current channel link which connects the French and British electricity networks[45]. Local substations are often unmanned and need to be kept dry to prevent corrosion. The boom in home swimming pools quickly led to a demand for dehumidification.

(b) *Energy saving*. Dehumidifiers which both ventilate the home and dry clothes have been developed and marketed[46]. However, limitations on clothes space, creases on drying, and the slow drying speed prevented a successful launch despite significant energy savings. Improved detail design will lead to a more satisfactory solution for both drying and airing clothes. The addition of a dehumidifier to a large commercial tumble dryer has been assessed[47]. Energy use was halved but the slow drying speed, the high capital cost, bulk and the relatively low annual running time of such dryers prevented commercial application. However, smaller, quieter units could be usefully built into highly-loaded driers which operate for long periods, for example as in a laundry.

Already available are units which dehumidify and cool and put the heat removed usefully into the domestic hot water cylinder. These methods are very popular in hot, steamy kitchens. Plans are already in progress to apply a dehumidifier to recover the latent heat released from a proprietory dishwasher handling 7000 dishes/hour. Such a dehumidifier can reduce the electrical input from 113kW to 42kW and also, by eliminating much of the heat and moisture, introduce much more acceptable conditions to the kitchen[48].

The progressive development of high-temperature dehumidification is opening up a wide range of industrial applications from timber drying, malt drying, plaster drying, to food and grain applications. At high temperatures (>150°C) steam recompression looks particularly attractive and will take over the drying operation.

Recent work in the United States of America has highlighted the implications of a humid climate on the energy consumption of supermarkets. The traditional design approach has been for an air-conditioning engineer to design the store to operate at a maximum of 24°C 55% r.h. in summer while the refrigeration capacity for the food cabinets or shelves to maintain their deep-frozen temperature in such an ambient. The refrigeration engineer designs the refrigeration equipment to meet both the sensible cooling and the latent cooling. The latent cooling is from the heat of condensation of the water vapour in the air as it condenses on the cold surfaces and then the heat of fusion as it freezes. High humidities can therefore lead to high latent refrigerated cabinet load with a high energy cost and a risk of spoilage if food temperatures go too high.

If the humidity in the store can be lowered then the latent load on the refrigerated displays will be reduced and their energy consumption correspondingly lowered. Conventional air-conditioning equipment does not normally dehumidify well at low relative humidities. The solution is to dry the incoming fresh air, and two approaches are being used to achieve this. The first is an extension of the conventional refrigeration design with much lower refrigerant evaporation temperatures for this special air inlet treatment plant[49]. The second is the use of a regenerative solid desiccant dryer for the inlet air[50-52].

Preliminary measurements show energy savings of 15% achieved for the refrigerant solution but feasibility studies suggest even greater savings possible with versions of the desiccant system.

(c) *New needs*. New needs for very dry conditions constantly appear in the packaged food and packaged pharmaceutical fields. The shelf life of dried products such as soup powder or antibiotic drugs can be strongly influenced by the dryness of the product when packed. Very dry conditions usually prolong the useful life of the stored product.

The most recent identification of a new market is in horticultural greenhouses. Quality control, planned growth and growing schedules have led to a revolution in horticultural techniques. Modern greenhouses are usually double- or triple-glazed, tightly-built with planned ventilation, and used throughout the year. The main problem is the rapidly-rising relative humidity at the onset of dusk. In such well-insulated houses some condensation occurs on the plants as well as the windows. This activates

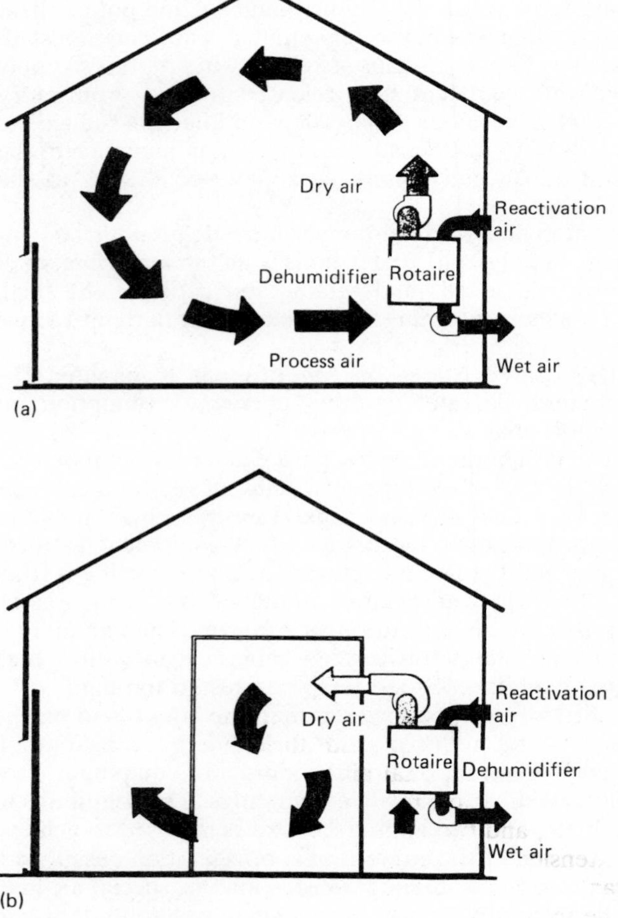

Figure 9.24 Simple plastics screening can protect the drying zone. (a) Normal operation: the dehumidifier recirculates and dehumidifies the air inside the store. (b) Selective dehumidification: sensitive materials are enclosed in a simple plastics tent. Air from the store is dried, pumped through the tent and back into the store (courtesy of Rotaire, 1984)

the fungal invasion of botrytis[53,54]. Guidelines to the heat-pump solutions are now available[55].

Corrosion control in warehouses is a further possibility. As warehouses become more automated then the goods can be stored dryer and colder. Pioneer trials showed that in very large buildings the bulk of the moisture release came from the drying out of the concrete floor. This can take two to three years if the building is relatively cool. The dehumidifiers were invaluable during this prolonged drying but air infiltration provided adequate if less effective moisture control normally. Dehumidifiers will appear in this market but only when our building techniques are able to provide an airtight space.

Corrosion control in factories by means of dehumidification is being helped by a research project exploring the critical relative humidity above which the corrosion rate accelerates. A special electrochemical cell has been constructed which can be placed in the environment being examined[55]. It operates at different relative humidities and records the likely chemical activity. The management can then see the importance of humidity control in their own particular climate. Dusty and corrosive atmospheres require a lower relative humidity to avoid rapid corrosion.

Selective zones within a factory can be isolated and kept very dry. This technique is growing and is used particularly for engineering items such as electric welding rods which require the flux bonded to the rod to be kept very dry. The technique is illustrated in *Figure 9.24*.

9.5 References

1 Martinex, A.R. (ed). *Solar Cooling and Dehumidifying*. Pergamon Press, Oxford, 1981

2 Asami, K., Ishijima, K. and Tanaka, H. 'Improvements of noise and efficiency of rolling piston type refrigeration compressor for household refrigerator and freezer'. (R. Cohen, ed). Purdue Compr Techy Conf, 1982, *Proc*, 268-274

3 Matsuo, K., Senshu, T., Hayashi, M. and Kokuba, H. 'How can heat pumps be made more cost competitive?'. Intern Energy Agency Heat Pump Conf, May 1984, *Proc*, 87-96. Graz, Austria. Pubd by Technische Universität, Graz, 1984

4 Ikegawa, M., Sato, E., Tojo, K., Arai, A. and Arai, N. 'Scroll compressor with self-adjusting back pressure measurement'. *ASHRAE trans* **90**, No 2A, 314-326, 1984

5 Goricke, P. 'Steurbare Warmepumpenverdichter - Rollkolben und Wankelverdichter'. *Elektrowärme* im Technischen Ausbau, Edition A, **38**, A4/5, 232-236, 1980

6 Curwen, P. W. and Liles, A. W. 'Development of a free piston, variable stroke compressor for load following electric heat pumps'. *Elektrowärme* im Technischen Ausbau, Edition A, **38**, A4/5, 243-252, 1980

7 Mann, B. 'ERA to study pole amplitude modulation motors'. *Htg & Air Condg Jnl*, pp 40, Feb 1982

8 Toshiba Technical Leaflet, 'Inverter controlled air conditioning', Toshiba, 1986

9 Jaster, H. and Miller, S. 'Steady state and seasonal efficiencies of air-to-air heat pumps with continuously speed-modulated compressors'. *Elektrowärme* im Technischen Ausbau, Edition A, **38**, A4/5, 237-240, 1980

10 Browne, F. D. 'Feedback control of evaporator pressure'. *ASHRAE Jnl*, 41-42, Sept 1984

11 Paul, J., Schmitt, K. and Strehl, U. 'Speed-controlled heat pumps'. Intern Inste of Refrign Con 'Heat pumps and air circulation in conditioned spaces'. *Proc* of the Mtgs of Commissions B1, B2, E1, E2, 113-122. Essen, W. Germany, Sept 1981

12 Kandpal, T. C. 'Improved efficiency compressors for air conditioning'. Purdue Compr Techy Conf (ed J. F. Hamilton) 1978, *Proc*, 151-153

13 Anon. 'Flooded evaporators'. *Intern Heat Pump Bull*, **3**(1), 7, 1985

14 Kamei, S., Mitzushima, T., Kifune, S. and Keto, T. 'Research on the frost formation in a low temperature cooler condenser'. *Japanese Scic Rev*, **2** 317-326, 1952

15 Schneider, H. W. 'Equation of the growth rate of frost forming on cooled surfaces'. *Intern Jnl of Heat & Mass Tranfer,* **21**, 1019-1024, 1978

16 Barrow, H. 'Personal communication'. Research in progress at Dept of Mech Engg, Univ of Liverpool, 1985

17 Sanders, C. 'Personal communication'. Research in progress at Blg Res Sta (Scotland), Glasgow, 1985

18 Maczek, K. and Krolicki, Z. 'Non-adiabatic process in throttling capillary tubes used in packaged units'. Intern Inste of Refrign Conf 'Heat pumps and air circulation in conditioned spaces'. *Proc* of the Mtgs of Commissions B1, B2, E1, E2, 49-57. Essen, W. Germany, Sept 1981

19 Danfoss Ltd. 'The appliance of Danfoss hermetic compressors'. *Danfoss Jnl*, 1-7, Aug 1981

20 Bonne, U. and Mueller, D. A. 'Advanced control systems'. *Elektrowärme* im Technischen Ausbau, Edition A, **39**, 130-137, 1981

21 Bonne, U., Patani, A., Jacobson, R. D. and Mueller, D. A. 'Electric driven heat pump systems: simulations and controls'. *ASHRAE Jnl*, Feb 1980

22 Honeywell Corp. 'Advanced heat pump control system application manual'. Doc RE/REV 10-79/71-5100, 1979

23 Anon. 'Modern motor design'. *Engg*, 824, Nov 1984

24 Sensair Ltd, 22 Kenilworth Rd, Basingstoke, Hants RG23 8JL, 1985

25 Perry, E. J. 'Drying by cascaded heat pumps'. Inste of Refrign Mtg, London, Oct 1981

26 Brundrett, G. W. and Blundell, C. J. 'An advanced dehumidifier for Britain'. *Htg & Ventg Engr*, 6-7, Nov 1980

27 Tschaikorsky, B. and Kuznetsov, A. P. 'Investigations of mixtures of refrigerants in compression refrigeration machinery'. *Kholod Tech*, **40**, 9-11, 1963

28 Cooper, W. D. and Borchardt, H. J. 'The use of refrigerant mixtures in air-to-air heat pumps'. 15th Intern Cong of Refrign, Venice, Italy, 1979

29 Connon, H. A. and Drew, D. W. 'Estimation and application of thermodynamic properties for a non-azeotropic refrigerant mixture'. Intern Inste of Refrign Conf 'Heat pumps and air circulation in conditioned spaces'. *Proc* of the Mtgs of Commissions B1, B2, E1, E2, 91-100. Essen, W. Germany, Sept 1981

30 Kruse, H. 'The advantages of non-azeotropic refrigerant mixtures for heat pump applications'. *Intern Jnl of Refrign*, **4**(3), 119-125, 1981

31 Rojey, A. 'Pompe à chaleur fonctionnant avec un mélange de fluides'. Intern Inste of Refrign Conf. *Proc* of the Mtgs for Commissions B1, B2, E1, E2, Mons, Belgium, 1980

32 Kruse, H. and Jakobs, R. 'The importance of non-azeotropic binary refrigerants for use in heat pumps and refrigerating plant'. *Klima und Kalte Ingenieur*, 253-260, Jly/Aug 1977. Elecy Ccl trans, OA 1760: 1980

33 Haselden, G. G. and Klimek, L. 'An experimental study of the use of mixed refrigerants for non-isothermal refrigeration'. Inste of Refrign, *Proc*, **54**, 127-154, 1957

34 Johannsen, A. 'Performance simulation of a solar air conditioning system with liquid desiccant'. *Intern Jnl of Ambient Energy*, **5**(2), 59-88, 1984

35 Szokolay, S. V. 'Experience with an active solar air conditioning system'. First Intern Conf on Bldg Energy Managet, Oporto, Portugal, May 1980

36 Reay, D. A. and Macmichael, D. B. A. *Heat Pumps:Design and Applications*. Pergamon Press, Oxford, 1979

37 Gandhidasan, P. 'Comparative study of two types of solar regenerators for liquid absorption dehumidification systems'. ASHRAE transactions, **90**, No 2A, 78-83, 1984

38 Worsoe-Schmidt, P. 'Modern trends in heat pump development'. Intern Inste of Refrign Conf 'Heat pumps and air circulation in conditioned spaces'. *Proc* of the Mtgs for Commissions B1, B2, E1, E2, 15-22. Essen, W. Germany, Sept 1981

39 Trommelmans, J., Bulck, E. van den, and Berghmans, J. 'Factors influencing the performance of a domestic absorption heat pump'. Intern Inste of Refrign Conf 'Heat pumps and air circulation in conditioned spaces'. *Proc* of the Mtgs for Commissions B1, B2, E1, E2, 377-386. Essen, W. Germany, Sept 1981

40 Didion, D. A. 'Personal communication'. Blg and Environl Div, Nat Bureau of Standards, Gaithersburg, Maryland, USA, 1985

41 Farrell, T. 'Thermoelectric heat pumping', Elecy Ccl Res Cen, Capenhurst, Rep 844, 1975

42 Brundrett, G. W. 'Vortex tube application'. *Design Engg*, 71-73, Dec 1968

43 Iles, T. 'The Brayton-cycle heat pump for industrial process applications'. *Elektrowärme im Technischen Ausbau*, Edition A, **38**, A4/5, 285-294, Jly/Sept 1980
44 Dubinsky, M. G., Hekhoroshev, V. M. and Stavissky, A. Y. 'Application of the air turbo refrigerating machine as a heat and cold generator for pre-dried agricultural products freezing'. Intern Inste of Refrign Conf 'Heat pumps and air circulation in conditioned spaces'. *Proc* of the Mtgs for Commissions B1, B2, E1, E2, 310-316. Essen, W. Germany, Sept 1981
45 Anon. 'Channel link contract'. *Htg & Ventg Engr*, 11, 7 Jly 1984
46 Capaldi, B. 'Units to ventilate the home and to dry clothes'. *Elecl Rev*, 428-429, 3 Oct 1975
47 Ruiter, J. P., Lentvaar, G. and Zeypstra, A. H. 'Tumble dryer with heat pump'. *Elektrotechnik*, 58 (4), 224-229, 1978
48 Stroder, W. 'Use of heat pumps in large dishwashing installations'. *Elektrowärme im Technischen Ausbau*, Edition A, **40**, 3, 108-111, 1982. Elecy Ccl trans, OA 2565: 1982
49 Whitehead, E. R. 'Outdoor air treatment for humidity control in supermarkets'. ASHRAE *Proc*, **91**, No 1B, 434-440, 1985
50 Calton, D. S. 'Application of a desiccant cooling system to supermarkets'. ASHRAE *Proc*, **91**, No 1B, 441-445, 1985
51 Manley, D. L., Bowlen, K. L. and Cohen, B. M. 'Evaluation of gas-fired desiccant-based space conditioning for supermarkets'. ASHRAE *Proc*. **91**, No 1B, 447-456, 1985
52 Burns, P. R., Mitchell, J. W. and Beckman, W. A. 'Hybrid desiccant cooling systems in supermarket applications'. ASHRAE *Proc*, **91**, No 1B, 457-468, 1985
53 Bailey, B. J. 'Limiting the relative humidity in insulated greenhouses at night'. *Acta Hort*. **148**, 1-11, 1983
54 Royle, D. 'Humidity key to poinsettia disorder'. *Grower*, 29 Nov 1984, page 35
55 Electricity Council. 'Heat pumps and heat recovery techniques in agriculture and horticulture'. Tech Inf Rep, AGR 10, 1984
56 Moore, B. 'Personal communication'. Elecy Ccl Res Cen, Capenhurst, 1985

Chapter 10

Economics

10.1 Introduction

There is no universal optimum for a system design because each customer's problem is different. However, it will be useful to consider the economic factors from at least four viewpoints:

(1) *The dehumidifier designer*. He sets out to produce an effective design at low capital cost.
(2) *The project engineer*. He takes a built-up dehumidifier and applies it to his particular drying problem.
(3) *The cost accountant*. He wants to know the total cost of the drying operation.
(4) *The engineering director*. He wishes to check that the dehumidifier is more cost-effective than its competitors.

Let us consider these four requirements in turn and finally consider the potential markets.

10.2 The dehumidifier designer: basic manufacturing cost of the dehumidifier

The price of the components of a dehumidifier varies with size and quantity ordered. The list price for a popular, high-quality, mass-produced compressor/condenser unit is illustrated in *Figure 10.1* as a function of nominal electrical power.

The cost of the sets can be expressed by the relationship

$$\text{Cost} = £213 \times (\text{compressor power kW})^{0.38}$$

This relation is true for a range of sizes from 90 kW to 500 kW. Earlier studies showed that the exponent 0.38 was more likely to be 0.6 for the larger semi-hermetic and open compressors[]].

The manufactured cost is the sum of the costs of the components together with the assembly cost and overheads. In the domestic and small commercial market mass-production techniques cut the assembly costs to a

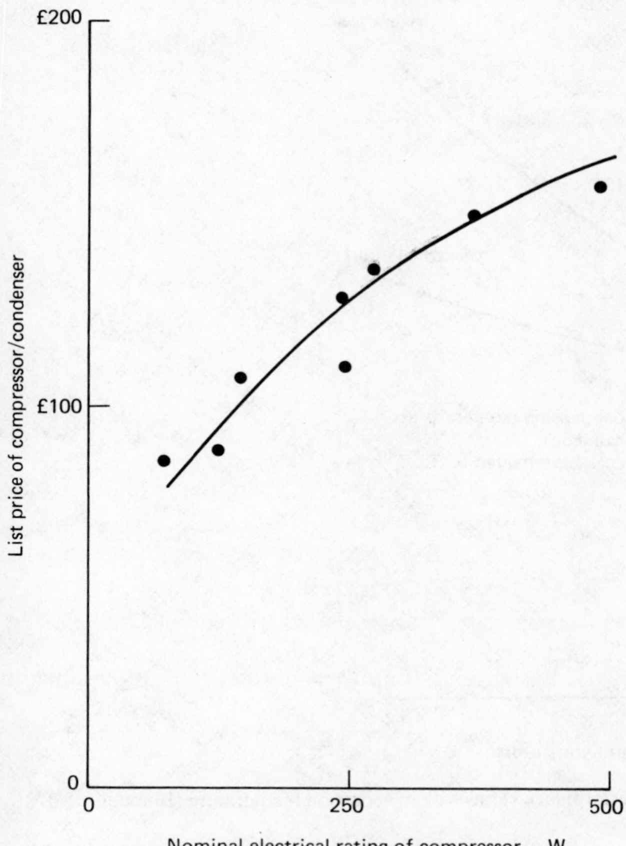

Figure 10.1 List price for hermetic compressor/condensing sets. Cost of compressor/condensing set = £213 (compressor power in kW)$^{0.38}$

small fraction of the total cost. The manufactured cost is therefore little more than the sum of the components. In the industrial market the machines are more expensive and tend to be built on a batch basis for particular orders. The Belgian study[1] showed that for the larger semi-hermetic and open machines the manufactured price was approximately double that of the sum of the components.

The actual design of the dehumidifier benefits from the use of a computer model of the system. Small changes in one factor interact with the performance of the other components. Some form of design and sensitivity analysis is now essential. Precise answers are not yet achievable because full performance characteristics of all the components are not normally known. However, the models are excellent at identifying trends and the use of them is highly commended. The larger producers of dehumidifiers or of compressors have their own confidential models.

The National Bureau of Standards, Washington, USA, have a well-established and proven refrigerant circuit computer model but at

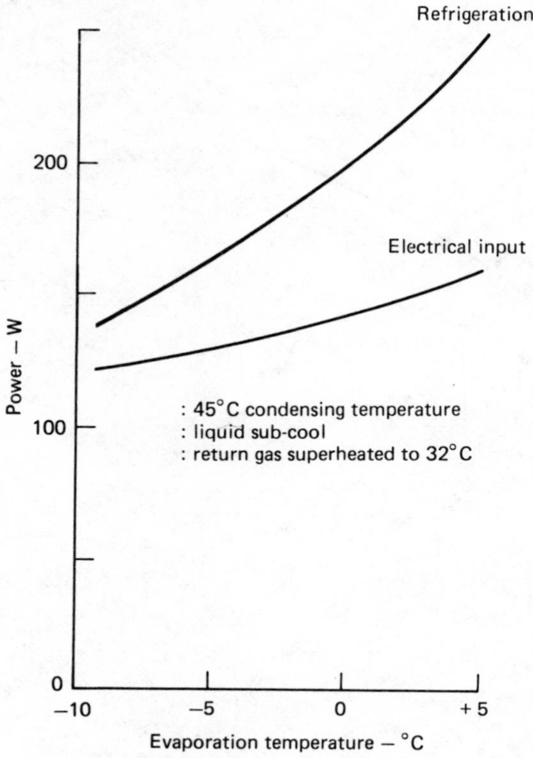

Figure 10.2 Compressor performance varies with evaporation temperature (Blundell, 1978)[3]

present this does not deal specifically with dehumidification[2], but it can be a very valuable first step. The Elecricity Council Research Centre, Capenhurst, UK, has a highly-developed model which deals with domestic, commercial and industrial dehumidification. An outline of the technique is available[3]. Performance data from the compressor manufacturer is the starting point. An example of a small hermetic compressor is illustrated in *Figure 10.2*. The computed influence of evaporator area on the effectiveness of dehumidification is shown in *Figure 10.3*[3] for one air temperature and relative humidity. Such relationships are plotted for the range of working conditions under which the unit will operate.

A satisfactory optimization can be reached for any one design condition. This is particularly true for industrial processes where the operating conditions are known, specified and do not change. The designers of the mass-produced domestic and commercial units aim for a much wider spread of reasonable performance. However, the emphasis varies. Designers for swimming pool machines intend them to perform at their best in warm and very humid conditions. The North American machines tend also to be designed for rather warm summer conditions. The Japanese market is for cooler conditions and British-made machines are usually designed for cold conditions.

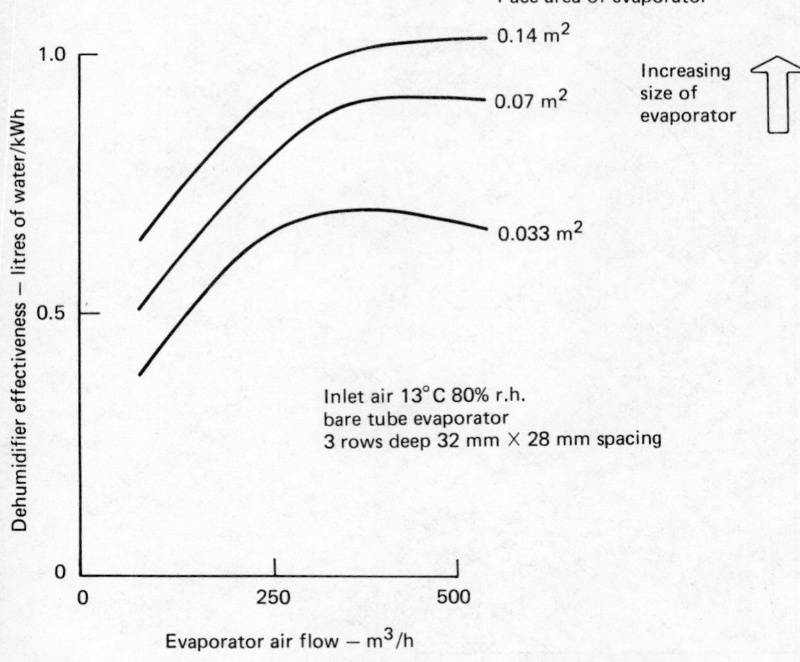

Figure 10.3 The influence of evaporator size on effectiveness (Blundell, 1978)[3]

The mathematical model can also be used to define unsatisfactory operating conditions[4]. Finned evaporators are used in some machines partly to reduce cost but also to reduce the size of the machine. However, these are particularly sensitive to air flow. At high air flows much of the finned surface can be above dewpoint and therefore plays an active part in heat transfer but little in dehumidification. An example of the small domestic dehumidifier, used earlier with plain tubes in the evaporator, is given in *Figure 10.4*[4]. This assumes that the same total area of heat transfer is supplied in each case. The very close space finning has a low maximum effectiveness and a very rapid decline in it with increasing air flow.

The manufactured dehumidifier can then be used on its own as a drying device or it can be incorporated into a drying system. The drying systems are essentially industrial, agricultural or swimming pool designs.

10.3 The system designer: running cost

While the refrigerant circuit is strongly influenced by its operating temperatures at the evaporator and condenser there is another very important running cost factor once a dehumidifier is introduced as a component of a drying cycle. This is the pumping power which goes into the recirculating air drying circuit. In many cases, particularly in grain

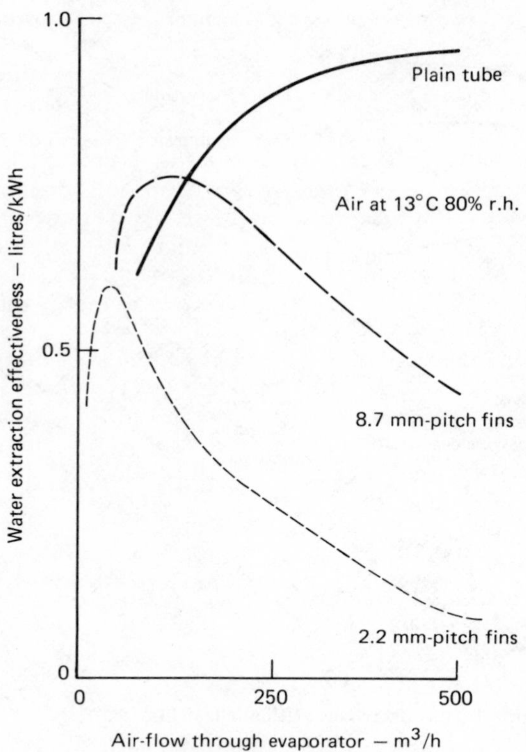

Figure 10.4 Caution with finned evaporation tubes at high air-flows (Blundell, 1978)[3]

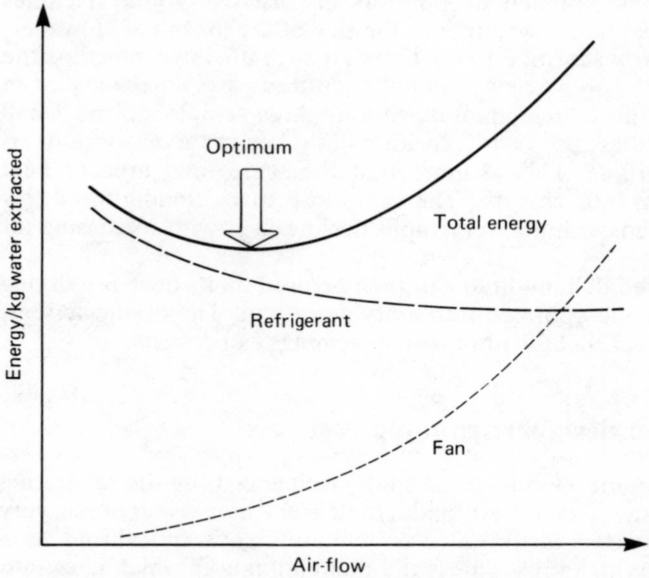

Figure 10.5 System optimization for air-flow (Flikke, Cloud and Hustrulid, 1957)[5]

drying where the air is forced through a bed of grain, this pumping power can equal the refrigeration circuit power.

Experimental results on a fixed bed of grain showed the relationship between dehumidification effectiveness and recirculating air flow. This is illustrated in *Figure 10.5*[5]. Increasing the air velocity increased the heat transfer from the air to the refrigerant circuit. This lowered the temperature difference between air and refrigerant and permitted a higher evaporating temperature. This led to a more effective refrigerant circuit. Unfortunately the pressure drop penalty of achieving a high air-flow rate increased the fan power at a faster rate than the improvement in the refrigerant circuit. This meant that the optimum recirculation rate was soon exceeded.

Dryers operating on a wide range of materials deserve special attention to the thickness of the bed. The pressure drop through beds of cereals is directly proportional to density but inversely proportional to the cereal size. Bed depth should be adjusted to keep the circuit near its optimum. Pressure-drop characteristics for a range of cereals are illustrated in *Figure 10.6*[6].

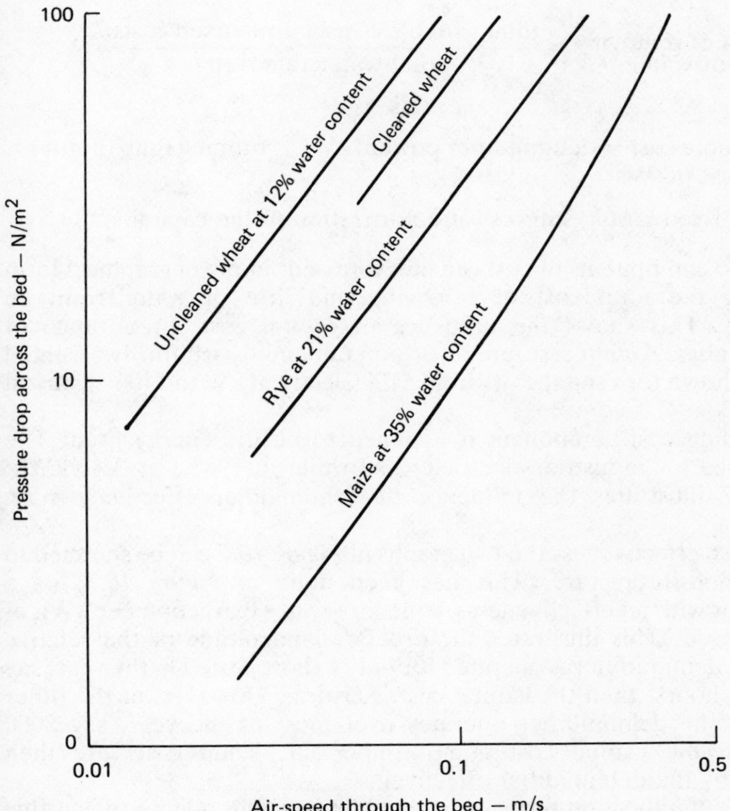

Figure 10.6 Pressure drop through a 1-m-high bed of cereal (Kroll, 1959)[6]

Close liaison between dehumidifier designer and the project engineer of the drying circuit is essential.

10.4 The cost accountant: total cost

Total cost of dehumidification is made up of two kinds of basic cost[6,7]:

(1) *Fixed-cost elements*. These are the items unrelated to the amount of dehumidification achieved over the year. The machine cost is the primary element because once purchased the interest or amortization of the capital has to be repaid whether or not the machine is actually used. The item would also include maximum demand charges for the electricity supply. While these would be paid only if the unit was operated, the basic charge is not sensitive to the duration of operation.
(2) *Variable costs*. These are the costs which progressively increase as the dehumidifier is run. Its main element is the energy used but it could also include a maintenance element. The actual cost depends upon the product of the energy cost and the effectiveness of the dehumidifier.

The equation is

$$\text{Total cost of removing one litre of water} = \frac{\text{total variable costs} + \text{total fixed costs}}{\text{total water removed}}$$

where

total variable cost = dehumidifier power (kW) × running time (hours) × energy cost p/kWh

and total fixed cost = interest or amortization of the capital

These two components of cost can be expressed simply in graphical form to quantify the total cost of removing one litre of water from an atmosphere. This shows the influence of capital cost for a range of operating hours. An interest rate of 10% per annum is arbitrarily assumed and this is shown for capital costs from £100/electrical kW to £400/electrical kW.

The running cost component is assumed to be the energy used. The average price for industrial electricity in Britain in 1985 was 3.4p/kWh. *Figure 10.7* illustrates the influence of dehumidifier effectiveness on running cost.

For a given effectiveness the two graphs in *Figure 10.7* can be summed to give a composite picture. This has been done in *Figure 10.8* for a dehumidifier with an effectiveness of one litre water extraction per kWh of electricity used. This illustrates the orders of magnitude of the relative costs. If the dehumidifier is operated for only a short period in the year, say below 2000 hours, then the capital cost is critical. However, at the other extreme, if the dehumidifier operates over most of the year, say 8000 hours, then the capital cost is not important. Total costs are then dominated by the dehumidifier effectiveness.

In all dehumidification processes there will be some release of sensible heat. If this sensible heat gain is useful, as in a swimming pool, then credit

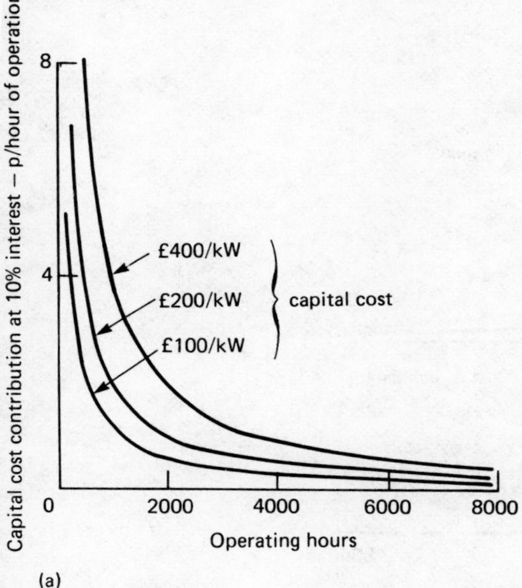

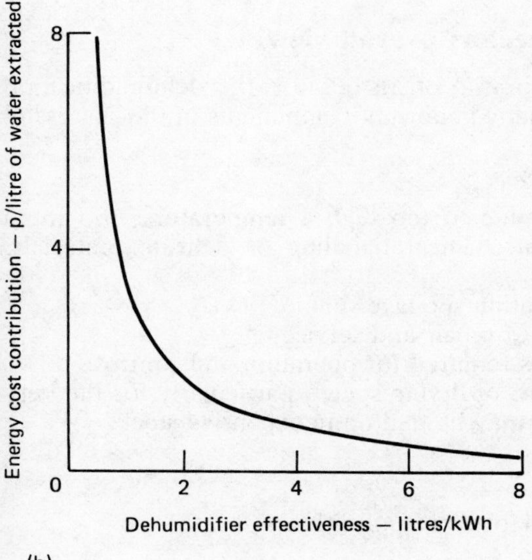

Figure 10.7 Total cost is the sum of the capital contribution and the running cost. (a) Capital-cost influence, and (b) running-cost influence (electricity at 1985 price, 3.4p/kWh)

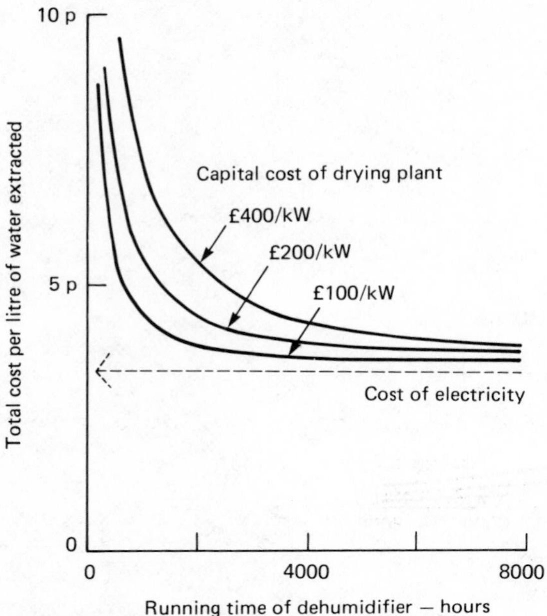

Figure 10.8 Total cost of dehumidification. Assumption: effectiveness = 1 litre water/kWh

for the space-heating energy saved can be offset against the dehumidifier running cost.

10.5 The engineering director: overall view

This is the most difficult appraisal of all because the dehumidification process will be only one of many important components in the successful production of the product.

These other factors include:

(1) Risks of drying damage due to too high a temperature, too rapid dehydration, too vigorous mechanical handling of delicate materials, non-uniformity.
(2) Possibilities for contamination spoilage.
(3) Plant reliability and ease of repair and service.
(4) Skill and manpower levels required for operation and control.
(5) The economic implications of drying speed, particularly for the very slow processes where finance may be tied up in expensive stock.
(6) Space availability.
(7) Scale of operation.

These have to be considered for each application.

10.6 Market size

A significant factor in final price is the selling route. High-volume, popular domestic products sell through highly-competitive High Street shops at

TABLE 10.1 Market size and other characteristics for dehumidifiers

Market	*Annual moisture removal* 10^6 tonnes of water	*Number of customers* $\times 10^3$	*Typical size of dehumidifier* kW	*Operating temperature* °C	*Load factor*	*Sales prospects*	*Competition*
Homes	70.0	19000	0.2	15	winter	excellent	ventilation
Paper making	9.0	0.01	1000.0	80	all year	good	steam
Compressed air	5.0	180.0	3.0	2	all year	excellent	none
Brick making	2.0	0.1	50.0	80	all year	good	hot air
Plaster drying	1.0	0.01	50.0	60	all year	good	hot air
Pools	0.9	2.0	50.0	25	most year	excellent	ventilation
Grain drying	0.5	0.1	50.0	45	summer	poor	sunshine
Hairdressers	0.4	34.0	0.5	20	all year	excellent	ventilation
Timber drying	0.2	1.0	10.0	60	all year	excellent	hot air
Launderettes	0.1	4.5	0.5	20	all year	good	ventilation

very low cost margins. This profit is essential from the high sales turnover. Specialist domestic products have to advertise widely and often require personal customer visits to make the sale. The on-cost above the manufacturer's factory price has to be considerably higher than for the popular products.

The commercial and industrial market is well organized to deal in small specialist pieces of equipment. Suppliers usually deal in one area and have a well-established reputation.

The potential sizes and types of markets are listed in *Table 10.1*[8].

Appendix

Assumptions for *Table 10.1*.

No formal figures for evaporation quantities have been identified; therefore the figures given in *Table 10.1* are personal estimates. The assumptions behind these estimates are as follows:

(1) *Homes*

Britain has 19 million dwellings and with normal occupancy four people release 7 kg of moisture/day. Home laundry at three washing-machine loads per week will release a further 21 kg/wk.

$$\begin{aligned} \text{Evaporation/year} &= 19 \times 10^6 \times (49 + 21) \times 52 \text{ wks} \\ &= 69 \times 10^6 \text{ tonnes} \end{aligned}$$

(2) *Paper and board manufacture*

Approximately 4.5×10^6 tonnes of paper and board are manufactured in Britain each year and the drying operation reduces the moisture content by 200%.

$$\begin{aligned} \text{Evaporation/year} &= 4.5 \times 10^6 \times 2 \\ &= 9 \times 10^6 \text{ tonnes} \end{aligned}$$

(3) *Compressed air*

Practically all of the industrial factories use at least one compressed air supply. Assuming a typical plant size of 1000 m^3/h air compressed to 7 bar with a 35°C intercooler, the water which should be removed would be approximately 6 litres/h at design or half that over the year.

$$\begin{aligned} \text{Dehumid. needed} &= 180000 \text{ factories} \times 3 \text{ litres/h} \times 24 \times 7 \times 52 \text{ kg/yr} \\ &= 5 \times 10^6 \text{ tonnes/yr} \end{aligned}$$

(4) *Bricks*

Approximately 16×10^6 tonnes of brick are made each year and have a drop in water content of 15%.

$$\begin{aligned} \text{Evaporation/year} &= 16 \times 10^6 \times 0.15 \\ &= 2 \times 10^6 \text{ tonnes} \end{aligned}$$

(5) *Plaster drying*

Annual production of plaster and plasterboard in Britain is 2×10^6 tonnes with a moisture content drop of 45%.

$$\begin{aligned}\text{Evaporation/year} &= 2 \times 10^6 \text{ tonnes} \times 0.45 \\ &= 0.9 \times 10^6 \text{ tonnes}\end{aligned}$$

(6) *Swimming pools*

Britain has approximately 1000 sports centres with a pool and a further 1000 public individual pools. Pool evaporation rates are typically $0.25\,\text{kg/m}^3/\text{h}$ when occupied and $0.1\,\text{kg/m}^3\,\text{h}$ unoccupied. An average pool is $350\,\text{m}^2$ of water surface with 10h occupancy.

$$\begin{aligned}&\text{Evaporation/year} \\ &\text{occupied} &&= 2000 \text{ pools} \times 350\text{ m}^2 \times 0.25\text{ kg/m}^2\text{h} \times 10 \text{ hours} \times 365 \text{ days} \\ & &&= 0.6 \times 10^6 \text{ tonnes/yr} \\ &\text{unoccupied} &&= 2000 \text{ pools} \times 350 \times 0.1 \times 14 \times 365 \\ & &&= 0.3 \times 10^6 \text{ tonnes/yr} \\ &\text{Total evap./year} &&= 0.9 \times 10^6 \text{ tonnes/yr}\end{aligned}$$

(7) *Grain drying*

Approximately 26×10^6 tonnes of grain are harvested annually and about 10×10^6 tonnes are stored for some time by government and commercial bodies. The maximum moisture content for storage without cost penalty is 15%. If 15% moisture is removed from the grain, i.e. from 20% moisture content harvested to 15% in store, then

$$\begin{aligned}\text{Evaporation/year} &= 10 \times 10^6 \text{ tonnes} \times 0.05 \\ &= 0.5 \times 10^6 \text{ tonnes}\end{aligned}$$

(8) *Hairdressers*

There are 34000 registered hairdressers in Britain. If the moisture generation rate was five times that in a home, then for a six-day week

$$\begin{aligned}\text{Evaporation/year} &= 34000 \times 35 \text{ kg/day} \times 6 \text{ days} \times 52 \text{ wks} \\ &= 0.4 \times 10^6 \text{ tonnes}\end{aligned}$$

(9) *Timber drying*

Approximately 0.3×10^6 tonnes of softwood and 0.2×10^6 tonnes of hardwood are dried each year in Britain. The reduction in their moisture content is 45% for softwood and 20% for hardwood. Therefore,

$$\begin{aligned}\text{Evaporation/year} &= 0.3 \times 10^6 \times 0.45 + 0.2 \times 10^6 \times 0.2 \\ &= 0.135 \times 10^6 + 0.04 \times 16^6 \\ &= 0.2 \times 10^6 \text{ tonnes}\end{aligned}$$

(10) *Launderettes*

There are approximately 4500 launderettes in Britain. If each has three dryers in use for a 10-h day and released 7kg of moisture per hour per machine, and on average half the machines are in use, then

$$\begin{aligned}\text{Evaporation/year} &= 4500 \times 3 \text{ machines} \times 7 \text{ kg} \times 10 \text{ h} \times 300 \text{ days} \times \tfrac{1}{2} \\ &= 0.1 \times 10^6 \text{ tonnes}\end{aligned}$$

10.7 References

1 Looveren, A. van, Verelst, J., Berghmans, J. and Gelders, L. 'Determining the capital cost of industrial heat pumps by correlation'. Intern Symp on the Indusl Appls of Heat Pumps. BHRA, Mar 1982

2 Petersen, S. R., Kelly, G. E. and Didion, D. 'Economic analysis of improved efficiency for central air conditioners'. Nat Bureau of Standards Rep, NBSIR 80-1993, Jun 1980

3 Blundell, C. J. 'A computer model of an advanced dehumidifier'. Elecy Ccl Res Cen, Capenhurst, ECRC/M1303, 1979

4 Blundell, C. J. 'Heat exchanger design for a domestic dehumidifier'. Elecy Ccl Res Cen, Capenhurst, ECRC/M1166, 1978

5 Flikke, A. M., Cloud, H. A. and Hustrulid, A. 'Grain drying by heat pump'. *Agricl Engg*, 592–597, Aug 1957

6 Kroll, K. *Trockner und Trocknungsverfahren (Drying and Drying Processes)*. Springer Verlag, W. Berlin, 1978

7 Marrett, A. J. and Sykes, A. *The Finance and Analysis of Capital Projects*. Longmans, London, 1965

8 Hodgett, D. L. 'Efficient drying using heat pumps'. *Chem Engr*, 510–512, Jly/Aug 1976

Chapter 11

Further sources of information

11.1 Journals

ASHRAE Jnl
Am Soc of Htg, Refrign, and Air Condg Engrs, 1791 Tullie Circle NE, Atlanta, Georgia, GA 30329, USA

Bldg Services Engg Research and Technology
CIBS Delta House, 222 High Rd, London, SW12 9BS

Bulletin of the Intern Inste of Refrign
177 Boulevard Malesherbes, F 75017, Paris, France

Drying Technology
Marcel Dekker Jnls, PO Box 11305, Church St Sta, New York, NY 10249, USA

Electrical World (USA)
McGraw Hill, New York, NY 10020, USA

Elektrowärme International
Postbox 103962, D-4300 Essen, W Germany

Energy and Buildings
Elsevier Sequoia SA, Lausanne, Switzerland

Energy Research
John Wiley & Sons Ltd, Baffins Lane, Chichester, W Sussex PO19 1UD

Environmental Science and Technology
Am Cheml Soc, 1155 16th St N W, Washington DC, USA

Intern Bldg Services Abstracts
BSRIA, Old Bracknell Lane, Bracknell, Berks RG12 4AH

Intern Heat Pump Bulletin
Climadata Press, 57 High St, Fareham, Hants PO16 7BG

Intern Jnl of Energy Research
John Wiley & Sons Ltd, Baffins Lane, Chichester, W Sussex PO19 1UD

Intern Jnl of Heat and Mass Transfer
Pergamon Press, Headington Hill Hall, Oxford OX3 OBW

Intern Jnl of Refrign
Intern Instn of Refrign, 177 Boulevard Malesherbes, F 75017, Paris, France

Process Engineering
Morgan-Grampian Ltd, Calderwood St, London SE18 6QH

11.2 Design of refrigeration equipment

11.2.1 Professional bodies

Air Condg and Refrign Inste
1815 North Fort Myer Dr, Arlington, Virginia, USA 22209

Air Moving and Condg Assoc
205 W Touhy Ave, Park Ridge, Illinois, USA

Am Soc of Htg, Refrign and Air Condg Engrs
1791 Tullie Circle NE, Atlanta, Georgia, GA 30329, USA

Chartered Instn of Bldg Services Engrs
222 Balham High Rd, Balham, London SW12 9BS

Intern Inst of Refrign
177 Boulevard Malesherbes, F 75017 Paris, France

11.2.2 Research

(a) Compressors

Delft Univ of Technology
Lab for Refrigg Engg, Delft, The Netherlands Dr S. Touber: compressor design

Inste of Refrign Machine Construction
USSR Scientific Research Dept, Moscow, USSR Dr A.V. Bykov: turbo compressor development

Ray W. Herrick Labs
Purdue Univ, W Lafayette, Indiana 47907, USA
Prof R. Cohen: advanced compressor development

Univ of Strathclyde
16 Richmond St, Glasgow, Scotland G1 1XQ
Prof J.F.T. MacLaren: compressor design

(b) Heat exchangers

National Engg Labs
East Kilbride, Renfrewshire, Scotland G75 0QU
Mr M.M. Daniel: icing of heat exchangers

TNO Organisation for Industrial Research
PO Box 342, Apeldoorn, The Netherlands
Ing K.W.H. Schol: icing of heat exchangers

Univ of Liverpool
Dept of Mechanical Engg, Brownlow Hill, Liverpool, Merseyside
Dr H. Barrow: icing of heat exchangers

(c) Controls

École Supérieure d'Ingénieurs en Électrotechnique et Électronique
81 Rue Falquiere, F 75015 Paris, France
Mr J. Ehrhart: microprocessor control

The Polytechnic of Central London
115 New Cavendish St, London W5M 8JS
Prof D.R. Wilson: microprocessor control

VEB Kombinat Luft und Kaltetechnik
Dresden Stammbetrieb Forschung und Technik, Dresden, German Democratic Republic
Dr S. Nowotny: microprocessor control

(d) Refrigerants and lubrication

Battelle Institut
Am Roemerhof 35, Postfach 900-160, D-6000 Frankfurt, W Germany
Dr H.A. Janssen: absorption pairs

Du Pont Co
Louviers Building, Wilmington, Delaware 198 98, USA
Mr P.Y. McCormick: refrigerants

Electricity Ccl Research Centre
Capenhurst, Chester, Cheshire CH1 6ES
Dr C. Lopez-Cacicedo: high-temperature refrigerants

Électricité de France
Les Renardieres, Moret-sur-Loing, France
Dr G. Laroche: high-temperature lubricants

Imperial Chemical Industries PLC
Runcorn, Cheshire
High-temperature refrigerants

Institut du Génie Chimique
Chemin de la Loge, 31078 Toulouse Cedex, France
Dr A. Salazar: computation of absorption pairs

Institut Français due Pétrole
1–4 Avenue de Bois-Preau, 92502 Rueil-Malmaison, France
Dr A. Rojey: non-azeotropic refrigerants

National Bureau of Standards
Centre for Bldg Technology, Gaithersburg, Maryland, USA
Dr D.A. Didion: equation of state for non-azeotropic fluids

Scientific Research Instn of the Refrigg Industry
Moscow, USSR
Dr V.P. Latyshev: absorption refrigerants

Technical Univ of Hanover
Hanover, W Germany
Prof H. Kruse: development of non-azeotropic refrigerants

Thermotechnisch Institut
Katholieke Universiteit Leuven, Heverlee, Belgium
Prof J. Trommelmans: absorption pairs

(e) Electric and gas-driven motors

British Gas Corpn
Research Dept, Watson House, Peterborough Rd, London SW6 6HN

Electrical Research Assoc Ltd
Cleeve Rd, Leatherhead, Surrey KT22 7SA
Mr M. Webb: electric motor development and control

Electricity Ccl Research Centre
Capenhurst, Chester, Cheshire CH1 6ES
Mr W.P. Baker: electric motor design and control

N.V. KEMA
Utrechtsweg 310, 6800 ET Arnhem, The Netherlands
Mr H. Wolf: electric drives

(f) Modelling and testing

Électricité de France
Les Renardieres, Moret-sur-Loing, France
Mr M. Delandre: test chamber

Electricity Ccl Research Centre
Capenhurst, Chester, Cheshire CH1 6ES
Mr F. Sharman: modelling

Institut für Angewandte Thermodynamik und Klimatechnik
Univ Essen, Essen, W Germany
Dr F. Steimle: refrigerant development

Inste of Refrign
Sofia, Bulgaria
Dr D. Itcheva: modelling

Intern Energy Agency Heat Pump Centre
Petersgasse 45, A-8010 Graz, Austria
Dr W. Hochegger: equipment testing

Intern Research and Development Co Ltd
Fossway, Newcastle upon Tyne, Tyne and Wear NE6 2YD
Dr D.A. Reay: equipment development

National Bureau of Standards
Gaithersburg, Maryland, USA
Dr D.A. Didion: computer modelling: test cells

New Univ of Ulster
Mechanical Engg Dept, Coleraine, Co Londonderry, Northern Ireland BT52 15A
Dr J.T. McMullan: equipment development

Ontario Hydro
Toronto, Canada
Mr J.M. Bell: testing cells

Ray W. Herrick Labs
Purdue Univ, W Lafayette, Indiana 47907, USA
Prof R. Cohen: research and development

Refrigeration Lab
Technical Univ of Denmark, DK-2800 Lyngby, Denmark
Prof P. Worsoe-Schmidt: development and testing, modelling of absorption

Refrign Research Inc
525 N Fifth St, Brighton, Michigan 48116, USA

Research and Development Authority
Ben Gurion Univ of the Negev, Beer Sheva, Israel
Dr I. Yaron: development

Royal Inste of Technology
Stockholm, Sweden
Prof E. Granryd: development and test

Technical Univ of Wroclaw
50–370 Wroclaw, Wybrzeza Wyspianskiege 27, Poland
Dr Z. Krolick: modelling components

VEG-Gas Instituut NV,
Apeldoorn, The Netherlands
Dr M.F.G. van der Jagt: gas-engine development

(g) Manufacturers of dehumidifiers

Airscrew Howden Ltd
Weybridge, Surrey KT15 2QR (Tel 0932 45511, Telex 929515)

ANCO Products Ltd
Daish Way, Dodnor Industrial Est, Newport, Isle of Wight (Tel 0983 521465)

Andrews Industrial Equipment Ltd
Dudley Rd, Wolverhampton, W Midlands WV2 3DB (Tel 0902 58111, Telex 336737)

Bry Air Inc
PO Box 269, Sunbury, Ohio, USA
Dessicant

Carrier Air Condg
London SW7 1RB (Tel 01–589 8111, Telex 914688)

Compair Industrial Ltd
PO Box 7, Broomvale Works, High Wycombe, Bucks HP13 5SF (Tel 0494 21181, Telex 837371)

Daikin Industries Ltd
Osaka, Japan
Dr K. Tanaka

A/S Dantherm
DK 7800, Skive, Denmark (Tel 07 524144, Telex 66712)

Denco Refrign Ltd.
Whitworth Road, Southampton, Hants SO9 1WS
(High-pressure gas dehumidifier)

Eaton Williams Group Ltd
Station Rd, Edenbridge, Kent TN8 6EG (Tel 0732 863447, Telex 95493)

Ebac Ltd
Bishop Auckland, Co Durham DL14 9TF (Tel 0388 5061, Telex 558292)

Ebco Manufacturing Co
265 N Hamilton Rd, Columbus, Ohio 4213, USA
Mr D.I. Jakeway, General Manager, International (Tel 614–861–1350, Telex 246637)

Environheat Ltd
Letts Rd, Far Cotton, Northampton (Tel 0604 66341)

Happel GmbH c/o Conservatherm Ltd
3 Lansdown Close, Horsham, W Sussex R12 4GN (Tel 0403 57388)

Haydon Air Distribution Ltd
221 Old Christchurch Rd, Bournemouth, Dorset BH11 1PG (Tel 0202 24592, Telex 418473)

Hitachi Ltd
Tsuchiura, Japan
Dr K. Matsuo: advanced domestic dehumidifier

Kathabar Systems Europe
PO Box 220, AE Zoetermeer, The Netherlands (Tel 31–7921, Telex 31736)

Modern Technological Products Ltd
53 Back Sneddon St, Paisley, Renfrewshire, Scotland (Tel 041 848 1784)

Pall Pneumatics Ltd
Europa House, Havant Street, Portsmouth, Hants PO1 3PD (Tel 0705 753545)

Menerga Apparatebau GmbH
Gutenbergstrasse 51, D-4330 Mulheim, a.d. Ruhr 12, W Germany (Tel 0208 76966, Telex 856028)

Mons Precision Services (Co-op) Ltd
Unit 2, Hillfoot Industrial Est, Hoyland Rd, Sheffield, S Yorks S3 8AB (Tel 0742 339253)

Novatherm RSD Products Ltd
Units 1 and 2, The Maltings, Alton, Hants

Qualitair (Air Cond) Ltd
Castle Rd, Eurolink, Sittingbourne, Kent ME10 3RH (Tel 0795 75461, Telex 965023)

Seveso
Officine di Seveso, Via Orobia 3, 2013 Milan, Italy

Siemens AG
Erlangen, W Germany

Stiebel Eltron
Dr Stiebelstrasse, D-3450 Holzminden, W Germany

Temperature Ltd
192–206 York Road, London SW11 3SS

Toshiba UK Ltd
Frimley Rd, Camberley, Surrey GU16 5JJ

Trembath Air Condg
414 Purley Way, Croydon, Surrey CR9 4BT (Tel 01 688 2285, Telex 946895)

York Division of Borg Warner
PO Box 1592, York, Pennsylvania 17405, USA

York Division of Borg Warner Ltd
Gardiners Lane S, Basildon, Essex SS14 3HE (Tel 0268 287676, Telex 99105)

Walker Air Condg Ltd
18c Buckingham Ave, Slough Trading Est, Slough, Berks SL1 4QB (Tel 0753 3647)

11.3 Domestic applications

11.3.1 Professional bodies

Am Soc of Htg, Refrign and Air Condg Engrs
1791 Tullie Circle NE, Atlanta, Georgia, GA 30329, USA

Chartered Inste of Bldg Service Engrs
222 Balham High Road, London SW12 9BS

Congres Intern due Bâtiment (CIB)
704 Weena, Rotterdam 3, The Netherlands

The Inst of Energy
18 Devonshire St, London W1N 2AU

Réunion International des Laboratoires d'Essais et de Recherchés (RILEM)
Sur les Matériaux et les Constructions, 12 rue Brancion, 75737 Paris, CEDEX 15, France

Royal Inste of Brit Architects (RIBA)
66 Portland Place, London W1N 4AD

11.3.2 Research

Brit Gas Corpn
Research Dept, Watson House, Peterborough Rd, London SW6 6HN
Dr D. Fishman: comfort and humidity

Building Research Sta
Bucknalls Lane, Garston, Watford, Herts WD2 7JR
Dr S.J. Leach: moisture in buildings

Building Research Sta (Scotland)
Kelvin Ave East Kilbride, Renfrewshire, Scotland G75 ORZ
Mr C. Saunders: condensation in housing/dehumidifier testing

Building Science Dept
The Univ, Newcastle upon Tyne, Tyne and Wear NE1 7RU
Prof A.C. Hardy: condensation in housing

Calder Campus, Liverpool Polytechnic
Dowsefield Lane, Liverpool, Lancs L18 3JJ
Dr M. Blackmore: moisture in housing

Cement and Concrete Assoc
Wexham Springs, Slough, Berks SL3 6PL
Mr P.J. Witt: moisture in concrete buildings

Centre Scientifique et Technique du Bâtiment
Ave Jean Jouris, Champs-sur-Marne, France
Mr J. Borel: moisture in building materials

Centre Scientifique et Technique de la Construction
Rue du Lombard 41, B-1000 Bruxelles, S 110683, Belgium
Mr R. De Bruyckere: moisture in buildings

College of Home Economics
Univ College, Llantrisant Rd, Cardiff, S Glam, Wales
Mrs A.M. Rees: moisture in the home

Danish Bldg Research Inste
Postbox 119, DK 2970 Horsholm, Denmark
Dr G. Christensen: moisture in houses

Electricity Ccl Research Centre
Capenhurst, Chester, Cheshire CH1 6ES
Dr G.W. Brundrett: domestic dehumidifier development

Inste of Applied Physics TNO-TH
Stieltjesweg 1, Delft 2208, PO Box 155, The Netherlands
Ir G.J. Beernink: moisture measurement/modelling

Laboratoire due Physique du Bâtiment
Univ of Liége, 4000-Liége, Belgium
Prof. J. Lebrun: modelling responses

MPTJ kaf Tjeplotechniki
Moskovskaja Ob1. 141001, Mitischtji-1, USSR
Mr P. Brdlik: heat and mass transfer

Norwegian Bldg Research Inste
7034 NTH, Trondheim, Norway
Mr A. Tveit: moisture in building materials

Sheffield Polytechnic
Pond St, Sheffield, S Yorks S1 1WB
Dr I. Denman: domestic dehumidifier development

TNO
Postbox 49, Delft, The Netherlands
Dr B.H. Vos: moisture movement

11.4 Swimming pools

11.4.1 Professional bodies

Inste of Baths and Recreational Management
36–38 Sherrard St, Melton Mowbray, Leics LE13 1XJ

Inste of Water Pollution Control
53 London Rd, Maidstone, Kent ME16 8JH

Instn of Environmental Health Officers
Chadwick House, 48 Rushworth St, London SE1 ORB

Instn of Occupational Safety and Health
322 Uppingham Road, Leicester LE5 OQG

11.4.2 Research

Building Research Sta
Bucknalls Lane, Garston, Watford, Herts WD2 7JR
Mr N. Milbank: field tests

Centre Scientifique et Technique du Bâtiment
Ave Jean Jouris, Champs-sur-Marne, France

Electricity Ccl Research Centre
Capenhurst, Chester, Cheshire CH1 6ES
Dr D.J. Dickson: air movement and moisture

Rheinisch-Westphalisches Elektrizitätswerk AG
Anwendungstechnik, Essen, W Germany
Mr K. Biasin: field tests

Univ of Bremen
Bremen, W Germany
Mr J. von Dusseln/U. Lahl: health and air quality

11.5 Industrial applications

11.5.1 Professional bodies

Am Chem Soc
1155 16th St N W, Washington DC, USA

Am Soc of Htg, Refrign and Air Condg Engrs
1791 Tullie Circle NE, Atlanta, Georgia, GA 30329, USA

The Inste of Energy
18 Devonshire St, London W1N 2AU

The Inste of Physics
47 Belgrave Sq, London SW1X 8QX

Inste of Refrign
76 Mill Lane, Carshalton, Surrey SM5 2JR

Instn of Chemical Engrs
165–171 Railway Terrace, Rugby, Warwicks CV21 3HQ

Instn of Mechanical Engrs
1 Birdcage Walk, London, SW1

Instn of Corrosion Science and Technology
14 Belgrave Sq, London SW1X 8PS

11.5.2 Industrial research

Agricultural Engg Department
Univ of California, Davis, California 95616, USA
Dr R.P. Singh: models for food drying

Brit Food Manufacturing Industries Research Assoc
Randalls Road, Leatherhead, Surrey
Miss A. Millidge: practical food drying

Brit Hydromechanics Industrial Research Assoc
Cranfield, Beds MK43 OJA

Campden Food Preservation Research Assoc
Chipping Campden, Glos GL55 6LD
Mr N. Lawson: food preservation

Centre Technique de l'Industrie des Papiers cartons et Celluloses
Boîte Postale 175X, 38042 Grenoble, France
Mr P. Turel: paper technology

Corrosion Centre
National Physical Lab, Teddington, Middlesex
Dr T.J. Quinn: prevention of corrosion

Électricité de France
Les Renardieres, Chalons-sur-Marne, France
Mr M. Delandre: industrial dehumidification

Electricity Ccl Research Centre
Capenhurst, Chester, Cheshire CH1 6ES
Dr C. Lopez-Cacicedo: high-temperature industrial dehumidifier

LABORELEC
B-1640 Rhode St Genese, Belgium
Mr B. Geeraert: industrial drying

Luikov Inste for Heat and Mass Transfer
Minsk, BSSR, USSR
Mr O.G. Martynenko: industrial drying

Nederlands Instituut voor Zuivelonderzoek
Kernhemseweg 2, Ede, Netherlands
Dr Ing. T.E. Galesloot

Rheinisch-Westphalisches Elektrizitätswerk AG
Anwendungstechnik, Essen, W Germany
Mr P. Kalischer: industrial dehumidifiers

Salford University
Dept of Cheml Engg, Salford, Gtr Manchester M54 WT
Prof F.A. Holland: crop drying with dehumidifiers

Shirley Institute
Didsbury, Gtr Manchester M20 8RX
Mr J.H. Black: textile drying

Scientific Instruments Research Assoc Inste (SIRA)
South Hill, Chislehurst, Kent BR7 5EH
Mr B.J. Berry: measurement of humidity

Wool Industries Research Association
Headingley Lane, Leeds, W Yorks LS6 1BW
Mr R. Crowther: wool drying

11.6 Horticulture and storage

11.6.1 Professional bodies

Am Soc of Htg, Refrign and Air Condg Engrs
1791 Tullie Circle NE, Atlanta, Georgia, GA 30329, USA

British Mycological Soc
Dept of Plant Sciences, Wye College, Wye, Ashford, Kent TN25 5AH

National Inste of Agricultural Engrs
West End Rd, Silsoe, Beds MK45 4DU

Inste of Refrign
76 Mill Lane, Carshalton, Surrey SM5 2JR

Royal Horticultural Society
Horticultural Hall, Vincent Sq, London SW1P 2PE

11.6.2 Research

Georgia Experiment Sta
Univ of Georgia, Athens, Georgia, USA
Food storage

Glasshouse Crops Research Inste
Worthing Rd, Rustington, Littlehampton, W Sussex BN16 3PU
Mr G.F. Sheard: moisture in greenhouses

Long Ashton Research Assoc
Long Ashton, Bristol BS18 9AF
Mr C.V. Cutting: crop propagation

National Inste of Agricultural Engg
Wrest Park, Silsoe, Beds MK45 4HS
Mr B.J. Bailey: dehumidification in greenhouses

National Vegetable Research Sta
Wellesbourne, Warwicks CV35 9EF
Moisture in horticulture and storage

Pest Infestation Control Labs
London Rd, Slough, Berks SL3 7HJ
Mr R.H. Thompson: moisture and insects

Rothampstead Experimental Sta
Harpenden, Herts AL5 2JQ
Mr P.H. Needham: moisture in plants

Scottish Inst of Agricultural Engg
Bush Estate, Penicuik, Midlothian, Scotland EH26 OPH
Moisture in greenhouses

Stockbridge House Experimental Horticulture Station
Cawood, Selby, N Yorks YO8 OTZ
Mr R.E. Butters: moisture in greenhouses

11.7 Compressed gases

11.7.1 Professional bodies

Am Soc of Htg Refrign and Air Condg Engrs
1791 Tullie Circle NE, Atlanta, Georgia, GA 30329, USA

Brit Compressed Air Society
8 Leicester St, London WC2H 7BN

Brit Compressed Gases Association
21 St James Sq, London SW1Y 4JU

Chartered Instn of Bldg Service Engrs
222 Balham High Rd, London SW12 9BS

The Compressed Air and Gas Inste
122 East 42nd St, New York, NY 10017, USA

11.7.2 Research

Ray W. Herrick Labs
Purdue Univ, W Lafayette, Indiana 47907, USA
Prof R. Cohen: compressor design, training, noise treatment

TABLE 11.1 Summary of dehumidifier manufacturers

Manufacturer	*Type**	*Domestic*	*Commercial*	*Industrial*	*Pools*	*Compressed air*	*Timber*
Airscrew Howden	R						√
Anco Products	R				√		
Andrews Indusl	R	√	√	√			
Bry Air Inc	D			√			
Carrier Air Condg	R				√		
Compair Indusl	R					√	
Daikin Indusl	R	√	√				
Dantherm	R	√	√	√	√		
Denco Refrign	R					√	
Eaton Williams	R	√	√	√	√		
Elac Ltd	R	√		√			√
Ebco Manufg	R	√					
Environheat Ltd	R		√				
Happel GmbH	R				√		
Haydon Air	R	√	√	√			
Hitachi	R	√					
Kathabar	L		√				
Mod Tech Prod	R	√					
Pall Pneumatics	D					√	
Menerga	R				√		
Mons Precision	R	√					
Novatherm	R				√		
Qualitair	R					√	
Seveso	R	√					
Siemens	R				√		
Stiebel Eltron	R				√		
Temperature Ltd	R		√	√			
Toshiba	R	√					
Trembath	R	√					
York	R				√		
Walker	R	√	√	√	√		

*Type: R = refrigerant; L = liquid sorbent; D = dessicant

Index